Soap Opera History

CONTRIBUTING AUTHOR
MARY ANN COPELAND

PREFACE BY MARCY WALKER

FOREWORD BY MACDONALD CAREY

MALLARD PRESS

AN IMPRINT OF
BDD Promotional Book Company, Inc.

Louis Weber, C.E.O.
Publications International, Ltd.
7373 North Cicero Avenue
Lincolnwood, Illinois 60646

Permission is never granted for commercial purposes.

Printed in the U.S.A.

8 7 6 5 4 3 2 1

ISBN 0-7924-5451-0

Library of Congress Catalog Card Number: 90-63490

First published in the United States 1991 by The Mallard Press.

Front cover: (clockwise, from top left) Morgan Fairchild; Susan Sullivan and Robert Foxworth in *Falcon Crest;* Susan Seaforth Hayes and Bill Hayes in *Days of Our Lives;* Susan Lucci; Meg Ryan and Frank Runyeon in *As the World Turns;* Marcy Walker; Larry Hagman in *Dallas;* Tracey E. Bregman-Recht and Michael Damian in *The Young and the Restless;* Donna Mills and Ted Shackelford in *Knots Landing;* Macdonald Carey in *Days of Our Lives;* Katherine Kelly Lang and Ron Moss in *The Bold and the Beautiful;* and John Forsythe holding Joan Collins, with Linda Evans (back) in *Dynasty.*

Back cover: (top) *Twin Peaks* characters at Laura's funeral; (bottom left) Genie Francis and Anthony Geary in *General Hospital;* and (bottom right, left to right) Marcy Walker, Robin Mattson, and Robin Wright in *Santa Barbara.*

Mary Ann Copeland is an expert on and long-time fan of soap operas. She writes articles for the leading soap opera periodicals.

Marcy Walker currently plays Eden Capwell Cruz on *Santa Barbara;* she also appeared on *All My Children* as Liza Colby. She has been making forays into prime-time television. Ms. Walker has been nominated many times and has received an Emmy for her work on *Santa Barbara.*

Macdonald Carey has played Dr. Tom Horton on *Days of Our Lives* since 1965, and has received two Emmys for his work. He is also a respected stage and screen actor. Mr. Carey is also an author and has written three books of poetry and an autobiography.

John Kelly Genovese, consultant, is a leading authority on soap operas.

Special thanks to Polly Hazen of the National "Days" Fan Club and to Don Frabotta.

Contents

Preface

Stories. My Maw Maw (or most commonly referred to as Grandma anywhere but the South) and I would have long talks in her kitchen, and she would impart her wisdom to me while we snapped beans. She'd always say, "Always remember ... it's not nice to tell stories ... just remember that. Nobody likes to be known as a storyteller..." Now, she was talking about lies, of course, but anywhere but the South, stories are "STORIES." And little did I know I would dedicate nearly a decade to them.

Soap operas have been the most consistently entertaining and profitable form of television since they left radio, and the fans are the most dedicated and devout groups ever. I've been honored to have been involved with a couple of shows that have featured some of the best actors in our business. I was also quick to realize that every actor, from principal to extra, was an integral part of the foundation of any show.

I think one of the on-going struggles of daytime performers and producers was the fight for legitimate recognition. "Soap operas" were teamed with the word "housewife" for so long, and I'm glad that during the years *both* of those descriptive stereotypes have been given the respect and recognition they deserve. Of course, fan reactions have always been a major part of what propels the storylines and a character's popularity, so I'd like to give them part of the credit for changes over the years.

As *anything* evolves, we see bits of contemporary life infused into daytime shows. We have gone from swelling organ music to Top 10 tunes matched to beautiful montages of love scenes. (Some of those songs reached the top *because* they started as a couples' love song on a soap!) And the days of camera work being "two heads talking" are virtually extinct. Now we have handheld shots, cameras on cranes, fog machines, sets with pools and ponds, indoor beaches, and millions of dollars spent on location.

In the constant demand for better quality, more contemporary storylines, and beauty, adventure, and romance, soap operas have kept their pace. The fly-by-the-seat-of-your-pants style, like that of summer stock, can really be thrilling. Everyone relies on instinct, watching out for each other, and that—combined with mutual respect for your cast and crew mates— transforms just "shows" into "families." We tape 360 days a year, 12 hours a day. Hour shows tape about 90 pages a day and half-hours shows do just that, half that. That includes music, sound, lighting, rewriting, directing, camera work, props, memorization, makeup, hair, wardrobe. And somewhere in the middle of all that, you add stress and a sense of humor.

No matter what the efforts are, the rewards from the fans are worth cherishing. The audience is why we are successful. Because they feel a part of our family, going through the trials and tribulations of their favorite characters, they give more than any average spectator. I'd like to think on those turbulent days—when I feel that tears or jokes are not going to come easy—that they notice the extra effort. And you know, they always do.

So, to the fine people who have had an instrumental hand in allowing us the dignity of going to work every day, year after year, I dedicate this preface.

Thanks for all your support, love, and generosity. You make it *more* than worthwhile. No story.

Marcy Walker

Foreword

S omeone on the evening news said recently, "Americans see everything in life as drama. They just want to know who are the good guys and who are the bad guys."

We Americans start in life by playing "cowboys and Indians," or in these more ethnically conscious days, "cops and robbers."

Historically, people in the Western world had morality plays on the steps of the cathedrals in the Middle Ages. For centuries, there were bands of players doing plays about good and evil, traveling throughout every country in the world. In America, in the eighteenth, nineteenth, and early twentieth century, there were traveling acting companies—tent shows that played homespun dramas that taught moral lessons.

In the twentieth century, radio arrived and with it, the daily soap opera. People could become more involved in these dramas than in the tent shows. Through the miracle of radio, which came right into the home, the stories were more accessible. And the characters and situations were more recognizable. By 1950, television was here and we became even more involved in these daily dramas of other people's lives. And the dramas were about people just like us. We could identify with the situations the characters got into and we could live their emotions vicariously. Soap operas like *One Man's Family, The Guiding Light, General Hospital,* and *Days of Our Lives* had taken over our lives.

Now, of course, with VCRs, if you have to work or you have to attend class in school, you don't have to miss your show. It is there waiting for you at home at the end of the day or at the end of the week.

As trivial, as mundane as these soap operas seem to the regular viewer, the afficionado, the fan, the stories on these soap operas bring some sort of order to the chaos of everyday life. As a soap opera fan, I can escape into a world that is somehow better and more balanced than mine is. The soap opera gives me hope, it makes me feel life is not so bad after all.

In the Western world, there has been no change in basic ethics since the days of the Greeks. What was right and wrong then is right and wrong now. The family and what the family taught its children preserved those ethics through the years. The world of drama and the theater were the mirror of family ideals. Soap opera has for the most part been a reflection of what family life should be. The early radio soap operas ensnared the viewer from the beginning. The TV soap opera has really not changed very much from the days when it was just radio soap opera. It's basically the same. The stories revolve around a family and the family revolves to a great extent around the soap opera, both the day and the night versions.

Over 70 percent of daytime TV viewers are caught up in viewing soap operas (according to a 1985 survey by Helen Kaufman for Lazarsfeld's Bureau of Audience Research). It's there they find good old-fashioned stories, not in the movies, not in the situation comedies. The audience finds there what it asks for—entertainment, escape, and stories where good triumphs and evil is punished.

And where else can you find these things nowadays but in a soap opera?

Macdonald Carey

Macdonald Carey

Introduction

Although series with continuing storylines existed on radio before 1930, *Painted Dreams*, created by former Ohio schoolteacher Irna Phillips, is technically considered radio's first soap opera. It premiered on Chicago's WGN radio in 1930 and featured a multiplotted story that connected the lives of fictional characters living in a small town. The widowed Mother Moran was the serial's leading heroine. The formula for the soaps we know today was created with this serial.

By 1933, Irna Phillips had created a serial titled *Today's Children,* which was loosely based on *Painted Dreams,* for network radio. Two former advertising executives, Frank and Anne Hummert, were inspired by Phillips's success and began creating a batch of their own serials for a competing network. Several of their creations, including *Just Plain Bill, The Romance of Helen Trent,* and *Ma Perkins,* lasted for decades. The Hummerts boasted that their radio dramas were "true to life." The truth is they offered the pretense of real life ladeled with a heavy serving of fantasy. It was the Depression and housewives listening to the soaps while doing their daily chores looked forward to escape, even if only for 15 minutes. Helen Trent possessed a mind-numbingly boring personality, yet she led a glamorous life as a Hollywood dress designer who attracted one handsome suitor after another. Listeners identified with her and vicariously reveled in her romantic adventures.

Phillips attempted to match the prolific Hummerts' output by creating *The Guiding Light, Road of Life, Woman in White, The Right to Happiness,* and *The Brighter Day.* The difference with Phillips's serials was that she introduced a type of character, the professional. *The Guiding Light* and *The Brighter Day* centered on ministers. *The Road of Life* featured a doctor and *Woman in White* highlighted a nurse's life. Unlike the

Fran Carlon and Ed Pawley from the radio soap that later went to TV, Portia Faces Life.

Hummerts, Phillips shyed away from fantasy-based plots and allowed her stories to spring from the characters themselves.

Phillips is also responsible for creating the amnesia storyline. This plot device has been used on soaps from *The Guiding Light* in the thirties to prime-time television's *Dynasty* in the late eighties.

By the early fifties, television was emerging as a force to be reckoned with. A number of radio serials attempted to make the switch to television, including *The Guiding Light, When a Girl Marries, The Brighter Day, One Man's Family, Portia Faces Life, The Road of Life,* and *Young Dr. Malone,* but most of them failed and were quickly canceled. *One Man's Family, The Brighter Day,* and *Young Dr. Malone* were moderate successes and lasted a few years before being canceled. The only radio serial to survive on television still airs today, *The Guiding Light.*

Transplanted radio serials faced two major obstacles. In order to succeed, they needed to emphasize visual imagery over talky scripts. Unfortunately, the low budgets allotted for daytime television serials prevented writers from pursuing fantasy-adventure storylines and limited most scenes to two sets, the kitchen and the living room. *Search for Tomorrow,* an early soap created specifically for television, succeeded because it understood that viewers were willing to be drawn into quiet scenes between a recently widowed grieving mother and her young daughter, who were sharing a meal at their kitchen table. In 1956, Phillips created *As the World Turns* with the understanding that viewers wanted to become involved with the lives of other people; that they didn't watch soaps just to follow the next fantastic plot turn. Instead, she believed they wanted to experience the characters, to feel as if they were in the characters' homes.

By the early sixties, network radio serials no longer existed. The last four to air were *The Right to Happiness, Ma Perkins, Young Dr. Malone,* and *The Second Mrs. Burton.* Meanwhile, television serials were flourishing. CBS, with its line-up of such high-rated serials as *Search for Tomorrow, Love of Life, The Secret Storm, The Edge of Night, The Guiding Light,* and the number-one rated *As the World Turns,* was the leading network. It wasn't until the late sixties that NBC began to seriously challenge CBS's success with *Another World, Days of Our Lives,* and *The Doctors. Another World* won viewers with storylines that contained psychological undercurrents. *Days of Our Lives* featured a family of doctors, the Hortons, who encountered sexual dilemmas such as rape and incest. *The Doctors* provided viewers with a realistic look at operations, which were staged under the supervision of medical experts.

Meanwhile, ABC, after a series of false starts, finally had a hit with *General Hospital.* Creators Frank and Doris Hursley juxtaposed nurse Jessie Brewer's troubled marriage to the neurotic Dr. Phil Brewer with hospital crises. This created an effective blend of domestic and medical drama. Encouraged by the hospital-based soap's popularity, the third-place network became more aggressive in taking chances. In 1966, it offered a gothic serial titled *Dark Shadows* that featured vampires, witches, and werewolves as leading characters. Intrigued by the novelty of the serial, teenage viewers took an instant liking to it, thus creating a new audience of viewers. In 1968, *One Life to Live* premiered with storylines featuring characters from different class backgrounds and races.

CBS also tapped into the youth market by offering attractive young leads in their new serials, *Love Is a Many Splendored Thing* and *Where the Heart Is.* By 1969, NBC was also ready to take a chance on luring younger viewers by premiering a college-based soap, *Bright Promise.*

Daytime soaps changed in several significant ways during the seventies. In January 1970, ABC introduced *All My Children,* a serial that emphasized young love and the relationships between parents and their children. The serial also tackled real life issues such as the Vietnam War, abortion, wife abuse, child abuse, alcoholism, and drug abuse.

CBS took a bold step toward the future with the premiere of *The Young and the Restless* in March of 1973. On the surface, it presented a classic soap structure by featuring two families: one upper-class and the other working-class. What set *The Young and the Restless* apart was its willingness to feature young characters in sexual relationships who attempted to communicate their ambivalent feelings in a changing time. Young heroine Chris Brooks spoke candidly with her fiance, Snapper Foster, about whether they should engage in sexual relations before marriage. Impatient with Chris's desire to maintain her virginity, Snapper sought sexual release with a waitress, Sally McGuire. When Chris was raped, she worked through her feelings by talking. Fantasy returned and played a big part in the serial's success. A dowdy girl was transformed into a beautiful world-famous concert pianist through the magic power of love. A powerful, attractive millionaire found himself captivated by a sexy but earnest lower-class young woman who had always dreamed of wealth and glamour. Relevancy was included in the mix with storylines that confronted frigidity, impotence, a mother's mastectomy, and lesbianism.

An early cast photo from the long-running Days of Our Lives.

Motivated by *The Young and the Restless's* immediate success with viewers, CBS's older soaps tried to emulate it with mixed results. *The Secret Storm* and *Love of Life* were hardest hit. Their decline was so swift that neither serial lasted out the decade.

Another World expanded to a one-hour format with great success in 1974. By the end of the decade, *The Guiding Light, Days of Our Lives, General Hospital, All My Children, One Life to Live, As the World Turns,* and *The Young and the Restless* also expanded to an hour. Of the serials that remained in a 30-minute format, *The Edge of Night, Somerset, Search for Tomorrow,* and *The Doctors* began having a difficult time holding on to viewers, and were soon canceled. A few newer shows, *Loving* and *The Bold and the Beautiful,* remain.

By 1980, ABC had surpassed CBS as the number-one network in daytime. The top-rated *General Hospital* won millions of new young viewers with a storyline that featured a young herione, Laura Baldwin, who fell in love with mob-connected Luke Spencer soon after he raped her. Young people were suddenly presented in a new way on daytime serials and offered storylines that appealed to the adolescent fantasies of its new audience. Luke and Laura spent an entire summer on the run from the mob. In another storyline, they rescued their hometown from being frozen by a diabolical scientist. Other more conventional soaps, including *Days of Our Lives* and *As the World Turns,* tried to duplicate *General Hosptial's* success by copying its storylines.

Prime-time soaps also became extremely popular in the eighties. Until 1978, the only serial in the history of television that was popular in prime-time was *Peyton Place.* In March of 1978, CBS took a chance on a six-episode serial titled *Dallas* that followed the lives of a large oil family. By 1981, *Dallas* was the most popular show on television. *Dynasty, Falcon Crest,* and *Knots*

Landing also proved popular with viewers. The decline of prime-time soaps began in 1990. *Dallas* and *Knots Landing* managed to maintain respectable ratings, but *Falcon Crest* and *Dynasty* weren't as fortunate. In the spring of 1990, ABC introduced a new prime-time serial created by filmmaker David Lynch and Mark Frost, titled *Twin Peaks.* It maintains a cultlike following that seems to increase—though it may be that the serial is unconventional so it generates more press than other shows.

Today American daytime soaps are enjoyed all over the world. *The Bold and the Beautiful* is one of Greece's most popular series. Viewers in France clamor to follow *Santa Barbara. Loving* is a hit with audiences in Italy. The *Days of Our Lives* fan club has received applications from as far away as Nigeria.

In the early nineties, daytime soaps have returned to the basics, featuring plots that highlight romance and family. There is, however, more of an attempt to try and present life more realistically. "Daytime soaps gained by being more accurate and honest," said Ruth Warrick, who plays Phoebe Tyler Wallingford on ABC's *All My Children.* "It lost it when we threw all the rules out... and let all the young studs meet, score and into bed time after time just to record another notch in their belts. We in soaps have a certain responsiblity because we are role models, there's no question about it. But we do show that people will pay for irresponsible actions; that you won't win or get off scot-free. It's good that soaps are more honest and real, but for a time we went overboard, just like society did in terms of permissiveness. We've definitely pulled back from that; now with AIDS and the like, everyone thinks through relationships much more than they used to. Putting that in a story element makes it so much more immediate to people because many viewers relate to us as a family and mimic our actions."

Pat Falken Smith is a former headwriter of General Hospital. *She made TV soap history by creating the Luke and Laura storyline.*

Mary Linda Rapelye and Frank Runyeon played Maggie Crawford and Steve Andropolous on the long-running As the World Turns.

Major Soap Operas

Soap Operas have been around as long as radio. Once television was born, soaps were some of the first shows that translated from radio to the new medium. Not all made lasting impressions, but many have. Many people have raised their families while watching the families on the soap grow up. Many have had an important impact on our lives. And many have provided hours of entertainment and pleasure. Those that have run for many years, or have been innovative, are profiled here.

ALL MY CHILDREN

JANUARY 5, 1970–PRESENT ABC

A lost suitcase nearly prevented this serial from making it to television. Agnes Nixon created *All My Children* in her spare time, while writing for *The Guiding Light*. She wanted to write a story about the close friendship between three friends, two boys and a girl. She was particularly interested in exploring the relationship between the two boys. "I write a lot about friendship partly in protest against those who say everyone is so tough and you're not supposed to show emotions. Especially men," she explained to writer Dan Wakefield in his book, *All Her Children*. Nixon was also interested in writing about the relationships between parents and children.

During a Christmas vacation in St. Croix, she polished a presentation of the series and five sample scripts. When Nixon returned home, she discovered the suitcase containing her work was missing. Fortunately, a few months later, the suitcase resurfaced and she resumed work on *All My Children*.

When Nixon was confident her presentation was ready for others to see, she pitched it to Procter & Gamble. They purchased an option on the series, but later dropped it. The official explanation was they couldn't find an available slot on any of the networks. Convinced they had another reason for passing on her series, Nixon tucked it away in a drawer and forgot about it. A few months later, she took over as headwriter for *Another World*, a serial so low rated that NBC was seriously considering canceling it. Within a year, the revitalized soap shot up to second place in the Nielsen ratings.

Realizing Nixon was largely responsible for *Another World*'s sudden popularity, ABC approached her about creating a new serial. Instead of submitting her presentation on *All My Children*, Nixon decided to create something entirely fresh. She delivered *One Life to Live*, a serial that boasted three families of diverse ethnic and economic backgrounds. It also featured a storyline about a light-skinned black woman passing for white. *One Life to Live* was an immediate success, prompting ABC to request a second series from Nixon. Her husband suggested she submit *All My Children* and the rest is history.

When it premiered, *All My Children* centered on two families, the upscale, blue-blooded Tylers and the solid, middle-class Martins. Charles and Phoebe Tyler had two adult children, Anne and Lincoln. Chuck Tyler, Charles's orphaned grandson, also lived with the family.

Kate was the matriarch of the Martin family. She had two middle-aged sons, Joe, a widowed doctor, and Paul, a bachelor lawyer who was declared missing in action in Vietnam. Joe had three children: Bobby; Jeff, who followed in his father's footsteps and became a doctor; and Tara, a teenager. Bobby disappeared early in the series; he departed for a camping trip and never returned. No mention was ever made of him again.

Jeff Martin (Charles Frank) and Mary Kennicott (Susan Blanchard) finally married after Erica gave Jeff a divorce. Their happiness was fleeting; criminals killed Mary when they broke into her home.

Ruth Warrick plays Phoebe Tyler Wallingford, a good-hearted but meddling member of the community in Pine Valley.

Joe shared a close friendship with Ruth Brent, a nurse at Pine Valley Hospital. Ruth and her husband, Ted, had a teenage son, Philip. Early in the series, Ted was killed in an auto accident. Soon after, Ruth and Joe realized they loved one another and married.

Ruth's sister, Amy, was married to Lincoln Tyler. Rosemary Prinz, a popular actress from *As the World Turns,* played Amy. She received star billing during her six-month stint. Rounding out the cast were Mona Kane and her self-centered, spoiled teenage daughter, Erica.

During its 21-year history, young love has always been a central theme of *All My Children.* The friendship between Philip, Chuck, and Tara was a forerunner. Philip and Tara dated, while Chuck harbored a secret crush for Tara. Erica Kane resented Philip's growing love for Tara because she wanted him for herself. Erica accidentally overheard a conversation revealing that Philip was really the son of Amy Tyler, who'd had an affair with Nick Davis. Philip had been adopted at birth by Ruth and Ted. An eager Erica spilled the beans to Philip, who confronted his parents. They reluctantly confirmed Erica's story.

THE CAST

Original Cast

BOBBY MARTIN	MIKE BERSELL
TED BRENT	MARK DAWSON
LINCOLN TYLER	JAMES KAREN
RUTH BRENT	MARY FICKETT
CHARLES TYLER	HUGH FRANKLIN
TARA MARTIN	KAREN GORNEY
LOIS SLOANE	HILDA HAYNES
MONA KANE	FRANCES HEFLIN
NICK DAVIS	LAWRENCE KEITH
ERICA KANE	SUSAN LUCCI
JOE MARTIN	RAY MacDONNELL
AMY TYLER	ROSEMARY PRINZ
CHUCK TYLER	JACK STAUFFER
KATE MARTIN	KATE HARRINGTON
ANNE TYLER	DIANA De VEGH
JEFF MARTIN	CHRISTOPHER WINES

ALL MY CHILDREN

JANUARY 5, 1970–PRESENT ABC

Mistakenly believing that Nick was the one to spill the beans, Ted tore out of the house to confront Nick—but instead was killed in an automobile accident. A guilt-ridden Philip ran away to New York, where he found a low-paying job. Soon after moving to New York, Philip was involved in an accident, which caused amnesia. Embarrassed that the whole town now knew about her affair with Nick Davis, Amy packed her bags and moved away.

Feeling abandoned by Philip, Tara turned to Chuck for emotional support. Meanwhile, Philip was found and he returned home to Pine Valley. Nick tried to help his son regain his memory, but was unsuccessful. While in Pine Valley, Nick began seeing wealthy Anne Tyler. Realizing Philip had completely forgotten her, Tara believed they no longer had a future together, so she began dating Chuck. Eventually, Philip's amnesia lifted, and he tried to mend his relationship with Tara, but she no longer trusted him. She accepted Chuck's marriage proposal.

Angered that Tara had forsaken his son, a drunken Nick interrupted the young couple's wedding ceremony and slugged Chuck, who was rushed to the hospital. Tara and Chuck's wedding was postponed after doctors found that Chuck had a defective kidney. While Chuck was in the hospital receiving treatment, Nick encouraged Philip to see Tara. Still attracted to Philip, Tara secretly dated him. Philip received his draft notice, inspiring him to propose to Tara. On his last night in Pine Valley, the couple tried to find a minister to perform the ceremony. When their efforts failed, Tara and Philip married themselves in an empty church. They spent the evening making love. The following morning, Philip left for Vietnam.

A few weeks later, Tara learned she was pregnant. Unfortunately, Philip's family received word he was missing in Vietnam. By now, Chuck had been released from the hospital. Tara confided the truth to him about her marriage to Philip and that she was pregnant. A gallant Chuck offered to marry Tara and raise her baby as his own. The couple eloped, and then announced to their families they'd been married for several weeks. A few months later, Tara gave birth to a baby boy, Philip. Chuck proved to be such a good husband and father that a grateful Tara found herself falling in love with him.

A surprised and emotionally overwhelmed Ruth received word that Philip had been located. He was a P.O.W. in Vietnam. Philip returned to Pine Valley thinking he would resume his marriage to Tara. News that Tara was happily married to Chuck crushed Philip. Meanwhile, Ruth knew Philip was the father of Tara's child, but she didn't tell him.

Frank (John Danelle) and Nancy Grant (Lisa Wilkinson) were a realistic couple, they had daily ups and downs like most people.

18

Mike Roy (Nicolas Surovy) helped Erica (Susan Lucci) pen her autobiography, and fell in love with her in the process.

Accepting that his relationship with Tara was history, Philip turned his attention to Erica. In the years since her teenage crush on Philip, Erica had accumulated much life experience. Wanting to be a doctor's wife, Erica had married Tara's brother, Jeff. When she discovered she was pregnant, Erica secretly had an abortion. Complications led to her hospitalization. Jeff was angry when he learned about the abortion, but Erica promised to reform her selfish ways and become a loving wife. Jeff's hectic life as an intern, however, left Erica bored and unhappy.

Eventually, she became a professional model in New York City. She had an affair with Jason Maxwell, the powerful head of a thriving modeling agency. Frustrated by his marriage to

Erica, Jeff found true love with nurse Mary Kennicott. Jeff asked Erica for a divorce, but she was unwilling to free Jeff so he could wed Mary. Jason Maxwell was found murdered and Jeff became the main suspect. It was later discovered that Erica's mother, Mona, had accidentally killed Jason. Mona had blocked the experience from her memory. Erica finally agreed to divorce Jeff, and he quickly wed Mary. But their happy union didn't last long. Soon after their honeymoon, escaped criminals broke into their home, and killed Mary.

Flattered by Philip's attention, a lonely Erica decided to trick him into marriage by becoming pregnant. Although her scheme to become pregnant worked, Erica was forced to face the fact

Philip didn't love her. She decided to have a second abortion. Philip wasn't happy to find that Erica was planning an abortion and convinced her to marry him. An illness caused Erica to miscarry, sending her into a deep depression. Concerned for her mental health, Philip arranged to have her committed for psychiatric treatment.

With Erica temporarily out of the picture, Philip began spending his free time at Tara and Chuck's home. Forming a close friendship with little Philip, he finally put the pieces together and realized the boy was his son. Ruth reluctantly confirmed Philip's suspicion. Philip confronted Tara with the truth while Chuck was away at a medical convention. After Tara admitted the truth, the couple acknowledged they still loved each other and spent the night making love. Tara

planned to tell Chuck she wanted a divorce, but his kidney condition returned. With Chuck seriously ill, Tara pleaded with Philip to give her time before breaking the news about their relationship to Chuck. Suspecting that Tara planned to ask for a divorce, Chuck prolonged his illness by refusing to continue his dialysis treatment. And Erica wasn't thrilled to hear Philip was once again in love with Tara, so she refused to divorce him.

As time passed, Erica became bored playing housewife and decided to resume her career. A short time later, she agreed to Philip's request for a divorce. Chuck got involved with an emotionally needy ex-prostitute, Donna Beck. Realizing he loved Donna, Chuck set Tara free to marry Philip.

Tara and Philip's long-awaited marriage finally happened, but trouble soon followed. Conflicts arose over little Philip, who didn't accept Philip as his father and even changed his name to Charley (Chuck's full name is Charles). Tara also had a lingering interest in Chuck. This prompted the couple to separate for a short time. Eventually, they reconciled their differences and got back together. By this time, Philip had become a police officer and he was killed on duty in a helicopter crash. After working through her grief, Tara married little Philip's child psychologist, Jim Jefferson. Soon after their marriage, all three left town.

Following her divorce from Philip, Erica had an affair with Nick Davis. Erica desperately wanted to marry Nick, but his marriage to Anne Tyler left him sour on the idea. Distraught over Nick's rejection, Erica tried to kill herself. When Nick left town, Erica became involved with former professional football player Tom Cudahy. They eventually married. Once again, Erica's role as a wife took second place to her career. She lied to Tom about taking birth control; Tom very much wanted a child. Behind Tom's back, Erica auditioned for the role of spokeswoman for Sensuelle Cosmetics. When she was awarded the position, a furious Tom divorced her. Erica's next conquest was the married head of Sensuelle Cosmetics, Brandon Kingsley. Their affair was threatened by Kent Bogard, who was heir to Bogard International, Sensuelle's largest competitor. Frustrated by Brandon's unwillingness to divorce his wife, Sara, Erica broke off their affair and took up with Kent.

A woman claiming to be Erica's half-sister, Silver, showed up at Erica's New York apartment. Accepting Silver as her sister, Erica invited the young woman to move in with her. She soon came to regret her generous offer when Silver started

ALL MY CHILDREN

JANUARY 5, 1970–PRESENT ABC

Susan Lucci is reportedly the highest-paid performer in daytime soaps. She's an original cast member of *All My Children*, landing her role as Erica Kane when she was 20 years old. A graduate of New York's Marymount College, Lucci worked as a color girl for the *Ed Sullivan Show*. This meant that she arrived at the Ed Sullivan Theater in New York, sat on a stool, and tried her best not to fall off. "That's really what I did. I sat in front of a camera. They were developing a system of lighting color television."

Besides doing walk-ons on various daytime serials, Lucci also had a bit part in the feature films *Me, Natalie* and *Goodbye Columbus*. When the opportunity to audition for the role of the 15-year-old vixenish Erica presented itself, Lucci was reluctant to audition. "Soaps always made me laugh for the wrong reasons. Either relationships were melodramatic or they belonged in a Hallmark card," she said. After reading her audition scene, which involved an argument between a mother and daughter over boys and math grades, Lucci's opinion quickly changed. "I understood Erica immediately. It was a scene out of life."

Lucci's home life is nothing like the glamorous yet unsettled life of Erica. She married Helmut Huber in the early seventies and they have two children, Liza and Andreas.

In 1990, Lucci joined the cast of prime-time's *Dallas* in a recurring role. Occasionally, she has entertained thoughts of leaving *All My Children*, but hasn't yet acted upon it. "It's tempting," she said, "especially when I'm up against a wall with a contract renewal staring at me. But I'm also aware that in an actor's lifetime you're lucky if that one smashing part ever comes along."

sleeping with Kent. Feeling betrayed by Kent and blinded with rage, Erica accidentally killed him. She was sentenced to the electric chair, but was saved by Silver, who witnessed the murder. After clearing Erica, Silver confessed she was not Erica's half-sister.

Erica's exciting life inspired her to publish a biography. Writer Mike Roy assisted her, and their collaboration led to an affair. When the book was released, millionaire Adam Chandler purchased the movie rights. Erica wanted to marry Mike. But he decided to go to Tibet, where he intended to write another book. Erica married Adam on the rebound. After completing his book, Mike returned to Pine Valley and resumed his affair with a now-married Erica.

Susan Lucci plays the self-centered Erica Kane. Despite Erica's bad points, she has a vulnerable side that makes her lovable.

Jesse Hubbard (Darnell Williams) and Jenny Gardner (Kim Delaney) were close friends, they both had troubled childhoods and they seemed to understand each other.

Adam staged his own death because a former employee possessed a diary that implicated Adam in his first wife's death. This opened the door for Mike and Erica to marry. Adam eventually cleaned out the skeletons in his closet and resumed his life in Pine Valley. News that Erica married Mike shortly on the heels of his staged death infuriated Adam. When it became apparent that Erica chose to remain married to Mike, Adam vowed to destroy her. Later, Mike was killed trying to rescue Erica's half-brother, Mark Dalton, and Brooke Cudahy from drug lords.

A grief-stricken Erica traveled to Tibet, where she sought comfort from her pain. While there, Erica fell in love with a monk, Jeremy Hunter. The couple planned to marry, but trouble soon arose when Jeremy's former lover, Natalie,

arrived in Pine Valley. An already pregnant Natalie tricked him into sleeping with her and then pretended he was the father of her child. Erica proved that the real father of Natalie's baby was Jeremy's late father. Having a sudden change of heart about marrying Jeremy, Erica set her sights on millionaire Travis Montgomery. They fell in love, married, and had a daughter, Bianca.

Steven Andrews, a vengeful business associate of Travis's, arranged to have Bianca kidnapped. Erica's baby was returned, but when she discovered Travis was involved in the kidnapping, she fled the country, taking Bianca with her. Erica sought refuge in a cabin owned by Steven. Not realizing Steven was responsible for Bianca's kidnapping, Erica found herself attracted to him. When Travis finally managed to find Erica, she

ALL MY CHILDREN

JANUARY 5, 1970–PRESENT ABC

informed him she wanted a divorce. A fight erupted between Steven and Travis and Steven was killed. That same night, Travis was the victim of a violent mugging, which caused him to lose his memory.

In an attempt to help Travis regain his memory, he was admitted to Oak Haven, a rest home. Erica tried to patch up their relationship. But Erica lied to Travis, and so he ended any chance of a reconciliation. After his amnesia lifted, Travis fell in love with Skye, Adam Chandler's daughter, who was also an Oak Haven patient.

Erica became involved with Travis's younger brother, Jackson. Travis's love for Skye turned out to be infatuation. When he discovered Erica was involved with Jackson, he accused his brother of trying to steal his wife. Erica decided to remarry Travis, believing it was in Bianca's best interest, but she no longer loved him.

Nina Cortlandt's fairy tale romance to Cliff Warner was also a notable storyline. The early stages of their relationship were threatened by Nina's possessive, millionaire father, Palmer Cortlandt, and nurse Sybil Thorne, who wanted Cliff for herself. Sybil managed to sleep with Cliff and then informed him on his wedding day to Nina that she was pregnant. Nina backed out of the marriage and insisted Cliff wed Sybil, who eventually gave birth to a baby boy, Bobby. When Sybil turned up dead, Cliff was accused of killing her. The real killer was Tom Cudahy's black sheep brother, Sean.

Soon after Nina and Cliff's wedding, Nina had an affair with Steve Jacobi, a business associate. Nina and Cliff separated, but reconciled shortly after Nina ended her relationship with Steve, who later turned up dead in a plane crash. While performing medical work in South

Kim Delaney (left) played Jenny Gardner, the daughter of Opal Gardner, played by Dorothy Lyman (center). On the right is Susan Lucci, who plays the beautiful Erica Kane.

After Erica's divorce from Travis Montgomery, she fell in love with Travis's brother, Jackson (Walt Willey, left). Patrick Wayne (right) played the ship's captain.

America, Cliff would also be presumed dead in a plane crash. Unable to accept news of her husband's death, Nina traveled to South America with Matt Connolly, a mercenary friend of Jeremy Hunter's. They tried unsuccessfully to locate her husband.

Returning to Pine Valley, Nina fell in love with Matt and married him. Weeks later, Cliff returned home. Nina was tempted to reconcile with Cliff, but when she learned she was pregnant with Matt's child, she had a change of heart. Instead, she and Matt left town. Meanwhile, Cliff had an interracial romance with Dr. Angie Hubbard. Angie's husband, police officer Jesse Hubbard, was recently killed in the line of duty. Cliff eventually proposed to Angie and she accepted.

Weeks before the ceremony, Nina returned to town with her son, who was seriously ill. The boy needed a blood transfusion. When Cliff discovered that Matt didn't share the same blood type as the boy, and that he did, he realized he was the boy's natural father. Cliff canceled his wedding plans to Angie, while Nina filed for divorce from Matt. Nina and Cliff remarried and left Pine Valley with their children.

All My Children premiered as a half-hour serial. It expanded to a full hour in 1977. Actress Mary Fickett, who plays Ruth Martin, was the first daytime soap performer to win an Emmy. Besides providing its audience entertaining storylines, the serial has attempted to heighten their social awareness by tackling subjects such as homosexuality, abortion, AIDS, rape, drug abuse, child abuse, wife abuse, alcoholism, mental illness, and Vietnam and its effects.

Humor has also played a big role in *All My Children's* success. It has larger-than-life characters such as the self-centered and beautiful Erica Kane Montgomery, manipulative Palmer Cortlandt, ditzy Opal Gardner, overbearing Phoebe Tyler Wallingford, her ex-con-man husband Langly Wallingford, and ex-carny-girl turned mother-confessor Myrtle Fargate.

College students are attracted to the serial's younger characters, and make up a big part of its audience. Celebrity viewers include Carol Burnett (who has appeared on the serial in two different roles), Oprah Winfrey, Gladys Knight, Melba Moore, Joe Montana, Luther Vandross, and the L.A. Raiders.

"We never stirred things up for the sake of argument," said creator Agnes Nixon. "Always, the point was to entertain. We stuck to the old vaudeville chestnut: 'Make 'em laugh, make 'em cry, make 'em wait'." They've been doing that successfully for 20 years.

ANOTHER LIFE

JUNE 1, 1981–OCTOBER 5, 1984 CBN

"Take the soap operas in the afternoon!... They teach women how to run around on their husbands in a very sophisticated fashion and get by with it. So I say that television has become a vendor of perniciousness. And I think we need some men and women at the top who are not motivated by the gods of the almighty dollar," the Reverend Jerry Falwell told *Penthouse* magazine in the early eighties.

Enter *Another Life*, the Christian Broadcasting Network's (CBN) alternative to the "immoral" soaps broadcast on commercial television. Touted by CBN executives as the "soap with hope," this religious, half-hour serial premiered on June 1, 1981. It brought the uplifting message that positive solutions to any problem could be found through a strong relationship with God. More than 3,200 cable systems carried the half-hour drama, making it available to more than eighteen million households. It was also telecast on approximately twenty broadcast stations.

The Davidsons were the serial's prominent family. Six months after its premiere, patriarch Scott was killed in a tragic car accident. His surviving widow, Terry, worked as a nurse at Kingsley Hospital. They had two children: an emotionally fragile daughter, Lori, and a teenage son, Peter, whose Christian values were ridiculed by his rabble-rousing college classmates. Terry's sister, Nancy, was selfish and deceitful, in sharp contrast to Terry's own loving nature.

During the serial's three-year run, Lori, among others, would often find her faith in God challenged. An early storyline featured the dilemma she faced when she was falsely accused of sleeping with another woman's husband. Responsible for spreading the malicious rumor was the immoral, filthy rich Miriam Carpenter Mason. Miriam claimed that Lori was trying to destroy her family.

Later, Lori was involved in an automobile crash. She awoke in a hospital bed several days later and found out she was paralyzed. The handsome doctor Ben Martin cured Lori's paralysis. Lori and Ben fell in love and married. While the newlywed Lori struggled with the loneliness of being a doctor's wife, a new tragedy entered her life. A rapist attacked her, although he was unsuccessful at raping her.

After being kidnapped and held hostage for a large ransom, Miriam had a spiritual awakening. Although committed to turning over a new leaf, she discovered that old habits die hard. She would occasionally revert to her past bad behavior—especially when she was unsuccessful at getting what she wanted.

Playboy Russ Weaver also became a religious convert. In his case, a near-fatal shooting made him evaluate his life. While unconscious, Russ had an out-of-body experience, caught a glimpse of hell, and decided to make some major changes.

The cast of *Another Life* included several faces familiar to soap opera viewers. Michael Ryan, who appeared on *Another World* for fifteen years as John Randolph, played Vince Cardello, the ruthless head of an organized crime ring. Paul Tinder, also of *Another World*, played Dr. Brian Graham. Nick Benedict, who starred on *All My Children* and *The Young and the Restless*, played Cardello's right-hand man, Ron Washington. Debbie McLeod, formerly of *Search for Tomorrow*, played Lori Davidson Martin.

Below: *Ben and Lori Martin (Matt Williams and Debbie McLeod, left) were close to her family, which included her mother, Terry (Mary Jean Feton, right back), and brother, Peter (Darryl Campbell, right front). Lori's father had been killed in an auto accident.*

Opposite page, top: *Miriam Carpenter Mason (Ginger Burgett) was an unhappy, unkind person until she was kidnapped and held hostage. She had a religious conversion experience and tried to live a better life.*

Opposite page, bottom: *Lori and Ben faced many trials, but their faith kept their relationship solid.*

THE CAST

Cast

PAUL MASON	ROBERT BENDALL
RON WASHINGTON	NICHOLAS BENEDICT
SAMANTHA MARSHALL	DEE DEE BRIDGEWATER
ALEX GREELEY	BOB BURCHETTE
MIRIAM CARPENTER MASON	GINGER BURGETT
IONE REDLON	EDYE BYRDE
PETER DAVIDSON	DARRYL CAMPBELL
LUCILLE FIGGINS	FRANKIE CARDOZA
COURTNEY CARPENTER	SUSAN C. CAREY
STACEY PHILLIPS	KAREN CHAPMAN
SCOTT DAVIDSON	JOHN CORSAULT
TERRY DAVIDSON	MARY JEAN FETON
CARLA REDLON	ELAIN GRAHAM
HELEN CARPENTER	SUZANNE GRANFIELD
HUGO/JEREMY LANCELOT	KELLY GWIN
GENE REDLON	EDDIE HAILEY
BLUE NOBLES	CHANDLER HILL HARBEN
GIL PRESCOTT	J. MICHAEL HUNTER
BABS FARLEY	JULIE JENNY
CHARLES CARPENTER	RANDY KRAFT, JR.
LIZ CUMMINS	CAROLYN LENZ
BARBARA	LORI MARCH
CARRIE WEAVER	MARTY McGAW
JEFF CUMMINGS	MATT McGOWAN
LORI DAVIDSON MARTIN	DEBBIE McLEOD
	JEANETTE LARSON
NANCY LAWSON	NANCY MULVEY
MORA LINDSAY	NAOMI RISEMAN
RUSS WEAVER	CHRISTOPHER ROLAND
VINCE CARDELLO	MICHAEL RYAN
HAROLD WEBSTER	ALAN SADER
BECKY HEWITT	SUSAN SCANNELL
VANESSA FAZAN	DIANE SEELY
VICKI LANG	ANNAMARIE SMITH
KATE PHILLIPS CAROTHERS	DOROTHY STINNETTE
DAN MYERS	KIM STRONG
BRIAN GRAHAM	PAUL TINDER
DAVE PHILLIPS	TOM URICH
LEE CAROTHERS	JIM WILLIAMS
	PAUL GLEASON
BEN MARTIN	MATT WILLIAMS
AMBER PHILLIPS	PEGGY WOODY

ANOTHER WORLD

MAY 4, 1964–PRESENT NBC

This long-running serial was originally intended to be a spin-off of *As the World Turns*. Creator Irna Phillips pitched the concept to CBS, but the network passed on it because they had no available time slot. NBC heard about the series and quickly spoke to Phillips. Although the competing network made it impossible for Phillips to introduce her new characters on *As the World Turns*, she shrewdly titled her new creation *Another World*.

Set in the small town of Bay City, Michigan, the serial focused on the Matthews family. Wealthy attorney Will Matthews headed a successful accounting firm. He and Liz, his "nouveau riche" wife, were the parents of Bill and Susan. Will's brother, Jim, was a C.P.A. who led a less ostentatious lifestyle with Mary, his wife. They had three children: Russ, a college student; Pat, who was in love with the manipulative Tom Baxter; and Alice, a teenager. Will and Jim's sister, Janet, was having an affair with Tom's married father, Ken Baxter.

Several of the serial's shortcomings became obvious soon after its premiere. In her eagerness to see the show succeed, Phillips had projected fast-paced storylines involving a devastating family tragedy, a single-parent pregnancy, an illegal abortion, and a love relationship between a beautiful orphan and a wealthy young man (his disapproving, obsessive mother worked overtime to undermine the relationship). Unfortunately, the characters featured in the storylines seemed like second-rate copies of *As the World Turns*. Tom Donovan, the serial's first director, explained, "The story and the characters didn't always work together. Irna had Virginia Dwyer, as Mary Matthews, playing a kind of Nancy Hughes. But Mary never had the same importance as Nancy and tended to stagnate, mostly because Irna's melodrama didn't allow Mary Matthews the same range as Nancy Hughes."

Phillips stayed with the struggling serial for two years before turning the headwriting reins over to James Lipton. Lipton's first action was to eliminate several characters. Rather than improving the show's ratings, his efforts resulted in a bigger downward slide. Positive changes occurred when Lipton was replaced by Agnes Nixon in 1967. Nixon swiftly killed all the characters Lipton had

created. Once again, the Matthews were moved to the front. Alice was sent to nursing school and became a nurse in record time. Pat married successful lawyer John Randolph, and encountered problems with his insecure teenage daughter, Lee. Russ married self-centered, scheming Rachel Davis (originally played by Robin Strasser), who grew up poor and was determined to improve her lot in life.

Although this was several years before Nixon's *All My Children* premiered, she borrowed from the serial's already created bible, which was tucked away in her office filing cabinet. "I patterned Rachel after Erica Kane," she explained. "Rachel was a character with doom potential—meaning that she is destructive but was ultimately a greater threat to herself than other people."

Below: *In 1983, Mac Cory (Douglass Watson) and Rachel Davis (Victoria Wyndham), and Blaine Ewing (Laura Malone) and Sandy Cory (Chris Rich) sealed their marriage vows. Rachel and Mac divorced several times, but they were destined for each other and always remarried.*

Opposite page: *The cast of* Another World *poses for a group photo in 1979.*

It took a full year before Nixon was able to see the dramatic potential behind one of her original characters, Steven Frame. Nixon observed a unique chemistry when George Reinholt was in scenes with Jacqueline Courtney, who played Alice Matthews. Inspired by what she saw, Nixon decided to create a love story for Steven and Alice. Rachel, Alice's sister-in-law, complicated their romance.

Under Nixon's guidance, *Another World* skyrocketed to the top of the ratings and became a hit. In 1968, she resigned to launch *One Life to Live* on ABC. She was replaced by Bob Cendella. When the ratings fell, a succession of headwriters tried to turn things around by resorting to melodramatic plots. In 1971, Procter & Gamble, which owned *Another World,* took a chance on an untried talent in soap opera headwriting, novelist Harding ("Pete") Lemay. He saw rich, dramatic possibilities in the serial's class-conflict elements.

THE CAST

Original Cast

GRANDMA MATTHEWS	VERA ALLEN
JIM MATTHEWS	JOHN BEAL
JANET MATTHEWS	LIZA CHAPMAN
ALICE MATTHEWS	JACQUELINE COURTNEY
LIZ MATTHEWS	SARAH CUNNINGHAM
LAURA BAXTER	AUGUSTA DABNEY
MARY MATTHEWS	VIRGINIA DWYER
BILL MATTHEWS	JOSEPH GALLISON
KEN BAXTER	WILLIAM PRINCE
TOM BAXTER	NICHOLAS PRYOR
MELISSA PALMER	CAROL ROUX
SUSAN MATTHEWS	FRAN SHARON
RUSS MATTHEWS	JOEY TRENT
PAT MATTHEWS	SUSAN TRUSTMAN

ANOTHER WORLD

MAY 4, 1964–PRESENT NBC

Lemay's first major change was to develop new layers to Rachel's character. "I didn't feel it was necessary to keep Rachel a black-and-white character," he explained. "I saw her instead as a person who had always had bad breaks and who defeats herself because she is so used to failure. I wanted the audience to feel her pain as I felt it. I wanted the audience to feel her tears."

Viewers also learned more about Steven's background, which was similar to Rachel's. Relatives from his past moved to Bay City, allowing the audience to see how Steven related emotionally to characters other than Alice and Rachel. Steven was forced to confront the real possibility that his love for both women was based on fantasy rather than reality.

Lemay also introduced a new character who would have a major impact on Rachel's life, millionaire Mackenzie Cory (played by Douglass Watson). Complicating their relationship was Mac's obsessive daughter, Iris Cory Carrington (originally played by Beverlee McKinsey).

In 1974, *Another World* was the first serial to expand to a full hour. It's also presently the only daytime serial to spawn three spin-offs *(Somerset, Lovers and Friends,* and *Texas).* Several weeks after the show switched to a 60-minute format, Lemay implemented three changes that completely caught viewers off guard. George Reinholt was fired (allegedly because of backstage conflicts) and his character written off, presumed dead. Next, matriarch Mary Matthews suffered a fatal heart attack. Finally, Jacqueline Courtney was replaced by Susan Harney.

In 1979, *Another World* became the only serial in daytime history to expand to 90 minutes. Unfortunately, the extra half hour proved disastrous. Viewers had a difficult time following the story and began tuning out. In 1980, the serial returned to an hour format, but the damage had already been done. Meanwhile, an exhausted Harding Lemay stepped down as headwriter.

For the next several years, *Another World* floundered. By the mideighties, the emphasis had shifted away from the Matthews and three new families were introduced: the wealthy Loves, the down-to-earth McKinnons, and the combative Hudson brothers. Rachel's three children, Jamie, Amanda, and Matthew (all three had different fathers), also moved to the forefront.

In 1989, as the serial prepared to celebrate its twenty-fifth anniversary, tragedy struck. Longtime cast member Douglass Watson suffered a fatal heart attack while on vacation. Several weeks after the actor's death, Rachel learned her husband, Mac Cory, had died. Acknowledging Mr. Watson's death, *Another World's* headwriter, Donna Swajeski, said, "Douglass Watson was more than a wonderful performer. He embodied the essence of the good father, the loving husband, the intimate family man. To me he was a legend. A larger-than-life figure, who could make you cry and laugh, and remember him long after the TV was turned off for the day. His presence, his talent, will always be the foundation of our show."

Paying tribute to her costar, Victoria Wyndham (the current Rachel) said, "Our industry has lost a fine actor. Our company has lost a beloved colleague. And I have lost a friend."

Despite his death in 1989, Douglass Watson's presence is still felt by the cast and fans.

Victoria Wyndham is a sculptor and this was written into the show. Here she stands with Douglass Watson and the bust she sculpted of him.

During the late sixties and through the midseventies, the love triangle between Alice, Rachel, and Steven was featured prominently. When Rachel first met Steven, she was married to Alice's brother, Russ, who spent most of his time at the hospital as an intern. Steven was too preoccupied with Alice to notice Rachel's interest. An argument between Steven and Alice opened the door for Rachel to make her move. She showed up at Steven's apartment and succeeded in seducing him. By the time Rachel learned she was pregnant, Alice and Steven had cleared up their differences.

Cornering Steven alone, Rachel broke the news about her pregnancy and demanded he marry her. When Steven refused, Rachel told Russ she was pregnant with Russ's child.

Rachel chose Steven and Alice's engagement party to share the truth about her pregnancy with a stunned Alice. The next day, Alice broke her engagement to Steven and flew to Paris. Refusing to believe Alice would be gone forever, Steven proceeded with plans to build her dream

house. Time passed and Alice returned to Bay City, her wounds healed. She and Steven married and moved into their new house.

Once Russ realized Steven was the father of Rachel's son Jamie, he divorced her. Rachel next set her sights on Ted Clark, a hapless blackmail victim who got involved in criminal activities. They divorced soon after Ted was sentenced to a long prison term.

Steven tried to form a relationship with his son, Jamie, while taking care to avoid Rachel. It was at this time that Rachel's father, Gerald Davis, moved to Bay City. Feeling guilty for abandoning his daughter when she was a child, Gerald promised to help her win Steven. He urged Rachel to tell Steven he couldn't visit Jamie unless she was present. One night while Steven was with Rachel and Jamie, a pregnant Alice slipped off a stepladder and miscarried. Alice tried to locate Steven, but didn't know where he was. Later, Gerald arranged for Alice to see Steven and Rachel together. Upset and confused, Alice ran away to New York, but

ANOTHER WORLD

MAY 4, 1964–PRESENT NBC

Steven didn't know why. Consequently, Steven grew closer to Rachel. Steven divorced Alice and wed Rachel.

Alice found a job working as a private nurse for Dennis Carrington. Dennis was the son of writers Eliot and Iris Carrington, who were separated. Dennis suffered from a heart condition that required complicated surgery. Since Russ specialized in cardiac problems, Alice returned to Bay City with Dennis.

Fearing that Eliot was falling in love with Alice, Iris bugged his apartment to find out more about the true nature of their relationship. Iris taped a conversation between Alice and Steven clearing up their differences. Iris handed the tape over to Rachel. Discovering that Iris had bugged his apartment, Eliot threatened to have her arrested, but quickly changed his mind when she suffered a nervous breakdown. Once Iris recovered, Eliot offered to give their marriage another try. To his surprise, Iris was no longer interested and divorced him.

Steven managed to secure an illegal divorce from Rachel by lying in court. Alice's lawyer brother-in-law, John Randolph, represented Steven in the divorce. Realizing that Steven had lied placed John in an awkward situation. Unable to deal with it, he began drinking heavily.

Steven and Alice finally remarried, but the ceremony was interrupted by a drunken John, who finally exposed Steven's lies. Steven was sentenced to a short prison term for perjury. Angered at John, he withdrew all of his business and turned it over to Tim McGowan, a new lawyer in town. This encouraged John's alcoholism to progress. With Rachel's support, John eventually picked up new clients, set aside his drinking, and reunited with his family.

While Steven was in jail, Rachel demanded that Alice move out of the house so she and Jamie could move in. Believing Rachel was within her legal rights, a distraught Alice moved out and immediately had a nervous breakdown. She was sent to an institution for psychological treatment.

Below, left: *Larry Lau played Jamie Frame, the son of Rachel Davis and Steve Frame.*

Below right: *During the 1984 season, Cecile DePoulignac (Nancy Frangione) was having a secret affair with Cass Winthrop (Stephen Schnetzer, right), despite plans to marry Peter Love (John Hutton, left).*

Felicia Gallant (Linda Dano) had an affair with Cass Winthrop, but he was also having an affair with Cecile.

By the time Steven was released from prison, Alice's psychological problems were successfully treated. Unfortunately, Alice learned she would never be able to bear children. At first, she resisted reconciling with Steven, but they eventually resumed their marriage.

While Steven was in Australia on a business trip, Alice's mother died. Soon after, Alice received word that Steven had been killed in a helicopter crash.

Soon after Steven's death, Rachel got involved with Iris's father, Mackenzie Cory. Much to Iris's dismay, Mac fell in love with Rachel and married her. Marriage to Mac softened Rachel and she gave birth to a daughter, Amanda. Meanwhile, Iris continued scheming to break up the couple. Eventually, Mac and Rachel were torn apart. They divorced and remarried several times.

During one of their break-ups, Steven resurfaced in Bay City, much to everyone's surprise. A couple of years earlier, Rachel had given birth to a second son, Matthew. His father was Mitch Hobson, a former lover of Rachel's who

would continue to have an impact on her life for several years. Steven's reappearance in Bay City was especially unsettling for Alice, who was now engaged to marry Mac. Steven explained his reasons for staying away from Bay City and Alice accepted them. Seeing Steven again, Alice realized she was still in love with him and canceled her plans to marry Mac.

Alice, however, never had the opportunity to remarry Steven. Alone with Rachel at a construction site, Steven faced the fact he was still in love with her. Since this was one of the periods when Rachel was divorced from Mac, she believed she was also still in love with Steven. The couple made plans to marry and a rejected Alice left town. Ironically, Rachel was also denied the opportunity to remarry Steven. Weeks after they pledged their love, Steven was killed in a tragic car accident. His final appearance in Bay City was in 1989, when Alice communicated with his spirit in a dream.

Rachel and Mac's last marriage ceremony took place in 1983. They lived relatively happy with one another until the summer of 1989, when Mac died of a heart attack. In his will, Mac left everything to be divided between Rachel, their daughter Amanda, and Iris.

Iris had succeeded in completely destroying her relationship with her father. Mac's death made it impossible for Iris to reconcile their differences.

Soon after Mac's death, a mysterious stranger arrived in Bay City named Ken Jordan. Believing Ken had new information regarding Mac's death, Rachel befriended him. It wasn't long before a second will, supposedly written by Mac, materialized. The will was particularly disheartening for Iris because she wasn't included in it. Complicating matters for Rachel was the attraction she felt for Ken.

The nineties have seen the reemergence of the Frame family. The Corys and the Loves are also heavily featured.

Honoring the serial's twenty-fifth anniversary in 1989, David Bailey, who has a recurring role as Russ Matthews, said, "The show is as good now as it's been in all the years I've been here. I think it's very competitive with the other good shows in daytime. In the past, maybe one or two shows a week were good. Now it's three and four that are really excellent. I was here for the twentieth anniversary. I'd only been here two years then, and I didn't have a sense of what it meant to be part of a show that's been on the air for so long. But something's clicked in the last couple of years, and I really have a sense of pride that this show's been around so long."

AS THE WORLD TURNS

APRIL 2, 1956–PRESENT CBS

This serial premiered on the same day as *The Edge of Night*. Both were daytime television's first 30-minute serials. Irna Phillips created *As the World Turns* with the intention of placing character over plot. She believed people watched television soaps not to see what would happen next, but to experience the characters. As a result, most scenes took place between two characters seated at a kitchen table sipping coffee or on a living room sofa. Procter & Gamble backed the project and even agreed to Phillips's unprecedented stipulation that the serial not be canceled for an entire year, no matter how dismal its ratings.

As the World Turns was set in the medium-sized midwestern city of Oakdale, Illinois. It centered on two families, the Lowells and the Hughes. Patriarch Judge Lowell was a widower with an adult son, Jim. Jim and his wife, Claire, had a teenage daughter, Ellen. Jim was a partner in the family law firm, along with his friend Chris Hughes. Chris and his wife, Nancy, had four children: Donald, Penny, Bob, and Susan (who died in a freak accident when she was hit by lightning while swimming). Living with the Hughes was Chris's father, known affectionately as Grandpa Hughes. Chris's sister, Edith, also played an important role during the serial's first few years.

Helen Wagner, who has played Nancy Hughes since the serial's first episode, was fired by Phillips after thirteen weeks because of a contract dispute. The writer claimed her reasons for dismissing Wagner had to do with how the actress wore her hair, her style of clothes, and various other trivial gripes. Immediately following her departure, Wagner began performing in a play. Meanwhile, on the show Nancy was out of town vacationing. Once Phillips's temper cooled, she realized her mistake and requested that the actress return. Wagner agreed—with one stipulation. She wouldn't return immediately because of her commitment to the play's producers. "Irna loved being at my mercy," said Wagner, "and wanted me back on the show all the more."

Billy Lee, who originated the role of Grandpa Hughes, wasn't as fortunate. Phillips dismissed him after three episodes. His

replacement, Santos Ortega, remained with the show until his death on April 10, 1976. Hal Studer, who played Donald Hughes, was given a pink slip because the writer thought he was too short. He was replaced by Richard Holland.

An early storyline featured Jim Lowell's extramarital affair with Edith Hughes. Although it was tastefully handled, Procter & Gamble was nervous about the audience response. Phillips wanted Jim to divorce his wife and marry Edith. As a rule, Procter & Gamble vetoed divorce storylines, but gave the writer the go ahead to break up Jim and Claire. They drew the line, however, at having Jim marry Edith. They were concerned it would look like Jim was being

Below: *(left to right) Santos Ortega as Grandpa Hughes, Don MacLaughlin as Chris Hughes, Helen Wagner as Nancy Hughes, and William Johnstone as Judge James Lowell.*

Opposite page: *The love story between Kim Reynolds (Kathryn Hays) and Bob Hughes (Don Hastings) caused many problems when it began. Bob was married to Kim's sister when they met, and the audience was appalled. Many years later, in 1985, Kim and Bob finally married.*

rewarded for his adultery. Phillips was angered by Procter & Gamble's decision, but accepted it. A short while later, she sent Jim on a business trip to Florida and killed him in a boating accident. Viewers were jarred by Jim's sudden demise and immediately wrote the network letters expressing their dissatisfaction. Phillips's response was, "As the world turns, we know the bleakness of winter, the promise of spring, the fullness of summer, and the harvest of autumn . . . the cycle of life is complete. . . . What is true of the world, nature, is also true of man. He too has his cycle."

As the World Turns was the only soap in daytime television history to spin-off its own prime-time serial, *Our Private World*. It ran through the summer of 1965 and centered around an immensely popular character from the daytime serial, Lisa Miller Hughes, played by Eileen Fulton. Lisa left Oakdale to begin a new life in Chicago. But the prime-time serial proved

THE CAST

Original Cast

BOB HUGHES	BOBBY ALFORD
CLAIRE LOWELL	ANN BURR
JIM LOWELL, JR.	LES DAMON
ELLEN LOWELL	WENDY DREW
JAMES T. LOWELL	WILLIAM JOHNSTONE
GRANDPA HUGHES	BILLY LEE
CHRIS HUGHES	DON MacLAUGHLIN
MRS. TURNER	LEONA POWERS
DONALD HUGHES	HAL STUDER
JANICE TURNER	JOYCE VAN PATTEN
NANCY HUGHES	HELEN WAGNER
EDITH HUGHES	RUTH WARRICK

AS THE WORLD TURNS

short-lived, and Lisa returned to Oakdale and *As the World Turns*.

Phillips resigned as headwriter in 1970, terminating her contract with Procter & Gamble for health reasons. A few months later, she was hired as story consultant for *A World Apart*, an ABC soap created by her adopted daughter, Katherine Phillips. The soap ran for 15 months. In 1972, *As The World Turns* suffered a serious drop in ratings and Phillips was persuaded by Procter & Gamble to resume her role as headwriter.

Upon her return, Phillips was horrified by what she found. Elizabeth Talbot was being pursued by brothers Paul and Dan Stewart. Even more disgusting to the writer, Dan had a daughter by his wife, Susan, and a second daughter out of wedlock with Elizabeth. Things had certainly changed since Jim Lowell's affair with Edith! Ironically, Phillips didn't consider it progress.

Back at the helm, Phillips made immediate and sweeping changes in the serial's direction. Paul Stewart suffered a brain tumor and died off-camera. Elizabeth died from a fall upwards on a stairwell trying to rescue her daughter, Betsy. Dan was exiled to England. Susan's recent marriage to Dr. Bruce Baxter was annulled because he became sexually impotent.

Phillips also introduced a new character who would have a major impact on the lives of several people living in Oakdale, particularly Dr. Bob Hughes and his wife, Jennifer. Kim, a former professional singer, arrived in Oakdale to visit her newly married sister, Jennifer. A physical attraction developed immediately between Kim and Bob. It wasn't long before they found themselves involved in an affair. Later, Kim learned she was pregnant with Bob's child. Discussing Kim Reynolds with a reporter in 1973, Phillips provided viewers with an insight into her own personality when she said, "Everyone asks me how I got the idea for Kim Reynolds on the show, because she certainly is an unusual character. She's really me—at a much younger age. She's fiercely independent, as I was, and she won't settle for second best. She looks in the mirror and refers to herself as 'the lady in the mirror.' Well, that was her other self, which no one knew about: the true me, the person I always hid from the world. She's having a child out of wedlock, which will be only hers. I adopted two children—Kathy and Tommy—without having a husband. We're both the same. And she's going to have that child to prove that a woman can do it alone."

Phillips's storyline proved disastrous. Viewers were appalled that Bob would cheat on his wife—especially with his own sister-in-law. In their eyes, the character's integrity had been completely destroyed. They could no longer trust him. Thousands of letters flooded CBS complaining about the storyline. When the ratings took a nosedive, Procter & Gamble abruptly fired Phillips from the show she had created 17 years earlier. Six months later, Phillips, who was busy penning her autobiography, died in her sleep.

John Dixon (Larry Bryggman) is one of soap's longest-running villians, and when he married scheming Lucinda Walsh (Elizabeth Hubbard) the sparks really began to fly.

Penny Hughes (Rosemary Prinz) lost her husband, and in her grief she turned to Roy McGuire (Konrad Matthaei). They married but the marriage didn't last.

Nearly 18 years after her death, four of Phillips's creations are still running on network television. Besides *As the World Turns,* they include *The Guiding Light, Another World,* and *Days of Our Lives.* To date, no other single headwriter has matched her record.

The husband and wife team of Robert Soderberg and Edith Sommer replaced Irna Phillips as the serial's headwriters. Their most significant change was to transform Kim into a more traditional soap opera heroine.

While other network soaps were breaking barriers and offering racier, more daring storylines in the seventies, *As the World Turns* remained conservative. The Hughes family was still prominently featured and storylines progressed at their usual slow pace. In 1976, *As the World Turns* became CBS's first serial to expand to a full hour. To make way for the extra 30 minutes, the network dropped *The Edge of Night* (it was quickly snapped up by ABC).

By 1980, Procter & Gamble reluctantly decided to follow the latest trend in daytime soaps and began emphasizing younger characters. Suddenly, the Hughes became secondary characters. Nancy and Chris were reduced to making infrequent appearances and were completely dropped for a period of almost three years. Storylines moved at a faster pace and relied heavily on love triangles.

In 1986, Douglas Marland was appointed headwriter. His first step was to restore the Hughes to front-burner status. He also introduced a new family, the Snyders, who lived on a farm. For a brief period, the eldest Snyder son, Seth, was

engaged to Bob's daughter, Frannie. Their engagement ended when Seth thought he loved Bob and Kim's daughter, Sabrina, whose resemblance to Frannie was uncanny (the same actress played both parts). Seth's heart was broken, however, when Sabrina left town to marry an old flame in her native England. Marland was also responsible for introducing the first male homosexual character on daytime soaps.

A favorite character during the serial's early days was Chris and Nancy Hughes's daughter, Penny (played by Rosemary Prinz). Penny idolized her Aunt Edith and was devastated to learn she was having an extramartial affair with Jim Lowell. In an effort to create space from her family, a disillusioned teenaged Penny eloped with rebellious Jeff Baker (played by Mark Rydell). Nancy and Chris quickly moved to have the marriage annulled. A few years later, a more mature Penny and Jeff married again— this time with her parents' blessing. Penny and Jeff's plans to have a child were dashed when Penny discovered she couldn't conceive. Soon after, Jeff was killed in an automobile accident.

A short time after Jeff's death, Penny fell in love with Neil Wade (played by Michael Lipton), a former doctor. They married and opened a bookstore. Penny and Neil also made plans to adopt a child. Sadly, Neil's reason for giving up medicine surfaced. He resented his estranged natural father, Dr. Doug Cassen (Nat Polen), for pushing him into medicine. Like Jeff, Neil died in an automobile accident.

Overwhelmed by her second husband's death, Penny had a short, unhappy marriage to Roy McGuire. After her divorce, she left Oakdale and moved to England. She finally found happiness with a European racing champion. They adopted a young Eurasian girl and named her Amy. Occasionally, Penny makes visits to Oakdale, but she no longer figures prominently in the story.

Bob Hughes's first serious romance began in the summer of 1960, with the conniving Lisa Miller, a young farm girl from Rockford, Illinois. Phillips intended to feature their romance for the summer and write Lisa off in the fall. Eileen Fulton, who played the character, proved so popular that the writer changed her mind and increased Lisa's involvement in the serial.

Lisa snared Bob by seducing him and getting pregnant. Their elopement came as a complete surprise to Bob's parents, Chris and Nancy. Since Bob was still in college, his parents graciously opened their home to the young newlyweds. Soon after, Lisa gave birth to a baby boy, Tom.

AS THE WORLD TURNS

APRIL 2, 1956–PRESENT CBS

Marriage to Bob proved boring for Lisa. Leaving the care of her child to Nancy during the day, Lisa enrolled in college courses. She also found herself attracted to a successful shoe tycoon, Bruce Elliott. After the couple had an illicit affair, Lisa decided to divorce Bob, hoping to marry Bruce. Once her divorce was final, Bruce made it clear he had no intention of marrying Lisa. Alone and frightened, Lisa tried to talk Bob into remarrying her, but he wasn't interested. In an effort to get her life back on track, a despondent Lisa left young Tom with the Hughes and temporarily relocated to Chicago. After a brief marriage to a millionaire, Lisa returned to Oakdale.

Lisa's next lover was Michael Shea, who was married to Claire. Repeating old behavior patterns, Lisa got pregnant and tried to convince Michael to marry her. Michael was an insecure social climber who feared a divorce from Claire would cause him to lose status in Oakdale. When Claire discovered their affair, she immediately ended her marriage. Lisa's affair with Michael led to Claire's daughter, Ellen, developing a lifelong resentment toward her.

Lisa gave birth to a second son, Chuck. Now that his marriage with Claire was finished, Michael spent time at Lisa's developing a relationship with his son. Impulsively, Michael proposed marriage to Lisa, but she was no longer interested.

At this time, Lisa's first son, Tom, had returned from the Vietnam War a drug addict. Michael caught Tom trying to steal drugs from his cabinet and forced Tom to sign a written confession. Michael then used the confession to blackmail Lisa into becoming his wife.

Their marriage was a disaster. Lisa sexually tormented Michael and then would lock him out of their bedroom. Angered by Lisa's antics, Michael threatened to prove she was an unfit mother in court. Worried that she could lose Chuck, Lisa took her young son and ran off to Mexico.

Bob's second wife was model Sandy McGuire. She married the young doctor to provide security for her and her son, Jimmy. Realizing there was no real future for their marriage, Sandy eventually divorced Bob and moved to New York, where she intended to become a professional model.

Receiving word that her mother, Alma Miller, was critically ill, Lisa secretly returned to Oakdale. To her horror, Tom was on trial for killing Michael. Apparently, Tom confessed to the crime to protect his mother, who he suspected may have killed Michael. Lisa was so upset by Tom's trial that she developed amnesia. Later, authorities concluded that Michael was killed by a vengeful ex-lover. Lisa then regained her memory.

Once again Lisa found herself attracted to Bob, but he was interested in Jennifer Ryan, the widow of a doctor friend who had attended medical school with Bob. Not wasting any time, Lisa fell for Bob's brother, Donald. He admitted to Lisa he was attracted to her, but insisted marriage was out of the question.

Bob married Jennifer, but a number of problems soon developed. Jennifer's adult son, Dr. Rick Ryan, resented their marriage and took every opportunity to undermine their relationship. Jennifer also had an adult daughter, Barbara. Jennifer and Bob's marriage was further threatened by the arrival of Jennifer's sister, Kim.

The whole Hughes family, played by (front, left to right) Scott DeFreitas, Julianne Moore, (seated) Helen Wagner, Don MacLaughlin, (back) Hillary Bailey Smith, Gregg Marx, Don Hastings, and Kathryn Hays.

Bob's affair with Kim left her pregnant. When Kim discovered Jennifer was also pregnant with Bob's child, she accepted a marriage proposal from social-climbing Dr. John Dixon, who loved Kim and was willing to give her unborn child a name. Jennifer gave birth to a baby girl, Frannie. Meanwhile, Kim's daughter supposedly died. Years later, Kim and Bob would discover that the child was alive and had been adopted by a couple in England. They were finally introduced to their daughter, Sabrina, in 1986.

Believing her daughter was dead, Kim tried to divorce John, but he refused. Jennifer was diagnosed with a terminal disease and later died in an automobile accident. Although still married to John, Kim sought a separation and fell in love with Dr. Dan Stewart, grandson of the late Jim Lowell. Dan was already married to Susan, an alcoholic, and they had a daughter, Emily. (Years earlier, Dan fathered another daughter, Betsy, whose mother was the late Liz Talbot.)

After Dan secured a divorce from Susan and won custody of their daughter, he pressed Kim to divorce John. Unfortunately, an accident caused Kim to suffer amnesia and she unknowingly became sexually involved with John. Their encounter led to the birth of a son, Andy. Eventually, John agreed to divorce Kim. Her plans for a happy married life with Dan ended when he developed a fatal illness.

In the mideighties, Kim resumed her relationship with Bob and they finally wed. Kim and John's adolescent son, Andy, developed a drinking problem that had a serious effect on Kim's marriage to Bob. When Andy's alcoholism forced Kim to become closer to John, Bob felt neglected. One night he made the mistake of sleeping with Susan Stewart, now a recovered alcoholic who was on the brink of developing a drug dependency. Later, Bob confessed his indiscretion to Kim, seriously jeopardizing their marriage.

AS THE WORLD TURNS

APRIL 2, 1956–PRESENT CBS

Eileen Fulton moved to New York in 1956 with two desires: to succeed as an actress and a singer. Quicker than she could blink an eye, both desires were fulfilled. A minister's daughter, she graduated from Greensboro College, where she received acting awards for her performances in *Candide* and *Thirteen Clocks*. While studying acting, Fulton sold hats at Macy's department store and frequently modeled for photos used to accompany stories in *True Confessions* magazine. She also appeared in the feature film *Girl of the Night*, which costarred Anne Francis.

Fulton's role as Bob Hughes's status-conscious girlfriend, Lisa Miller, was originally projected to run for 13 weeks. At the end of her first day, Fulton wasn't even certain she would last the week. "I felt nervous that day," she remembered, "but only because the show was live. I felt sure the role was mine because I had signed a contract. But after we went off the air, Don MacLaughlin, who played Chris Hughes, came over to me and said, 'Eileen, you were wonderful. We think you're charming and love what you do. It's a breath of fresh air to see you act, but don't go out and buy that Rolls yet, because you still have Irna Phillips [the creator of *As the World Turns*] to deal with—this was your on-air audition for her.'"

Determined to win Phillips over, Fulton added dimensions to her character the writers hadn't anticipated. "The claws came out the second day I was on the show. I didn't want to play a nice, sweet girl. There was really no choice made by the writers about what they wanted her to be,

so I made the choice. I wanted to play a bitch—a character part. I thought, 'I'll move my wheels, use my inner monologue, and make it work.' I would do the words as written during rehearsal and when we went on the air, I would say the words but think wicked thoughts about Bob and how I was going to get him. I was changing the character as I was doing it and she was growing. Irna saw that on-screen and started writing for me."

During her 30 years on the serial, Fulton can only recall one storyline that unnerved her. It happened in the midseventies when Lisa experienced a hysterical pregnancy.

Like the famous television character she plays, Fulton has been married several times. "I'm disappointed my marriages didn't work out. The first one, when I came to New York, couldn't have worked because we were both too young.

"My second marriage disappointed me because I really loved him; he was the great love of my life. Our five years together were very happy, really wonderful, but something happened later on, and I don't know what. I don't mean it happened between us, but I rather think he changed because of some great personal stresses on him in business." She dismisses her brief third marriage as a "mistake."

When asked what she'd like to see happen to Lisa, Fulton said, "I'd like to see an exciting storyline and have her claws come out again. I think she should have a fabulous romance in her life, although not necessarily another marriage. But romance does spark things up."

Eileen Fulton plays the sometimes selfish, sometimes scheming Lisa. Lisa never seems happy until she has a man, but never is happy with the man she has.

BARE ESSENCE

FEBRUARY 15, 1983–APRIL 29, 1983 NBC

This short-lived, prime-time serial began as a CBS four hour mini-series that originally ran on CBS in October 1982. It starred Genie Francis, Linda Evans, Donna Mills, and Lee Grant. Impressed by its strong showing, NBC hoped a weekly version would be equally successful. Unfortunately, Linda Evans, Donna Mills, and Lee Grant weren't available to reprise their roles. Instead, well-known actresses Jennifer O'Neill and Jessica Walter were signed to costar with Genie Francis.

Francis, who played Laura Webber Spencer on daytime's *General Hospital,* starred as Tyger Hayes. She was a high-spirited young woman determined to succeed in the business world.

Describing her role, Francis said, "The nice thing about Tyger is that she's an active character. She may get herself into trouble, but she will get herself out again. She's responsible for herself. That's a quality most people—and certainly a lot of women—would like to have."

In the first episode, Tyger's wealthy husband, Chase Marshall, was killed in a racing car accident. Chase's father, Hadden Marshall, was the ruthless head of a huge, privately held conglomerate called Kellico. He opposed Tyger's drive to stake a claim in the family's business. Supporting Tyger's efforts was Hadden's sister, Margaret. She encouraged Tyger to try her skills on a new line of perfumes the company was

The cast of Bare Essence: *(front, left to right) Jennifer O'Neill, Genie Francis, Jessica Walter, (middle) Michael Woods, Jamie Lyn Bauer, Wendy Fulton, Jonathan Frakes, (rear) John Dehner, Susan French, and Ian McShane.*

Niko Theopolous (Ian McShane) romanced Lady Bobbi (Jennifer O'Neill) because he wanted revenge against her daughter's in-laws.

planning to manufacture. Ava, the widow of Hadden's son Hugh, feared that a perfume Tyger was developing might become successful—and subsequently strengthen her position at Kellico. Ava wanted her son, Marcus, to take over as head of Kellico. As a way of insuring this, Ava eventually married Hadden.

Meanwhile, across the continent, Tyger's mother, the beautiful Lady Bobbi, had fallen in love with Niko Theopolous, a Greek millionaire who had a score to settle with the Marshalls. Unknown to Lady Bobbi, Niko's primary reason for romancing her was directly related to a plot he was brewing to destroy the Marhall empire.

In the serial's final installment, viewers learned that Chase's death was no accident. Shortly before Chase's fateful race, Muffin Marshall, a vengeful in-law, had deliberately sabotaged his car.

Al Corley, who walked away from his role as Steven Carrington on the successful series *Dynasty* a season earlier, played Chase. Jaime Lyn Bauer, best known for her role as Lauri Brooks on daytime's *The Young and the Restless*, replaced Donna Mills as Barbara Fisher. Before joining *Dynasty* as Dex Dexter, Michael Nader played Alexi Theopolous.

Cast

ALAN	RICHARD BACKUS
BARBARA FISHER	JAMIE LYN BAUER
CATHY	LAURA BRUNEAU
CHASE MARSHALL	AL CORLEY
HADDEN MARSHALL	JOHN DEHNER
NATASHA	ANULKA DZIUBINSKA
MARCUS MARSHALL	JONATHAN FRAKES
MARGARET MARSHALL	SUSAN FRENCH
MUFFIN MARSHALL	WENDY FULTON
TYGER HAYES	GENIE FRANCIS
ROBERT SPENCER	TED LePLAT
NIKO THEOPOLOUS	IAN McSHANE
ALEXI THEOPOLOUS	MICHAEL NADER
LADY BOBBI ROWAN	JENNIFER O'NEILL
LARRY DEVITO	MORGAN STEVENS
AVA MARSHALL	JESSICA WALTER
SEAN BENEDICT	MICHAEL WOODS

THE BOLD AND THE BEAUTIFUL

MARCH 23, 1987–PRESENT CBS

Creator William Bell's *The Young and the Restless* had been CBS's top-rated serial for several years when the network approached him about developing a second serial. His credentials as a headwriter were impeccable. Prior to *The Young and the Restless*, he was headwriter of *Days of Our Lives*, co-headwriter of *Another World*, dialogue writer for *As the World Turns* and *The Guiding Light*, and co-creator of *Our Private World*. Bell was hesitant to begin work on another serial. He felt executive producing and scripting five one-hour episodes of *The Young and the Restless* were more than enough to keep him busy. But during the Christmas holiday season of 1985, ideas began surfacing in Bell's mind about a new serial. Suddenly excited by the idea of creating a new series, Bell and Lee Philip Bell, his partner-wife, isolated themselves in a hotel room and began developing the premise for *The Bold and the Beautiful*. When they were finished, he presented his proposal to CBS, and the network quickly snapped it up.

The fashion industry served as the backdrop for Bell's new half-hour serial. Set in Los Angeles, *The Bold and the Beautiful* centered on the successful Forrester family and the lower-class Logans. Patriarch Eric Forrester headed the multimillion dollar business, House of Forrester. He and his first wife, Stephanie, had four adult children: Ridge, Thorne, Felicia, and Kristen. After having been deserted by her unemployed husband, Steven, several years earlier, Beth Logan was left alone to raise their four children: Storm, Brooke, Donna, and Katie. Publishing magnate Bill Spencer's daughter, Caroline, was involved with Ridge.

Bell's original intention was to cast *The Bold and the Beautiful* with attractive faces that would be new to a daytime audience. To that end, he hired Ronn Moss, Clayton Norcross, Joanna Johnson, and Katherine Kelly Lang. As casting continued, Bell discovered "I couldn't find the right people to play all of the roles. Then I started to look back. Jim Storm—he was perfect on *The Young and the Restless* for awhile, he'd be perfect for Bill Spencer. The same with Lauren Koslow, she'd been on *The Young and the Restless* and now she'd be just right for Margo Lynley. Of course,

the central character, the one the other characters revolve around, is the most important because the balance of the show leads from the center. I called John McCook. I asked him to come to the office, not so much out of nostalgia but because I wanted to see what he looked like. He looked terrific. I told him I was coming up with a new show and I'd like him to think about it. He said he'd do just that and we agreed to get together after the first of the year. Frankly, John was a little younger than what I was thinking of for the role of Eric Forrester, but he's such strong support, such a good leader among actors that by Christmas I knew I wanted him for the role."

Bell reached back to his stint as headwriter of *Days of Our Lives* in the seventies for the perfect actress to play Eric's wife, Stephanie. He selected Susan Flannery, who made a strong impact on daytime audiences with her role as Laura Horton on *Days of Our Lives*.

Below: *The Forrester family: (clockwise, top left) Thorne (Clayton Norcross), Ridge (Ronn Moss), Kirsten (Teri Ann Linn), Eric (John McCook), and Stephanie (Susan Flannery).*

Opposite page: The Bold and the Beautiful *actors group for a cast photo.*

Two additions to the cast immediately caught the media's eye. They were Carrie Mitchum, granddaughter of Robert Mitchum, and Ethan Wayne, son of John Wayne. When *Soap Opera Digest* asked Bell if they were hired for their talent or as a publicity gimmick, he answered, "I asked myself the same question. When we read these young people, I backed up and said, 'Whoa, are we casting them because of their names or their talent?' If you go with the name, in the long run it hurts you and it hurts the show. When you're starting a new show, you've got to go with what works, not with what looks good. I'll admit, there's probably more media attention around these kids than would be normal because of their background, but they have real talent."

A year after the premiere of *The Bold and the Beautiful*, a new character was added who would become very popular with viewers, Sally Spectra (Darlene Conley). She was the formidable head of Spectra Creations, the ripoff rival of the House of Forrester. Ironically, Conley's role as Sally Spectra was only supposed to be short-term. "They needed someone or something to rival

THE CAST

Original Cast

BETH LOGAN	JUDITH BALDWIN
STEPHANIE FORRESTER	SUSAN FLANNERY
ROCCO CARNER	BRYAN GENESSE
CAROLINE SPENCER	JOANNA JOHNSON
MARGO LYNLEY	LAUREN KOSLOW
BROOKE LOGAN	KATHERINE KELLY LANG
KRISTEN FORRESTER	TERI ANN LINN
ERIC FORRESTER	JOHN McCOOK
DONNA LOGAN	CARRIE MITCHUM
RIDGE FORRESTER	RONN MOSS
THORNE FORRESTER	CLAYTON NORCROSS
DAVE REED	STEPHEN SHORTRIDGE
KATIE LOGAN	NANCY SLOAN
BILL SPENCER	JIM STORM
STORM LOGAN	ETHAN WAYNE

THE BOLD AND THE BEAUTIFUL

MARCH 23, 1987–PRESENT CBS

the House of Forrester designs," explained Conley. "I was supposed to come in as Clarke Garrison's former lover [Clarke was involved with Eric's daughter, Kristen], blackmail him, threaten Forrester, and go away." Impressed by the audience's overwhelmingly positive response to Conley's performance, Bell decided to hire her on a permanent basis. Acknowledging Bell's contribution to creating Sally Spectra, Conley said, "Other soaps have tried the older, outrageous woman, but have only picked up the eccentricities. They miss what makes her really special. With Sally, they created her and didn't miss. She's a successful businesswoman. She does function on several levels, and she laughs at herself. Believe me, no one laughs at Sally Spectra first. She's always making fun of herself."

Ridge Forrester's romance with Caroline Spencer was heavily featured during the serial's early years. When Ridge first proposed to Caroline, her father was outraged. Moments before the wedding ceremony, he presented Caroline with evidence proving Ridge had been sleeping with other women during their engagement. Caroline canceled the wedding.

Determined to stand on her own two feet, she left her father's home and found an apartment. Soon after, Caroline was raped by a casual acquaintance. Fearful of living alone anymore, Caroline accepted Brooke's offer to move in with her family. Ridge's brother, Thorne, served as a source of support to Caroline during the rapist's long trial. Believing she was in love with Thorne, Caroline married him. The marriage many not have happened if Brooke hadn't joined forces with Thorne to prevent Caroline from receiving a letter from Ridge professing his love for her. To Caroline's surprise, Brooke ended her relationship with police officer Dave Reed and become romantically involved with Ridge.

Caroline's mixed response to her former fiance's new relationship was minor compared to Ridge's mother, Stephanie. She viewed Brooke as a social climber who was only interested in Ridge for his money. When Caroline discovered Brooke's participation in thwarting her relationship with Ridge, she briefly cooled their friendship.

Thorne's marriage to Caroline was nearly jeopardized when they moved in with his family. One evening, Ridge pulled a prank on a drunken Caroline by slipping into her bed and pretending to be Thorne. Not realizing it was Ridge, Caroline made love to him. When Thorne inadvertently heard about Ridge's prank, he got drunk and shot his older brother. Ridge recovered from his injury with no memory of his attacker. Meanwhile, a protective Stephanie (who had witnessed the shooting) did her best to cover up the ugly incident. Like Ridge, Thorne completely erased the shooting from his mind. When Caroline learned of Thorne's involvement in Ridge's shooting, she divorced him.

Ridge came close to marrying Brooke when she informed him she was pregnant. The wedding was canceled after Brooke miscarried. Ridge and Caroline admitted their love for each other and finally married. Shortly after the ceremony, Caroline was diagnosed with a mysterious illness. To Stephanie's horror, Brooke recovered from her break-up with Ridge by getting involved with Eric. Even worse, Brooke was pregnant again—by Eric!

Opposite page: *Caroline loved Ridge, but she found out on her wedding day that he had slept with another woman. Thorne gave comfort to Caroline through all her trials, and he confessed he also loved her. They eventually married. Caroline, though, was still very much in love with Ridge, and in 1990, they finally wed. Their trials are not over yet; Caroline has a disease that may cause her death.*

Above: *Margo Lynley (Lauren Koslow), a designer at the House of Forrester, discusses business with Eric Forrester (John McCook).*

THE BRIGHTER DAY

JANUARY 4, 1954–SEPTEMBER 25, 1962 CBS

*I*n many respects, this serial resembled *The Guiding Light.* Both were created by Irna Phillips, both began on radio, and both featured clergymen as core characters. *The Brighter Day* first aired on radio in 1948. And from 1954 to 1956, viewers who missed the television broadcast could hear the same episode on radio later that afternoon. The early sixties marked the most significant difference between the *The Brighter Day* and *The Guiding Light.* While *The Brighter Day* struggled with a revised format, *The Guiding Light* continued to flourish.

The Brighter Day featured the Dennis family, who lived in Three Rivers. The Reverend Richard Dennis was a widower raising five children. The eldest daughter was Liz, who assumed the maternal role for her younger siblings. Althea valued material wealth over inner-peace. Grayling was the only son, Patsy was an average teenager, and Babby was the youngest child. Lending emotional support to the family was Aunt Emily Potter, who worked part-time writing an advice column for the local newspaper.

When the series premiered on television in 1954, a flood had destroyed Three Rivers, causing the Dennis family and their friends to settle in New Hope, Pennsylvania. Liz had left town and Althea was pursuing her newfound ambition to become a successful actress. It looked as if Althea might realize her goal when she was cast in a play. An unfortunate accident onstage one evening, however, sidelined Althea's budding career indefinitely (she was struck unconscious by a falling sandbag). Apparently, the accident affected Althea's mind because she soon began experiencing sudden mood swings. Alarmed by Althea's erratic personality changes, the Dennis family encouraged her to seek psychiatric counseling. A few sessions with Dr. Hamilton made it apparent to Althea she'd be better off with a self-help book. Rather than encouraging her to pursue acting, the doctor suggested she find a good man to marry and settle down as a housewife. Instead, Althea packed her bags and moved to New York City to become a Broadway star.

A more immediate problem at hand for Rev. Dennis was Grayling's progressive alcoholism. Complicating matters was Grayling's illicit involvement with an older woman. Shortly after their affair ended, Grayling met and fell in love with Sandra Talbot. To Grayling's horror, he discovered Sandra was a woman with a past—she'd once been romantically involved with his shady business partner. Clearing up their differences, Grayling and Sandra eventually married.

Insecure because of her inability to get pregnant, Sandra suffered a hysterical pregnancy. While Sandra attempted to cope with her mental difficulties, Grayling found himself drawn to her nurse, Lois Williams. Viewers weren't pleased when Grayling acted on his desires and had a sexual affair with Lois. Before the serial completed its run, Grayling successfully confronted his drinking problem.

Youngest daughter, Babby, who had grown into a teenager, wasn't having an easy time adjusting to adolescence. At every turn it seemed she was confronted with a new crisis, each more overwhelming than the last.

Preoccupied with her sibling's myriad of problems, Patsy began neglecting her own life, particularly in the area of romance. Feeling that he wasn't a priority in her life, Patsy's boyfriend, Alan Butler, turned to another woman for attention.

James Noble played Grayling Dennis after Hal Holbrook and before Forrest Compton. Noble later played Donald Hughes on As the World Turns, Ed Sims *on the short-lived* A World Apart, *but is probably most famous for his role of the governor on the TV sitcom* Benson.

Murial Williams played Lydia Canfield Herrick.

The Brighter Day peaked in 1956, when it was the highest-rated serial on television. By the late fifties, its audience had dwindled to a fraction of its former size. In an attempt to infuse the serial with new energy, the format was revised. Once again the Dennis family and their friends uprooted their lives and relocated to Columbus, a college town. It was hoped that new, younger characters would draw former viewers back.

Originally owned by Procter & Gamble, The Brighter Day was sold to CBS in the early sixties. The serial experienced multiple cast changes in 1961, when CBS moved the show from New York City to Television City, its new studio in Hollywood. The switch proved disastrous and The Brighter Day was canceled in 1962. The announcement from CBS was sudden and the serial had less than two weeks to tie up loose storylines. In the last episode, aired on September 29, 1962, Paul Langton, still in character as Uncle Walter Dennis, stepped forward. Addressing the camera, Langton explained to viewers how each character would eventually resolve their problems. His final words, "The microphone can't pick up their voices and soon the picture will fade. If on occasion you think of us, we hope your memory will be a pleasant one."

THE CAST

Original Cast

BABBY DENNIS	MARY LINN BELLER
ALTHEA DENNIS	BROOKE BYRON
GRAYLING DENNIS	HAL HOLBROOK
PATSY DENNIS	LOIS NETTLETON
RICHARD DENNIS	WILLIAM SMITH
RANDY HAMILTON	LARRY WARD

Final Cast

CHRIS HAMILTON	MIKE BARTON
EMILY POTTER	MONA BRUNS
GRAYLING DENNIS	FORREST COMPTON
RICHARD DENNIS	BLAIR DAVIES
PATSY DENNIS HAMILTON	JUNE DAYTON
JUDITH PORTER	BENNYE GATTEYS
CHARLES FULLER	DEAN HARENS
WALTER DENNIS	PAUL LANGTON
TOBY BALLARD	DON PENNY
SANDRA TALBOT DENNIS	NANCY RENNICK
MORT BARROWS	BENNY RUBIN

BRIGHT PROMISE

SEPTEMBER 29, 1969–MARCH 31, 1972 NBC

This Hollywood-based, half-hour drama served as a vehicle for film star Dana Andrews, who starred as college president Thomas Boswell. Considering the student unrest, sexual freedom, and drug experimentation taking place on college campuses all over America in the late sixties, a serial set in a college town seemed ripe with dramatic possibilities. Early storylines suggested *Bright Promise* was the perfect serial to explore subjects that previously had been relegated to the evening news. Several months after its premiere, however, low-ratings indicated viewers weren't interested. The serial's creators, Frank and Doris Hursley, who had also created *General Hospital* six years earlier, were replaced when the show implemented more traditional storylines. They shifted its focus from Bancroft College's students to the townspeople of Bancroft.

During the serial's two-and-a-half year run, a pivotal character was Sandy Jones Pierce. Her overwhelming drive to take the rotten hand she'd been dealt in life and parlay it into something closely resembled Lisa's underhanded manipulations on *As the World Turns* and Rachel's social-climbing tactics on *Another World*. Originally introduced as a student at Bancroft College, Sandy created a minor scandal by having an illicit affair with Bill Ferguson, a married professor.

Shortly after dropping out of college, Sandy was forced to endure a long trial after being falsely accused of murder. Once her name was cleared, Sandy married for a brief period, divorced, and then gave birth to an illegitimate baby. A rare illness almost cost Sandy her life, but the malady vanished as mysteriously as it had appeared. Before the serial ended, Sandy surprised

Dana Andrews played Thomas Boswell, the president of Bancroft College. Ultimately, the focus of the show shifted from the college and the Boswell family.

Before success as Luke on General Hospital, *Anthony Geary played David Lockhart on* Bright Promise.

everyone by marrying the conservative brother of Martha Ferguson. Sandy had coveted Martha's husband years earlier.

Like Sandy, Martha Ferguson also suffered through a long murder trial. She was unjustly charged with killing Sylvia Bancroft. Sylvia was the wealthy and mysterious natural mother of Martha's adopted son, David Lockhart, a teenage former mental patient. In the serial's final episode, Martha, who'd been found innocent, married Dr. Tracy Graham, played by film and television star Dabney Coleman.

After *Bright Promise's* cancellation, Gloria Monty worked on television movies. Several years later, she helped revitalize *General Hospital* and reunited several cast members of *Bright Promise.* Tony Geary, who played David Lockhart, became one of the most successful actors in daytime television for his role as Luke Spencer. Susan Brown, who played Martha Ferguson, appeared as Dr. Gail Adamson Baldwin. David Lewis, who played Martha's father, college dean Henry Pierce, appeared as patriarch Edward Quartermaine. Finally, Anne Jeffreys, who played Sylvia Bancroft, had a brief run in 1984 as Amanda Barrington.

Cast

JODY HARPER	SHERRY ALBERONI
THOMAS BOSWELL	DANA ANDREWS
MARTHA FERGUSON	SUSAN BROWN
TRACY GRAHAM	DABNEY COLEMAN
BRIAN WALSH	JOHN CONSIDINE
RED WILSON	RICHARD EASTMAN
CHARLES DIEDRICH	ANTHONY EISLEY
PROFESSOR MITCHELL	IVOR FRANCIS
DAVID LOCKHART	ANTHONY GEARY
SYLVIA BANCROFT	REGINA GLEASON
	ANNE JEFFREYS
ALBERT PORTER	PETER HOBBS
ANN BOYD JONES	GAIL KOBE
	COLEEN GRAY
ELAINE BANCROFT	JENNIFER LEAK
HENRY PIERCE	DAVID LEWIS
	TOD ANDREWS
WILLIAM FERGUSON	PAUL LUKATHER
	JOHN NAPIER
HOWARD JONES	MARK MILLER
SANDRA JONES PIERCE	PAMELA MURPHY
	SUSANNAH DARROW
CHET MATTHEWS	GARY PILLAR (CARPENTER)
STUART PIERCE	PETER RATRAY
ALICE PORTER	SYNDA SCOTT
JENNIFER MATTHEWS	NANCY STEPHENS
AMANDA WINNINGER	JUNE VINCENT
ISABEL JONES	LESLEY WOODS

CAPITOL

. . . .

MARCH 26, 1982–MARCH 20, 1987 CBS

*T*his half-hour serial, created by Stephen and Elinor Karpf, focused on two feuding families, the Cleggs and the McCandlesses. Although set in Washington, D.C., the Karpfs chose to steer clear of using their serial as a political forum. "It was basically a story about people with a background in Washington—that was the arena," explained Elinor. "The major developments in the characters' lives didn't revolve around politics," stressed Stephen. Instead, the serial emphasized the rivalries between the two families.

The wealthy Cleggs included powerful patriarch Sam, his ruthless wife, Myrna (originally played by Carolyn Jones and later by Marj Dusay); Sam's eldest son by a former marriage, Trey; oldest daughter, Julie; son, Jordy; and youngest daughter, Brenda.

The McCandless family was headed by Clarissa, a widow. She and her husband, Baxter, had five children: Tyler, an Air Force hero with political aspirations; Thomas, a handicapped doctor; Matt, an Olympic hopeful; Wally, a confused college student; and Gillian, still in her teens. Following Baxter's death, Clarissa's father, former political bigwig Judson Tyler, served as the family's patriarchal figure.

Playing an important role in Clarissa's life was longtime friend Senator Mark Denning. His unstable wife, Paula, was thought to be housebound. In fact, she pretended to suffer from agoraphobia as a way of holding onto her husband, who she feared was in love with Clarissa. Their daughter, Sloane, was a popular television newscaster.

The feud between the Tylers and the Cleggs began thirty years earlier, when Myrna discovered her lifelong friend Clarissa was going to marry the love of Myrna's life, Baxter McCandless. Vowing revenge, Myrna implemented her first evil deed against Clarissa's family by destroying Judson's political career. Exploiting the "Red Scare" that had overtaken the country, Myrna successfully convinced everyone that Judson was a closet communist.

The romance between Tyler McCandless and Julie Clegg figured prominently during the serial's first two years. When Julie suffered amnesia in a boating accident just weeks before her wedding to Tyler, Myrna took advantage of the situation by convincing Julie she was in love with Lawrence Barrington. Myrna approved of Lawrence because she thought he came from a wealthy family. In reality, he was a con man hoping to tap into the Cleggs' millions by marrying Julie. Eventually, Lawrence's true identity was exposed, Julie regained her memory, and she and Tyler finally wed. Soon after, a pregnant Julie had a miscarriage and learned she'd never be able to have children. Two different attempts to adopt children proved unsuccessful.

Myrna Clegg (Carolyn Jones, left) and Clarissa McCandless (Constance Towers, right) are the heads of two powerful families in Washington, D.C.

Julie Clegg (Kimberly Beck-Hilton) and Tyler McCandless (David Mason Daniels) were in love and planned to marry, despite the objections of their feuding families.

Meanwhile, Tyler's vendetta against organized crime resulted in criminals kidnapping Julie to punish Tyler. With Sloane's help, Tyler rescued Julie. Unfortunately, Julie's return home wasn't a time for celebration. Instead, she was accused of shooting Senator Mark Denning (he survived his wounds). It was later revealed that Jenny Diamond, a deranged woman with an amazing resemblance to Julie, was responsible. Before the serial ended, Julie and Tyler decided to separate.

Following an unhappy relationship with former prostitute Kelly Harper, Trey fell in love with Sloane. Unknown to Trey, Kelly left town pregnant—apparently with his child. Months after Trey married Sloane, Kelly returned and revealed they had a son, Scotty. To Sloane's disappointment, Trey decided to end their marriage so he could marry Kelly. Any chance Trey and Kelly had for happiness, however, was destroyed by Kelly's growing dependency on drugs.

After divorcing Kelly, Trey began a whirlwind romance with a young woman barely out of her teens, Angelica. They married, causing everyone in the Clegg family to question Trey's state of mind. The marriage was annulled months later when it was discovered Angelica's first husband was still alive. Single again, Trey realized he still loved Kelly. Although Kelly finally

Original Cast

JULIE CLEGG	KIMBERLY BECK-HILTON
WALLY McCANDLESS	BILL BEYERS
JUDSON TYLER	RORY CALHOUN
LAWRENCE BARRINGTON	JEFF CHAMBERLAIN
JORDY CLEGG	TODD CURTIS
SHELLY GRANGER/KELLY HARPER	JANE DALY GAMBLE
TYLER McCANDLESS	DAVID MASON-DANIELS
SAM CLEGG II	ROBERT SAMPSON
MATT McCANDLESS	SHEA FARRELL
FRANK BURGESS	DUNCAN GAMBLE
BRENDA CLEGG	LESLIE GRAVES
MYRNA CLEGG	CAROLYN JONES
SLOANE DENNING	DEBORAH MULLOWNEY
MARK DENNING	ED NELSON
JEFF JOHNSON	RODNEY SAULSBERRY
THOMAS McCANDLESS	BRIAN ROBERT TAYLOR
CLARISSA McCANDLESS	CONSTANCE TOWERS
SAM "TREY" CLEGG III	NICHOLAS WALKER
LISBETH BACHMAN	TONJA WALKER

CAPITOL

MARCH 26, 1982–MARCH 20, 1987 CBS

managed to kick her drug habit, Trey was devastated to discover Scotty wasn't his son. Thomas had been sexually involved with Kelly and was Scotty's true father.

Clarissa discovered that a man calling himself Jarrett Morgan was actually her presumed-dead husband, Baxter McCandless. An accident had disfigured Baxter years earlier, causing him to drop out of his family's life and assume a new identity. During his years away from the family, Baxter became involved with Interpol and was

helping the government crack a notorious spy ring operating in Washington. Eventually, Clarissa was able to work through her anger and love Baxter again.

Sloane got her mind off Trey by becoming sexually involved with the mysterious Zed Diamond. His presumed-dead wife Jenny was the Julie look-a-like who shot Mark Denning. To protect his unbalanced wife, Zed fled Washington with her. Under Zed's loving care, Jenny regained her memory, confessed to shooting Mark, and was

Below: *The cast of* Capitol *pose for a group photo.*

Opposite page: *Trey Clegg (Nicholas Walker) and Sloane Denning (Deborah Mullowney) were a hot couple for a time, but they eventually went their separate ways.*

54

CAPITOL

MARCH 26, 1982–MARCH 20, 1987 CBS

eventually set free. With everyone believing she was sane, an obsessed Jenny hatched a plot to kill Sloane, who she thought was still attracted to Zed. The scheme backfired, resulting in Jenny's death.

While covering a news story, Sloane was reunited with a former love, Prince Ali of Baracq. Political unrest in Ali's torn country made it impossible for him to marry Sloane. Instead, he married a woman named Yasmeen. On their wedding day, Yasmeen was killed by an assassin's bullet. To Sloane's horror, her father, who was a spy, was responsible. When orders were issued for Mark to kill his own daughter, he resisted and was murdered. Anxious to build a life with Prince Ali, Sloane gave up her career to marry him. On their wedding night, Ali was kidnapped by dissidents plotting to overthrow Baracq. In his absence, Sloane tried to run the country. In the final episode, Sloane found herself facing an execution squad.

Capitol was canceled in March 1987, one

week short of celebrating five years, and was replaced by *The Bold and the Beautiful.* Producer John Conboy ended the serial without tying up storylines, hoping ABC or NBC would pick it up, but he was unable to generate interest.

Responding to the cancellation, Constance Towers, who played Clarissa McCandless, said, "The show should have been moved because we were in a very tough time slot. In New York it was 2:30 to 3 p.m., when mothers go pick up their children at school. It was very tough and yet we were still making it. We were never out of tenth or eleventh place (out of approximately 25 daytime shows) in all the time we were on, which is rare for a new soap opera. I really felt like I lost a child because we gave five years of tremendous energy, caring, and love to the project. We all felt we finally had it in a position where the stories were wonderful. We were devastated that the network had the problem it had and that people who didn't know came on and made the decision [to cancel]."

Opposite page: *A weekend break in shooting is the perfect time for a picnic—very all-American! Partaking in the feast are (from bottom, clockwise) Kimberly Beck-Hilton, Nicholas Walker, Constance Towers, and Ed Nelson.*

Below: *Tammy Wynette joined the cast in 1986. She is joined by (left to right) Rory Calhoun, Marj Dusay, and Constance Towers.*

THE COLBYS

NOVEMBER 20, 1985–MARCH 26, 1987 ABC

This one hour weekly serial was a short-lived spin-off of *Dynasty*. Like its predecessor, *The Colbys* tracked the lives of the super rich. Underscoring their promise that this series would be bigger than life, the producers drafted Moses himself, Charlton Heston, to headline. Also lending star power were Barbara Stanwyck, who complained unmercifully about the poor quality of scripts, and Katherine Ross.

Ironically, it was English actress Stephanie Beacham who inspired viewers to sit up and take notice of the show. Praising Beacham's performance, *Soap Opera Digest* wrote, "Beacham has combined theatrical performing in London with a haughty sense of sardonic bitchery to create the show's most memorable character, Sable Colby. If Joan Collins is the rock on which *Dynasty* is built, Beacham, in her own way, and

Barbara Stanwyck and Charlton Heston played Constance and Jason Colby, a brother and sister who ran Colby Enterprises.

58

Top: *Fallon (Emma Samms), who was suffering from amnesia, married her husband's cousin Miles (Maxwell Caufield).*

Below: *Jason (Charlton Heston) was married to the manipulative Sable (Stephanie Beacham), but he was in love with Francessca, Sable's sister.*

THE CAST

Cast

JOHN MORETTI	VINCE BAGGETTA
SABLE SCOTT COLBY	STEPHANIE BEACHAM
HENDERSON PALMER	IVAN BONAR
NEAL KITTREDGE	PHILIP BROWN
HUTCH CORRIGAN	JOSEPH CAMPANELLA
MILES COLBY	MAXWELL CAUFIELD
SEAN McALLISTER	CHARLES VAN EMAN
CHANNING CARTER COLBY	KIM MORGAN GREENE
ROGER LANGDON	DAVID HEDISON
JASON COLBY	CHARLTON HESTON
CASH CASSIDY	JAMES HOUGHTON
GARRETT BOYDSTON	KEN HOWARD
JEFF COLBY	JOHN JAMES
DR. WAVERLY	GEORGANN JOHNSON
ANNA ROSTOV	ANNA LEVINE
LUCAS CARTER	KEVIN McCARTHY
ZACHARY POWERS	RICARDO MONTALBAN
WAYNE MASTERSON	GARY MORRIS
L. B. (LITTLE BLAKE) COLBY	ASHLEY MUTRUX BRANDON BLUHM
PHILLIP COLBY	MICHAEL PARKS
KOLYA (NIKOLAI) ROSTOV	ADRIAN PAUL
ADRIENNE CASSIDY	SHANNA REED
FRANCESSCA SCOTT LANGDON	KATHERINE ROSS
FALLON CARRINGTON COLBY	EMMA SAMMS
MONICA COLBY	TRACY SCOGGINS
SACHA MALENKOV	JUDSON SCOTT
CONSTANCE COLBY	BARBARA STANWYCK
ARTHUR CATES	PETER WHITE
SPIROS KORALIS	RAY WISE
BLISS COLBY	CLAIRE YARLETT

THE COLBYS

NOVEMBER 20, 1985-—MARCH 26, 1987 ABC

on her own terms, is creating that same sort of base in *The Colbys.* In a show that lumps together big-name veterans and inexperienced pups, she is, in this country, an anomaly, an accomplished newcomer—to American television and to soap stardom."

The series began with Jeff Colby, a popular character on *Dynasty,* accepting an offer from his Uncle Jason to work for Colby Enterprises, a multinational conglomerate with interests in oil, shipping, real estate, and the aerospace industry.

Jason and his wife, Sable, had three adult children: Miles, Monica, and Bliss. Jason's sister, Constance, lived with the family on their large estate overlooking Los Angeles. Zachary Powers was Jason's nemesis and business rival.

The series kicked off with Jeff arriving in Los Angeles to discover that his believed-dead ex-wife, Fallon, had married his cousin Miles. Since mysteriously dropping out of sight two years earlier, Fallon had suffered amnesia and now called herself Randall Adams. Taking Miles aside, Jeff revealed Fallon's true identity, but Miles wasn't interested. Under a doctor's advice, Jeff agreed not to pressure Fallon into trying to regain her memory. Meanwhile, Fallon chose not to pursue marital relations with Miles until she understood more about her past.

Other prominent storylines during the first season included Sable's plot to have Constance declared incompetent so she couldn't leave her shares of Colby Enterprises to Jeff; Constance's

Below: *Despite being Jason's enemy, Zachary Powers (Ricardo Montalban) seems to get along just fine with Sable.*

Opposite page: *The glamorous Colby women: (left to right) Bliss (Claire Yarlett), Sable, and Monica (Tracy Scoggins).*

THE COLBYS

NOVEMBER 20, 1985— MARCH 26, 1987 ABC

secret relationship with rancher Hutch; Zachary Powers's attempts to undermine Jason Colby, both professionally and personally; and Francessca's brief marriage to British diplomat Roger Langdon.

Jason's children also had their own problems to contend with. Unable to deal with Fallon's ultimate rejection, a despondent Miles raped her. Fallon then divorced Miles. Monica became romantically involved with blind country singer Wayne Masterson and record executive Neil Kittredge, who was still married. Bliss fell in love with environmentalist Sean McAllister. By season's end, Jeff had discovered that Jason was his father. Jeff and Miles were also accused of killing two of Jason's business associates. Fed up with his wife's manipulations, Jason started divorce proceedings against Sable and was later arrested for allegedly attempting to murder her.

During the second season, Sable's attempts to hold on to Jason proved unsuccessful. He proceeded with plans to marry Jeff's mother, Francessca. When Francessca's presumed-dead first husband, Phillip Colby (Jason's brother),

surfaced in Los Angeles, Francessca and Jason decided to call off the wedding. Instead, Miles walked down the aisle with reporter Channing Carter, who started out writing an expose on the Colbys but quickly changed her mind after becoming part of the story. Monica's sexual relationship with married Senator Cash Cassidy nearly destroyed his political career. Bliss became engaged to Russian ballet dancer Kolya Rostov, who made plans to defect to America. Constance Colby died in Nepal. Fallon gave birth to her second child, a girl—leaving Jeff and Miles to figure out who was the baby's father.

Borrowing heavily from the feature film *Close Encounters of the Third Kind*, the serial employed the most bizarre season cliff-hanger to date. While driving down a desolate country road, Fallon was abducted by aliens and pirated away in a spaceship.

Since *The Colbys* wasn't renewed for a third season, Fallon's story was resolved on *Dynasty*, where she was joined by Jeff. The following season, Sable and her daughter Monica also became regular players on the long-running series. Sable's new enemy was Alexis.

Opposite page: *Fallon finally regained her memory, and she remarried Jeff (John James).*

Below: *The cast of* The Colbys *accept an award for their show.*

63

DALLAS

· ·

APRIL 2, 1978–PRESENT CBS

When producer Leonard Katzman and creator/writer David Jacobs first got the go-ahead from CBS for their drama about a wealthy Texas family, they never intended to generate a prime-time serial. In fact, the original plan was to shoot a mini-series. Once in the production stages, though, the project was treated as an episodic series with each of the shows self-contained and resolved by the end of the hour. Only at the tail end of its trial run (mid-1978), almost by accident, did a continuing storyline emerge, making *Dallas* a prime-time soap opera.

Still, no one was convinced that this necessarily boded well because initial ratings weren't high. Additionally, it had been over a decade since a nighttime serial, ABC's *Peyton Place*, had provided a successful format. Few anticipated that by the end of its second season *Dallas* would have taken the world by storm. Nor did anyone expect that the serial would alter the course of television history.

The setting was Southfork Ranch, not far from Dallas, Texas. The primary story delved into the wide-reaching maneuvers of the Ewing family. The oil rich empire was headed by Jock Ewing, while his wife, Eleanor Southworth Ewing (Miss Ellie), was mother to their three sons: power hungry J.R., Jr. (the eldest); Gary, the black sheep of the family destined soon to depart Southfork; and Bobby, good-looking, upstanding, and always a threat to his plotting brother J.R. Also making their residence at the ranch were J.R.'s mistreated and alcohol-abusing wife, Sue Ellen; Gary's raucous teenage daughter, Lucy; and Bobby's pretty wife, Pamela. The latter provided the link to the Barnes family—Pamela Barnes Ewing was the daughter of Digger Barnes, ex-partner of Jock Ewing. Forty years before, Jock had blamefully outwitted Digger by usurping the Barnes share of a fortune along with Digger's romantic claim on Miss Ellie.

The rising pulse of the serial was sparked early in the 1978-79 season as Larry Hagman's inimitable portrayal of ruthless J.R. began to take shape. His long string of infidelities catapulted Sue Ellen into her own affair with Ewing rival Cliff Barnes, the son of Digger and brother of Pam. Petite Charlene Tilton's Lucy was also notorious for her affairs. She seduced—among others—

Ray Krebbs, the ranch's overseer, who was later revealed to be her uncle.

The second full season exploded into action with *Dallas* ranking in the top ten of all prime-time series. In rapid-fire succession, Gary Ewing departed to foster spin-off *Knots Landing*, Pam learned that Digger (Keenan Wynn) wasn't her father, and J.R. sired a son by Sue Ellen. The arrival of the baby, John Ross, shocked everyone into the discovery that he wasn't the offspring of Cliff Barnes. Multiplying the tension was J.R.'s

Jock (Jim Davis, left) and his son J.R. (Larry Hagman, right) discuss some business on Southfork.

Some members of the cast assemble for a photo: (front, left to right) Jenna Wade (Priscilla Beaulieu Presley), Miss Ellie (Barbara Bel Geddes), Clayton Farwell (Howard Keel), (back) Ray Krebbs (Steve Kanaly), Bobby (Patrick Duffy), Sue Ellen (Linda Gray), J.R. (Larry Hagman), and Cliff Barnes (Ken Kercheval).

affair with Sue Ellen's sister Kristin (Mary Crosby), not to mention his ongoing ploys to finacially harm brother Bobby. It shouldn't have come as any surprise on that season's cliff-hanging finale when someone shot J.R. (*Time* magazine dubbed him "that human oil slick.") The only question that remained was "Who shot J.R.?"

So unprecedented was the serial's success that a rash of similar prime-time soaps were immediately engineered, including ABC's *Dynasty*, NBC's *Flamingo Road,* and CBS's *Falcon Crest.* The revelation of Kristin as the villainess on November 12, 1980, was witnessed by an estimated 80 percent of television viewers, the largest audience recorded up to that date.

Clearly, the two-and-a-half-year-old *Dallas* had become a multinational megahit. For the first half of the eighties, the Ewings and their warring sons and daughters tromped the other prime-time serials in the race for popularity. Each season left devoted fans on the edge of their seats, where they would be forced to stay until the story resumed the following fall.

But in 1985, favor started to decline when Patrick Duffy's efforts to leave *Dallas* meant Bobby Ewing's death. Jock Ewing had been

THE CAST

Original Cast

GARY EWING	DAVID ACKROYD
WILLIE JOE GARR	JOHN ASHTON
LIZ CRAIG	BARBARA BABCOCK
ELEANOR SOUTHWORTH EWING	BARBARA BEL GEDDES
JOHN ROSS (JOCK) EWING	JIM DAVIS
BOBBY EWING	PATRICK DUFFY
SUE ELLEN EWING	LINDA GRAY
JOHN ROSS (J.R.) EWING, JR.	LARRY HAGMAN
RAY KREBBS	STEVE KANALY
CLIFF BARNES	KEN KERCHEVAL
JULIE GREY	TINA LOUISE
PAMELA BARNES EWING	VICTORIA PRINCIPAL
LUCY EWING	CHARLENE TILTON
VALENE EWING	JOAN VAN ARK
JEB AMOS	SANDY WARD
DIGGER BARNES	DAVID WAYNE

DALLAS

APRIL 2, 1978–PRESENT CBS

deceased since the 1981 death of actor Jim Davis and the role of Miss Ellie had been taken over in the 1984-85 season by Donna Reed. The public wasn't pleased.

Not even with the 1985 fall return of Barbara Bel Geddes as Eleanor, nor with Patrick Duffy back on the boards by fall of 1986, could *Dallas* reclaim all its previously amassed viewers. Nevertheless, in its short history the pioneering serial had swept down barriers and collected a core audience that would see Southfork and its inhabitants well into the nineties.

From the seeds of mayhem, planted in the first years that led up to J.R.'s shooting, had grown a mighty oak of a saga. After the eldest brother's recuperation (during which Bobby became the acting head of Ewing Oil), J.R.'s furor was focused on undoing his brother by many and sometimes illegal scams. Family shame was furthered when Ray Krebbs, one of Lucy's previous conquests, turned out to be Jock's illegitimate son, her uncle. Fortunately, Lucy had gone on to new love interest and then husband, Mitch Cooper. Ray married the influential Donna Carver.

Plagued by a host of affairs on both sides, J.R. and Sue Ellen's marriage dissolved into divorce only to later rebound in a remarriage. Pam, under ever-increasing emotional strain, separated from Bobby. They soon divorced. Lucy's marriage to Mitch didn't last long and she quickly rebounded in a fling with Mickey Trotter. That fun was fleeting as an intoxicated Sue Ellen caused a car accident in which Mickey almost died. In the hospital, Ray Krebbs shut off Mickey's life support system. Ray was convicted of manslaughter, though he was soon back in society.

Cliff Barnes, who rose to power as head of Barnes/Wentworth Oil, was busy planning economic vengeance against J.R. Cliff was beginning to resemble J.R. in personality, if not capability. The Ewing-Barnes feud, in fact, was actually rooted in events as long ago as 1860. Cliff's double-crossing half-sister Katherine Wentworth chased after J.R. but fell in love with Bobby. Katherine had no luck since Bobby had become the catch of his old flame Jenna Wade.

As J.R.'s acts of manipulation multiplied, many death threats were made against him. But this time, when a shot rang out and a body fell to the floor, the lingering question became "Who shot Bobby?"

Indeed, although the bullet was thought to be directed at J.R., Bobby was the target of the unrequited Katherine. Clouds of suspicion were lifted from Pam and Jenna. Ironically, Jenna was arrested for the murder of her tyrannical husband, Marchetta. After Bobby healed, he was able to help prove that she had been set-up.

In his never-ending quest to cross swords with J.R., Cliff received an extra load of ammunition. A Ewing cousin, Jamie, started working for Cliff to undermine her family. In retaliation, J.R. made sure Jamie was not welcome at Southfork. J.R. also nabbed the beautiful Mandy Winger, Cliff's love interest, for his own carnal desires.

An old document fell into Cliff's hands that indicated Jamie, as the daughter of Jock's brother Jason, was owed rightful shares in Ewing holdings. Just as he wagered a takeover by marrying Jamie, Cliff was presented with another document voiding the earlier one.

Below: *Sue Ellen and her sister, Kristin (Mary Crosby, rear), both slept with J.R. Kristin became one of the most famous characters in TV history when she shot J.R.*

Opposite page: The cast of Dallas: *(front, left to right) Susan Howard, Barbara Bel Geddes, Charlene Tilton, Victoria Principal, (center) Linda Gray, (rear) Steve Kanaly, Ken Kercheval, Larry Hagman, and Patrick Duffy.*

DALLAS

APRIL 2, 1978–PRESENT CBS

Following a series of sexual misadventures, Lucy remarried Mitch and the two left for Atlanta. Bobby's romance with Jenna was crumbling as he confronted his still-strong love for Pam. After spending a blissful night together, Bobby and Pam knew nothing of the awful fate that awaited them. A hit-and-run accident (the collision was meant to destroy Pam) harmed Bobby when he heroically tried to save her. The youngest Ewing son was pronounced dead.

A devastated Pam engaged in a relationship with former suitor Mark Grayson. Jenna became involved with Jack Ewing, Jaime's brother. J.R. had Sue Ellen committed to a mental institution. When, with the help of her mother, she emerged, Sue Ellen and J.R. waged a vicious fight for custody of young John Ross. Shockingly, a beleaguered Pam survived a South American emerald mine adventure and realized finally that Bobby wasn't dead. Instead, rather unbelievably, everything that happened to Pam that year, including her marriage to Mark, had all been a terrible dream.

heartbreaking dilemma evolved for him. Although he remarried Pam, part of his heart still belonged to Jenna, who was romantically linked with Ray Krebbs. Complicating Pam's situation was the fact that she hadn't been able to get pregnant by Bobby. Divorced from Donna, Ray later married Jenna and the two left the area. Pam wasn't able to hold on long to her spouse because on the very day that she learned she could conceive a child with Bobby, Pam's face was grossly disfigured in a car accident. Humiliated beyond all comfort, Pam divorced Bobby and disappeared.

Meanwhile, just as it seemed that J.R. was getting the best of Sue Ellen, she launched a fashion line of skimpy lingerie. Pouring salt on J.R.'s wounds, Sue Ellen succeeded in promoting her venture by employing Mandy as her chief model. Impressed with her business acumen, J.R. renewed his bond with Sue Ellen while an angry Marlena (J.R.'s latest love interest) was forced to face the truth that J.R. would never be legally hers to marry.

Ray Krebbs (Steve Kanaly), a ranch hand, is really an illegitimate son of Jock's. He married Donna Culver (Susan Howard) after her husband died, but they divorced and he married Jenna Wade.

Clint Ogden (Monte Markham) congratulates Sue Ellen on her remarriage to J.R., as J.R. looks on in triumph.

Another ghost from the past turned up in the guise of Parmalee, a ranch worker. He claimed to be Jock Ewing, risen from the dead. Proven a fraud, Parmalee had nevertheless caused much family anxiety. Miss Ellie, meanwhile, had long been married to Clayton Farlow. A misunderstanding over a platonic kiss upset Ellie enough for her to ask Clayton to leave. After he was framed and then freed for a murder he didn't commit, Clayton came back to Ellie and Southfork. Not much later, Lucy returned without Mitch.

J.R.'s skeletons were tumbling out of the closet when past misdeeds caught up with him. Entangled in a knotted web of international monopoly stratagies, he continued to implicate

Bobby and the rest of his family in his shady dealings. Even while he was being forced to give up a sizeable amount of his holdings, J.R. was masterminding a buy out of Westar stock. But Sue Ellen beat him to the punch with her own Weststar stock purchase. In utter rage, J.R. ousted her from Southfork and sent son John Ross to a boarding school. Turning to business partner and latest lover Nicholas Pearce, Sue Ellen took him with her as the two confronted J.R. about the location of the boarding school. Tempers heated up and J.R., gun in hand, forced Nick over a balcony railing. In seconds, Sue Ellen shot three times in J.R.'s direction and then called the police to report two deaths.

DALLAS

However, only Nick had died and no one was charged by the law. J.R. had only suffered a minor flesh wound. Yet again the two divorced. Although Sue Ellen gained custody of John Ross, she permitted the boy to stay with his father. Sue Ellen purchased a film company and she made a movie about the underhanded actions of her ex-husband. Before taking off for England with a new beau, Sue Ellen screened the movie for J.R. She left him with the understanding that if he misbehaved, she would show the film to the world.

The nineties have started with a whirlwind of storylines taking Ellie and Clayton off on a cross-country adventure, and bringing the focus on the next generation of Ewings.

During the absence of Barbara Bel Geddes because of health reasons, fans clamored for her return. After her health improved, she was able to resume her part in the serial. But Donna Reed was given such an abrupt notice by both the network and Lorimar Productions that she sued for breach of contract in the amount of 7.5 million dollars. The following year, Ms. Reed was diagnosed with cancer and she died a year later.

Viewers did not fail to notice the glaring inconsistency of Bobby's resurrection from death in the 1986-87 season. Too many unresolved storylines were left dangling when Pam suddenly realized everything surrounding his death had just been a dream. Criticism over the unfortunate choice in plotting coincided with a drop from top ten ratings.

Since leaving *Dallas* in 1988, Linda Gray has not been prominently featured in any TV shows or movies. Victoria Principal, who departed in 1986, has been seen in several made-for-TV movies. After honing her acting skills in the role of Jenna, Priscilla Presley went on to star in *The Naked Gun* and to be executive producer for the short-lived series *Elvis*.

The serial has offered many cast members, including Larry Hagman, Linda Gray, Patrick Duffy, and Steve Kanaly opportunities to direct episodes. When he left his role as Ray, Steve Kanaly concentrated his efforts on his television directing career. Actress Susan Howard, who played Ray's wife Donna, went on to write episodes for *Dallas*. Larry Hagman is presently the executive producer of the serial.

Famous names such as Alexis Smith as Jessica Montford, Morgan Brittany as Katherine

As the season moved toward its finale in the spring of 1980, more than a few characters had reasonable cause to shoot J.R Ewing. Still, as the last frame of the episode that showed an unidentified person shooting J.R. faded from view, the world was left for an entire summer to wonder, "Who shot J.R.?"

Was it lifelong rival Cliff Barnes? J.R.'s provoked mistress Kristin? Could it have been embittered wife Sue Ellen? Or possibly even one of his parents, Jock or Miss Ellie? How about the cheated financier Vaughn Leland? Lucy's ex-husband Alan Beam had motivation to kill J.R. For that matter, so did Sue Ellen's lover Dusty, except that he was presumed dead. Rumors spread that J.R. had actually pulled the trigger on himself. In the meantime, there was another problem. Was J.R. dead or just wounded?

"*Dallas* Fever" swept the globe. Bets were placed in Las Vegas. Security at the studio had to be reinforced. Six different resolutions were shot so that the actors themselves didn't know the answer. Hysteria heightened when Larry Hagman's contract negotiations were stalled. Even Hagman didn't know who shot J.R.

At long last, on November 21, 1980, as 83 million viewers (in the United States alone) waited breathlessly, the culprit was revealed to be the vengeful Kristin. And yes, J.R. was very much alive. Garnering a 54.3 rating and a 76 share, the event went down in television history as the highest numbered audience ever recorded up to that time.

J.R. in pain after the shot that shocked TV-land. Millions of fans had to wait until the next season premiere to find out "Who shot J.R.?" and if he survived his attack.

DALLAS
. . . .
APRIL 2, 1978–PRESENT CBS

Wentworth, and Leigh Taylor Young as Kimberly Cryder have made guest appearances in and around Southfork.

In writing about the extraordinary impact of *Dallas*, Richard Katzman said, "This is an American program, designed for Americans and presented in a thoroughly American perspective of what entertainment should be, and yet these special qualities of *Dallas* have allowed the show to cross every cultural boundary. While the dialogue is translated in any non-English speaking country, the woes and troubles and fun and joy of the Ewing family remain the same. In short, the Ewings have been accepted by every economic group and every social structure, including millions of people worldwide who have never seen or done any of the things they see on the show. This universal appeal is but one of the firsts we have been extremely proud to be a part of."

A handful of prime-time serials would go on to break the records of those many "firsts" that *Dallas* trailblazed. But nowhere, before or after, has there been another anti-hero as all consuming as J.R. Ewing. Without a doubt, he is the man that TV audiences love to hate—and fans are hoping they will get to see him for many more years.

Below: *Bobby pushes Pamela to safety, but he is injured and dies. Of course, it all turned out to be Pamela's dream and he was alive after all.*

Opposite page: *J.R. is the villian TV viewers love to hate.*

In 1976, prior to being hired for a new prime-time serial called *Dallas*, Larry Hagman hadn't worked since his part on *I Dream of Jeannie*. Leasing out his Malibu home, he took his family to live with his famous mother, Mary Martin, in Palm Springs. Then things changed rapidly.

As the venomously power-hungry J.R. Ewing, Larry Hagman captured the role of a lifetime. During the 1980 fervor caused by the international echo of the question, "Who shot J.R.?" the actor was also able to negotiate the contract of a lifetime. Rumored to be in excess of a million dollars that would triple before long, plus a guaranteed percentage of *Dallas* merchandise sales, the coup looked to have been masterminded by someone as conniving as J.R. himself.

But had Hagman really transformed into his on-camera persona? The actor denied the comparison as he commented that J.R. would have criticized the deal. "J.R. would say to me," said Hagman, "'You dope, you had 'em by the throat; why didn't you squeeze a little harder?' That's not my style."

Presently, as executive producer of the serial he almost turned down, Hagman devotes any spare time to private moments of reflection and the quiet company of family and friends.

DARK SHADOWS

"My name is Victoria Winters. I am going on a journey that will bring me to a strange, dark house on the edge of the sea at Widow's Hill. There, I am going to be a governess to a young boy and the companion of a mysterious woman."

So began the first episode of *Dark Shadows* on July 27, 1966. The serial that introduced vampires, ghosts, and werewolves to daytime television began, appropriately, with a dream. "I awoke suddenly in the middle of a strange dream," recalled producer Dan Curtis. "The bedroom was pitch black, yet I could see the dream clearly. My dream was about a girl riding on a train. She was reading a letter and gazing out the window."

In the dream, the girl's voice explained that she'd been hired as a governess at an old mansion along the New England seacoast. The final image Curtis recalled seeing was the girl left alone in the empty station at twilight—as the train continued on its way. Forcing himself awake, Curtis replayed the dream in his mind. "I thought about it and it was brilliantly logical to me." Executives at ABC agreed and gave Curtis the green light to develop a gothic soap opera.

Collaborating with writer Art Wallace, Curtis gave the young woman in his dream a name, Victoria Winters. He set her in Collinsport, Maine, where she was hired by wealthy matriarch Elizabeth Collins Stoddard to care for her troubled young nephew, David Collins, at Collinwood mansion. The boy's stuffy father, Roger, was a widower. Also living on the estate was Elizabeth's rebellious teenage daughter, Carolyn. Maggie Evans, a local waitress, rounded out the cast. Maggie lived with her widowed father, Sam, an alcoholic artist.

Elizabeth's dead husband, Paul, figured prominently in the serial's early storyline. Elizabeth had killed her husband with a poker when she discovered that he tried to steal jewelry their daughter Carolyn was to inherit. Jason McGuire, Paul's accomplice, convinced Elizabeth not to confess her act to the police. Instead, he helped Elizabeth conceal her husband's body in a trunk. Then he blackmailed her. Carolyn became incensed when she discovered her sexy boyfriend, Burke Devlin, was making moves on her cousin's new governess.

The serial took a turn toward the supernatural when it introduced its first ghost, Bill Malloy. A few months later, David's late mother, Laura, made her spiritual presence known. She was followed by another ghost, Josette DuPres. Locked away in a secret room of the old house was the ghost of a little girl who became David's playmate. "We found that dealing with the supernatural seemed to increase the audience," said producer Robert Costello. "We got a better response to the show."

Although experimenting with the soap opera format was beginning to attract a larger share of the audience, the serial's ratings still weren't high enough to impress ABC. The network ordered Dan Curtis to make extreme changes or the show would be canceled. To save his faltering series, Curtis turned to a vampire for help. "I'd always felt that a vampire was as spooky as we could get," explained Curtis, "that if the viewers bought it, we could get away with anything. If it didn't work, I figured we could always drive a stake through his heart."

Below: *Jonathan Frid as the vampire Barnabas Collins.*

Opposite page, top: *Angelique (Lara Parker) views a picture of a Collins ancestor.*

Opposite page, bottom: *Kate Jackson played Daphne Harridge and Jonathan Frid also played Bramwell Collins.*

THE CAST

Cast

BALBERITH	HUMBERT ALLEN ASTREDO
NICHOLAS BLAIR	HUMBERT ALLEN ASTREDO
CAROLYN STODDARD	NANCY BARRETT
ELIZABETH STODDARD COLLINS	JOAN BENNETT
PHILLIP TODD	CHRISTOPHER BERNAU
MRS. JOHNSON	CLARICE BLACKBURN
CHRIS JENNINGS	DON BRISCOE
TOM JENNINGS	DON BRISCOE
HALLIE STOKES	KATHY CODY
JOE HASKELL	JOEL CROTHERS
ELLIOT STOKES	THAYER DAVID
COUNT PETOFI	THAYER DAVID
MATTHEW MORGAN	THAYER DAVID
JEFF CLARK	ROGER DAVIS
NED STUART	ROGER DAVIS
ROGER COLLINS	LOUIS EDMONDS
SAM EVANS	DAVID FORD
	MARK EVANS
FRANK GARNER	CONARD FOWKES
RICHARD GARNER	HUGH FRANKLIN
BARNABAS COLLINS	JONATHAN FRID
BURKE DEVLIN	ANTHONY GEORGE
	MITCHELL RYAN
JULIA HOFFMAN	GRAYSON HALL
DAVID COLLINS	DAVID HENESY
DAPHNE HARRIDGE	KATE JACKSON
WILLIE LOOMIS	JOHN KARLEN
	JAMES HALL
PHYLLIS WICK	DORRIE KAVANAUGH
TONY PETERSON	JERRY LACY
VAMPIRE GIRL LILY	MARSHA MASON
AMANDA HARRIS	DONNA McKECHNIE
OLIVIA COREY	DONNA McKECHNIE
LAURA COLLINS	DIANA MILLAY
VICTORIA WINTERS	ALEXANDRA MOLTKE (ISLES)
	BETSY DURKIN
AMY JENNINGS	DENISE NICKERSON
ANGELIQUE DuVALL COLLINS	LARA PARKER
CASSANDRA COLLINS	LARA PARKER
JASON McGUIRE	DENNIS PATRICK
PAUL STODDARD	DENNIS PATRICK
	JOEL FABIANI
JEB HAWKES	CHRISTOPHER PENNOCK
SEBASTIAN SHAW	CHRISTOPHER PENNOCK
SABRINA STUART	LISA RICHARDS
ADAM	ROBERT RODAN
GEORGE PATERSON	ALFRED SANDOR
	VINCE O'BRIEN
	DANA ELCAR

DARK SHADOWS

JULY 27, 1966–APRIL 2, 1971 ABC

Barnabas Collins, played by Canadian actor Jonathan Frid, made his first appearance on April 14, 1967. He arrived on Elizabeth's doorstep claiming to be a long lost cousin from England and the descendant of the original Barnabas Collins. At first, Barnabas was depicted as an evil vampire. He kidnapped Maggie Evans, who reminded him of his lost love Josette, and then he went after Victoria Winters.

A few months after Barnabas's arrival, Dr. Julia Hoffman was introduced as a character who figured out his secret and tried to cure him. The late Grayson Hall, who played Julia, decided to expand the character by adding her own unique interpretation. She told a reporter, "What happened is that I played this doctor filled with all these technical things that I had to talk about, and to not make it so dry I made a decision all by myself that I would be in love with Barnabas.... I decided that instead of being a serious dedicated doctor, I would be a serious dedicated doctor in love with a patient; a patient who happened to be a vampire."

A later storyline, set in 1795, showed Barnabas to be a sympathetic character by tracing his origins as a vampire. The audience learned Barnabas had been hexed by a treacherous witch, Angelique, who condemned him to eternal life as a vampire.

Barnabas fell in love with Josette, a recent arrival from Martinique, when he first met her in 1795. This displeased Josette's handmaiden, Angelique, who secretly loved Barnabas. Employing black magic, Angelique influenced Josette to fall in love with Barnabas's cousin. Before Barnabas knew it, the bewitched couple was married. Devastated by the news, Barnabas challenged his cousin to a duel and killed him. Angelique followed Barnabas to the old house, where he lived in mournful solitude. She promised to cure his ailing young sister, Sara, if he'd marry her. Once they were married, Barnabas learned Angelique was a witch who had created Sara's illness to manipulate him into marriage. Angered, Barnabas confronted Angelique, making it clear he detested her. Angelique retaliated by wrecking havoc on the Collins family, which resulted in young Sara's death. Unable to deal with this new loss, Barnabas shot Angelique. Fearing that she was dying, Angelique hexed Barnabas, who was attacked by a bat. Angelique recovered, but

Barnabas's mysterious bat attack proved fatal. Realizing Barnabas was doomed to return as one of the living dead, Angelique visited his tomb to prevent his new incarnation. Trapping Angelique in the mausoleum, Barnabas finally exacted his revenge by killing her.

When Barnabas's horrified parents learned their son was a vampire, they tried in vain to cure him. Finally, Barnabas's father shot him. Realizing his last effort was futile, he chained his son during daylight inside a coffin hidden away in a secret area of the Collins family crypt. After his parents died, Barnabas remained in the coffin for nearly 200 years until he was freed by Jason McGuire's accomplice, Willie Loomis.

Barnabas was over 200 years old, and at one point reverted to his true age. He recovered and regained immortality.

Top: *Grayson Hall (left) played Dr. Julia Hoffman, who was in love with Barnabas and was searching for a cure for his vampirism. Nancy Barrett played Carolyn Stoddard.*

Bottom: *Victoria Winters (Alexandra Moltke) was the innocent governess who was surrounded by vampires, witches, and ghosts at Collinwood mansion.*

Cast Continued

MAGGIE EVANS	KATHRYN LEIGH SCOTT
QUENTIN COLLINS	DAVID SELBY
GRANT DOUGLAS	DAVID SELBY
SARAH COLLINS	SHARON SMITH
HARRY JOHNSON	CRAIG SOLOCUM
GERALD STILES	JAMES STORM
BRUNO HESS	MICHAEL STROKA
EZRA BRAITHWAITE	ABE VIGODA
EVE	MARIE WALLACE
MEGAN TODD	MARIE WALLACE
ROXANNE DREW	DONNA WANDREY
DAVE WOODARD	RICHARD WOODS
	ROBERT GERRINGER
	PETER TURGEON

1795 Cast

MILLICENT COLLINS	NANCY BARRETT
NAOMI COLLINS	JOAN BENNETT
ABIGAIL COLLINS	CLARICE BLACKBURN
MAUDE BROWNING	VALA CLIFTON
NATHAN FORBES	JOEL CROTHERS
BEN STOKES	THAYER DAVID
PETER BRADFORD	ROGER DAVIS
SUKI FORBES	JANE DRAPER
JOSHUA COLLINS	LOUIS EDMONDS
ANDRE DuPRES	DAVID FORD
BARNABAS COLLINS	JONATHAN FRID
JEREMIAH COLLINS	ANTHONY GEORGE
NATALIE DuPRES	GRAYSON HALL
DANIEL COLLINS	DAVID HENESY
RUBY TATE	ELAINE HYMAN
GREGORY TRASK	JERRY LACY
VICTORIA WINTERS	ALEXANDRA MOLTKE (ISLES)
	BETSY DURKIN
ANGELIQUE DuVALL COLLINS	LARA PARKER
JOSETTE DuPRES	KATHRYN LEIGH SCOTT
NOAH GIFFORD	CRAIG SOLOCUM
SARAH COLLINS	SHARON SMYTH

DARK SHADOWS

JULY 27, 1966–APRIL 2, 1971 ABC

Shortly after Barnabas appeared, the ratings took off. It was a particular favorite of students, who rushed home from school every afternoon to catch the latest episode. Louis Edmonds, who played Roger Collins, recalled his astonishment at seeing hundreds of children standing in front of the studio hoping to catch a glimpse of the actors. "We knew we had something bigger than life on our hands," he said. Attempting to explain the serial's appeal, the *New York Times* wrote, "There is something mysterious about the way Jonathan Frid as vampire Barnabas Collins attracts millions of viewers to his vampire character.... His 'Barnabas' has a lost, forlorn look, almost as if the actor can't remember his lines, and is trying to read them from a teleprompter." Alexandra Moltke, who played Victoria Winters, didn't think the paper's tongue-in-cheek appraisal was too far off target. "That faraway look that Barnabas used to get was really a desperate searching for the teleprompter," she concurred. "However, a whole other personality developed out of that. People thought that he was just a lost, unhappy, well-meaning vampire when, in fact, he wasn't supposed to be that way at all."

Lara Parker, who played Angelique, credits Jonathan Frid with discovering new dimensions to Barnabas that the writers hadn't intended. "He made himself a reluctant vampire and that gave people something to identify with. However, every time he became the vampire, he was just as scary as he ever was. When he was the human being, your heart went out to him, because you saw how much he suffered.... I think the fact that all the *Dark Shadows* characters were multi-dimensional made the show so popular. They really caught the viewers' imagination."

After appearing in nearly every episode for two years, Frid found himself exhausted. He met with Dan Curtis and pleaded with him "to get somebody else on this show. Another Monster to help take some of the weight off me, as well as help me!" A few weeks later, *Dark Shadows* introduced a new male character who proved extremely popular. Quentin Collins, played by David Selby, was first conceived as an evil spirit fighting to win possession of young David Collins's soul. When viewers responded favorably to Quentin, the writers decided to develop a whole storyline around him.

In an attempt to contact Quentin's spirit,

Barnabas was transported back to 1897, when Quentin is still alive. During this period, matriarch Edith Collins, who was in her nineties, was nearing death. Edith had four adult grandchildren: Edward, Carl, Quentin, and Judith. Soon after Barnabas's arrival, Edith died of natural causes. Before her will was read, Quentin, who enjoyed gambling and drinking, intercepted the will and discovered his grandmother hadn't left him a cent. Quentin tried to doctor a forged will, but his efforts were thwarted by Barnabas. With the help of satanist Evan Hanley, a vengeful Quentin tried to conjure up the devil to destroy Barnabas, but instead Angelique materialized. Meanwhile, Angelique wasn't thrilled to learn Barnabas had adjusted to 1897 and was romancing the Collins's governess, Rachel Drummond.

Unknown to Quentin, his first wife, Jenny, was still alive. When he ran off with Edward's wife, Laura, Jenny went crazy and was confined to secret quarters by Edward and Judith. Escaping from her room, Jenny tried to locate Quentin. To her horror, she discovered him seducing Beth Chavez, a maidservant. In a blind fury, Jenny plunged a knife into a shocked Quentin's chest.

Audiences didn't buy the storyline when Jonathan Frid played Bramwell Collins, he was too closely identified with Barnabas.

Barnabas at Collinwood mansion.

Seeing Quentin's body, Barnabas realized he'd have to be brought back to life—otherwise his premature death could have potentially disastrous effects on future Collins descendants. Ultimately, Angelique offered to help Barnabas. She'd make Quentin "rise and talk," provided Barnabas return an unspecified favor at a future date. When Barnabas agreed, Angelique stood by her promise and made Quentin "rise and talk." But she made him a whacked-out zombie, with which she intended to terrorize Rachel Drummond. Eventually, a bizarre exorcism succeeded in reuniting Quentin's body and soul.

Quentin's out-of-body experience had little effect on raising his spiritual consciousness. Once again, he was caught by Jenny trying to seduce Beth Chavez. Once again, Jenny tried to kill him. This time, Quentin strangled Jenny.

News of her sister's (Jenny) death didn't please Magda Racosie—a gypsy fortune teller who once worked for Edith Collins. She placed a curse on Quentin and transformed him into a werewolf. The curse was also meant for Quentin's male descendants.

Magda regreted her curse when she discovered Jenny had secretly given birth to twins belonging to Quentin—a girl and a boy. A horrified Magda embarked on a desperate search

Cast Continued
1897 Cast

EVAN HANLEY	HUMBERT ALLEN ASTREDO
CHARITY TRASK	NANCY BARRETT
JUDITH COLLINS TRASK	JOAN BENNETT
MINERVA TRASK	CLARICE BLACKBURN
TIMOTHY SHAW	DON BRISCOE
BETH CHAVEZ	TERRY CRAWFORD
COUNT PETOFI	THAYER DAVID
VICTOR FENN-GIBBON	THAYER DAVID
SANDOR RACOSIE	THAYER DAVID
CHARLES DELAWARE TATE	ROGER DAVIS
DIRK WILKINS	ROGER DAVIS
EDWARD COLLINS	LOUIS EDMONDS
BARNABAS COLLINS	JONATHAN FRID
MAGDA RACOSIE	GRAYSON HALL
JULIA HOFFMAN	GRAYSON HALL
GARTH BLACKWOOD	JOHN HARKINS
JAMISON COLLINS	DAVID HENESY
EDITH COLLINS	ISABELLA HOOPES
CARL COLLINS	JOHN KARLEN
GREGORY TRASK	JERRY LACY
AMANDA HARRIS	DONNA McKECHNIE
KING JOHNNY ROMANO	PAUL MICHAEL
NORA COLLINS	DENISE NICKERSON
VALERIE COLLINS	LARA PARKER
RACHEL DRUMMOND	KATHRYN LEIGH SCOTT
KATHRYN HAMPSHIRE	KATHRYN LEIGH SCOTT
QUENTIN COLLINS	DAVID SELBY
WIDOW ROMANO	LANA SHAW
ARISTEDE	MICHAEL STROKA
JENNY COLLINS	MARIE WALLACE

DARK SHADOWS

JULY 27, 1966–APRIL 2, 1971 ABC

to find a cure for Quentin. Her journey led to the discovery of the mummified hand of Count Petofi, a powerful occultist who had also been a werewolf. The hand had been severed as a payment to gypsies for curing the count. To Magda's frustration, the hand had no effect on Quentin's condition. But once Count Petofi was reunited with his hand, he enlisted the help of artist Charles Delaware Tate to cure Quentin. Tate painted a portrait of Quentin that changed to a werewolf every full moon while Quentin remained human. The portrait also made Quentin immortal. A convoluted plot development, however, cost Quentin his immortality.

During the 1897 storyline, Dan Curtis directed a feature length film titled *House of Dark Shadows*. The movie was filmed on-location in Tarrytown, New York, in six weeks. Many of the actors who appeared in it continued to tape daily episodes of the serial in New York City. Jonathan Frid was reportedly unhappy that Barnabas was depicted in the movie as an evil vampire. When a sequel, *Night of Dark Shadows*, was made one year later, Frid chose not to be included. Instead, David Selby starred as Quentin Collins.

Since *Dark Shadows* relied heavily on special effects, there usually wasn't enough time left for the actors to adequately rehearse their scenes. The serial was performed live on tape, which meant whatever mistakes happened would be broadcast to millions of viewers. In one episode, a lamp fell three feet from Josette while she was lost in thought while writing a letter. Kathryn Leigh Scott, who played Josette, never flinched. In another episode, Josette's dress got caught on a tree branch and uprooted the tree, forcing the actress to drag the tree with her during the entire scene. During the closing credits, Jonathan Frid was once seen by viewers gathering his clothes to leave the studio. Another time, Louis Edmonds was in the process of changing into his street clothes when he was suddenly summoned back on the set to tape another scene, which ended up being shot with a tight close-up of Edmonds's face. To keep themselves from giving in to the pressure, the actors tried to remain good natured. "We laughed and fooled around a lot on the set," explained David Selby. "Many times when the camera cued in on us for a look of absolute horror on our faces before the commercial, we opened our eyes up wide in horror...and then completely cracked up when the

little red light on the camera went off, telling us we were no longer being seen by the viewers."

By 1971, *Dark Shadows* had become so convoluted with its various time travel storylines that frustrated viewers began tuning out. Dan Curtis reacted to the drop in ratings by quickening the show's pace, which only made the serial more confusing for viewers. Finally, ABC canceled the series. Today, reruns of *Dark Shadows* are available in syndication as well as on videocassette. Dan Curtis also filmed an updated, made-for-TV movie version for NBC in 1990 with a completely new cast.

Below: *Barnabas loved Victoria. He gazes at her neck longingly, but he restrains himself from biting her.*

Opposite page: *Barnabas was turned into a vampire by the witch Angelique, who was in love with him.*

DARK SHADOWS

JULY 27, 1966–APRIL 2, 1971 ABC

Jonathan Frid was preparing to move to California when his New York agent called and asked if he'd be interested in auditioning for the part of a vampire on a daytime serial. Sensing Frid's disinterest, his agent quickly said the gig would only be for a few weeks and that the extra money he earned would come in handy as he adjusted to his new life in California. Frid reluctantly agreed to audition. The role ended up lasting four years and made Frid one of the most famous faces in daytime television.

Viewers of *Dark Shadows* responded to Frid's sympathetic portrayal of vampire Barnabas Collins. The ratings skyrocketed, Frid began receiving bushels of fan mail, and hordes of teenage fans waited outside the studio for his autograph.

"Barnabas was the first sympathetic vampire," explained Frid in the *Dark Shadows Tribute*, published by Pioneer Press. "He was a man with an addiction who drank blood only to survive. The audience felt pity for him, and many of the women wanted to mother him. There was a love/hate relationship between the audience —particularly children—and Barnabas. In some ways, he was looked upon as a darker version of Santa Claus; friendly enough that you were intrigued by him, yet mysterious enough that he frightened you."

Frid landed his first acting role when he was 15 years old while attending a prep school in his hometown of Hamilton, Ontario. He played "old" Sir Anthony Absolute in Sheridan's *The Rivals*. "Of course the most important role in my life was the first one," he said. "It was during *The Rivals* that I thought, 'Yes, acting is what I can do.'" Five years later, while Frid was serving a stint in the navy, the thought first occurred to him to actually become a professional actor. He trained briefly at the Royal Academy in London, but dropped out after discovering Canadian actors were being paid handsomely to play Americans. After appearing in the feature film *The Third Man* and performing as Dr. Sloper in a Canadian production of *The Heiress*, he enrolled at Toronto's Academy of Radio Arts. He then studied at the Yale Drama School, where he received a Master's Degree in Fine Arts in 1957.

Moving to New York, Frid appeared in *The Golem, The Burning, Romeo and Juliet, Macbeth,* and *Richard III.* But it was his role as Barnabas Collins on *Dark Shadows* that made him a household name. Frid said he was too busy performing five episodes a week at the studio to realize the impact his performance was having on American television viewers.

In 1970, he starred in the feature film *House of Dark Shadows.* He wasn't happy with the movie because it depicted Barnabas as an evil vampire. When a sequel, *Night of Dark Shadows,* went into production a year later, Frid chose not to participate.

By 1971, Frid sensed the serial's cancellation was imminent. "Every time the show went up another notch, I figured it was peaking and that it would start to go down. It lasted a hell of a lot longer than I thought it would.... We started repeating ourselves and the show burned out."

Following the serial's demise, Frid appeared in Oliver Stone's *Seizure* and ABC's *The Devil's Daughter* before taking an extended leave from acting. By 1980, Frid became comfortable with the public's fascination of *Dark Shadows* and began making guest appearances at various conventions across America. Frid's reassociation with the public inspired him to launch a live show. "It's shaping up nicely," he said. "I've had my vacation from show business and now it's time to get back to brass tacks."

Barnabas became a sympathetic vampire when Jonathan Frid added a guilty conscious to Barnabas's personality.

DAYS OF OUR LIVES

NOVEMBER 8, 1965–PRESENT NBC

In a word, this nearly three decade old serial can be described best as family. It was created and produced through the years by the Corday family, followed by an ardently loyal family of fans, and adheres closely to the stories of its featured families. *Days of Our Lives* was born on a sunny afternoon, in a front porch discussion. Shop-talking with colleague Irna Phillips, one of soap opera's great matriarchs, Ted Corday received welcomed input about a daytime drama he hoped to launch. Phillips soon after coined the unforgettable opening line for the serial: "Like sands through the hourglass, so are the *Days of Our Lives.*" In addition to those words and the consistency of storylines that would evolve over the coming generations, *Days of Our Lives* would be known for its pulse-quickening, heart-thumping, knee-quaking sexiness.

Set in the town of Salem, the early story followed the days of the lives of the Horton family. The lineage began with Dr. Tom Horton, University Hospital's head of Internal Medicine, his wife, Alice Horton, and their five children. Son Tommy, the twin of Addie, was thought to have been a casualty in the Korean War. Addie ran off to Europe with her husband, superficial banker Ben Olson. They left their daughter, Julie, to the care of her grandparents. Completing the list of Alice and Tom's offspring were Marie, Bill, and Mickey. Bill was a doctor and Mickey a lawyer.

Even though *Days of Our Lives* premiered with juicy plot possibilities and film veterans Macdonald Carey as Tom and Frances Reid as Alice, its first season was rocky. Indeed, out of the 34 daytime serials on the air, the fledgling show ranked 32 in 1966. And worse, tragedy struck before the first year was over when creator/producer Ted Corday died. But Betty Corday, Ted's widow, sprang into action to try to save her husband's creation. Sure enough, with the contributions of new headwriter William J. Bell, the serial got on its feet and was soon giving the other soaps stiff competition.

One of Bell's earliest scintillating inventions was the forbidden, incestuous attraction between Marie and a man who was revealed to be her missing brother, Tommy. His war injuries caused amnesia and resulted in plastic surgery. Next came what would be hailed as television's best and

longest kept secret as to who really was the father of Dr. Laura Spencer's son, Michael. Throughout the tangled web of the tempestuous triangle between Laura (Susan Flannery), husband Dr. Bill Horton (Edward Mallory), and brother Mickey Horton (John Clarke), the serial's popularity continued to swell. By 1971, *Days of Our Lives* had ascended the ratings ladder and even managed to unseat long time champ *As the World Turns* from the coveted number one spot.

The Hortons and their entourage provided enough cliff-hangers for the serial to hover near or at the top for the first half of the seventies. In 1973, Pat Falken Smith, a previous underling writer to William J. Bell, took over as headwriter. Bell went on to write for his newly created serial *The Young and the Restless.*

Below: *Alice Horton (Frances Reid), Tom Horton (Macdonald Carey, top), and their son Mickey (John Clarke, right) are members of the leading family in Salem.*

Opposite page: *The 1989 cast of* Days of Our Lives.

For the next two years, Falken Smith's adept handling of storylines and her witty dialogue kept the praise coming. So ardent was the critical acclaim that a *Time* magazine cover story (bearing the picture of Bill and Susan Seaforth Hayes—Salem's Doug and Julie Williams) called *Days of Our Lives* "the best soap." The serial dominated in the Emmy Awards as yearly—from 1973 to 1978—it gobbled up nominations, recognition, and wins.

Unfortunately, however, dominance began to ebb in 1975, when an ill-fated choice on the part of NBC aided the downslide. In rewarding the success of the decade old serial with an expanded format (from a half hour to a full hour), the network positioned it against *As the World Turns.* Furthermore, when Falken Smith abandoned her headwriting post because of contract problems, the once sizzling soap could no longer compete with the daytime dramas captivating younger

Original Cast

TOM HORTON	MACDONALD CAREY
TONY MERRITT	RICHARD COLLA
JULIE OLSON	CARLA DOHERTY
JIM FISK	BURT DOUGLAS
ADDIE HORTON OLSON	PAT HUSTON
BEN OLSON	ROBERT KNAPP
STEVE OLSON	FLIP MARK
CRAIG MERRITT	DICK McLEAN
ALICE HORTON	FRANCES REID
A DETECTIVE	ROBERT J. STEVENSON

DAYS OF OUR LIVES

NOVEMBER 8, 1965–PRESENT NBC

audiences. By the end of 1979, the bland condition of *Days of Our Lives* led NBC executive Fred Silverman to demand total renovations.

This led from the frying pan into the fire. Tempers were flaring behind the scenes. Spats between cast and crew raged under the stress of multiple firings by new producer Al Rabin. More than a dozen characters were killed or written off by incoming headwriter Nina Laemmle. Insiders referred to this aspect of the overhaul as the "Valentine's Day Massacre."

Despite all the bloodshed, the revamping plan backfired when even the most loyal fans felt jilted by the loss of favorite characters. This dependable portion of the audience fell by the wayside. The only perk to come out of a new regime of characters was Gloria Loring's Liz Chandler. Within three years, Loring obtained freedom from restrictions in her contract that limited outside appearances. In so doing, she pioneered a new era of contractual rights for daytime actors.

In the meantime, Pat Falken Smith returned for a short period (after her lauded writing on *General Hospital*) to give *Days of Our Lives* a shot of adrenaline. This infusion of energy from Falken Smith's writing came in the form of new character Roman Brady, a cop, played by ex-*Dynasty* actor Wayne Northrop. By matching him up with Dr. Marlena Evans (Deidre Hall), and introducing the blood-chilling epic of the Salem Strangler, the serial found itself with a romantic couple who followed in the footsteps of *General Hospital's* Luke and Laura.

After co-writer Margaret DePriest was handed headwriting chores by Falken Smith, *Days of Our Lives* continued to heat up in intensity and popularity. By 1984, it ranked as NBC's number one soap opera. This was due mainly to its youth-oriented romantic intrigues and the latest of delicious duos, Bo Brady (Peter Reckell) and Hope Williams (Kristian Alfonso). Although Doug and Julie Williams left that year for greener pastures, the eighties saw the serial gain a steady momentum of success.

Recently, the series has dealt with the love-on-the-run story of Kayla Brady (Mary Beth Evans) and Steve Johnson, also known as Patch (Stephen Nichols). While many dynasties have been spawned, great-great grandparents Tom and Alice Horton still remain the foundation upon

which *Days of Our Lives* stands. Actors Macdonald Carey and Frances Reid still have star billing. The current producer is Ken Corday, son of Ted and Betty.

During the serial's first decade, Alice and Tom were plagued by the woes of all their children, particularly by sons Bill and Mickey, who were embroiled in a battle for the heart of Dr. Laura Spencer. Although Laura and Bill were engaged, Bill suddenly disappeared from Salem when a hand malady that would have prevented him from performing surgery was detected. Upon his recovery and return, Bill was met with a worse discovery. In her loneliness, Laura had married his brother Mickey.

The love affair between Kayla (Mary Beth Evans) and Patch (Stephen Nicols) has been a viewer favorite.

Bill couldn't contain his passion and, against Laura's will, forced her into having sex with him. Her pregnancy, she believed, was a result of the rape. Her father-in-law had informed her that Mickey (unknown to Mickey) was sterile. Tom Horton agreed not to confront Bill about the incident in order to protect Mickey from being destroyed about his sterility. The real father of Laura's baby boy, Michael, was kept a secret.

After Marie Horton found out her new love interest, Dr. Mark Brooks, was really her brother Tom; Marie ran off to become a nun. Tom attempted to settle down to a normal life with his wife, Kitty. It wasn't long, however, before meddling Kitty located a tape with the truth of Michael's parentage. Bill tried to retrieve the tape from her. In the course of their argument, weak-hearted Kitty suffered cardiac arrest and died. During the murder trial, Bill refused to reveal the information that would hurt his brother Mickey and was sentenced to jail.

Addie's daughter, Julie, had struggled through a difficult adolescence, tainted by her nasty rivalry with Susan Martin. A recent heiress, Susan had been courted by Doug Williams, a prison acquaintance of Bill Horton. Spurning Doug's golddigging advances, Susan devised a way to demolish Julie's marriage to Scott Banning— by hiring Doug to do it. Instead, love bloomed at first sight for Doug and Julie. Then, Addie returned from Europe and caught a fancy for Doug.

Just as Julie was about to leave Scott for Doug, Addie ran off with Doug. A living nightmare raged for Julie—she was in love with a man who was married to her mother. More traumas lay in store for Julie when Scott died shortly after that. Addie soon gave birth to Hope, Doug's daughter and Julie's half-sister. Reconciled to her sad fate, Julie decided to marry Bob Anderson. Bob was a successful and wealthy businessman who had left his wife, Phyllis, during a mid-life crisis.

DAYS OF OUR LIVES

NOVEMBER 8, 1965–PRESENT NBC

While strolling with baby Hope, Addie was struck by a car after pushing the stroller out of danger. The baby lived but Addie died. Although Doug was now a single father, Julie was imprisoned in a loveless marriage. Doug and Julie seemed destined to be star-crossed.

Meanwhile, Laura's private testimony after Bill's prison release allowed him to return to his medical practice. Mickey's fear that Laura and Bill were having an affair led him to an affair with his secretary, Linda Patterson. This caused tension between him and his son, Michael. A confrontation sparked a massive heart attack in Mickey, which was followed by a stroke. When Mickey awoke, he had no memory. He wandered out of the hospital unnoticed. He eventually made his way to a distant farm and took on a new identity. Mickey Horton became Marty Hanson, husband of the sweet, crippled beauty Maggie Simmons.

Later, Michael was hurt in an accident and needed blood. When Mickey found out his blood was not compatible, he remembered everything and figured out that Bill was Michael's natural father. In anger, Mickey tried to shoot Bill and was committed to a mental institution. Laura, too, was crumbling from the emotional pain. Michael was angry at his "real parents" for shielding the truth from him. In time, and with the help of psychiatrist Marlena Evans, Laura and Mickey would both mend.

One of the most popular storylines involved a terrifying murderer known as the Salem Strangler. Marlena became suspicious when she received a series of crank phone calls. The police sent Detective Roman Brady to protect her. The two found themselves attracted to each other.

Thinking that he was about to nab his prey during Roman's absence, the Salem Strangler murdered Marlena. When Roman discovered

Below left: *Dave (Don Frabotta) promotes the teenage horror movie that is being filmed in Salem in 1990.*

Below right: *Julie Williams (Susan Seaforth Hayes) and Dave at Doug's Place in 1974.*

Doug and Julie's marriage was a time of much rejoicing in Salem.

Marlena dead, he swore vengeance against the psychopath. Roman was shocked when he found Marlena alive. The dead woman was Marlena's unstable twin sister, Samantha. Just as everything was settling down, Roman was framed for murder. Barely a newlywed to Marlena, Roman was forced to go into hiding.

Beautiful 18-year-old Hope Williams had also been enjoying the company of a handsome Brady man. In her case it was Bo, Roman's brother. When Hope's father, Doug, walked in on the two of them in bed together, he suffered a heart attack.

Just before their wedding, Bo and Hope left Salem to assist Roman in his all-out war against the demonic Stefano DiMera, who possessed the potentially disastrous prisms. Before long, Marlena was in on the chase and eventually justice would be served. At least in the short run—since this villain refused to die. A tragic death lurked around the corner, however, for Marlena. She lost her life in an airplane crash.

Many of the members of the Salem community who left or were thought to be dead abruptly resurfaced in 1989. Bo, Hope, Julie, and

DAYS OF OUR LIVES

NOVEMBER 8, 1965–PRESENT NBC

Macdonald Carey has received two Emmys for his role as patriarch Dr. Tom Horton on the long-running *Days of Our Lives*. Prior to joining the daytime serial in 1965, he enjoyed a successful career in theatre, radio, and film. He received his college education at the University of Iowa and the University of Wisconsin. Radio presented him with his first opportunity to showcase his singing and acting talents. He appeared on such radio serials as *Stella Dallas*, *John's Other Wife*, *Just Plain Bill*, *Ellen Randolph*, *Woman in White*, and *Young Hickory*.

Following a critically acclaimed performance in Broadway's *Lady in the Dark*, Carey moved to Hollywood in 1942 and became a contract player for Paramount Pictures. He was seen in such feature films as *Dr. Broadway*, *Wake Island*, *Suddenly, It's Spring*, *Dream Girl*, *Streets of Laredo*, and *The Great Gatsby*.

In the early fifties, Carey began guest-appearing on television. He also starred in his own series, *Dr. Christian*, in 1956. During the sixties, he guest-starred on such popular series as *Ben Casey*, *Burke's Law*, *Mr. Novak*, *The Outer Limits*, and *Lassie*. After joining the cast of *Days of Our Lives*, Macdonald occasionally found time to guest-star in such series as *Owen Marshall*, *McMillan and Wife*, and *Police Story*.

This prolific actor is also the author of three books of poetry. His autobiography, *The Days of My Life*, will be published in 1991.

even producer Al Rabin have either resumed their roles or returned for brief stints on the serial. Steve Johnson, with and without his eyepatch, and wrongfully convicted wife, Kayla, struggled to be reunited. The nineties continue to focus on the Hortons and their friends and foes.

Days of Our Lives has had some exciting events behind the scenes, also. It won an Emmy Award for Outstanding Daytime Drama in 1978. In 1975, Susan Flannery won for Outstanding Actress. Bill and Susan Seaforth Hayes—real life husband and wife—fell in love on the set of the soap opera.

Macdonald Carey as Tom Horton is Salem's most respected doctor.

Diana Colville (Genie Francis) and Mike Horton (Michael Weiss). Soap viewers may recognize Genie Francis, she made soap history as Laura on General Hospital.

The serial tackled controversial social issues and taboo subjects, exploring a wide range of aspects related to sexuality such as storylines involving interracial couples, incest, lesbianism, and male homosexuality. At the same time, it was criticized by women's groups for portraying women as victims.

Celebrity singer Al Jarreau was a familiar face when he made a guest appearance on *Days of Our Lives.* What's more, Patch's alter ego Stephen Nichols, now a sex symbol, is a Rhythm and Blues singer. Sadly, Nichols has announced plans to leave the show.

When honored by the Academy of Television Arts and Sciences for her achievement in daytime drama, Susan Seaforth Hayes said to the cast and crew of *Days of Our Lives,* "I practically grew up with you. You were there during the most important moments of my life. Mac and Frances, you were like my second mother and father. I fell in love with my leading man [Bill Hayes]. Wes Kenney, our producer, came to my wedding. You beautiful people—you are my family."

Her feelings are certainly reflected by the fans who have been attached to the serial. They feel as if they are part of the family.

THE DOCTORS

. . . .

APRIL 1, 1963–DECEMBER 31, 1982 NBC

This show, which premiered on the same day as *General Hospital*, was created by former *Ma Perkins's* writer Orrin Tovrov and began as an anthology series set at Hope Memorial Hospital. Each day a new story would be introduced by one of the series' four regulars: Dr. Jerry Chandler (Richard Roat), Dr. William Scott (Jack Gaynor), Dr. Elizabeth Hayes (Margot Moser), or Reverend Sam Shafer (Fred J. Scollay), the hospital's chaplain. By summer, the stories had expanded to a full week. Guest stars included Mercedes McCambridge, Sylvia Sidney, and Dyan Cannon.

One story featured James Pritchett as a top-level business executive suffering from back problems. The producers were so impressed with Pritchett's performance they offered him a regular role and reintroduced him a few weeks later as Dr. Matt Powers. On March 2, 1964, *The Doctors* switched to a continuing storyline and began focusing on the personal problems of Hope Memorial's staff of doctors and nurses. Eight years later, in 1972, it was the first daytime soap to win an Emmy for best overall program.

The town location was not named until 1976, when it was revealed to be the fictional New England town of Madison. An early storyline centered on Dr. Matt Powers's attraction to a new doctor at Hope Memorial, Dr. Maggie Fielding. Matt was a workaholic widower who was raising his 16-year-old son, Mike. Matt was at first unable to admit his true feelings for Maggie. Complicating matters was Maggie's troubled marriage to sexually impotent Alec Fielding. Ironically, Matt was responsible for performing the surgery that made it possible for Alec to resume sexual relations with Maggie. Soon after the operation, Alec was killed in a car accident. Although Maggie was now free to marry Matt, he wasn't forthcoming with a proposal. He believed his first wife had killed herself because of his preoccupation with work. He secretly feared a marriage to Maggie would inspire her to follow a similar course of action.

Realizing Matt wasn't ready for marriage, Maggie turned to wealthy Kurt Van Allen for comfort. After marrying Maggie, Kurt's true colors surfaced. He made her life a living hell and then deserted her. Pregnant by Kurt, Maggie felt uncomfortable turning to Matt for support.

Following the birth of her daughter, Greta, Maggie received news Kurt had been stabbed to death in the South Seas. This paved the way for a reunion with Matt. As Maggie and Matt made plans to marry, Kurt's sister, Theodora, arrived in town wanting custody of Greta. Greta was the sole heir to Kurt's vast fortune. Maggie managed to keep custody of her daughter by agreeing to sign over Greta's inheritance to Theodora. Finally, three years after their first meeting, Maggie and Matt wed.

Following in his father's footsteps, Mike became a medical student. While pursuing his medical studies, Mike fell in love with Liz Wilson. Creating obstacles in their relationship was Liz's overbearing mother, Harriet, who disapproved of Liz getting involved with men. Mike used Liz to experiment with a new drug he had developed, nearly killing her. The drug temporarily rendered

Below: James Pritchett (seated), (left to right) Adam Kennedy, Ellen McRae, Elizabeth Hubbard, and Gerald O'Loughlin starred in The Doctors.

Opposite page, top: *Carolee Campbell played nurse Carolee Aldrich.*

Opposite page, bottom: *David O'Brien played Dr. Steve Aldrich.*

THE CAST

Original Cast
(as a continuing story)

NORA HANSEN ANDERSON	JOAN ANDERSON
NURSE BROWN	DOROTHY BLACKBURN
EDIE BARCLAY	PATRICIA HARTY
STEVE LLOYD	CRAIG HUEBLING
BROCK HAYDEN	ADAM KENNEDY
MRS. McMURTRIE	RUTH McDEVITT
JUDY STRATTON LLOYD	JOANNA PETTET
MATT POWERS	JAMES PRITCHETT
SAM SHAFER	FRED J. SCOLLAY
MICHAEL POWERS	REX THOMPSON
MAGGIE FIELDING	ANN WILLIAMS

Final Cast

ERICH ALDRICH	MARK ANDREWS
NATALIE BELL	JANE BADLER
KIT McCORMICK	HILLARY BAILEY
STEPHANIE ALDRICH	ANNE ROSE BROOKS
MAGGIE POWERS	LYDIA BRUCE
MIKE POWERS	STEPHEN BURLEIGH
IVIE GOODING	CHRIS CALLOWAY
KATY WHITNEY	MAIA DANZIGER
PHILIP MANNING	JAMES DOUGLAS
HOLLIS RODGERS	DONNA DRAKE
GRETA VAN ALLEN POWERS	LORI-NAN ENGLER
PAUL REED	MARK GODDARD
ALTHEA DAVIS	ELIZABETH HUBBARD
M. J. MATCH CARROLL	AMY INGERSOLL
THEO WHITNEY	TUCK MILLIGAN
STEVE ALDRICH	DAVID O'BRIEN
DANNY MARTIN	JOHN PANKOW
MATT POWERS	JAMES PRITCHETT
CAROLEE ALDRICH	JADA ROWLAND
FELICIA/ADRIENNE HUNT	NANCY STAFFORD
JEFF MANNING	MICHAEL J. STARK
LUKE DANCY	FRANK TELFER
NOLA DANCY ALDRICH	KIM ZIMMER

THE DOCTORS

APRIL 1, 1963–DECEMBER 31, 1982 NBC

Liz insane. Hospital board member Philip Townsend was obsessed with Liz. When he discovered she was about to leap off a ledge at Hope Memorial, he swiftly prevented her near suicide and then kidnapped her. Eventually, Liz was rescued, her sanity restored, and she was reunited with Mike.

Prior to marrying Maggie, Matt was briefly involved with Dr. Althea Davis, the new head of the outpatient clinic at Hope Memorial. Althea was a recent divorcee raising two children, Penny and Buddy. The arrival of brash brain surgeon Dr. Nick Bellini forever altered Althea's life. Two people couldn't have been more different. Althea was a blueblood New Englander and Nick had a poor childhood spent in a Chicago ghetto. Despite their differences, Althea and Nick were immediately drawn to each other. While they were away for the weekend making love, Althea's son, Buddy, contracted spinal meningitis. His sudden death caused a distraught and guilt-ridden Althea to break up with Nick. Once she worked through her grief, Althea had a change of heart and agreed to marry Nick. This delighted Penny because she adored Nick. But their union was short lived. Nick and Althea realized their personalities made marriage between them impossible and decided to divorce. Blaming Althea for the breakup, Penny left town to live with her father, Dave Davis.

Althea's third husband was Dr. John Morrison, Hope Memorial's Chief of Psychiatry. Though a psychiatrist, he was none too stable himself. Realizing Althea and Nick were still drawn to each other, John struggled to keep them apart. His dirty deeds included faking paralysis and murder. When Althea discovered the truth about her husband, she attempted to expose him. An automobile accident, however, left Althea comatose. Nick came to her rescue and successfully performed brain surgery on her. Later, John was killed by a deranged patient.

Wealthy playboy Dr. Steve Aldrich made a dreadful mistake by becoming involved with the unbalanced Dr. Karen Werner. His seduction left Karen pregnant and when she tried to kill herself, Steve agreed to marry her. Soon after the birth of their son, Erich, the couple divorced. Karen was later killed in a plane crash trying to return to her native Germany with Erich. The baby survived and was raised by Steve. Reverting to his former playboy ways, Steve had a fling with good-natured nurse Carolee Simpson. A misunderstanding prompted Carolee to keep her pregnancy secret. For the sake of her baby, she agreed to marry Dr. Dan Allison, who secretly suffered from a terminal heart condition. When it became clear to Dan that Carolee was still in love with Steve, a vengeful Dan decided to take his own life and make it look like Steve had killed him. Just as Steve was about to be sentenced for Dan's murder, Carolee found her dead husband's diary and used it to clear Steve. Their marriage soon followed.

Nola (Kathleen Turner) congratulates her sister, Sara (Dorothy Fielding), on her marriage to Mike Powers.

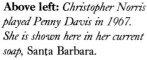
Steve's mother, Mona, disapproved of Carolee. She tried to start an affair between Steve and his former girlfriend, Dr. Ann Larimer, who had once been engaged to Nick. Finding Ann in Steve's arms one day, Carolee assumed they were involved and fled to New York City, where she had a mental breakdown. With Carolee out of the picture, a deserted Steve turned to Ann for emotional support and subsequently married her. Finding Carolee in a hospital, Ann arranged to secretly have her committed to a faraway mental institution. Her plan was discovered by Steve, who immediately ended their marriage and resumed relations with a recovered Carolee. After Steve remarried Carolee, Ann gave birth to Steve's baby in Brazil. Ann decided not to return, and she told Steve the baby was dead. A short time later, Carolee and Steve had a baby girl, Stephanie.

In the late seventies, the downtrodden Dancy family became an integral part of *The Doctors.* Their arrival in Madison would have a major impact on the lives of many of the doctors and nurses working at Hope Memorial. Matriarch Virginia Dancy worked as housekeeper for Steve's mother, Mona. Virginia and her husband, Barney, had five adult children: Jerry, Nola, Luke, Sara, and Joan.

Jerry fell in love with a now-adult Penny and married her. His inability to make ends meet created problems for Penny, who was accustomed to a higher standard of living. Joan was a drug addict being treated by Matt. When someone pulled the plug on Joan's respirator, Matt was charged with her death. Jason, a lawyer and Steve's brother, defended Matt. Jerry's obsession with finding his sister's killer was the final straw for

95

THE DOCTORS

APRIL 1, 1963–DECEMBER 31, 1982 NBC

Opposite page: *Ellen Burstyn was known as Ellen McRae when she played Dr. Kate Bartok on* The Doctors. *This picture is from a scene in one of her later films,* The Resurrection.

Above: *A cast photo taken in 1978.*

Penny. Ending their marriage, Penny packed her bags and moved to Japan. Althea soon followed. When Penny died in a horrible accident, Althea returned to her friends at Hope Memorial. Meanwhile, Jason managed to clear Matt of murder by exposing Dr. Paul Summers as Joan's killer.

The social climbing Nola Dancy saw an opportunity for a better life in Jason. Realizing his marriage to his wife, Doreen, was shaky, Nola seduced him. After successfully putting an end to his marriage, Nola manipulated Jason into marrying her. Hearing that Nola had cheated on him, Jason left town. Learning that Nola was pregnant, he later returned. Blood tests indicated Jason wasn't the father of her daughter, Jessica—prompting him to once again leave town. Meanwhile, Mona noticed a birthmark on Jessica that confirmed Jason was her father. Unfortunately,

news had reached them that Jason had been killed. Unable to deal with Nola raising her granddaughter, Mona legally sought custody of Jessica. When it became apparent she might lose her case, Mona kidnapped Jessica and fled to Italy. In the meantime, everyone learned Jason was still alive. Soon after, Mona returned with Jessica. Then, Jason was shot and killed by a deranged woman who claimed to love him.

Like his sister Nola, Luke was determined to overcome his humble beginnings. To achieve that goal, he romanced two older wealthy women. Luke turned over a new leaf, however, when he met and fell in love with young Missy Palmer. Luke wanted to make love to her, but Missy had a fear of sex because she had been raped by her father. Eventually, Missy was able to overcome her fear and the couple married. Their happiness

THE DOCTORS

APRIL 1, 1963–DECEMBER 31, 1982 NBC

Kathleen Turner's role in *Body Heat* launched her film career. Ironically, the part was first offered to Kim Zimmer, who replaced Turner as Nola Dancy on *The Doctors* in 1979. Unfortunately, the producers weren't willing to give Zimmer time off from the serial to film *Body Heat*. To this day, Zimmer experiences twinges of regret over losing the part that made Kathleen Turner famous. "It could've been me. I could have been doing the kinds of roles that she is doing; you can't help but think that," said Zimmer.

Rick Jacobs, who hired Turner to play Nola, knew she was destined for film stardom. "She wasn't as beautiful then as she is now," said Jacobs. "There was a bit of baby fat in the face. And she was a bit more in herself then. But you could feel her ambition—you could see her thinking about the next step."

While Turner played the starring role in *Body Heat*, Zimmer managed to take enough time off from *The Doctors* to appear as Mary Ann, the woman whose identity Turner assumed at the end of the film.

Before Kathleen Turner played Nola Dancy, Kathryn Harrold appeared in the role.

The Doctors was unable to successfully weather change. Six different teams of writers in four years were unable to get the serial back on track. The departure of key cast members also caused viewers to desert the once popular soap. When NBC moved it to a new time slot, the audience didn't follow.

Below: *Kathleen Turner played the conniving Nola Dancy.*

Opposite page: *Mike Powers (John Shearin) married Sara Dancy, but Sara soon died from a mysterious disease.*

ended abruptly when Missy was kidnapped by a psychopathic leader of a cult group and was killed.

The last Dancy sibling, Sara, married Mike Powers. But her happiness was not secure. She was diagnosed with a mysterious illness and died.

As *The Doctors* drew to a close, grave robbers unleashed a plague from the Aldrich crypt. Before a cure was found, the plague counted Mona among its victims. It was also revealed that a youth serum was keeping 60-year-old Felicia Hunt young enough to pass for her daughter, Adrienne. A series of misunderstandings had caused a separation between Maggie and Matt. Realizing they were still in love, they announced plans to remarry on New Year's Eve.

DYNASTY

Richard and Esther Shapiro created this one-hour weekly serial with an eye toward capturing the romance they remembered from movies they grew up with in the forties. "Stories where the audience pulled for men and women to fall in love and walk off into the sunset holding hands; stories with characters who dreamed of, pursued, and found their romantic ideal," wrote Esther Shapiro in *The Authorized Biography of the Carringtons.*

When *Dynasty* premiered in 1981, critics didn't acknowledge the show's romance, instead they accused the Shapiros of copying the most successful soap in prime-time television history, *Dallas.* The comparison was understandable: Both serials featured wealthy, powerful families involved in the oil business. What became *Dynasty's* unique calling card was its heavy emphasis on style. How characters lived was as important as the problems they faced. Describing *Dynasty*, *Soap Opera Digest* wrote, "[the series] teaches about clothes, about horses, about champagne, caviar and cars. It teaches about manners.... you learn what not to do as much as you learn what to do when, let's say, you are attending a lavish ball, where everyone is a multimillionaire. Looking at *Dynasty*, you learn about style, even if it's not your style."

Set in Denver, the serial centered on the Carrington family. Patriarch Blake was president of Denver Carrington, a major oil corporation. His recent bride, Krystle, had been his secretary. Fallon was Blake's self-centered, spoiled daughter and Steven his confused homosexual son. Matthew Blaisdel was a top geologist who worked for Blake and was Krystle's ex-lover. Matthew was stuck in a stormy marriage with his unbalanced wife, Claudia. They had a teenage daughter, Lindsay, who was preoccupied with boys and sex. A major source of trouble for Blake was Cecil Colby, the head of a rival oil company, Colbyco. Cecil's nephew, Jeff Colby, was attracted to Fallon, but she was too busy with Michael Culhane, the family's chauffeur, to notice. Creating problems for Krystle at home was Blake's snooty majordomo, Joseph Anders, who made it clear he was responsible for running the estate.

In the first season, it looked like Blake's life was headed toward disaster. Besides seeing his business fall apart, Blake was convinced Krystle still loved Matthew. Michael was given his walking papers after Blake uncovered his affair with Fallon. Cecil promised Fallon he'd bail Blake out of financial trouble if she'd marry Jeff. Anxious to rescue her father's failing business, Fallon agreed to a loveless marriage. Steven, who was involved in a love affair with Ted Dinard, questioned his homosexuality after sleeping with Claudia. Blake was incensed to discover his son in a romantic embrace with Ted. They quarreled and Ted was accidentally killed. During Blake's trial for murder, the prosecution introduced an unexpected witness. This twist served as the first season's cliff-hanger. Curious viewers had to wait until September to learn the identity of the mysterious, veiled woman.

Below: *Blake Carrington (John Forsythe) is the head of the Carrington family. He married his secretary Krystle (Linda Evans) in the first episode of* Dynasty.

Opposite page: Dynasty *was known for its fashions. The cast gathers for a photo in full regalia.*

The second season started with Blake surprised to discover that his vengeful ex-wife, Alexis, had swept into town to testify against him. Alexis told the court that Blake had a history of violence. Years earlier, his temper had left her former lover, Roger Grimes, a cripple. Despite Alexis's damaging testimony, Blake was put on probation for killing Ted Dinard. Claudia was shattered to receive news that her husband and daughter were left for dead in a Peruvian jungle. Frustrated by Krystle's icy attitude toward him, Blake's pattern for violence continued when he raped her. Later, Krystle learned she was pregnant. Mobsters retaliated against Blake for a botched business deal by blinding him. Blake's sight miraculously returned, but he pretended otherwise hoping to win back a sympathetic Krystle.

Fallon's world was turned upside down when she learned that Cecil Colby might be her father. Distraught by the possibility, Fallon ended up in a violent car crash. She was nursed back to health by sexy Dr. Nick Toscanni. After recovering from her

THE CAST

Original Cast

JOSEPH ANDERS	LEE BEGERE
CLAUDIA BLAISDEL	PAMELA BELLWOOD
CECIL COLBY	LLOYD BOCHNER
STEVEN CARRINGTON	AL CORLEY
KRYSTLE GRANT CARRINGTON	LINDA EVANS
BLAKE CARRINGTON	JOHN FORSYTHE
MATTHEW BLAISDEL	BO HOPKINS
JEFF COLBY	JOHN JAMES
LINDSAY BLAISDEL	KATY KURTZMAN
FALLON CARRINGTON	PAMELA SUE MARTIN
MICHAEL CULHANE	WAYNE NORTHROP
WALTER LANKERSHIM	DALE ROBERTSON
TED DINARD	MARK WITHERS

DYNASTY

JANUARY 12, 1981–MAY, 4, 1989 ABC

injuries, Fallon cheated on Jeff by sleeping with Nick. By the season's end, she gave birth to Jeff's son, Little Blake.

A pool accident nearly signaled the end for Steven, but he survived. Still confused over his sexuality, Steven compensated by marrying Krystle's low-class, oversexed niece, Sammy Jo. Realizing the marriage was doomed, Steven initiated a separation, announced to his family he was homosexual, and then left town. A pregnant Krystle lost her unborn baby in a fall from a horse masterminded by an envious Alexis.

The season ended with Alexis hitting pay dirt when Cecil proposed marriage. While making love, Cecil suffered a heart attack. Concerned that her gravy train was about to come to end before it even started, Alexis quickly arranged a wedding in Cecil's hospital room. Cecil died shortly after the

ceremony. Having ended his affair with Fallon, Nick battled with Blake for Krystle's affection. During a hurricane, Nick left an unconscious Blake for dead, while a terrified Krystle desperately tried to locate him.

The third season began with Krystle rescuing Blake. Immediately after the couple decided to reconcile, Fallon's son, Little Blake, was kidnapped. At first everyone believed Claudia, who was becoming crazier, had kidnapped the infant. Suspicion was nearly confirmed when Claudia was found on the rooftop of an office building, where she sent her "baby" hurling toward the ground. Everyone's heartbeat quickly returned to normal after discovering the "baby" was a plastic doll. Eventually, Little Blake was returned and the kidnapper apprehended. It was Alfred Grimes, father of Alexis's former lover,

On Blake and Krystle's wedding day, Steven (Al Corley) and Fallon (Pamela Sue Martin) celebrate their father's vows.

Alexis (Joan Collins) awakens Jeff Colby (John James) to tell him how she thinks he should run his life correctly.

Roger Grimes—the man Blake was responsible for crippling.

The kidnapping caused painful memories to surface for Blake and Alexis. Their first son, two-year-old Adam, was kidnapped in 1957. They had given up hope of ever seeing their son again when he suddenly materialized at Blake's office as a grown man. At first, Blake believed he was an imposter, but soon came to accept Adam as his son. Alexis immediately greeted Adam with open arms. Hurt by his father's initial rejection, a vengeful Adam worked as a lawyer for his mother's company, Colbyco. Jealous of Jeff's relationship with the Carringtons, Adam tried to kill Jeff with poisonous paint. Following his divorce fom Fallon, Jeff got involved with Joseph Anders's daughter, Kirby. This angered Adam because he was attracted to Kirby. One night, while Jeff was away, Adam raped her. When a distraught Kirby discovered she was pregnant, she led everyone to believe the baby was Jeff's and manipulated him into marrying her. Suffering from toxemia, Kirby lost the baby. Finally facing up to the fact that Jeff still loved Fallon, Kirby divorced him. In a strange turn of events, she became involved with Adam.

The Carringtons were devastated to receive word that Steven had been killed in a Southeast Asia oil rig disaster. Blake was so overwhelmed with grief that he refused to believe his son was dead. Blake's faith paid off when Steven returned home very much alive. However, it was difficult for the family to recognize Steven because he had a completely new face. He had suffered such severe burns in the fire that a plastic surgeon was forced to completely alter his features. (Actually, Al Corley, who played Steven, quit the series over a storyline dispute. He was replaced by Jack Coleman.) In the third season's cliff-hanger, Alexis and Krystle were trapped in a burning cabin.

As the fourth season opened, Alexis and Krystle were rescued by Mark Jennings, Krystle's first husband. To Krystle's surprise, Mark informed her that their "quickie" Mexican divorce wasn't legal. Meanwhile, police discovered that the fire had been set by Joseph Anders, who wanted Alexis dead. Apparently, he feared she had information about his past that could destroy his daughter, Kirby. After legalizing her divorce from Mark, Krystle proceeded with plans to remarry Blake. Sammy Jo returned to Denver just long enough to dump her son, Danny, in Krystle's lap.

103

DYNASTY

Sammy Jo's next destination was New York City, where she hoped to become a successful model. Concerned that she was becoming too attached to Danny, Krystle turned him over to Steven.

As if Alexis wasn't enough to contend with, Krystle soon discovered she had a new rival for Blake's love, Tracy Kendall, who worked at Denver Carrington. To Blake's credit, he saw through Tracy's manipulations and happily remarried Krystle. When news reached Blake that Steven was living with another gay man—his lawyer, Chris Deegan—Blake tried to win legal custody of Danny. Desperate to keep his son, Steven rushed into marriage with Claudia, who'd just been released from a mental institution. The newlyweds succeeded in gaining custody of Danny. Concerned over Adam's growing attachment to Kirby, Alexis convinced her possible daughter-in-law to begin a new life alone in Paris.

A sophisticated, beautiful black singer, Dominique Deveraux, arrived in Denver claiming to be Blake's half-sister. She became an immediate enemy of Alexis. The season cliff-hanger ended with a few plots unresolved. Alexis was accused of killing Mark Jennings—he was found dead after a heated fight with Alexis on her penthouse terrace. Fallon entered a whirlwind romance with wealthy Peter DeVilbus but abruptly ended it after realizing she still loved Jeff. The reunited couple planned an elaborate wedding. Moments before the ceremony, Fallon, who was suffering from head pains, disappeared in her car during a thunderstorm.

The fifth season opened with the Carringtons receiving news that Fallon had apparently left town with Peter DeVilbus and was believed dead after a fiery plane crash. A distraught Jeff turned to DeVilbus's grieving widow, Nicole Simpson, for comfort. Moments before his death, Blake's father, Tom Carrington, confirmed that Dominique Deveraux was Blake's half-sister.

Alexis represented herself at her trial and was convicted of murdering Mark Jennings. Later, the real killer was discovered. Harboring a grudge against Alexis, psychotic congressman Neal McVane dressed himself up in women's clothing, donned a dark wig, and pushed Jennings off Alexis's penthouse terrace. Many eyewitnesses, including Steven, thought they had seen Alexis kill Jennings. Now freed from prison, Alexis quickly put the ugly ordeal behind her by

accepting a marriage proposal from sexy Farnsworth "Dex" Dexter, who was several years her junior. Complications soon developed when Alexis's daughter, Amanda, returned to town and immediately found herself attracted to Dex.

Dynasty increased its glamour quota by signing two major Hollywood stars to appear as regulars. Rock Hudson played millionaire Daniel Reece, who had romantic designs on Krystle and was Sammy Jo's natural father. Ali MacGraw appeared as Lady Ashley Mitchell, yet another woman who thought she was in love with Blake. Despite her sexual overtures, Blake chose to stay with Krystle, who gave birth to their daughter, Krystina. Claudia cheated on Steven with another man and they divorced. Steven began to question his sexuality again when he found himself attracted to Luke Fuller. With Steven out of Claudia's life, Adam became her new bed partner.

Below: Dominique Deveraux (Diahann Carroll) showed up in Denver, claiming to be Blake's half-sister. Here she is with Brady Lloyd (Billy Dee Williams).

Opposite page: Daniel Reece (Rock Hudson)—who died soon after—confers with Krystle. Although he is actually Sammy Jo's father, he left Krystle in charge of his estate.

DYNASTY

JANUARY 12, 1981–MAY, 4, 1989 ABC

Following Daniel Reece's death, Sammy Jo returned to town and attempted to weasel money out of Krystle, who served as executor of Reece's estate. Angered that Krystle didn't fall for her manipulations, Sammy Jo schemed to get her out of the way. She hired a woman named Rita to impersonate Krystle so that Rita could sign over Reece's estate to her.

In the season cliff-hanger, Amanda prepared to marry Prince Michael of Moldavia. The marriage was arranged by Alexis and Michael's father, King Galen. The Carrington family traveled to Moldavia for Amanda's wedding. Shortly before the ceremony, Jeff proposed marriage to Lady Ashley—not realizing that Fallon had surfaced in Los Angeles, a victim of amnesia. While Amanda and Michael exchanged wedding vows, terrorists sprayed the church with bullets.

Dynasty concluded its season as television's highest-rated series. The following season it would veer off-course, causing millions of viewers to defect. Meanwhile, the producers had their hands full trying to launch *The Colbys,* a spin-off of *Dynasty.* Fallon and Jeff left *Dynasty* to star in *The Colbys.* Jeff left Denver to work for his uncle Jason Colby.

When the sixth season opened, viewers learned that Lady Ashley Mitchell and Steven's boyfriend, Luke, were killed in the attack. Aware they were no longer safe in their own country, Prince Michael and King Galen traveled to America. They used Denver as their new home base. In her misguided attempt to rescue King Galen, Alexis disguised herself as a nun and affected a French accent. Krystle was held hostage in a Moldavian dungeon for several weeks by Defense Minister Warnick. Immediately after her

Dominique was finally accepted as a member of Blake and Krystle's family.

release, Krystle found herself held captive again—this time by Joel Abrigore, a greasy acquaintance of Sammy Jo's. While Joel tried to force himself on Krystle, Blake was being served poisoned soup by Rita, who had successfully impersonated Krystle. To add even more confusion, several characters from *The Colbys* popped up and then moved over to their own series.

Alarmed by *Dynasty's* dramatic dip in audience, the producers did an abrupt change and shifted gears. In quick succession, Sammy Jo admitted her part in Krystle's kidnapping, Blake recovered from his poisoning, Rita and Joel were arrested, Amanda and Prince Michael dissolved their marriage, and Alexis quit her obsession to become Queen of Moldavia.

Amanda (Catherine Oxenberg) lived with her mother, Alexis, and fell in love with her mother's lover, Dex.

Getting back to basics, the producers devised a storyline where Alexis once again found herself drawn to Blake and began making sexual advances toward him. Blake, however, was too wise and experienced to fall for Alexis's tricks. Furious at his rejection, Alexis plotted revenge. Assisting Alexis was Blake's brother, Ben, who had been living in Australia. They devised a complicated scheme to cheat Blake out of his father's inheritance. During a legal hearing, Ben accused Blake of playing a role in their mother's death. Ben won a $125 million settlement. Disgusted by Alexis's manipulations, Dex turned to alcohol for comfort. Amanda stepped up her efforts to win Dex, but eventually was forced to accept that Dex wasn't in love with her. After a botched suicide attempt, Amanda fell for Clay Fallmont. Competing for Clay's affection was Sammy Jo. Adam and Claudia took their relationship a step further by marrying. Claudia suffered emotional problems when Blake wouldn't sign over rights to an oil well she believed belonged to her family. Alexis was reunited with her sister, Caress, who wrote a best-selling expose about their relationship, titled *Sister Dearest*.

In the season cliff-hanger, Dominique announced her engagement to an old flame, Garrett Boydstrom. Separated from Adam, Claudia took up residence at the La Mirage, where she accidentally set the place on fire. Thanks to Ben's help, Alexis finally succeeded in destroying Blake's business. Following Dominique's engagement party, Krystle and Blake returned to their mansion, only to be evicted by Alexis, who held the lease. An enraged Blake grabbed Alexis by the neck and began strangling her.

The following season, Ben's wife, Emily Fallmont, provided Blake with information proving Ben was responsible for their mother's death. Before her death in a car crash, Emily revealed to Ben that Clay was his son. Thanks to Emily's information, Blake managed to win his company back from Alexis. Claudia perished in the fire at La Mirage and Blake was blamed for the fire, but was later cleared of all charges.

Dominique canceled her wedding plans to Garrett Boydstrom after discovering he lied about having been married several years earlier. A pregnant Sammy Jo married Clay. Doctors discovered that Blake and Krystle's three-year-old daughter, Krystina, suffered from a potentially fatal heart ailment and needed a heart transplant. The donor's mother, Sarah, kidnapped Krystina in a twisted attempt to replace her dead child. Fortunately, Krystina was returned safely to the Carringtons.

DYNASTY

JANUARY 12, 1981–MAY, 4, 1989 ABC

Former chauffeur Michael Culhane returned to Denver bent on destroying Blake. Not realizing Michael hated Blake, Amanda had a brief affair with him. When she discovered Michael's real reasons for sleeping with her, she returned to London. While inspecting an oil rig in Hong Kong with Ben and Alexis, an explosion caused Blake to lose his memory. Taking advantage of the situation, Alexis convinced Blake they were still married. Before Alexis succeeded in making love to Blake, Krystle arrived. Seeing Krystle suddenly jarred Blake's memory and the couple was happily reunited.

Putting their differences aside, Blake and Ben tried to work toward a healthier relationship. Ben's bitter daughter, Leslie, moved to Denver. She had spent her entire life blaming Ben for her mother's unhappiness. When Leslie began to accept Ben wasn't completely responsible, the two were able to heal old wounds. It didn't take long for Clay to find himself disillusioned in his marriage to Sammy Jo. Attracted to Leslie, he turned to her for comfort. After the two became physically involved, they discovered they might be brother and sister. When blood tests proved inconclusive, Clay left town.

Adam fell in love with Blake's assistant, Dana Waring. The two knew each other in high school, when Adam thought he was Michael Torrence. Released from prison, ex-congressman Neal McVane returned to Denver with evidence that Adam wasn't a Carrington. In order to keep Neal quiet, Adam reluctantly provided him with insider trading secrets. Dominique accepted a wedding proposal from a former lover, Nick Kimball, and made plans to move to New York City. The pressure of being blackmailed caused Adam to drink heavily and eventually destroyed his marriage. Finally, an emotionally-overwhelmed Adam confessed to Blake and Alexis he wasn't their son. To Adam's relief, Blake and Alexis made it clear to him that he was now their son.

In the season cliff-hanger, Alexis's car plunged into the river shortly after she had an emotional confrontation with her ex-husband Dex. Adam and Dana decided to remarry. Matthew Blaisdel (Claudia's ex-husband, who was believed dead) crashed the ceremony with armed gunmen and attempted to reclaim Krystle. Meanwhile, in California, Fallon was apparently abducted by a UFO.

The seventh season opened with Matthew Blaisdel holding the Carringtons hostage in their mansion. Steven rescued everyone by killing Matthew. Alexis was rescued from her accident by a handsome stranger, Sean Rowan. Alexis fell in love with her rescuer. After a brief courtship, they eloped to Mexico. What Alexis didn't realize was that Sean had ulterior motives for entering her life. Sean was seeking revenge against the entire Carrington family. His late father, Joseph Anders, was formerly employed as Blake's majordomo. Sean blamed the Carringtons for Joseph's death. He held an even bigger grudge against Alexis, who forced his sister Kirby to move to Paris. Fallon surfaced in Denver, where she was soon joined by Jeff. Their marriage began to crumble because Jeff was unable to accept his wife's story that she'd been kidnapped by a UFO. Jeff's one-night stand with Leslie Carrington was the final blow for Fallon, who quickly initiated divorce proceedings.

Below: *Blake and Krystle admire their new daugther, Krystina.*

Opposite page: *Krystle and Alexis were both married to Blake, but that is all they had in common. Alexis continually tried to interfere in Krystle and Blake's marriage.*

DYNASTY

Adam and Dana learned that Dana was unable to have children. Desperate to raise a child of their own, the couple located a surrogate mother, Karen Atkinson. Sean decided to complicate the situation by paying Karen's estranged husband, Jesse, to press for a reconciliation. Once they resumed their marriage, Jesse convinced Karen to fight for custody of the baby. Realizing they could lose the baby, an enraged Adam was beside himself. Unable to deal with Adam's response, Dana separated from him. Before the custody battle was settled, Sean compounded their grief by kidnapping the baby. With Steven's help, Adam rescued the child. To

his disappointment, the court awarded custody to Karen. The reason Dana wasn't able to have children was because of an illegal, unsafe abortion she secretly had as a teenager. A one-night encounter with a drunken Adam (then known as Michael Torrence) left her pregnant. Michael didn't remember their lovemaking, so Dana sought an abortion. Sean got wind of the abortion and blackmailed Dana. Eventually, she revealed the truth to Adam. His cold response at learning Dana "killed his baby" didn't help their relationship.

Blake decided to run for governor. His leading opponent was Alexis. This thrilled Sean

Jeff and Fallon (Emma Samms) had an on again, off again relationship. She first married him to save her father's business, but later found that she loved him.

Joan Collins's success on *Dynasty* is a classic example of one hand washing the other. Each contributed greatly to the other's popularity. The British-born actress was trained at the Royal Academy of Dramatic Arts. She made her stage debut when she was nine-years-old as a boy in Ibsen's *A Doll's House.* A series of roles in British-produced plays and feature films followed. Her first American movie roles were in *Land of the Pharoahs* and *The Virgin Queen.*

After film roles became scarce, Collins began accepting offers to appear in episodic television. Her credits include *Run for Your Life, Batman, Space:1999,* and *Star Trek.* She also appeared in the television mini-series *The Moneychangers.*

In the late seventies, she starred in two low-budget films, *The Bitch* and *The Stud,* based on novels by her sister, Jackie Collins. Referring to those days, Joan said, "To be perfectly honest, I wasn't exactly being offered the cream of the crop in roles. It's called 'can't get a job.' Some say I lowered my standards with these films. I suppose I did. But they served a purpose. They gave a boost to my career. I knew precisely what I was doing, and I exploited myself as much as I could for a reason—to make myself into the kind of actress who would be considered to do other things. And that is what has happened."

The Dynasty *cast accepts an award for their show.*

because it left him in charge of Colbyco. The campaign forced Blake to turn his own company over to Adam, Fallon, and Steven, who spent more time fighting than conducting business. During a heated debate, Alexis was shot (the bullet was intended for Blake). Unknown to everyone, Sean was the gunman. Alexis survived her wound and continued her campaign. Alexis and Blake lost to a third candidate. Steven and Sammy Jo resumed their relationship. It was short-lived; Sammy Jo soon gave into the sexual advances of football player Josh Harris. Josh suffered from a cocaine addiction and an overdose left him dead. Finally realizing that his homosexual desires made it impossible for him to have a successful relationship with a woman, Steven split from Sammy Jo.

Sean devised a scheme he believed would ruin Blake. Traveling to Natumbe, West Africa, Sean planted illegal guns and rocket launchers on one of Blake's oil rigs to make it look like Blake

was involved in international gun-running. Dex figured out what Sean was up to and also discovered that Sean was Joseph Anders's son. He warned Alexis about her husband and then traveled to Natumbe with Blake to inspect Blake's oil rigs. At the moment they discovered the shipment of weapons, Sean attempted to blow up the rig. Blake and Dex survived, but Sean was believed killed in the explosion.

As the season drew to a close, Sean resurfaced in Denver and showed up at Alexis's home, armed with a gun. Dex arrived, a scuffle ensued, and the gun went off. Following his divorce from Fallon, Jeff fell in love with Sammy Jo. Jeff proposed marriage, but Sammy Jo wasn't convinced they had much of a chance for a successful life together. Jealous of Jeff's interest in Sammy Jo, Fallon succeeded in seducing him. Immediately after they made love, Sammy Jo arrived at Jeff's home to announce she wanted to accept his proposal. Unknown to Sammy Jo, Fallon was hidden away

DYNASTY

JANUARY 12, 1981–MAY, 4, 1989 ABC

in Jeff's bedroom. Krystle began suffering from a mysterious psychological illness. One night Blake returned home to find his home in shambles. Even worse, Krystle had left him.

In the serial's final season, Blake managed to locate Krystle in Ohio, where she was living with her cousin, Virginia. A former head injury was responsible for Krystle's strange behavior. She explained her only chance for survival was a potentially life-threatening operation. Krystle made Blake promise he'd file for divorce if the operation resulted in her becoming a vegetable. When Blake received word the operation wasn't successful in restoring Krystle's health, he reluctantly left her in Switzerland and carried through on his promise to divorce her.

Realizing it was time to move forward with her life, Fallon graciously stepped aside, giving Jeff the space he needed to marry Sammy Jo. Before the ceremony took place, however, Sammy Jo fell in love with Tanner McBride, a priest. Meanwhile, Fallon started a relationship with Sergeant Zorelli. Complicating the involvement was Zorelli's investigation into the twenty-five-year-old murder of Roger Grimes, whose body was discovered in a lake on Carrington property. The murder was linked to valuable art pieces hidden on the estate. Years earlier, Blake's father had assisted Nazi war criminals, who paid him with stolen art. Blake didn't want anyone to know about his father's horrendous past and thwarted Zorelli's investigation. His behavior led Zorelli to believe he had something to hide.

Viewers learned that when Roger was alive, he had witnessed Tom hiding the treasures. Roger had stolen some of the paintings and even gave one to Alexis, who was his lover and Blake's wife at the time. Police Captain Handler was interested in getting his hands on the hidden treasure and framed Blake for murder. In return for squelching evidence against Blake, Handler wanted Blake to secretly relinquish the treasure to him. When Blake passed on Handler's offer, the police captain shot him.

To Fallon's horror, she remembered killing Roger when she was a little girl. Apparently, she was so traumatized by seeing Roger knock Alexis unconscious that she shot him. While on a walk around the Carrington estate with her baby sister, Krystina, Fallon found an old mine shaft, where she discovered the treasure. Roger's son, Dennis,

who was a former cop, was already at the sight trying to steal the loot. A fight ensued and Fallon shot him. The gunshot caused the mine shaft to cave in, leaving Fallon and Krystina trapped inside with Dennis, who wasn't dead.

Soap viewers will recognize Emma Samms; not only did she play Fallon on Dynasty, *but she also played Holly on* General Hospital.

Adam Carrington (Gordon Thomson) married Dana Waring (Leann Hunley) and it looked like Adam would reform his evil ways. But their inability to have children caused problems in their marriage and they eventually split.

Alexis and Dex tried to rekindle their romance, but old conflicts kept surfacing. Instead, Dex turned his attention to Sable Colby, Jason Colby's ex-wife, who was now living in Denver. Seeking revenge against her former nemesis, Alexis, Sable actively worked to undermine both her professional and personal life. In retaliation, Alexis revealed to Sable's daughter, Monica, that Jason Colby wasn't really her father. Sable's affair with Dex led to her becoming pregnant.

Fed up with Adam's abusive behavior, Dana left Denver. Adam next got involved with Krystle's cousin, Virginia. When Adam discovered she was an ex-prostitute, he began treating her like dirt.

Angered by Adam's shabby treatment of Virginia, Blake ordered him off the Carrington estate. To get even with Blake, Adam joined forces with Alexis. Dex proposed marriage to Sable, but she was worried he still loved Alexis. In the serial's final episode, Dex and Adam got into a fight on Alexis's balcony. The railing broke, causing Alexis and Dex to tumble over. Blake was shot by a corrupt cop involved with the Nazi treasure.

The producers chose not to resolve the storylines, hoping that ABC would air a special two-hour movie. Attempts to reunite the cast proved impossible and plans for the TV movie were shelved.

EASTENDERS

1987–PRESENT PBS

This half hour serial, which began in Britian in 1984, is considered the most popular series in British television history. American viewers have had the opportunity to watch it twice a week on various PBS stations throughout the country since 1987. *Eastenders* is about London's changing East End and the problems faced by the people who live there. Much of the action takes place in the Queen Victoria Pub, located in fictional Albert Square. The neighborhood's diverse, working-class residents congregate in the pub to exchange gossip and air their troubles.

Den Watts and his wife, Angie, own the pub. Residents consider Den a con man, but he's fair to his staff. Angie's constantly pushing Den to improve his lot in life and aspire to the ranks of the middle class. Both dress flashy in an attempt to make people believe they're better off than they are. They have an adopted 14-year-old daughter, Sharon, who attends a private school and is embarrassed that her family lives in a pub.

Seventy-year-old Louise (Lou) Beale has lived in the Square longer than anyone else. She's a plump, funny widow with an obsessive loyalty to her family and a passion for playing bingo. Living with Lou is her daughter Pauline, son-in-law Arthur Fowler, and their two teenage children, Mark and Michelle. Since Arthur is unemployed, Pauline struggles to support the family by working the morning shift at the Launderette on Bridge Street. Pauline's twin brother, Pete, visits Lou on a regular basis. Pete runs a fruit and vegetable stall outside the Queen Victoria Pub. He and his wife, Kathy, have a teenage son, Ian. Rounding out the cast are Indian immigrants, a Turkish Cypriot, and a gay couple.

"Our storylines really reflect life," said Wendy Richard, who plays Pauline Fowler. "We don't pull punches when we approach issues like teenage pregnancy, unmarried mothers, and drugs. We often show racial tensions, problems with unemployment, and with the social services..."

To lend authenticity to the serial's gritty sets, the producers designed everything from location to make-up with a clear emphasis on realism. This eye toward realism includes props used on the show. The Queen Victoria's tap is capable of pouring beer, while the washing machines in the coin-operated Launderette wash loads of soiled clothing. Actors are hired by their similarity of background, ethnicity, and accents of the characters they play.

Eastenders *has been successful because the characters are authentic, and could be our next door neighbors.*

Top: *Paul J. Medford plays Kelvin Carpenter.*

Bottom: *Shreela Ghosh plays Naima Jeffery.*

THE CAST

Cast

NICK COTTON	JOHN ALTMAN
SIMON WICKES (WICKSY)	NICK BERRY
JAMES WILLMOTT-BROWN	WILLIAM BOYDE
DOT COTTON	JUNE BROWN
DEBBIE WILKINS	SHIRLEY CHERITON
MARY SMITH	LINDA DAVIDSON
ANDY O'BRIEN	ROSS DAVIDSON
SHARON WATTS	LETITIA DEAN
PETE BEALE	PETER DEAN
ANGIE WATTS	ANITA DOBSON
HAROLD LEGG	LEONARD FENTON
ETHEL SKINNER	GRETCHEN FRANKLIN
NAIMA JEFFERY	SHREELA GHOSH
DEN WATTS	LESLIE GRANTHAM
EDDIE	SIMON HENDERSON
TONY CARPENTER	OSCAR JAMES
SAEED JEFFERY	ANDREW JOHNSON
KELVIN CARPENTER	PAUL J. MEDFORD
SUE OSMAN	SANDY RATCLIFF
PAULINE FOWLER	WENDY RICHARD
PAT WICKS	PAT ST. CLEMENT
ALI OSMAN	NEJDET SALIH
MARK FOWLER	DAVID SCARBORO
KATHY BEALE	GILLIAN TAYLFORTH
ARTHUR FOWLER	BILL TREACHER
MICHELLE FOWLER	SUSAN TULLY
LOFTY (GEORGE) HOLLOWAY	TOM WATT
LOU (LOUISE) BEALE	ANNA WING
IAN BEALE	ADAM WOODYATT

THE EDGE OF NIGHT

APRIL 2, 1956–NOVEMBER 28, 1975 CBS
DECEMBER 1, 1975–DECEMBER 28, 1984 ABC

*D*aytime television's first mystery serial premiered the same day as *As the World Turns*. Both were owned by Procter & Gamble and both were television's first half-hour serials. Since the early fifties, Procter & Gamble had expressed interest in developing a mystery serial. In the midfifties, the company tried to buy the television rights to *Perry Mason*, which it had sponsored as a daytime radio serial. But creator Earle Stanley Gardner wasn't interested in seeing his crackerjack lawyer restricted to a soap opera format. Procter & Gamble next turned to Irving Vendig, a former writer on the *Perry Mason* radio serial, and gave him the green light to develop a new serial featuring a lawyer similar to Perry Mason.

Vendig's serial centered on Mike Karr, a policeman who soon passed his bar exam and joined the District Attorney's office. John Larkin was hired to play Karr; his previous experience included playing Perry Mason on the old radio series. Mike Karr's love interest was Sara Lane, whose personality was similar to Perry Mason's secretary, Della Street. Sara came from a large family, which included an immature brother, Jack, played by Don Hastings (viewers today know him as Dr. Bob Hughes on *As the World Turns*), and a corrupt uncle, Harry Lane.

The Edge of Night quickly became television's top-rated daytime serial, attracting nine million viewers. It held on to that position until the early sixties, when it was supplanted by *As the World Turns*. Fans included Bette Davis, Eleanor Roosevelt, and Tallulah Bankhead. Its late afternoon time slot also attracted a large number of male viewers, as well as students returning home from school.

The Edge of Night's first storyline involved Mike Karr waging war against a notorious crime syndicate—which included Sara's brother Jack among its members—operating in Monticello. When he wasn't fighting crime, Mike was busy romancing Sara. Eventually, they married. A short time later, Sara gave birth to their daughter, Laurie Anne. Although Mike's career was fraught with danger, his homelife was idyllic. A tragic event, however, altered Mike's life. Attempting to rescue their two-year-old daughter from an onrushing car, Sara was killed. After two years of grieving,

Mike fell in love with reporter Nancy Pollock. They later married.

Anxious to open his own law firm, Mike stepped down as assistant district attorney. His close friendship with Police Chief Bill Marceau made it possible for Mike to be informed about the latest criminal activities in Monticello. Widowed Bill Marceau was father and mother to a troubled teenage daughter, Judy. Realizing he was in love with his secretary, Martha Spears, Bill proposed marriage. By this time, his daughter was an adult ready to start a new life in a different town. Since Martha was interested in experiencing motherhood, the middle-aged couple decided to adopt a teenage girl, Phoebe Smith. At first, Phoebe was unable to trust their love and she made their lives miserable. When the Marceaus made it clear to Phoebe they weren't going to abandon her, she straightened out.

Wealthy divorcee Nicole Travis breezed into Monticello and immediately set her sights on happily married Mike Karr. Meanwhile, her business partner, Susan Forbes, was attracted to Mike's associate lawyer, Adam Drake. To Susan's disappointment, Adam was drawn to Nicole.

Below: *Nancy (Ann Flood) and Mike Karr (Forrest Compton) were the leading family in Monticello.*

Opposite page: *Nancy was Mike's second wife. She left him one time, because of his obsession with fighting crime, but they eventually reconciled.*

Nicole's father, Senator Ben Travis, was secretly involved in a loan-shark racket. Among its victims was Stephanie Martin, whose life was horribly scarred by Travis's crime syndicate. Her husband and daughter were killed in a car accident arranged by Travis's henchmen. When another daughter, Debbie, was diagnosed as autistic, Stephanie became unbalanced. By this time, Travis's connection to the underworld had been exposed and he was serving time in prison. Convinced that Nicole was just as corrupt as her father, a deranged Stephanie sought revenge. She sent Nicole poisoned chocolates and deadly spiders. At night, Stephanie would dress in men's clothing, put a stocking over her head, and sneak around Nicole's home. To get closer to Nicole, Stephanie got a job in Nicole's dress shop and pretended to be her friend. Adam, who was casually dating Nicole, sensed something was amiss with Stephanie. He advised Nicole to be careful.

Meanwhile, Nicole's former husband, Duane Stewart, moved to Monticello and tried to rekindle his relationship with Nicole. This infuriated Duane's second wife, Pamela, and she plotted to kill Nicole. At the same time, Adam succeeded in gathering enough evidence to prove Stephanie was responsible for terrorizing Nicole. While on his way to see Nicole to present the evidence, Pamela mistook Stephanie for Nicole and stabbed her in the back with a large knife. Encountering Stephanie's bloodied body, a horrified Nicole was too shaken to immediately

THE CAST

Original Cast

SARA LANE	TEAL AMES
CORA LANE	SARAH BURTON
MATTIE LANE	BETTY GARDE
HARRY LANE	LAUREN GILBERT
WINSTON GRIMSLEY	WALTER GREAZA
JACK LANE	DON HASTINGS
MIKE KARR	JOHN LARKIN
BETTY JEAN LANE	MARY MOOR
MARILYN	MARY ALICE MOORE

Final Cast

DIDI BANNISTER	MARIANN AALDA
JULIANA STANHOWER	AMANDA BLAKE
BRIAN MURDOCK	PHILIP CASNOFF
MIKE KARR	FORREST COMPTON
JEREMY RHODES	MICHAEL CONFORTI
LAURIE ANN KARR	LINDA COOK
LIZ CORELL	MARCIA CROSS
MILES CAVANAUGH	JOEL CROTHERS
JODY TRAVIS	KARRIE EMERSON
JOHN "PREACHER" EMERSON	CHARLES FLOHE
NANCY KARR	ANN FLOOD
BETH CORELL	SANDY FAISON
RAVEN ALEXANDER WHITNEY	SHARON GABET
DEL EMERSON	ROBERT GERRINGER
MARK HAMILTON	CHRISTOPHER HOLDER
MITZI MARTIN	LELA IVEY
GERALDINE WHITNEY	LOIS KIBBEE
CALVIN STONER	IRVING LEE
SCHUYLER WHITNEY	LARKIN MALLOY
DEREK MALLORY	DENNIS PARKER
LOGAN SWIFT	TOM TAMMI
CHRIS EGAN	JENNIFER TAYLOR
CLIFF NELSON	ERNEST TOWNSEND
GARY SHAW	A.C. WEARY

THE EDGE OF NIGHT

APRIL 2, 1956–NOVEMBER 28, 1975 CBS
DECEMBER 1, 1975–DECEMBER 28, 1984 ABC

phone the police. Also on the scene was Stephanie's daughter, Debbie, who was equally horrified. Suddenly finding her voice, Debbie screamed for Nicole to remove the knife from Stephanie's back. Stunned to hear Debbie speak, Nicole pulled the knife out and left her fingerprints on it. Nicole was charged and tried for the murder. Adam served as Nicole's lawyer and succeeded in proving her innocent. Now in love with Adam, Nicole hoped they would marry. To her disappointment, Adam wasn't yet prepared to part with bachelorhood.

The presence of the Whitney clan in Monticello would have a major impact on the Karr family. Former Senator Gordon Whitney and Geraldine, his domineering wife, had two adult sons: Colin, an ambitious junior senator whose political career left his wife, Tiffany, feeling neglected, and Keith, a schizophrenic. Desperate to keep herself amused, Tiffany had an affair with Ron Christopher, who was married to Nancy Karr's sister, Cookie. When Cookie learned of her husband's infidelity, she became mentally unbalanced and had to be committed to a mental institution.

Meanwhile, Laurie, now a young adult, had become romantically involved with a mysterious, bearded young man named Jonah Lockwood. But Jonah was really Keith Whitney—a multiple-murderer. Sensing Jonah was potentially dangerous— and suspicious of Keith's past—Adam Drake visited a tropical island Keith once called home. Adam discovered that Keith had killed his former wife. Adam hurried back to Monticello to warn Laurie—but Keith had already shepherded Laurie away and was about to push her off a high turret. Losing his footing, Keith fell to his death.

A few years later, Gordon and Colin Whitney were killed in a tragic accident, leaving Geraldine and Tiffany to adjust to their new lives as widows. In the meantime, Cookie regained her sanity and was reunited with her husband. Cookie and Ron moved to a new town.

Laurie fell in love with Mike's new associate, Vic Lamont, and they married. Vic's preoccupation with his career left Laurie feeling bored and lonely. Despite Vic's objection, Laurie took a job working part-time at the New Moon Cafe, owned by former convict Johnny Dallas. What started as friendship between Laurie and Johnny blossomed into love and they became sexually involved.

Adam finally proposed marriage to Nicole. This angered her new boss, Jake Berman, who was in love with Nicole. Jake arranged to have himself shot by Johnny Dallas to make it look like Adam had pulled the trigger. The plan backfired when Jake was found dead. Meanwhile, Adam was tried for his murder. Phoebe's boyfriend, Kevin Jamison, enlisted the help of his detective buddy, Joel Gantry, to clear Adam. It was revealed that Jake had been married to Joel's late mother, Edith Berman. Joel had proof that Jake murdered Edith, so Joel avenged his mother's death by killing Jake. Police authorities discovered the truth and Adam was cleared of any wrong doing. He and Nicole married in a ceremony on Mike and Nancy's patio.

After Adam's death, Nicole (Jayne Bentzen, seated) fell in love with Miles Cavanaugh (Joel Crothers). His dying wife, Denise (Holland Taylor), killed herself but made it look like Miles and Nicole were responsible.

Phil (Ray MacDonnell) and Louise Capice (Mary K. Wells) were an important couple in the first decade of the show. Louise was a spoiled rich debutante. Then she met Phil, who often was involved in Mike's detective work, and she matured.

Unfortunately, Adam's trial caused Laurie's marriage to disintegrate when it was revealed Laurie had slept with her boss, Johnny Dallas. After divorcing Laurie, Vic became involved with wealthy divorcee Kay Reynolds. To Mike and Nancy's sadness, Laurie resumed her affair with Johnny. Mike suspected Johnny was still tied up with the mob. In a sense, Mike's suspicions were warranted. In fact, the mob had infiltrated Johnny's business—but it was against Johnny's wishes.

The reemergence of the mob in Monticello also created problems for Chief of Police Bill Marceau and his wife, Martha. Now that Phoebe was an adult, Martha was obsessed with adopting another child. Martha and Bill unknowingly got involved with a black market lawyer and adopted a baby girl, Jennifer. Once they became emotionally attached to Jennifer, the mob made their presence known. Bill was given a choice:

submit to blackmail or lose his beautiful new baby daughter.

In a twisted desire to replace her sons, Colin and Keith, Geraldine Whitney turned her attention to Adam Drake and Kevin Jamison. With Geraldine's backing, Adam made a bid for the Senate. Kevin accepted Geraldine's generous offer to move into her mansion.

The mob wasn't pleased to learn of Adam's political plans. They arranged for Nicole's father, Ben Travis, who was terminally ill, to be released into Nicole's custody. Ben was to keep Adam from running for the senate. Ben male nurse, Morlock Sevingy, was hired by the mob to keep an eye on Ben. When Ben failed, the mob ordered Morlock to kill Adam. While Adam and Nicole were vacationing on a boat in the Caribbean, the boat sunk. Adam survived, but Nicole was reported drowned.

THE EDGE OF NIGHT

APRIL 2, 1956–NOVEMBER 28, 1975 CBS
DECEMBER 1, 1975–DECEMBER 28, 1984 ABC

Fed up with being manipulated by the mob, Bill resigned from the police force. Worried that the ex-chief of police would turn against them, the mob arranged to have Jennifer's natural mother, Taffy Sims, materialize and demand custody of her daughter. After losing Jennifer, Martha showed up at Taffy's home and pleaded to see the baby. When Taffy denied her request, a desperate Martha reached for a nearby gun and threatened her. The gun went off and Taffy fell. Martha made a hasty exit. With Taffy dead, authorities returned Jennifer to the Marceaus. Believing their problems with the mob were over, Bill again became chief of police. Meanwhile, Morlock was caught trying to kill Adam and was arrested. Visiting Martha, representatives from the mob threatened to expose her as Taffy's killer unless she convinced Bill to release Morlock. Surprising the mob, Martha went to the police and confessed her involvement in Taffy's death. Martha was charged with premeditated murder.

Determined to find Nicole's killers, an obsessed Adam gave up his campaign for the senate. Assisting Adam in his quest to track down Nicole's killers was a beautiful new assistant district attorney, Brandy Henderson. Guilt-ridden over his daughter's death, Ben decided to finger members of the mob, but was killed by Morlock.

Johnny's best friend and bartender at the New Moon Cafe, Danny Micelli, married Johnny's top waitress, Babs Werner. When Babs inadvertently learned of the mob's involvement in Nicole's death, Morlock ordered her killed. Angered by Babs's death, Johnny agreed to become an undercover agent against the mob. With her parents' blessing, Laurie finally agreed to marry Johnny.

Adam succeeded in clearing Martha of Taffy's murder. Martha was set up by the mob—the gun she used the day Taffy died contained blanks. After Martha fled Taffy's home, the mob killed Taffy.

In a scuffle with Babs's husband, Danny, Morlock was shot. Believing he was about to die, Morlock confessed to all his criminal activities, including Nicole's death.

Adam's relationship with Brandy continued to grow and the happy couple decided to marry. As their wedding day approached, however, Adam received news that would have a major impact on the couple's marriage plans. His wife Nicole was still alive! She'd been in a prolonged coma in a Paris hospital. Regaining consciousness, Nicole returned to Monticello—causing Brandy and Adam to break their engagement. Eventually, Nicole and Adam resumed their married life. A short while later, Nicole informed Adam she was pregnant. Before the baby was born, Adam was killed by the mob.

Until the early seventies, *The Edge of Night* continued to rank as one of daytime television's highest-rated serials. A sudden shift to an earlier time slot in 1972 caused its audience to erode.

Nicole's half sister, Jody Travis (Lori Loughlin), first fell in love with Nancy's nephew, then with Gavin Wylie (Mark Arnold). Neither relationship lasted very long.

A cast photo in 1975.

When CBS expanded *As the World Turns* to an hour in 1975, it decided to drop *The Edge of Night*, which was quickly picked up by ABC and returned to its former late afternoon time slot. Although the serial managed to attract a respectable audience, its late afternoon slot now worked against it. Local affiliates carrying it realized they could make more money airing their own programming and dropped the show, causing its overall ratings to plummet. Henry Slesar, who was the serial's headwriter for nearly two decades, said, "If you took city-by-city ratings, *Edge* was remarkably successful. Very often, it was second in its time slot. But without station clearance, you don't get an audience. And a lower overall rating doesn't encourage new stations. So it became a case of the snake swallowing its own tail."

During the show's last years, several new characters arrived in Monticello, revitalizing the serial. They included Nicole's half-sister, Jody; Dr. Miles Cavanaugh, who would later become Nicole's second husband; Nancy Karr's nephew Kelly McGrath; and Derek Mallory, who replaced Bill Marceau as chief of police.

Two new characters, in particular, enjoyed front-burner storyline status up until the show's final episode on December 28, 1984. They were Schuyler (Skye) Whitney, who was Geraldine's nephew, and Raven Alexander, whose mother, Nadine, was a close friend of Geraldine's.

Before the series ended, Mike and Nancy Karr's marriage took a big step into the eighties when they exchanged their twin beds for a large double.

FALCON CREST

· ·
DECEMBER 4, 1981–MAY 17, 1990 CBS

This one-hour weekly serial had the luck of following the high-rated *Dallas* through nearly all its eight-season run. Like *Dallas, Falcon Crest* focused on the rich as they struggled to hold on to their power and wealth. Oscar winner Jane Wyman was lured out of retirement to star as Angela Channing.

Fictitious Tuscany Valley, located in the Napa Valley region outside San Fransisco, was the setting. Much of the action centered around the wine-making industry. The manipulative and cunning Angela Channing, who headed Falcon Crest Wines, was a leading force in the town. Her highly principled, upstanding nephew Chase Gioberti served as a constant thorn in her side. Ruthless newspaper owner Richard Channing was another nemesis.

In the serial's first episode, Chase arrived in town from New York to manage the fifty acres of vineyards he had inherited from his father, Angela's brother Jason. Angela immediately felt threatened by Chase infringing on her territory. She had grown accustomed to running the family business her way. She also believed the land Chase inherited should have gone to her. To begin his new life in Tuscany Valley, Chase brought along his wife, Maggie, and their two children, Cole and Victoria.

Angela decided that the best way to rid herself of Chase was by making his life miserable. Unknown to Chase, she tried to thwart his bid for a badly needed bank loan. She also tried to undermine Chase's relationship with his son, Cole, by intimating to Cole it was possible he could one day become the sole inheritor of Falcon Crest. When it became obvious to Angela she wouldn't be taking over Chase's land, she urged her playboy grandson, Lance Cumson, to marry Melissa Agretti, whose family also owned a large winery. It was Angela's hope that by consolidating Agretti and Falcon Crest wineries, she would gain enough control to render Chase powerless. Ironically, by the first season's end, Chase succeeded in legally wrestling control of Falcon Crest away from Angela, who vowed to get even.

Chase's stint as head of Falcon Crest was in marked contrast to Angela's rule. Whereas Angela exploited her workers and involved herself in unethical business dealings, Chase struggled to act in everyone's best interest. His primary concern was to prevent the power-hungry fat cats from taking over Tuscany Valley. When he was made county supervisor, his first order of business was halting Angela's plan to monopolize the town's water supply. Chase realized Angela's plan would result in bankrupting the struggling wineries in the area. Chase's mother, Jacqueline Perrault (played by film star Lana Turner), assisted Chase in his battles with Angela. Having shared a history with Angela, Jacqueline understood her better than anyone else and welcomed the opportunity to offer her son advice on how to handle Angela.

Jane Wyman came out of retirement to play Angela Channing, the ruthless head of Falcon Crest wineries.

Lance Cumson (Lorenzo Lamas) was forced by his grandmother to marry Melissa Agretti. Angela hoped to consolidate the family wineries.

Lance Cumson longed to be powerful like his grandmother Angela, but his privileged background left him unwilling to work. He resented Angela's hold over him, but seemed unable to stand on his own two feet. Lance's ambitious wife, Melissa, recognized Lance's insecurity and encouraged him to be more forceful. Angela sensed the influence Melissa had over Lance and found herself growing less fond of her. To compensate for his low self-esteem, Lance continued sleeping with other women. Meanwhile, a hurt Melissa turned to Cole for comfort. When Lance learned that Melissa's newborn baby, Joseph, was fathered by Cole, he left town with an old girlfriend, Lori Stevens. A lack of funds eventually brought Lance back to his wife and his rich lifestyle.

When Angela's ex-husband, newspaper mogul Douglas Channing, died, his son Richard arrived in town to take over *The San Francisco Globe*. Richard inherited 50 percent of the paper, while the other half was divided between Angela's two daughters, Julia and Emma. A greedy Richard wasn't content with owning half. He also wanted the shares belonging to his half-sisters, as well as Carlos Agretti's land and Falcon Crest. Assisting Richard was Jacqueline, whom he was later told was his mother. One scheme Richard employed to take over Falcon Crest involved joining forces with Julia, who was easily manipulated by Richard's charm. Ultimately, the plan backfired. Richard's next step was to secure a permit to

THE CAST

Original Cast

CHAO-LI	CHAO-LI CHI
JULIA CUMSON	ABBY DALTON
DOUGLAS CHANNING	STEPHEN ELLIOTT
PHILLIP ERICKSON	MEL FERRER
CHASE GIOBERTI	ROBERT FOXWORTH
EMMA CHANNING	MARGARET LADD
LANCE CUMSON	LORENZO LAMAS
COLE GIOBERTI	WILLIAM R. MOSES
MAGGIE GIOBERTI	SUSAN SULLIVAN
VICKIE GIOBERTI	JANE ROSE
ANGELA CHANNING	JANE WYMAN

Final Cast

PILAR CUMSON	KRISTIAN ALFONSO
CHAO-LI	CHAO-LI CHI
MICHAEL SHARPE	GREGORY HARRISON
EMMA CHANNING ST. JAMES	MARGARET LADD
LANCE CUMSON	LORENZO LAMAS
LAUREN DANIELS CHANNING	WENDY PHILLIPS
RICHARD CHANNING	DAVID SELBY
DANNY SHARPE	DAVID SHEINKOPF
GENELE ERICSON	ANDREA THOMPSON
ANGELA CHANNING	JANE WYMAN

FALCON CREST

DECEMBER 4, 1981–MAY 17, 1990 CBS

build a race track in the Tuscany Valley, a move that was sure to herald the demise of the area's wine industry.

In the second season's cliff-hanger, Chase and Jacqueline were both shot by Angela's daughter, Julia Cumson, who proved to be psychotic. Melissa Agretti's father, Carlos, was an earlier victim of Julia's. (Melissa's lover, Cole, had been tried for her father's death.) Julia's misguided actions were prompted by a twisted desire to protect her mother. Jacqueline's gunshot wound proved fatal, while Chase was left paralyzed. Julia was sentenced to a long prison term and then transferred to a mental institution.

Chase's recovery from paralysis was helped by the professional expertise of Dr. Michael Ranson, a highly regarded neurosurgeon and nephew of Jacqueline's. Meanwhile, Chase wasn't pleased to learn his wife, Maggie, had accepted an offer from Richard to join his newspaper staff as a reporter. Maggie's sister, Terry Hartford, who secretly worked as a high-priced call girl, moved to town. She quickly fell in love with Michael. She later moved in with him. Julia escaped from the mental institution, but was presumed dead after being trapped in a cabin that went up in flames. To fulfill a final request of Julia's, the Channings and Giobertis boarded a plane for Italy. The plane plummeted toward a crash landing as the third season drew to a close. Casualties from the crash included Cole's new wife, Linda; Angela's shrewd and powerful lawyer, Phillip Erickson; and Dr. Michael Ranson.

The serial's fourth season veered toward violence. A major storyline focused on a mysterious international crime syndicate known as "The Cartel," which was headed by Gustav Riebmann. The Cartel had been co-founded by the late Jacqueline. It surfaced in Tuscany Valley because it believed a large fortune once belonging to the Nazis has been buried on Falcon Crest land. Residents endured a series of plane crashes, bombings, and buggings before the crime ring was destroyed.

Angela finally got revenge against Richard by taking over the *Globe.* Her first course of action was to appoint Lance editor. Richard retaliated by framing Lance for the attempted murder of Angela, but Lance was cleared of all charges. Richard also acquired one-third of

Falcon Crest from Angela's half-sister, Francessca. Melissa divorced Lance, married Cole, and then constantly fought with him. Cassandra Wilder arrived in Falcon Crest and began a one-woman vendetta against Angela for wrongs Angela supposedly inflicted on her family.

Cassandra succeeded in causing the financial ruin of both Angela and Richard. Angela turned to a former lover, wealthy shipping magnate Peter Stavros (played by Cesar Romero), for assistance. Before Peter was able to help Angela, he was abducted by his daughter Sophia, who wanted the money he had earmarked for Angela. Once Peter managed to free himself, he proposed to Angela. Realizing she could become Peter's wife or allow him to be her

Angela married Peter Stavros (Cesar Romero) to save her home and fortune.

Cole (William R. Moses) married Melissa (Ana Alicia) after her divorce from Lance. Their marriage broke up, also.

landlord, a practical Angela accepted his proposal. Following Peter to Tuscany Valley was Peter's adult son, Eric. Richard's efforts to rebuild his own financial empire included siphoning money from the Tuscany Downs racetrack. Maggie's sister, Terry, uncovered Richard's shady activities and threatened to expose him if he didn't marry her.

Richard's new female lawyer, Jordan Roberts, suffered from a split personality—at night she was Monica, a professional hooker. Maggie became a victim of amnesia and through her fog wrote a thinly veiled, fictional expose about the residents of Tuscany Valley. After her book was published, Maggie was pursued by a crazed book publicist, Jeff Wainwright, who later raped her.

Unable to have another baby together, Melissa and Cole hired a surrogate mother, who successfully seduced Cole and then decided to keep the baby. Emma became obsessed with a trucker named Dwayne, while Lance fell for a rock singer, Patricia "Apollonia" Kostero, much to his grandmother's displeasure. The season ended with a major earthquake hitting Tuscany Valley.

Criminal activities were at the forefront of the serial's fifth season. Richard hired a private investigator named Miss Jones to help him get information on business rivals. Miss Jones betrayed Richard by framing him for murder. She also tried to kill Chase and was responsible

FALCON CREST

DECEMBER 4, 1981–MAY 17, 1990 CBS

for the death of Jeff Wainwright, Maggie's obsessed publicist. Soon after Richard had Miss Jones imprisoned in Borneo, her sister Meredith surfaced in Tuscany Valley seeking revenge against him. Melissa attempted to launch a singing career and she kidnapped Maggie's newborn baby, Kevin.

Emma's life became even more bizarre when she got involved with a con artist named Karlotti, who claimed to be a spiritualist in touch with the late Dwayne's spirit. A woman claiming to be Peter's long-lost daughter, Skylar, turned out to be an imposter named Kit Marlowe, who was running from a devious Eastern billionaire, Roland Saunders. His life came to an end when Kit offered him a poison cigar moments before Peter fatally struck him on the head with a wrench. Dan Fixx showed up on Angela's doorstep saying he was a relative. Angela gladly accepted him into the family fold, but this caused Lance to be insecure about his status.

In the season cliff-hanger, Peter decided to return to Greece and he divorced Angela. Before leaving town, he left Angela with news that would have a major impact on her life: Richard Channing was really *her* son. Chase drowned trying to rescue his kidnapped baby.

The seventh season began with Maggie grieving the loss of her husband. Moving on with her life, Maggie admitted to her feelings for Richard and accepted his marriage proposal. Their life was complicated by Richard's involvement with an international crime ring known as "The Thirteen." While Maggie fretted over her husband's possible criminal activities, their lives were endangered by a series of bombings taking place on Richard's estate. Disappointed by Dan's romantic involvement with Melissa, Angela successfully lured a despondent Lance back into her clutches. Angela decided Melissa was a threat and devised a scheme to drive her insane. She hired a special effects artist to rig Melissa's home. Melissa thought she was seeing ghosts.

Emma inadvertently got mixed up in a prostitution ring and then turned her story into a screenplay. Maggie's daughter Vickie married Peter's son Eric, who turned out to be a compulsive gambler. After losing badly in a poker game with Richard, Eric turned over a deed of land in Nevada. He then traveled to Monte Carlo with Vickie, where he continued to accumulate gambling debts—partly thanks to Richard and "The Thirteen." Richard's plan backfired, however, when he learned Vickie had been kidnapped by a Yugoslavian white slavery ring. Eventually, Richard managed to rescue Vickie—leaving everyone in Tuscany Valley thinking he was a hero. Thanks to Maggie's quick marriage to Richard, Angela inherited the Gioberti vineyards. Discovering Richard's involvement in Vickie's horrible experience, Maggie divorced him. A reformed Richard went to the FBI and shared everything he knew about "The Thirteen." Melissa got her hands on a key that once belonged to Chase. The key was to a safe deposit box that held the deed to Falcon Crest. To Melissa's surprise, the deed was made out to her family. Once Melissa proved that the deed was legal, she headed for Angela's to take over Falcon Crest.

Maggie's sister, Terry Hartford (Laura Johnson), had been a high-priced call girl before coming to Tuscany Valley.

After Chase's death, Maggie (Susan Sullivan) married Richard Channing. She got to know him well while working on his newspaper.

Upset by Richard's testifying against "The Thirteen" at a Senate hearing in Washington, Rosement, who headed the crime ring, put a contract out on his life. Realizing his family's life was in danger, Richard offered his own life so that theirs would be spared. "The Thirteen" drugged Eric and then ordered him to kill Angela. Fortunately, Richard managed to rescue her. His heroic act inspired the former rivals to reconcile their differences. A short while later, Eric shot Richard. Both Maggie and Angela attended his funeral. The season cliff-hanger had Melissa moving into Falcon Crest. Meanwhile, Angela secretly met with a bearded man and asked him, "When are you going to tell Maggie you're alive?"

Maggie was incensed to learn Richard had duped her into believing he was dead. Richard explained that it was part of the government's plan to protect him until they were able to crack "The Thirteen." Working through her anger, Maggie agreed to reconcile with Richard. Although Melissa was ensconced at Falcon Crest, she was by no means happy. Realizing she wasn't capable of running the winery, Melissa had a nervous breakdown, leading her to douse Falcon Crest in gasoline and torch it. Melissa died in the fire. Nick Agretti was appointed executor of her estate. Angela reclaimed her home by finally proving the deed Melissa held was a fraud.

Lance renewed his relationship with Pilar Ortega. The couple had known each other since childhood, but class differences always prevented them from having a successful relationship. Lance was surprised to discover that a one night stand between them ten years earlier had resulted in the birth of a baby daughter, Lisa. Emma

FALCON CREST

DECEMBER 4, 1981–MAY 17, 1990 CBS

married R. D. Young, a mystery writer who later committed suicide.

Business dealings over Falcon Crest caused Angela and Richard to become enemies again. When Maggie realized her husband hadn't changed, she divorced him. Richard used Maggie's history of alcoholism to win custody of her young sons. Turning his attention to Falcon Crest, Richard kidnapped Angela and put her in an apartment in San Fransisco. He then hired a woman who looked exactly like Melissa to spend time with Angela. After Melissa's double helped Angela escape, Angela tried to convince everyone Melissa was still alive. When Angela couldn't prove she had actually seen Melissa, Richard persuaded the authorities that she had lost her mind and Angela was committed to a mental institution. Richard then proceeded with plans to take over Falcon Crest. When a judge declared Angela mentally incompetent, Angela quickly persuaded Frank Agretti to marry her.

To Richard's disappointment, Frank was appointed conservator of her affairs. Tracking down Melissa's double, Samantha Ross, Angela convinced her to testify against Richard, who was convicted of stock fraud and kidnapping. In the season cliff-hanger, Richard was carted off to prison.

Maggie was surprised to receive a four-carat diamond ring from an imprisoned Richard. While trying to retrieve her sons' toys from the pool, Maggie put her finger through the drain and her ring got stuck. Her attempt to reclaim the ring resulted in her drowning. Michael Sharpe, a business rival of Richard's, bribed a judge to have Richard's sons put in the custody of Michael's sister, Lauren.

Emma fell in love with charmer Charley St. James. After they married, Charlie turned out to be a wife beater. In an effort to gain control of Falcon Crest, Charley put Angela in a coma after trying to suffocate her. Despite Frank's

Below: *Angela plots with Greg Reardon (Simon MacCorkindale).*

Opposite page: *Maggie loved Richard, but his underhanded dealings broke up their marriage.*

128

129

FALCON CREST

DECEMBER 4, 1981–MAY 17, 1990 CBS

marriage to Angela, a judge ruled that Emma should be appointed conservator of Angela's affairs. Richard was freed from prison and tried to win back his sons from Lauren and Walker Daniels. Realizing that his wife, Lauren, had become romantic with Richard, Walker tried to kill them both, but instead killed himself. Charley St. James duped Emma into selling Michael Falcon Crest for 14 million dollars. When a pregnant Emma discovered she had been set up by her husband, she pulled a gun and shot him. A judge ruled that Emma acted in self-defense and Emma decided to leave Falcon Crest.

Pilar and Lance's marriage was tested when Pilar allowed herself to be blackmailed for sex by Lance's business rival, Ned Vogel. Michael Sharpe's son, Danny, arrived in Tuscany Valley to work for his father. Danny fell in love with Charley St. James's sister, Sydney. Angered that Sydney double-crossed him in a business deal favoring Richard Channing, Michael arranged to have her killed. Unfortunately, his son became the victim and almost died. As Danny recovered from his wounds, Michael's ex-wife, Anne Bowen, learned that Michael was responsible for her son's accident. Disgusted by this information, she told Michael that she'd had an affair with Richard Channing and that he was Danny's real father. Angela recovered from her coma and joined forces with Michael to destroy Richard.

In the serial's final episodes, Danny learned from Anne that Richard was his father. Richard was unwilling to accept Danny as his son. Richard proposed marriage to Lauren and she accepted. In a desperate attempt to stop the fighting between Michael and Richard, Danny threatened to jump off a roof, but was rescued by both Michael and Richard. Angela was delighted when Richard, who had been suffering financial setbacks, finally turned Falcon Crest back over to her. Angela's first order of business was persuading Lance and Pilar to change their mind about leaving town. Lance agreed to serve as vineyard manager for Angela—provided he retain 10 percent of Falcon Crest. Emma returned to town with her new baby girl. Lance was thrilled to hear from Pilar that she was pregnant.

At Lauren and Richard's wedding, Michael attempted to reconcile with Danny by revealing he was responsible for Danny's accident. Danny responded by slugging Michael. Afterward, the two men embraced. Richard and Lauren walked down the aisle. Meanwhile, Angela gave a private toast to Falcon Crest, the only place she'd ever truly called home.

Commenting on why the serial concluded with an episode that tied up all the loose ends, executive producer Jerry Thorpe said, "We didn't want to frustrate the loyal hard-core fans by giving them the unknown, the unexplored, and someone in trouble."

Below: *Francesca Gioberti (Gina Lollobrigida), Angela's half sister, gave half of Falcon Crest to Richard Channing. Angela eventually regained her whole empire.*

Opposite page: *The cast of* Falcon Crest *assemble for a photo.*

FLAMINGO ROAD

JANUARY 6, 1981–JULY 13, 1982 NBC

One thing is certain about this one-hour weekly serial, the outstanding cast couldn't be held responsible for its failure. Morgan Fairchild starred as spoiled rich girl Constance Weldon. Joining her were Howard Duff, Mark Harmon, John Beck, David Selby, Barbara Rush, and Stella Stevens.

Based on Robert Wilder's novel, *Flamingo Road* was also a 1949 feature film starring Joan Crawford. The film centered on Crawford's character, Lane, a former carnival girl who became a powerful force in a corrupt town. But the serial emphasized Morgan Fairchild's character, Constance, and her turbulent marriage to Fielding Carlyle. The small town of Truro, Florida, was the setting. Crafty Sheriff Titus Semple, who had intimate knowledge of every skeleton hiding in every resident's cluttered closet, was largely responsible for keeping the plot moving.

The Weldons, who resided on ritzy Flamingo Road, were Truro's wealthiest family. Claude Weldon founded the family's successful paper mill, but had recently handed the reins over to his son Skipper. Thanks to Sheriff Semple's help, Fielding Carlyle was elected to the state senate. Semple pushed Fielding to wed Connie, correctly deducing that if Fielding married into the Weldon family it would help his political career. Despite the marriage, Fielding still carried strong feelings for his first true love, Lane Ballou, who sang at Lute-Mae Sanders's casino/bordello. Lane was romantically attached to Sam Curtis, a prosperous construction-company developer.

The serial's second season introduced cold-hearted business tycoon Michael Tyrone, whose arrival would have major impact on the lives of several Truro citizens, particularly the Weldons. When Michael was a young man, his father was executed for a murder he didn't commit. Realizing his father was set up, Michael was determined to avenge his death. To achieve his goal, Michael even employed black magic. When it became apparent that his sister, reporter Sande Swanson, didn't approve of his underhanded methods, he had her killed. Before her death, Sande had an tumultuous affair with Fielding. Meanwhile, Michael became sexually involved with both Lute-Mae and Constance. Viewers discovered that Constance was actually Lute-

Mae's illegitimate daughter. With the exception of her brother, Skipper, Constance succeeded in sleeping with every leading male character on the serial.

Skipper surprised his family by falling in love with Alicia Sanchez. Realizing his parents were resistant to his romance, Skipper eloped with Alicia.

In the final episode, Michael faked his own murder—making it look as if his longtime nemesis, Sheriff Semple, had killed him. The final scene revealed Michael—now believed dead—hidden away in a monastery.

Below: The wealthy Weldon family: (left to right) Skipper (Woody Brown), Eudora (Barbara Rush), Claude (Kevin McCarthy), and Constance (Morgan Fairchild).

Opposite page: Fielding Carlyle (Mark Harmon, standing) loved Lane Ballou (Cristina Raines) but Titus Semple (Howard Duff) pushed him to marry Constance Weldon.

132

Morgan Fairchild's career in television began in 1973 when she joined the cast of daytime's *Search for Tomorrow* as the wicked Jennifer Pace. Following her four-year stint on the serial, Morgan moved to Hollywood, hoping to break into feature films or land a role in a prime-time television series.

In the late seventies, she appeared as the original Jenna Wade on *Dallas*. Soon after, she was cast as the sexy Constance Carlyle on *Flamingo Road*. Her starring role in the serial looked as if it might propel her to the super-star status of such well-known performers as Donna Mills, Joan Collins, Linda Evans, and Michelle Lee. Unfortunately, the serial never picked up steam and was canceled after two seasons. She returned to series television with a starring role in ABC's *Paper Dolls* in the mideighties. The series was canceled after a half-season run.

Despite roles in short-lived series, Morgan remains optimistic about her acting career. "I've worked hard for many years but because of the way I look, people just assume I'm just another blonde who's where I am because I have the right look at the right moment," she said. "But I'll tell you this, I'm here to stay."

THE CAST

Cast

JULIO SANCHEZ . . . . FERNANDO ALLENDE
SAM CURTIS . . . . JOHN BECK
SKIPPER WELDON . . . . WOODY BROWN
ELMO TYSON . . . . PETER DONAT
TITUS SEMPLE . . . . HOWARD DUFF
CONSTANCE WELDON . . . . MORGAN FAIRCHILD
CHRISTIE KOVACS . . . . DENISE GALIK
ALICIA SANCHEZ . . . . GINA GALLEGO
FIELDING CARLYLE . . . . MARK HARMON
BETH MacDONALD . . . . SANDRA KEARNS
CLAUDE WELDON . . . . KEVIN McCARTHY
LANE BALLOU . . . . CRISTINA RAINES
JASPER, THE BUTLER . . . . GLENN ROBARDS
ALICE KOVACS . . . . MARCIA RODD
EUDORA WELDON . . . . BARBARA RUSH
MICHAEL TYRONE . . . . DAVID SELBY
DEPUTY TYLER . . . . JOHN SHEARIN
SANDE SWANSON . . . . CYNTHIA SIKES
LUTE-MAE SANDERS . . . . STELLA STEVENS

THE FORSYTE SAGA

OCTOBER 5, 1969–MARCH 29, 1970 PBS (FORMERLY NET)

This twenty-six part English serial, produced by the BBC in 1967, was based on John Galsworthy's series of books chronicling the lives of an upper-class English family over fifty years and three generations. It was played against the changing backdrop of Victorian and Edwardian life. Viewers who were too embarrassed to admit they watched *As the World Turns* or *All My Children* took great pleasure in exclaiming that *The Forsyte Saga* was their favorite television program.

The show was broadcast in more than 50 countries, including Zambia, Taiwan, and the Soviet Union. It was so popular that in England ministers protected churchgoers from missing a single episode by rearranging the hours of their church services. In Israel, the station carrying *The Forsyte Saga* wasn't allowed to show it on the sabbath. In the Netherlands, athletic events and public meetings were rescheduled so as not to conflict with it. When actress Susan Hampshire, who played Fleur Forsyte Mont, visited Oslo to promote the series, 40,000 fans jammed the stadium where she was appearing and 2,000 more lined the streets. In Holland, a flower was named after her character.

American fans included novelist James A. Michener and actress Helen Hayes, who was guest-lecturing at the University of Illinois when the serial first ran in the United States. Arriving in Chicago on Sunday evenings—the same night *The Forsyte Saga* aired, Miss Hayes would go directly to a television set, plant herself in front of it, and refused to talk to anyone until the latest installment was over.

The producers took care to incorporate Galsworthy's dialogue into scripts, built sets and designed costumes that accurately reflected the period, and inserted appropriate newsreel footage depicting the Edwardian era. This underscored the authenticity of the series.

A character any daytime serial would be proud to call its own was self-centered, misunderstood Fleur Forsyte Mont. In one episode, Fleur set fire to her family's home and in another she accidentally caused her father's death. At his deathbed, she promised to become a better person. Prior to her role on *The Forsyte Saga*, Susan was known for the sweet roles she played in Disney features. "I played all those very

one-dimensional girls," she said. "...soppy, boring girls who just stand there and say 'yes, yes' to the guy."

An episode titled "Dinner at Swithin's" was indicative of the serial's tone. It showed how the Forsytes assembled for a ritual meal. On the surface, nothing dramatic occurred, but by the episode's end, viewers felt they knew the Forsytes better. In a *TV Guide* article praising the series and its characters, Michener wrote, "They were real people, and if their problems were self-centered and petty, they were nevertheless, problems in which we became involved."

Michael Mont (Nicholas Pennell) has an argument with his obstinate wife, Fleur (Susan Hampshire).

Top: *The cast of* The Forsyte Saga.

Bottom: *Winifred Forsyte (Margaret Tyzack) and Soames (Eric Porter), her brother, discuss alarming news in the evening paper.*

THE CAST

Cast

MONTY DARTIE . . . . TERRY ALEXANDER
JUNE FORSYTE . . . . JUNE BARRY
BOISINNEY . . . . JOHN BENNETT
MARJORIE . . . . CAROLINE BLAKISTON
VAL . . . . JONATHAN BURN
ANN FORSYTE . . . . FAY COMPTON
CHARLES FERRAR . . . . BASIL DINGNAM
FRANCIS WILMOT . . . . HAL HAMILTON
FLEUR FORSYTE MONT . . . . SUSAN HAMPSHIRE
FRANCIS . . . . URSULA HOWELLS
JON FORSYTE . . . . MARTIN JARVIS
MRS. HERON . . . . JENNY LAIRD
LAWRENCE MONT . . . . CYRIL LUKHAM
JO FORSYTE . . . . KENNETH MORE
HELENE HILLMER FORSYTE . . . . LANA MORRIS
HOLLY . . . . SUZANNE NEVE
JOLYON FORSYTE . . . . JOSEPH O'CONNOR
ANNETTE LAMOTTE FORSYTE . . . . DALLIA PENN
MICHAEL MONT . . . . NICHOLAS PENNELL
MAC GOWAN . . . . JOHN PHILLIPS
SOAMES FORSYTE . . . . ERIC PORTER
IRENE HERON FORSYTE . . . . NYREE DAWN PORTER
BICKET . . . . TERRY SCULLY
WINIFRED FORSYTE DARTIE . . . . MARGARET TYZACK
JAMES FORSYTE . . . . JOHN WELSH
SWITHIN . . . . GEORGE WOODBRIDGE

FROM THESE ROOTS

· ·

JUNE 30, 1958–DECEMBER 29, 1961 NBC

This serial was so well-written that playwright Tennessee Williams was a fan. Its talented cast included *Soap's* Robert Mandan, *The Waltons's* Richard Thomas, *Facts of Life's* Charlotte Rae, *The Edge of Night's* Ann Flood, *As the World Turns's* Henderson Forsythe, and *Another World's* Barbara Berjer.

Set in the small New England town of Strathfield, the serial primarily focused on the Fraser family. In the opening episode, reporter Liz Fraser returned to her hometown from Washington, D.C., after receiving word her father, Ben, had suffered a heart attack. While Ben recuperated, Liz became acting publisher for her father's newspaper, *The Strathfield Record.* For awhile, Liz was romanced by young Dr. Buck Weaver. When Buck realized Liz was drawn to playwright David Allen, he turned his attention to Liz's best friend, Maggie Barber. After a brief engagement, Buck and Maggie married.

A memorable storyline involved Buck and Maggie's attempt to adopt a child. When they finally found a infant they wanted to adopt, the adoption agent, Hilda Furman, persuaded them to also take the infant's teenage brother, Richard. Unfortunately, Richard suffered from psychological problems and was a constant source of trouble.

Soon after Liz married David, he allowed himself to be seduced by alcoholic, self-centered actress Lynn Franklin. Complicating matters even more was Lynn's sexual relationship with her director, Tom Jennings.

A standout episode involved a live television broadcast of "Madame Bovary," starring Lynn Franklin and directed by Tom Jennings. The soap audience was taken backstage as Lynn changed into costume, got made up, and made her entrance in front of the live cameras. Meanwhile, Tom—having learned of Lynn's relationship with David—was shown in the control booth, struggling to push aside his personal feelings for his leading lady.

Ben's oldest daughter, Emily, was married to a mill runner, Jim Benson, who had a roving eye. His most notorious extramarital affair was with Luisa Corelli, whose sister, Rose, was married to Emily's brother, Ben, Jr. Shortly after Jim was found murdered, Emily fell in love with district attorney Frank Teton and eventually married him.

Emily and Jim had two children, Lyddy and Tim. Lyddy's most notable romance was with Don Curtiss, who was confined to a wheelchair. Tim married Peggy, daughter of Laura and Nate Tomkins, the wealthiest family in town. After Nate's unexpected death, Laura fell for a dishonest politician, Stanley Kreiser.

In the serial's final episode, David finally establishes himself as a successful writer. Kass, the Fraser's loyal housekeeper, received a $200,000 check settling her late husband's estate. Lyddy brought joy to the Fraser family by announcing she was going to have a baby. Meanwhile, Ben, now the mayor of Strathfield, and his district attorney son-in-law, Frank Teton, announced that they rid the town of organized crime.

Liz (Ann Flood) runs the newspaper during her father's illness, while her niece Lyddy (Sarah Hardy) helps out after school.

Ann Flood and David Sanders (top), and Mary Alice Moore and Sanders (bottom) in scenes from From These Roots.

THE CAST

Cast

GLORIA SAXON	MILLETTE ALEXANDER
KASS	VERA ALLEN
LYNN FRANKLIN	BARBARA BERJER
ARTIE CORELLI	FRANK CAMPANELLA
JIMMY HULL	JOHN COLENBACK
NATE TOMKINS	WARD COSTELLO
LIZ FRASER	ANN FLOOD
	SUSAN BROWN
JIM BENSON	HENDERSON FORSYTHE
LYDDY BENSON	SARAH HARDY
JAMIE	ALAN HOWARD
TOM JENNINGS	CRAIG HUEBLING
ROSE CORELLI FRASER	TRESA HUGHES
	JULIE BOVASSO
STANLEY KREISER	LEON JANNEY
LAURA TOMKINS	AUDRA LINDLEY
BEN FRASER	JOSEPH MacAULEY
	ROD HENDRICKSON
	GRANT CODE
GEORGE WEIMER	DONALD MADDEN
PEGGY TOMKINS BENSON	ELLEN MADISON
	URSULA STEVENS
	MAE MUNRO
DAVID ALLEN	ROBERT MANDAN
BEN FRASER, JR.	FRANK MARTH
JACK LANDER	JOSEPH MASCOLO
ENID ALLEN	MARY ALICE MOORE
HILDA FURMAN	CHARLOTTE RAE
BRUCE CRAWFORD	BYRON SANDERS
EMILY FRASER BENSON	HELEN SHIELDS
FRED BARNES	TOM SHIRLEY
FRANK TETON	GEORGE SMITH
LUISA CORELLI	DOLORES SUTTON
RICHARD	RICHARD THOMAS
MAGGIE WEAVER	BILLIE LOU WATT
BUCK WEAVER	LEN WAYLAND

GENERAL HOSPITAL

APRIL 1, 1963–PRESENT ABC

*D*estined to become an unparalleled phenomenon, as well as ABC's first successful soap opera, this serial had its debut on the same day as NBC's *The Doctors*. Both networks attempted to capitalize on the popularity of the nighttime medical dramas *Dr. Kildare* and *Ben Casey*. ABC killed its working title of *Emergency Hospital* and devised (from *Kildare's* Blair General and *Casey's* County General Hospital) the name *General Hospital*.

The serial revolved around the lives, loves, and deaths associated with the hospital's seventh floor, the internal medicine department. The provocative yet always platonic friendship between doctor Steve Hardy and nurse Jessie Brewer has been a mainstay of the serial. Steve Hardy's personal concerns stemmed from the chronic ups and downs with love interest Audrey March, a stewardess turned nurse. Jessie's persistent woes were due mainly to the indiscretions of her wayward husband, cardiologist Dr. Phil Brewer. The head of student nurses, Lucille March (sister of Audrey), provided comic relief with her bossy but affectionate banter. Additional intrigue was supplied by Dr. Tom Baldwin; his brother Lee, an attorney; Lee's wife, Meg; and her son, Scotty.

Created by Frank and Doris Hursley, who were credited with reviving an ailing *Search for Tomorrow* (and who continued to write for both serials during *General Hospital's* first six months), this newest attempt by ABC didn't seem to have the network's vote of confidence. Having consistently come in last to the other two networks, ABC had yet to score anything successful during daytime. The prevailing sentiment was—why should *General Hospital* turn out any differently?

The budget was so low on the show that early producer/director Jim Young asked John Beradino (Steve Hardy) to consider a decrease in his weekly $1,500 salary in order to allot more money to the construction of sets. Young had to be desperate to ask that of the proud, Italian, ex-professional baseball player Beradino. Plus, there was the added pressure of live taping—there were no re-takes. It was no wonder that Beradino and Emily McLaughlin (Jessie Brewer) developed ulcers.

Despite behind-the-scenes headaches (and tummy aches), *General Hospital* began, almost immediately, to garner an audience. This was due to the complex characters, the tear-wrenching stories created by the Hursleys, and the contribution of medical authenticity by consultant Dr. Franz Bauer. Of particular interest was the rapport between Steve Hardy and Jessie Brewer, with its romantic innuendo that never quite came to fruition. Emily McLaughlin remembered, "I used to throw my arms around him and cry on his shoulder. It was all very platonic, but there was always the intimation that something could happen. We were both washing dishes in my apartment one evening. I was single and Audrey was in Vietnam, and Steve said, 'Jessie, we're both free...' Just then the phone rang. Afterward we got tons of mail."

Below: *Dr. Steve Hardy (John Beradino) and nurse Jessie Brewer (Emily McLaughlin) flirted with the idea of a romance, but they were both married to other people. They have stayed good friends through the years.*

Opposite page: *Amy Vining (Shell Kepler), Jessie Brewer, and Bobbie Spencer (Jacklyn Zeman) confer at the nurse's station at General Hospital.*

Bigger surprises were yet to come. By 1972, *General Hospital* had become the top-rated daytime drama, having toppled *Days of Our Lives* and *As the World Turns* from their top positions. Popularity peaked as the storyline regarding Audrey (Rachel Ames) took place, including her rape by her husband Tom Baldwin (Paul Savior), subsequent child of that ill-fated union, and her plans for remarriage to Steve. A kidnapping of son Tommy, a murder, and a trial quickly ensued.

Unfortunately, and for what were not readily explained reasons, ratings had begun to slide by 1973. The writers and producers tried unsuccessfully to turn the trend around. Even with the revival of the ever popular drama between Jessie and Phil Brewer, who'd been presumed dead, the show couldn't seem to recapture its lost magic. Maybe the focus on the hospital setting was becoming too confining or maybe the melodrama had grown stale. But the best that could be attained was a fan following for

THE CAST

Original Cast

STEVE HARDY	JOHN BERADINO
AL WEEKS	TOM BROWN
ROY LANSING	ROBERT CLARKE
CYNTHIA ALLISON	CAROLYN CRAIG
EDDIE WEEKS	CRAIG CURTIS
PHILLIP MERCER	NEIL HAMILTON
PRISCILLA LONGWORTH	ALLISON HAYES
LENORE WEEKS	LENORE KINGSTON
MIKE COSTELLO	RALPH MANZA
JESSIE BREWER	EMILY McLAUGHLIN
KEN MARTIN	HUNT POWERS
PEGGY MERCER	K. T. STEVENS
PHIL BREWER	ROY THINNES

139

GENERAL HOSPITAL

APRIL 1, 1963–PRESENT ABC

new character Diana Maynard, played by Valerie Starrett. Diana suffered at the hands of Phil Brewer, as had Jessie, and went on to marry Dr. Peter Taylor (Craig Huebing), as had Jessie.

Other than these minor flare-ups of excitement, a downward spiral made way for a changing of the guards, marked by Jim Young's and the Hursleys' departures. The Hursleys handed the reins to their daughter and son-in-law, Bridget and Jerome Dobson (who later created *Santa Barbara*), but they had little success. Tom Donovan took over the producer's post, while a succession of new headwriters (Richard and Suzanne Holland, Eileen and Robert Mason Pollock, Irving and Tex Elman, the Hollands again) were brought in. The Hollands concentrated on using the untapped potential of actress Denise Alexander, who, two years before, had been wooed away from *Days of Our Lives* to play Dr. Lesley Williams. Before being replaced by the Pollocks, the Hollands began writing an unfolding scenario for Lesley that would eventually save the show from cancellation. In finding out that her daughter Laura (played first by Stacy Baldwin, later by Genie Francis), believed to have died in early childhood, was still alive, Lesley became increasingly desperate to fulfill her mothering role.

During the time the Pollocks were writing, several risky changes were implemented in Port Charles, New York. At the request of Fred Silverman, then head of ABC daytime programming, the serial was lengthened from 30 to 45 minutes. He thought viewers wouldn't want to tune in 15 minutes late to competing networks. The Pollocks got rid of almost 20 regular characters and introduced new ones, of whom the members of the Webber family were to have lasting interest. The storyline, written with notoriously heavy-handed dialogue, involved a volatile love triangle between Jeff Webber (Richard Dean Anderson), his wife, Monica (Patsy Rahn briefly, then Leslie Charleson), and his brother, Rick Webber (Michael Gregory, then Chris Robinson).

By mid-1977, with *General Hospital* facing certain cancellation six months down the road, ratings had plummeted. Grabbing at straws, the latest headwriters focused on a youthful plot for teenage Laura and young Scotty Baldwin (Kin Shriner). Still, the serial did nothing more than take a few drowning gasps until fate and three strokes of genius intervened.

The first saving grace came in the form of Gloria Monty, who was the former director of *The Secret Storm*. As the new producer, Monty started what would be hailed as her revolutionary producing of *General Hospital* on the first day of 1978. The second inspiration was in ABC daytime vice-president Jackie Smith's selection of Douglas Marland as headwriter. The third and hotly debated choice was in expanding from 45 minutes to an hour. So outlandish was Fred Silverman's strategy that Doug Marland asked him, "Why would you take a sick 45 minutes and turn it into an hour?" Maybe Silverman had consulted with an oracle and knew the show was about to make soap opera history.

Edward (David Lewis) and Lila Quartermaine (Anna Lee) may have a crazy family, but they have an abiding love that keeps them together.

Gloria Monty's gamble was to dump those first five hour-long episodes (hundreds of thousands of dollars worth) down the drain and to revamp all aspects of production. The antiquated live-tape techniques were replaced by the latest camera technology, which used the process of shooting segments out of order and follow-up editing. Lighting, sets, and music were completely overhauled under Monty's guidance. So noticeable was the facelift that the actual construction workers were, out of sheer necessity, caught by the camera during tapings. New scripts included references to repairs being done at the hospital.

Of greater impact was Marland's tantalizing treatment of Laura's seduction by an older man, her subsequent murder of him, and Lesley's confession to Laura's crime. Add to that the jealous devices of new character Bobbie Spencer (Jackie Zeman) who wanted Scotty Baldwin all to herself.

Within a year, the serial had climbed to number-three position in the ratings: a miracle. More miracles were ahead. The serial became the darling of the media, setting ratings records that blew the roof off.

Although the sensationalism of *General Hospital* in the nineties is barely recognizable to the viewers who have clung on since its first decade, the duo that began all the hubbub in 1963—Steve Hardy and Jessie Brewer—remain. The action of the first ten years covered Jessie's turbulent trials with husband Phil Brewer, the tragic death of their child, their resulting divorce, his own presumed death, and later reappearance. Also prominent were events in Steve's personal life; his marriage to Audrey March and her pregnancy by artificial insemination. With Steve driving, a car accident caused the unborn baby to die.

GENERAL HOSPITAL

APRIL 1, 1963–PRESENT ABC

Steve and Audrey divorced and she departed for Vietnam. She returned home and married Tom Baldwin, while denying that she was still in love with Steve. Refusing to allow the repugnant Tom to engage in sexual relations with her, Audrey was raped by him and became pregnant. Confronting her true feelings for Steve, she divorced Tom and went away to deliver her child.

By the time she returned, Audrey was forced to hide the child's existence, claiming the baby boy had died. She and Steve made plans to remarry. When Tom discovered her lies about his son, Tommy, Audrey was forced to resume her marriage to Tom, whose paranoia influenced him to mastermind the kidnapping of their son. Audrey was shattered.

Meg Baldwin, Lee's wife, had also suffered a series of devastating events. After a nervous breakdown and a stay in a mental institution, she became healthy just as she was stricken by high blood pressure, for which she was under the care of Dr. Lesley Williams. Sadly, even the dedicated Dr. Williams couldn't save Meg, whose death left Lee and stepson Scotty without a wife and mother.

Not very long after Phil Brewer had come back on the scene, he was found dead, his corpse being embraced by Jessie. As she awaited trial for his murder, everyone was shocked when Diana Taylor admitted to the crime. Creating a whirl of investigative frenzy, Diana's confusing confession led Peter Taylor and Lee Baldwin to peg nurse Augusta McLeod as the true villain.

After an exhaustive search, Lesley finally located her daughter Laura. Previously thought dead, Laura was being raised by Barbara and Jason Vining. In a custody suit against the Vinings, Lesley won permission for Laura to stay with her and her new husband, manipulative millionaire Cameron Faulkner, until more decisive action was taken. Trouble continued to brew when Laura, though enchanted by the Faulkners uppercrust lifestyle, cried out for Barbara Vining.

With the Webber family newly arrived to General Hospital, a torrid triangle between brothers Rick and Jeff Webber and his wife Monica soon raised its ugly head. Complicating matters was Heather Grant, who worked as household help for Peter and Diana Taylor, and who managed not only to seduce Jeff but to get pregnant by him. Much to Heather's chagrin, she

couldn't break up Jeff and Monica. She left Port Charles with a desperate plot to sell her son, Steven Lars, to the unwitting, childless Taylors. They were duped into adopting him and they renamed him P.J. In despair over the supposed death of his baby, Jeff, having divorced Monica, invited Heather to return and become his wife.

Although Monica had tried to come between the recently widowed Lesley Faulkner and Rick Webber, causing Lesley to miscarry Cam's baby, Lesley and Rick married. The two looked forward to a happy homelife raising Laura. Danger began to lurk when Rick's old friend, David Hamilton, visited. Hamilton made an illicit pass at Lesley.

Edward, his son, Alan (Stuart Damon), and daughter-in-law, Monica (Leslie Charleson), listen at the door to a conversation that is none of their business—but that has never stopped them before!

Spurned by her, Hamilton seduced the underage Laura. He then told Lesley he'd used Laura to make her jealous. Unknown to either, Laura heard the cruel admission and was driven to the brink. She hurled a statue at him, a blow that knocked his head against the fireplace and rendered him unconscious. Laura ran off shortly before Lesley came upon the dead Hamilton. To protect her beloved daughter, Lesley claimed to have commited the crime and was soon sentenced to prison. Laura mentally blocked the incident. Upset, she disappeared from Port Charles.

The romance between Laura (Genie Francis) and Luke (Anthony Geary) helped regenerate General Hospital, *which was on the downslide.*

No one was more surprised at this daytime heartthrob's rise to international stardom than the actor himself. His comment was, "My face is not the face of a sex symbol," then he added, "but Luke Spencer isn't interested in being pretty."

Reared in the tiny town of Coalville, Utah (population 300), Anthony Geary dreamed about becoming an actor. To that end, he pursued and attained a scholarship to the University of Utah's drama program. It was there that he captured the attention of guest director Jack Albertson, who cast him in *The Subject Was Roses.*

A professional tour of the play soon followed, and 18-year-old Geary's dream began to materialize. He headed for the bright lights of Hollywood. Still, he maintained a back-up plan—if acting failed to pan out, then he could always return to Coalville as a theatre arts instructor.

Such was not his fate. After 13 years of slugging it out in minor television roles, he defied the odds by becoming daytime's number-one leading man: Luke Spencer.

Since his permanent departure from *General Hospital* in 1984, Tony Geary has gone on to do feature films, television guest appearances, and several stage productions. Presently, he has no intention of returning to daytime drama.

When she was finally located, Laura was led home by Scotty Baldwin, whose romantic feelings for her had been growing over the years. Laura's confession to Hamilton's murder won Lesley immediate release from prison. Just when life began to look a little brighter for the Webbers, trouble-making Bobbie Spencer decided get revenge against Laura, who'd stolen Scotty from her. Scheming with her devious brother, Luke, Bobbie put the young lovers through ploy upon ploy. Now the wife of Alan Quartermaine, Monica poured salt on Webber wounds by having an affair with Rick. Her pregnancy would become the source of a paternity dilemma.

Equally disastrous was the fact that newlywed Laura Baldwin had developed a powerful attraction to Luke Spencer. Having become platonically attached to him and innocently involved in his underworld activities, vulnerable Laura was unable to stop him from kissing her and then throwing her on the dance floor and raping her. Before Luke had a chance to go through with

GENERAL HOSPITAL

APRIL 1, 1963–PRESENT ABC

his wedding to Jennifer (sinister mob boss Frank Smith's daughter) on board a yacht, Scotty Baldwin found out about Luke's conquest of Laura. Scotty went after Luke with a vengeance. Thrown overboard by the blows, Luke was left to drown but was washed ashore where Laura came to his side. Together they went into hiding.

After dodging hit man Hutch (who later became an ally) and the more lethal Sally Max (a man dressed as a woman), both in the service of underworld figure Frank Smith, Luke and Laura consummated their mutual desire and made plans for Laura to divorce Scotty when they returned to Port Charles. In the confusion about divorcing Scotty that followed their homecoming, Luke mistakenly believed Laura had changed her mind. Broken-hearted, Luke wanted nothing to do with her.

Alexandria Quartermaine, presumably working for Alan's father and her uncle, the affluent Edward Quartermaine, was secretly searching for the Ice Princess. It was a small statue formed by a massive uncut diamond that also held an incredible formula—a way to produce synthetic diamonds. Engaging the services of Luke, without telling him about the formula, Alex sent him into the clutches of adversaries Tony Cassadine and Robert Scorpio. In a surprise turn of events, Robert and Luke became allies when it was revealed that Alex was conspiring with both Tony and his brother Victor Cassadine. The notorious three were plotting to take over the world with the Ice Princess, which was in the hands of Victor.

Terror compounded for stowaways Luke and Robert as the Cassadines' yacht sailed away with

Below: *John Beradino and Emily McLaughlin pose with one of the many student nurses that have passed through the halls of* General Hospital.

Opposite page: *Bobbie Spencer has been looking for true love, but can't seem to find it. She married D. L. Brock (David Groh), but the marriage didn't last.*

GENERAL HOSPITAL

APRIL 1, 1963–PRESENT ABC

the statue. The yacht was headed to the Cassadine's tropical isle, where it would be met by wicked brother Mikkos. Fear turned to shock when Laura was also found to be hiding on the yacht. While Laura and Luke experienced romantic bliss on the island, Robert unraveled the plan of world destruction being masterminded by the Cassadines. He saw to it that all culprits were either jailed or executed.

In rapid succession, the dashing Dr. Noah Drake became involved with Bobbie Spencer, Scotty and Laura were divorced, Luke and Laura were married, Noah and Bobbie broke-up, and

Laura vanished into thin air. When journalist Jackie Templeton teamed up with Luke, they were led to villain David Gray. He was responsible for Laura's death and Luke killed him during a fight. Luke soon became romantically linked to Jackie.

After further devastating intrigues, Luke's odyssey appeared to be over. Port Charles even elected him mayor. And then, the most shocking circumstance occurred: Laura, very much alive, returned. Reunited at last, the ecstatic sweethearts left Port Charles for good, much to the chagrin of their thousands of fans.

Below: *Robert Scorpio (Tristan Rogers) and Anna Lavery (Finola Hughes) fight crime in Port Charles.*

Opposite page: *Celia Quartermaine (Sherilyn Wolter) left her college sweetheart to be with Jimmie Lee Holt (Steve Bond).*

GENERAL HOSPITAL

APRIL 1, 1963–PRESENT ABC

With Luke and Laura no longer in the spotlight, the serial focused on the dramas involving Robert Scorpio and Frisco Jones. Meanwhile, *General Hospital* ceased to be referred to as "The Luke and Laura Show."

Ironically, Genie Francis's Laura might never have come to life had her father succeeded in stopping her plans to become an actress. At the same time, one of Anthony Geary's first quips to Gloria Monty before agreeing to come on as Luke was "I hate soap operas."

Young audiences, teenagers, and college students have become a mainstay of the serial's popularity. During peak periods, the Nielsons have reported as high as 75 percent of viewers falling into the age bracket of 18 to 34. In 1981, a *General Hospital* rally at Harvard University had the same kind of feverish attendance as a Beatle concert in the sixties.

Celebrity fans of the serial include Lady Bird Johnson, the Kansas City Royals baseball team, Milton Berle, and the late Sammy Davis, Jr. Both Davis and Berle appeared as guest stars. Elizabeth Taylor's love for the show led to her much touted appearance.

General Hospital created instant stardom for many of its regulars—who couldn't go out in public without being mobbed. Anthony Geary was hailed early on as the Tom Selleck of daytime. Pop musician Rick Springfield used his role as Noah Drake to revive his musical career. Emma Samms (Holly) gained popular acclaim and was whisked away by nighttime's *Dynasty*. Demi Moore's Jackie was her vehicle into feature films.

Perhaps the biggest name to emerge from almost 30 years on the air is that of Gloria Monty, a name synonymous with *General Hospital.* Monty orchestrated an array of innovations that, for better or worse, influenced the rest of the daytime drama world. In fact, the general consensus is that when Gloria Monty sneezes, all other soap opera producers get colds.

The *Newsweek* issue of September 28, 1981, with Genie Francis and Tony Geary on the cover, said it all, "TV's Hottest Show—Luke and Laura of *General Hospital.*"

Experts clamored to find out just how this strange phenomenon had occurred. How had a serial set in the world of medicine blasted off to exotic places and catapulted the lives of two romantically entwined characters into soap opera immortality?

Many pointed to Gloria Monty's brilliant casting of Tony Geary in the role of Luke Spencer. Others claimed that the storyline, written by Pat Falken Smith (who replaced headwriter Doug Marland), of Luke's controversial rape/seduction of Laura was the source of the dramatic upswing in the ratings. Another camp held that the riveting espionage story, along with the tantalizingly luscious sets, had allowed Luke and Laura to become America's number-one sweethearts.

No less of a consideration in the success was the 1981 appearance by Elizabeth Taylor at Luke and Laura's wedding. Whatever the actual cause, the serial had captured a viewership of 14 million homes (audience share of 52). Never before had this been achieved in daytime drama, and it would, in the coming years, set the pace and tone for every other serial on the air. Needless to say, Luke and Laura led the way.

Luke and Laura's wedding day was a history-making event in daytime TV; over 14 million homes watched them tie the knot.

GENERATIONS

MARCH 27, 1990–PRESENT NBC

This half-hour serial was promoted as television's first fully integrated daytime soap. It focused on the relationship between two Chicago families: the Whitmores and the Marshalls. Their association began several decades ago when Vivian Potter was housekeeper and nanny for Rebecca Whitmore and her three children: Laura, Stephanie (nicknamed Sam), and J.D. Vivian's young daughter, Ruth, lived with her in the Whitmore mansion.

When Ruth grew up, she married Henry Marshall, who owned and operated five moderately successful ice cream parlors. With Ruth's urging, Henry enlisted the help of business mogul Martin Jackson, who marketed Marshall's ice cream nationwide. The move proved so successful that Ruth was able to buy the Whitmore mansion. Ruth and Henry have three children, Chantal, a lawyer; Jacquelyn Marshall Rhymes, a homemaker and mother; and Adam, a junior executive with the Hale Hotel chain. Living with the Marshalls is Ruth's mother, Vivian.

Like Ruth Marshall, Rebecca Whitmore also had a challenging past to overcome. Unknown to Rebecca, her ex-husband stole her inheritance. Determined to move forward with her life, a middle-aged Rebecca enrolled in law school and succeeded in becoming one of the nation's leading attorneys. When the serial premiered, her daughter Laura was married to advertising executive Trevor McCallum. Realizing that Trevor was cheating on her, Laura ended the marriage. They had an adult daughter, Monique.

Although Rebecca was saddened by the break-up of her oldest daughter's marriage, she was happy to see her granddaughter, Monique, marry photographer Jason Craig. Soon after their marriage, Jason inherited a multimillion dollar fortune, making him a murder target. Rebecca's youngest daughter, Sam, accepted a position as model and spokesperson for the upscale Hale Hotel chain. Sam's boss, the dastardly Jordan Hale, expressed an interest in Sam that went beyond business. Police Lieutenant Kyle Masters was also wildly attracted to Sam. Shortly after *Generations* premiered, J.D. left town.

Also playing an important role in the serial is Doreen Jackson, a recovering drug addict who was married to Martin Jackson. Following a brief fling with Adam Marshall, Doreen found herself pregnant. Before their daughter, Danielle, was born, the relationship died. Doreen next took up with her doctor, Daniel Reubens (played by Richard Roundtree). He resurfaced in Chicago in 1990 with his daughter, Maya Davis—alias Diana Reubens (played by Vivica Fox)—after falsely being accused of killing his wife.

Describing Doreen Jackson, Jonelle Allen said, "She's vain, conniving, but also vulnerable and has a great comedic side. She can be very nasty yet she's a strong, smart woman. To be able to show all those sides is rare for white or black actors and I feel I have been given the opportunity to do that on *Generations*.

Below: *Vivica A. Fox plays Maya Daniels and Kristoff St. John plays Adam Marshall.*

Opposite page: *(right) Kelly Rutherford plays Sam Whitmore and (left) Richard Roundtree plays Daniel Reubens.*

"I grew up watching—and still do—the old movies on television. I think there's a lot of panache and flair in Doreen, because those are the kinds of things I like to watch—those fabulous women in the classics of the '30s and '40s. So in this role, I get a chance to be bitchy, to be seductive, to be all sorts of things—and I get to wear great clothes. If I had only one word to describe Doreen, I'd say she was *swell*."

Joan Pringle, who plays Ruth Marshall, said, "The fact that the show would set a precedent was a big factor in taking the role, but the main reason was I loved the character of Ruth. I really enjoy playing her and it's the first time in a long time in television I've actually got to do a woman with any dimension.

"Ruth is trying to get a piece of the American pie for herself and her family through hard work and perseverance. Since Ruth didn't have much when she was growing up, she not only wants material things, but power, recognition, and security."

Richard Roundtree, who plays Dr. Daniel Reubens, said, "It's really wonderful to be involved with a show that chronicles three generations of a black family."

Besides heavily featuring on-camera black talent, *Generations* employs black workers in key positions behind the scenes. Judi Ann Mason is the

THE CAST

Original Cast

JASON CRAIG	TONY ADDABBO
DOREEN JACKSON	JONELLE ALLEN
HUGH GARDNER	JACK BETTS
HENRY MARSHALL	TAUREAN BLACQUE
CHANTAL MARSHALL	SHARON BROWN
REBECCA WHITMORE	PATRICIA CROWLEY
ROB DONNELLY	GEORGE DELOY
MARTIN JACKSON	RICK FITTS
SONNY	JAIME GOMEZ
VIVIAN POTTER	LYNN HAMILTON
MURRAY STEIN	PHILIP HOFFMAN
JOEL RESNICK	RICK LOHMAN
TREVOR McCALLUM	ANDREW MASSETT
RUTH MARSHALL	JOAN PRINGLE
LAURA McCALLUM	GAIL RAMSEY
JESSICA GARDNER	BARBARA RHOADES
LEONARD COOPER	RICHARD ROAT
SAM WHITMORE	KELLY RUTHERFORD
MONIQUE McCALLUM	NANCY SOREL
ADAM MARSHALL	KRISTOFF ST. JOHN
WALLY	MYLES THOROUGHGOOD

GENERATIONS
· ·
MARCH 27, 1990–PRESENT NBC

first black writer to pen scripts for a network soap. "I don't feel as though I'm General Black America in there," laughed Mason, acknowledging her unique position. "I think that would be a mistake, if I were to feel that as the black authority. It has been a very even exchange for us. If by any chance something were to come up where we'd be dealing with a type of racial situation, I think the writers would rehash it and discuss it first among ourselves before we'd go and try to put it on the imaginary characters. That's how we're working—from the inside out."

"It's a show that dares to be different," said Mason, "because it's going to deal with some subjects and say some things that have never been said before. You'll see black people who say they're black. You don't see this on other soap operas—they float around and don't address any issues that directly affect them. This is an attempt to woo the black audience, to tell them that it's acceptable to be who you are. You'll hear people who acknowledge the fact that they're different, that this isn't an imaginary world of soapdom where everybody is not aware of what really goes on around them in society. You'll find audience members who might be uncomfortable seeing a white person and a black person having dinner together. These characters can feel free enough to acknowledge the fact that can bother someone, but it might not bother them."

About the racial bigotry storyline, creator Sally Sussman said, "What the Marshalls are going through is very personal to them. We are dealing with a family and their personal struggles and how racism affects them, and that's why I think the storyline is powerful.

"We're trying to create something special. We're doing something very different and gutsy here and we're committed to making it work."

One interesting bit of trivia concerns the actor who now plays Chantal. Debbi Morgan, best known for her role as Angie on *All My Children*, played a role in a short-lived CBS nighttime soap called *Behind the Screen*. That soap was about the lives of the actors in a soap called *Generations*. Now Morgan is not just playing an actor playing on *Generations*, she is truly an actor on a real soap called *Generations*.

Below, left: *Doreen (Jonelle Allen) has been fighting drug and alcohol problems.*

Below, right: *Rob (George Deloy) married Jessica for her money, but he loved Sam.*

Opposite page: *Debbi Morgan plays Chantal. Soap fans will recognize her as Angie from* All My Children.

THE GUIDING LIGHT

JUNE 30, 1952–PRESENT CBS

This serial, created by Irna Phillips, has the distinction of being the longest-running series in broadcasting history. It began as a 15-minute radio serial in 1937, and premiered on television in 1952. For four years, it ran on both radio and television. Charita Bauer, who joined the series in 1950 and stayed until her death in 1985, said, "I was sad when the radio show stopped. It was the end of an era—and besides, we were going to lose that extra 40 dollars a show!"

The transition from radio to television wasn't easy for *The Guiding Light*. Only one month before the television version began, the radio serial was using techniques that would become dated on TV. The announcer's role, for example, was reduced on TV. On radio, it made sense for the announcer to lead listeners into a commercial by interjecting, "You're about to say something to Bertha, aren't you Bill? This habit of hers of attempting to direct other peoples lives can be a destructive one. I wouldn't want to be in your shoes, not for anything—because—well, we'll learn about this in a moment." In television, such an intrusion would not work.

When *The Guiding Light* first aired on radio, the Reverend Dr. Rutledge was the leading character. The setting was a fictional town—Five Points, California. Dr. Rutledge's frequent sermons gave the serial a spiritual tone. Contributing to the program's religious overtones was the use of organ music, which carried over to television.

By the time the series moved to television, Dr. Rutledge was phased out in favor of the Bauer family. Eventually, the serial's location also changed from Five Points to Springfield, a midwestern city. Immigrants Papa and Mama Bauer (originally played by Gloria Brandt on the radio version) had three adult children: Bill, Meta, and Trudy. Before the series reached television, Mama Bauer died. Not long after the move to television, Trudy was written out of the series.

Bill's marriage to the self-centered Bert was met with disapproval from his parents. Bert pushed her husband mercilessly and constantly complained that they weren't living well enough. Early in their marriage, Bert gave birth to two sons, Michael (originally played by Christopher Walken) and Edward (originally played by Pat

Collins). Frustrated by his inability to provide for his family, Bill turned to alcohol. As his disease progressed, Bert's selfishness diminished and she struggled to hold her family together. Her efforts caused the citizens of Springfield to reevaluate her. It wasn't long before people were turning to Bert for emotional support when their problems became overwhelming.

Bert's character wasn't the only one to undergo a dramatic transformation during *The Guiding Light's* early television days. In the radio version, Meta was a colorful character, raising eyebrows by pursuing a career as a professional model. When her young son Chuckie died, a grief-stricken Meta blamed her husband and shot him. When the serial was brought to television, Meta's carefree days were over. Instead, Meta learned from her past indiscretions and changed. The devilish behavior was passed to her sixteen-year-old stepdaughter, Kathy Roberts.

Papa Bauer (Theo Goetz) gives Bert (Charita Bauer) some advice.

When Ellen Demming was cast to play Meta, she was 29 years old. To make her look matronly, Ted Corday, the serial's director, altered her physical appearance. "They had my hair swept up into a chignon and they grayed the temples—for years," revealed Demming. "It looked strange and hilarious, but I guess it worked. Charita called them 'little white wings.' They painted the hair at my temples clown white, then I'd meet my husband for dinner after the show and he'd be mortified to be seen with this lady with white hair."

Kathy's marriage to Richard (Dick) Grant was a prominently featured storyline during the fifties. The marriage came to an abrupt end when Kathy confessed that Bob Lang, Kathy's first husband, was the real father of her young daughter, Robin. Shortly after the death of Meta's husband, Joe Roberts, Meta fell in love with Mark

THE CAST

Original Cast

META ROBERTS	JONE ALLISON
BERT BAUER	CHARITA BAUER
KATHY ROBERTS	SUSAN DOUGLAS
PAPA BAUER	THEO GOETZ
TRUDY BAUER	LISA HOWARD
DICK GRANT	JAMES LIPTON
JOE ROBERTS	HERB NELSON
BILL BAUER	LYLE SUDROW
LAURA GRANT	ALICE YOURMAN

THE GUIDING LIGHT

JUNE 30, 1952–PRESENT CBS

Holden (played by Whitfield Connor), a business associate of Bill Bauer's. Competing for Mark's afffections was Meta's stepdaughter, Kathy.

In 1958, creator Irna Phillips decided she'd had enough of Kathy and killed her in a car accident. CBS was swamped with angry letters from disgruntled viewers. An unfazed Phillips responded to their protests with a form letter that stated, "You have only to look around you, read your daily papers, to realize that we cannot, any of us, live with life alone..."

In 1958, Agnes Nixon was appointed headwriter. Her major influences on *The Guiding Light* were to inject spicier characters and storylines, and to introduce social issues. Nixon was responsible for creating the first important black character in a daytime serial, nurse Martha Frazier (originally played by Cicely Tyson).

Bert Bauer's brave battle with uterine cancer occupied the 1961-62 season. Bert's life was saved by early detection. "Bert was the perfect ostrich, the perfect prototype of the woman who does not go to an obstetrician after her last baby is born. And I thought Charita, herself, was the perfect actress to carry this message," explained Agnes Nixon in *Guiding Light, A 50th Anniversary Celebration*, published by Ballantine Books. "We did the story in stages. When Paul Fletcher learned that Bert hadn't had a physical since Ed was born, he suggested that she come in for a complete examination. Bert was like so many women, 'I'm healthy, nothing can happen to me. I'm invulnerable.'

"But she went ahead with the examination—I remember this scene so well because I had to write the scene six months before it actually happened to get it past the censors. Dr. Fletcher said we're going to do a Pap-smear test and Bert asked, what was that? He explained in detail, and later told her she had irregular cells. Eventually, Bert had the surgery, which saved her life."

Female viewers from across the country wrote letters thanking *The Guiding Light* for its realistic storyline. A significant number added that their own lives had been saved by having the examination. Nixon's own doctor said the show inspired a half-dozen patients he hadn't seen for years to come in and have the examination. "I was surprised by the strong audience reaction," said Nixon, "but it was probably a shock to a few

executives at Procter & Gamble. They were very much against doing this story. And so was CBS."

Bert's oldest son, Michael, took center stage as the serial's leading romantic figure in the early sixties. Michael's first serious romance was with Robin Holden (Kathy's daughter). Bert disapproved of Robin and did her best to undermine the relationship. Later, Mike married Julie Conrad (originally played by Sandra Smith). They were blessed with a daughter, Hope (originally played by Jennifer Kirschner). Once again, Bert interfered in Michael's life by offering unsolicited advice on child-rearing. Mike and Julie's marriage was challenged when Julie suffered a nervous breakdown. While committed to a mental institution, Julie committed suicide.

Anthony Call played Dr. Joe Werner and Millette Alexander played Dr. Sara McIntyre.

156

The Bauer family: (left to right) Leslie (Barbara Rodell), Mike (Don Stewart), Ed (Martin Hulswit), Papa (Theo Goetz), and Bert (Charita Bauer).

Agnes Nixon left *The Guiding Light* in 1966 to take over as headwriter of the low-rated *Another World*. *The Guiding Light* began airing in color on March 13, 1967. It expanded from 15 minutes to a half hour on September 9, 1968. By this time, the serial had switched to videotape and was no longer broadcast live.

The half-hour format was launched with a dramatization of a heart transplant—chalking up yet another first for the show. Bert's husband, Bill, was the patient.

The serial was carried into the seventies with a storyline featuring brothers Mike and Ed fighting over the same woman, Leslie Jackson (originally played by Lynne Adams). Ed was the first Bauer to marry Leslie. Like his father, Ed was an alcoholic. Unable to cope with Ed's disease, Leslie turned to Mike for support. When Leslie

discovered Ed's affair with Janet Mason (played by Caroline McWilliams), she confessed to Mike that she loved him. Leslie intended to divorce Ed, but he pleaded with her to give their marriage another chance. Learning that Leslie was pregnant with Ed's child, Mike became involved with the scheming Charlotte Waring (originally played by Victoria Wyndham) and later married her. Leslie was distraught by the news of Mike's marriage; but she divorced Ed anyway. When her son was born, she named him Frederick (after Mike and Ed's grandfather, Papa Bauer).

By the midseventies, Jerome and Bridget Dobson were *The Guiding Light's* headwriters. Their primary goal was to make the long-running serial more contemporary. In 1977, the show expanded to a full hour. Ed's relationship with Holly Norris (originally played by Lynn

THE GUIDING LIGHT

JUNE 30, 1952–PRESENT CBS

Deerfield) was a viewer favorite during the Dobson's tenure. Soon after they married, Holly became pregnant. Ed thought the baby was his, but Holly was having an affair with the evil Roger Thorpe (played by Michael Zaslow). Holly gave birth to a baby girl, Christina. An emergency blood transfusion for the ailing Christina served as the catalyst for Holly to reveal the truth to Ed about her affair with Roger. An enraged Ed found comfort in the arms of Rita Stapleton (played by Lenore Kasdorf), a new nurse at Cedars hospital. Their relationship grew and eventually Ed proposed marriage. Shortly after the ceremony, Rita was raped by her old flame and Ed's old nemesis, Roger Thorpe!

Roger became such a popular character that the serial's writers had a hard time killing him off. After marrying Holly, Roger also raped her. Holly pressed charges against him. When Holly lost her case, she killed Roger. A year later, Roger resurfaced in Springfield, obviously having survived Holly's attempt on his life. Once again, Roger was busy making both Holly and Rita's lives miserable. In 1980, viewers watched as Roger fell to his death from a cliff in the Dominican Republic. For several years, it looked as if Roger was really dead. To everyone's surprise, he resurfaced again in 1988.

The Dobsons were also responsible for creating the super-wealthy Alan Spaulding (originally played by Chris Bernau). He moved to Springfield with his long-suffering wife, Elizabeth (played by Lezlie Dalton), and their son, Phillip (originally played by Jarrod Ross). Elizabeth's closest friend was Jackie Marler (originally played by Cindy Pickettt). Unknown to Elizabeth, Jackie was Phillip's natural mother.

Following the arrival of the Spauldings, a complicated series of romantic musical chairs ensued. Jackie found herself attracted to Mike Bauer, but he was in love with Elizabeth. When Elizabeth's marriage to Alan ended, Jackie married him, hoping to get closer to her son, Phillip. Alan and Jackie's marriage was short-lived, however. He divorced her and married Mike's daughter, Hope. Meanwhile, Elizabeth married Jackie's ex-husband, Dr. Justin Marler (originally played by Tom O'Rourke), Phillip's natural father.

In 1980, Douglas Marland succeeded the Dobsons as headwriter. Marland was responsible for helping make *General Hospital* daytime television's top-rated soap in the late seventies. He quit the serial when Gloria Monty insisted he move to California, where the series was based. Marland took an inventory of *The Guiding Light's* characters and decided the show had become too upper-middle class. To inject contrast, he created the poor but noble Reardons.

Widowed Bea Reardon (originally played by Lee Lawson) ran a boarding house. She had five adult children: Tony (played by Gregory Beecroft), Maureen (originally played by Ellen Dolan), Jim (originally played by Michael Woods), Nola (originally played by Lisa Brown), and Chelsea (originally played by Kassie Wesley).

Ed (Peter Simon) and Maureen Bauer (Ellen Parker) have had their ups and downs, but in 1990 they remarried and now seem happy.

Left: *Michael Zaslow plays Roger Thorpe. He has become famous in the soap world for playing villians.*

Right: *Kim Zimmer plays Reva Shayne Lewis. She won an Emmy for her outstanding acting.*

In the beginning, Nola was considered the most colorful Reardon. Jealous of young Dr. Kelly Nelson's (originally played by John Wesley Shipp) relationship with the fragile Morgan Richards (originally played by Kristen Vigard), Nola schemed to undermine it. One evening she succeeded in taking a drunken Kelly to bed. Nola led Kelly to believe he made love to her, which was untrue. Later, Nola seduced Floyd Parker (originally played by Tom Nielsen) and got pregnant. Nola used the pregnancy to break up Morgan and Kelly by leading everyone to believe the child was Kelly's. Her plan nearly worked, but her mother learned the truth and revealed that Floyd was the father of Nola's child. Later, Kelly married Morgan. After working through her feelings for Kelly, Nola fell in love with millionaire Quinton Chamberlain (originally played by Michael Tylo). Soon after their marriage, the characters were written off.

Douglas Marland also introduced Carrie Todd (originally played by Jane Elliot), who suffered from a split personality. Marland was excited about the story he had created for Carrie, but producer Allen Potter insisted it be dropped. He also abruptly terminated Jane Elliot's contract. Upset by Potter's extreme steps, Marland resigned.

For a brief period, *The Guiding Light's* ratings tumbled as a series of different headwriters worked to get the serial back on track. For the first time in the serial's long history, the Bauers were no longer the leading family. In 1983, newly appointed producer Gail Kobe hired Pamela Long and Richard Culliton as headwriters. They expanded upon a family Marland had created, the oil-rich Lewises. Patriarch H. B. Lewis (originally played by Larry Gates) had three adult children: Billy (originally played by Jordan Clarke), Trish (originally played by Rebecca Hollen), and Josh

THE GUIDING LIGHT

JUNE 30, 1952–PRESENT CBS

The late Charita Bauer has the distinction of playing a single character for the longest period of time in the history of serials. She joined radio's *The Guiding Light* in 1950, one year before the serial would begin airing on television.

Bauer made her professional acting debut at age nine in Broadway's *Thunder on the Left*. While attending the Professional Children's School, she continued appearing in various Broadway productions, most notably as the original Little Mary in Claire Boothe Luce's *The Women*.

Her soap opera career included roles on such radio soaps as *Our Gal Sunday, The Aldrich Family, Lora Lawton, Maude's Diary, The Right to Happiness, Second Husband,* and *Young Widder Brown.*

A marriage in the forties produced a son, Michael Crawford, who was born in 1946. (In 1951, her television character, Bert, also gave birth to a son named Michael.) Bauer received an Emmy for Lifetime Achievement in 1983.

In 1984, Bauer began experiencing physical difficulties. An operation was performed to amputate part of her leg. After recovering from surgery, she returned to *The Guiding Light* in an emotional storyline involving Bert's own adjustment to an artificial limb. "It was a difficult situation all around," said *The Guiding Light's* producer at that time, Gail Kobe. "We told her she could work, we would certainly provide her with work and make every effort to make it comfortable for her on the set. I suggested the prosthesis story to her because I knew she had something to contribute and I wanted her to know she was needed on the show.... The scene in which Bert dropped a cup and couldn't bend over to pick up the pieces really got to me. It was clear Bert did not burst into tears out of self-pity, but sheer frustration. It was a story of courage."

With her health continuing to decline, Bauer made her last appearance on *The Guiding Light* on December 10, 1984. On February 28, 1985, she died. A year later, Bert Bauer died off-camera. "We waited exactly a year to deal with Bert's death," explained Gail Kobe. "And we celebrated Bert and Charita with a service and montage of pictures of her on the show through the past 35 years."

Below: *Beth Raines (Judi Evans) and Lujack (Vincent Irizarry) were proof that opposites attract. She was educated, sweet, and innocent, and he was an uneducated street hood.*

Opposite page: *Theo Goetz and Charita Bauer will never be forgotten by* The Guiding Light *fans. Though deceased, both live on in memory.*

(originally played by Robert Newman). Billy had a teenage daughter, Mindy (originally played by Krista Tesreau). All three Lewis men were smitten by Reva Shayne (played by Kim Zimmer). Reva's true love, however, was Josh. Their romance began when they were teenagers. In 1989, Josh and Reva freed themselves of all romantic entanglements and exchanged wedding vows. Soon after, Reva's long-lost son, Dylan (originally played by Morgan Englund), surfaced in Springfield. A year later, Kim Zimmer decided to step down from her role as Reva and the character was written out.

As *The Guiding Light* approaches its fortieth anniversary, it continues to be one of the most popular serials on daytime television.

HOW TO SURVIVE A MARRIAGE

JANUARY 7, 1974–APRIL 18, 1975 NBC

NBC touted this short-lived seventies sudser as "a new concept in daytime drama aimed at the growing army of divorced women who were trying to adjust to the single life after their marriages had broken up."

Describing the serial's initial storyline, Lin Bolen, then Vice President of Daytime Programming for NBC, said, "The heroine of the story, Chris Kirby, is a 32-year-old woman who has separated from her husband, Larry, after 12 years of marriage. She finds herself faced with the challenge of making a new life for herself, and she must cope with situations she has never before faced—job hunting, apartment hunting, and serving as mother and father to her young daughter. Both husband and wife must adjust to their new lifestyles as they try to learn to live apart from one another.... They must learn to date again in a new singles society from the one they knew 12 years ago."

The special 90-minute premiere episode explored such titillating subjects as promiscuity, impotence, female masochism, and how children are affected by divorce. It also contained the first nude scene ever on a daytime soap (the couple was shown in bed and were supposedly naked under the covers). Instead of hooking divorced women, the show's adult themes—and late afternoon time slot—attracted large numbers of teenagers who were arriving home from school at the same time the series aired.

While Chris was busy coping with the aftermath of divorce, her best friend, Fran Bachman, was adjusting to life as a widow. Fran's husband, Dave, died from a sudden heart attack after declaring bankruptcy. Fran's anguish over her husband's unexpected death inspired more than a thousand viewers to write sending their support and sympathy.

A year after Chris and Larry's divorce, a new team of writers decided to have the couple remarry. This time around, Larry's infidelity was no longer the issue. Instead, it was Chris's growing alcoholism.

Rosemary Prinz, who was best known for her role as Penny Hughes on *As the World Turns*, played hip psychologist Dr. Julie Franklin. She quit after six months. Film actors Brad Davis,

Armand Assante, and F. Murray Abraham also appeared as featured performers.

A switch to an earlier time slot proved to be the final blow for the faltering series, which had weathered multiple cast changes during its 14-month run. It was replaced by an expanded, 60-minute version of *Days of Our Lives*.

Chris (Jennifer Harmon) and Larry Kirby (Michael Landrum) divorced, which left their daughter, Lori (Suzanne Davidson), confused and unhappy.

Top: *Ken Kercheval would later go on to fame as Cliff Barnes in* Dallas. *In* How to Survive a Marriage, *he took over the role of Larry Kirby from Michael Landrum.*

Bottom: *Rosemary Prinz played hip psychologist Dr. Julie Franklin.*

THE CAST

Cast

JOSHUA BROWNE	F. MURRAY ABRAHAM
JOHNNY McGHEE	ARMAND ASSANTE
TERRY COURTLAND	PETER BRANDON
FRAN BACHMAN	FRAN BRILL
ROBERT MONDAY	GENE BUA
MONICA COURTLAND	JOAN COPELAND
ALEXANDER KRONOS	BRAD DAVIS
SUSAN PRITCHETT	VELEKA GRAY
LORI KIRBY	CATHY GREENE
	SUZANNE DAVIDSON
CHRIS KIRBY	JENNIFER HARMON
PETER WILLIS	BERKELEY HARRIS
	STEVE ELMORE
LARRY KIRBY	MICHAEL HAWKINS
	KEN KERCHEVAL
	MICHAEL LANDRUM
RACHEL BACHMAN	ELISSA LEEDS
SANDRA HENDERSON	LYNN LOWRY
DAVID BACHMAN	ALLAN MILLER
JOAN WILLIS	TRICIA O'NEIL
MOE BACHMAN	ALBERT OTTENHEIMER
JULIE FRANKLIN	ROSEMARY PRINZ
MAX COOPER	JAMES SHANNON
CHARLES MAYNARD	PAUL VINCENT
TONY DeANGELO	GEORGE WELBES
MARIA McGHEE	LAUREN WHITE

163

KNOTS LANDING

. . . .

DECEMBER 27, 1979–PRESENT CBS

This long-running prime-time serial was first pitched to CBS by creator David Jacobs in the summer of 1977. He envisioned a one-hour weekly drama about four families living in a middle-class Southern California community. Network executives liked the idea, but asked if Jacobs could broaden its scope—make it more ambitious. "They thought since there was nothing like it on TV, they wanted to start off with something bigger and promotable, a little more of a saga," Jacobs told a reporter in 1990. "As soon as they said saga I thought of Texas." At a follow-up meeting, Jacobs pitched *Dallas*, which premiered on the network one season later.

After *Dallas* took off, becoming television's number one hit, a CBS executive retrieved Jacobs's proposal for *Knots Landing*. He asked Jacobs to develop it as a spin-off of *Dallas*. Jacobs took two characters from the popular series, Gary and Val Ewing, and moved them to Knots Landing.

Knots Landing premiered during the Christmas holiday season of 1979 without much fanfare. In *Knots Landing: The Saga of Seaview Circle*, Jacobs wrote, "*Knots Landing* had trouble making ends meet for awhile. Though never a failure, it wasn't a success, either; it just hung in, with no identity of its own, either ignored in the press or seen as *Dallas's* tagalong little brother who could never live up. Still, it did what it had to do to get along; it was a survivor."

By 1990, *Knots Landing* was television's most popular prime-time serial. Besides outlasting *Dynasty* and *Falcon Crest*, it finally succeeded in surpassing "big brother" *Dallas* in the ratings. "I always thought *Knots Landing* had the potential to last longer than *Dallas* and even more so than *Dynasty*," said Jacobs. "Those two shows were very much connected with the era of the eighties —the Reagan era. *Knots Landing* is the kind of show that is downscaled."

"We keep the show as middle-class as possible," explained co-executive producer Lawrence Kasha. "They are not rarefied people or spoiled rich people. They share all of the problems that everyone can identify with—marriage, relationships, raising kids. Our rule is whatever happens in life could happen on *Knots Landing*."

"Our characters have histories and back stories," said Michele Lee, who plays Karen Fairgate MacKenzie. "There is also a sense of future. They are three dimensional and are honest and decent."

Jacobs believes some of the rare times the serial strayed from its down-to-earth roots was when Larry Hagman (J.R. Ewing on *Dallas*) made guest appearances. "There's no better actor on television than Larry Hagman, yet when he'd come to visit Knots Landing every once in awhile, we'd invariably find ourselves with an episode that didn't work. The scale was all wrong. J.R. is bigger-than-life, as in *Dallas* (the show and the city); he's a Them who too easily overpowers the Us gang on *Knots Landing*."

Gary (Ted Schackelford) and Valene Ewing (Joan Van Ark) left Dallas to get away from his wealthy family. They moved to Knots Landing in middle-class Southern California.

The cast of Knots Landing: *(back row, left to right) Michele Lee, Constance McCashin, John Pleshette, Donna Mills, (middle) Kim Landford, James Houghton, Julie Harris, Ted Schackelford, Joan Van Ark, and (front) Claudia Lonow.*

When Michele Lee was offered her role on the serial in 1979, she almost turned it down. Lee was interested in appearing regularly on a television series, but something more along the lines of situation comedy. Reading *Knots Landing's* pilot script, Lee found herself perplexed. One scene involved a fierce battle between Karen's husband, Sid Fairgate, and his rebellious daughter from an earlier marriage, 18-year-old Annie, who was sleeping with a married neighbor down the street. After reading the script, Lee thought to herself, "This is not Mary Tyler Moore." At a friend's urging, Lee tuned into *Dallas* and got a clearer idea of what the producers were trying to accomplish. She decided *Knots Landing* "was sort of like a modern day *Peyton Place.*"

At the close of *Knots Landing's* second season, Lee received startling news from David Jacobs, who was then executive producer. He told her Don Murray had decided to leave the series. Lee's immediate response was, "Omigod, what's going to happen to the show?" Lee recalled that Jacobs

THE CAST

Original Cast

ANNIE FAIRGATE . . . . KAREN ALLEN
VALENE EWING . . . . JOAN VAN ARK
JASON AVERY . . . . JUSTIN DANA
KENNY WARD . . . . JAMES HOUGHTON
GINGER WARD . . . . KIM LANDFORD
KAREN FAIRGATE . . . . MICHELE LEE
DIANA FAIRGATE . . . . CLAUDIA LONOW
LAURA AVERY . . . . CONSTANCE McCASHIN
SID FAIRGATE . . . . DON MURRAY
MICHAEL FAIRGATE . . . . PAT PETERSON
RICHARD AVERY . . . . JOHN PLESHETTE
GARY EWING . . . . TED SCHACKELFORD
ERIC FAIRGATE . . . . STEVE SHAW

KNOTS LANDING

DECEMBER 27, 1979–PRESENT CBS

was taken aback by her response. "He thought I'd be thrilled that Karen would now have a stronger role in the series. But I've always seen *Knots Landing* as a lot of intricate pieces. Some are larger than others, but they're all pieces of a puzzle that is well-constructed. I viewed Don's departure with incredible trepidation."

Knots Landing's third season opened with Sid's death. Lee was disheartened to discover her instincts were on the money; the show's ratings quickly dropped.

"The audience was upset," explained Lee. "They let the network know they were not pleased that the producers had broken up Mr. and Mrs. Everyday-Middle-America's marriage. Don's character exemplified what a man should be in a marriage and the women were not happy that he was off the series."

To Lee's relief, the producers gave her character an appropriate period to grieve Sid's death. "They purposely had a period of mourning so the audience could come down from the disaster," said Lee. "As an actress, I had fun that year. Karen was put through the process of finding herself."

By the beginning of the fourth season, it was decided Karen should fall in love again. "When the decision was made to involve Karen with another man my first concern was, how am I ever going to find an actor I can have the same kind of camaraderie I shared with Don?" said Lee. "What if I hate him? Even worse, what if the audience hates him? This person was going to have some big shoes to fill."

Lee was relieved to learn the producers had selected an actor worthy of facing the challenge, Kevin Dobson. He was introduced as police detective Mack Mackenzie, who was investigating Sid's mysterious death in an automobile accident. "Kevin is different in his portrayal of Mack than Don was as Sid," observed Lee. "The producers, rightfully so, didn't want him to play the same kind of character. By the time Karen and Mack were married, the audience had fully accepted their relationship. When the producers toyed with the idea of Mack having an extra-marital affair a few seasons ago, thousands wrote letters voicing their disapproval. As someone who also watches *Knots Landing* faithfully every Thursday night, I understood. If Mack ever slept around, I'd kill him," she teased.

Knots Landing's first season opened with the alcoholic black sheep of the Ewing family, Gary, and his naive, trusting wife, Valene, escaping the pressure of Dallas and his formidable family by moving to Southern California. Describing her character, Joan Van Ark said, "She's close to the bone, simple and direct. There's goodness in Valene." Meanwhile, Valene and Gary's daughter, Lucy, remained in Dallas.

The newly transplanted Ewings immediately began interacting with their neighbors who lived on the same cul-de-sac in the peaceful small community of Knots Landing. Gary even

Karen (Michele Lee) and Sid Fairgate (Don Murray) had a happy marriage, but Sid died after a mysterious accident.

Karen found happiness again when she met and later married Mack MacKenzie (Kevin Dobson).

managed to find work with neighbor Sid Fairgate, who owned Knots Landing Motors, a local classic car dealership. Sid and Karen had three teenage children: Diana, Eric, and Michael. In the first episode, Sid's 18-year-old daughter, Annie, was visiting the Fairgates.

Two other couples who figured prominently in the series were Kenny and Ginger Ward and Laura and Richard Avery. Kenny was a young record executive and Ginger was a kindergarten teacher. Richard had a roving eye and was an unfocused, unscrupulous lawyer. He envied his wife's success as a real estate broker. Laura and Richard had a young son, Jason.

During the serial's second season, Sid's divorced sister, Abby Cunningham (played by Donna Mills), moved into the cul-de-sac with her two children, Olivia (played by Tonya Crowe) and Brian (originally played by Bobby Jacoby). Abby made a quick enemy of Laura Avery by making no secret of her interest in Richard.

Soon after moving into Knots Landing, a sober Gary attended Alcoholics Anonymous meetings. A new member, Earl Trent (played by Paul Rudd), was impressed by Gary's recovery and asked Gary to be his sponsor in the program. Gary ultimately betrayed Earl's trust by having a brief affair with Earl's passionate wife, Judy.

KNOTS LANDING

DECEMBER 27, 1979–PRESENT CBS

The third season opened with Sid being paralyzed in a car accident. He later died from his injuries. A widowed Karen took over the family business. Val tapped into her creative energies and wrote a thinly veiled novel about the Ewings, titled *Capricorn Crude*. Her mother, Liliemae Clements (played by Julie Harris), arrived and moved in with Val and Gary. Val's novel was published and became an instant best-seller. Unfortunately, Val wasn't able to fully enjoy her success because Abby had managed to steal Gary away from her. Abby's primary interest in Gary was the recent fortune he inherited from his late father, Jock Ewing. A hurt Val divorced Gary, freeing him to marry Abby.

Soon after, Val began dating reporter Ben Gibson (played by Douglas Sheehan). Val's press agent, Chip Roberts (played by Michael Sabatino), had an affair with Karen's daughter, Diana, while also sleeping with singer Ciji Dunne (played by Lisa Hartman). When Ciji informed Chip she was pregnant, he panicked and killed her. Circumstantial evidence, however, resulted in Gary being arrested for the crime. Blinded by love, Diana fled Knots Landing with Chip, but later returned and moved in with Abby. A short while later, Chip was arrested, and Gary was released. Not long after, Chip escaped from prison and manipulated Diana into resuming their relationship. He died in a freak accident at Gary's ranch where he was hiding out with Diana. Following his death, Diana left town.

By this time, Richard Avery's marriage to Laura and his career had completely unraveled. Laura considered leaving Richard, but postponed taking action because of her pregnancy and his nervous breakdown. Richard talked Gary and Abby into financing a restaurant, Daniel's, but it failed. Upset by Richard's relationship with Abby, Laura finally divorced him. Devastated by the divorce, Richard left town.

Abby, meanwhile, was busy building a power base. Sid's death left her part owner of Knots Landing Motors, while her marriage to Gary made her a partner in Gary Ewing Enterprises. Abby was also heavily involved in the Lotus Point real estate development. Behind Gary's back, she began sleeping with the charismatic, wealthy State Senator Gregory Sumner (played by William Devane), who was tied to an organized crime ring. Sumner was an old friend of Mack Mackenzie,

who had married Karen Fairgate. Believing Mack's loyalty to an old friend would overrule his honesty, Greg offered him a position as crime commissioner. Greg realized Mack valued integrity over loyalty to a corrupt friend. This seriously threatened Greg's schemes, so he attempted to discredit Mack. Kenny and Ginger left Knots Landing to start their lives over in a new town.

The fifth season presented major dilemmas for three of *Knots Landing's* female characters. Karen was shot, but the bullet was intended for Gary. Karen found herself paralyzed for a brief period. Abby was held hostage by mobster St. Clare, who was eventually killed by Greg. Val gave birth to twins (the result of an emotional one-night encounter with Gary). In a complicated storyline, Val's babies were stolen from the hospital and sold to a black market baby operation. It took an entire season for Val to reclaim them.

Gary (left) was fascinated with Ciji Dunne (Lisa Hartman) and was accused of killing her. Kenny (James Houghton, right) was a record producer who was trying to help her with her career before she died. Kenny and his wife, Ginger, left Knots Landing soon after Ciji's death.

Val's brother, Joshua Rush (Alec Baldwin), was a TV evangelist in love with Cathy Geary (a Ciji look-alike, played by Lisa Hartman).

To Greg's dismay, Mack headed an investigation to expose Paul Galveston's illegal business practices. Greg also tried to ace Gary out of the Empire Valley development project. Greg's mother, Ruth Galveston (played by film star Ava Gardner), also figured in the storyline. When Paul suffered a fatal heart attack, Ruth left town. On a brighter note, Greg fell in love with Laura and married her.

The sixth season opened with the arrival of Val's preacher half-brother, Joshua Rush (played by Alec Baldwin). Seduced by the lure of fast money, Joshua gave up being a preacher in favor of becoming a television personality. He fell in love with on-camera talent Cathy Geary (a Ciji Dunne look-a-like, also played by Lisa Hartman), and proposed to her on the air. When it became apparent to Joshua that Cathy's show-biz career was moving faster than his, he suffered a nervous breakdown and committed suicide.

Abby's confused daughter, Olivia, became heavily addicted to drugs. Val married Ben, but their marriage was soon threatened by flirtatious Cathy, who was interested in Ben. Abby became sexually involved with Peter Hollister (played by Hunt Block), who claimed to be Greg's brother.

The seventh season featured a political race for the Senate between Gary Ewing and Peter Hollister. Gary lost the race—and also his wife—to the young Hollister. A small-time thug bent on revenge against Mack kidnapped Karen. To Mack's surprise, he had a sexy teenage daughter, Paige (played by Nicollette Sheridan)—the result of a love relationship with the wealthy Ann Matheson (played by Michelle Phillips). A restless Paige slept with Karen's son, Michael, and then moved on to Peter Hollister.

Abby worked overtime to help Olivia kick her drug dependency and even enlisted ex-husband Gary's help. The season ended with Peter's death. Realizing Olivia had an unrequited crush on Peter, Abby feared she killed him. In a misguided effort to protect her daughter, Abby attempted to dispose of Peter's body.

An investigation into Peter's death opened the serial's eighth season. To cover for Olivia, Abby confessed to the murder. Later, it was determined Paige was accidentally responsible for Peter's death. Abby rekindled a romance with her first serious love, millionaire Charles Scott (played by Michael York). To Abby's disappointment, she discovered Charles was only pursuing her because of his interest in the expansion of the Lotus Point Marina. Trying to influence Abby to back the expansion, a divorced Charles presented her with an engagement gift for two million dollars. He promised the amount would cover the debts she'd incur if she agreed to the expansion. Abby accepted the gift and quickly married Charles. The day after their wedding, Abby had the marriage annulled. Her attorney threatened to slap Charles with a lawsuit for fraud if he didn't agree to the annulment. Charles reluctantly signed the papers and a vindictive Abby succeeded in adding an additional three million to her savings account.

Following Charles's departure from Knots Landing, mobster Manny Vasquez muscled in to see the expansion move forward. Accompanying Manny was his thug nephew, Harold (played by Paul Carafotes). To Abby's consternation, Olivia fell in love with Harold. Gary focused his romantic interest on the late Peter's sister, Jill Bennett (played by Teri Austin), a former lover and work associate of Mack's. Val's husband, Ben, mysteriously disappeared in South America and was believed dead. Shortly after giving birth to a daughter, Meg, Laura developed a brain tumor and died. Overwhelmed by Laura's death, Greg turned Meg over to Mack and Karen to raise as their own.

Moving into Laura's former house on the cul-de-sac were Patricia and Frank Williams and

KNOTS LANDING
. . . .

DECEMBER 27, 1979–PRESENT CBS

"It may surprise viewers who see Abby as an immoral schemer, but I like her. Her main purpose on the show, of course, was to stir up trouble," wrote Donna Mills in *TV Guide.*

Chicago born Donna Mills arrived in New York and soon landed work on various prime-time television shows. A seven-month run on daytime's *The Secret Storm* led to her role as former nun Laura Donnelly on *Love Is a Many Splendored Thing.*

In 1970, she left the series to try her luck in Hollywood. She soon landed guest-star roles on such popular shows as *Gunsmoke, Police Story,* and *SWAT.* She also co-starred with *Dallas's* Larry Hagman in a short-lived situation-comedy titled, *The Good Life.* One of her most famous roles was in the classic Clint Eastwood film, *Play Misty for Me.*

Mills joined *Knots Landing* in 1981 and quickly became a viewer favorite. After nine seasons, she decided to leave the series and pursue other projects. "I'm looking forward to the new projects I have lined up and to having a personal life again," she wrote in *TV Guide.* "*Knots Landing* was never one of those shows that was cranked out with assembly-line efficiency. I look back on it and think, 'Did I really get up all the time at five o'clock in the morning? Did I really work 16-hour days?'... For so long, I have known exactly what I would be doing. But part of the excitement lies in the unknown. I need some uncertainty in my life. It causes creativity."

their adolescent daughter, Julie. The entire family was struggling to begin new lives given to them by the federal Witness Protection Program. Paige's former boyfriend, Johnny Rourke (played by Peter Reckell), surfaced in Knots Landing. She resumed a casual affair with Johnny, but quickly ended it when she realized she was in love with Greg. Meanwhile, Johnny found work as a courier for mobster Manny. A trip to Mexico nearly cost Paige, Johnny, and Michael their lives when Manny had them held hostage in an attempt to keep Karen, Mack, and Gary from going to the police about his illegal drug activities.

Jill became jealous of Gary's interest in Val. When Val finally acknowledged Gary was the father of her twins, Jill initiated a devious scheme designed to cost Val her life. First, Jill sent forged letters to Val from Ben. Next she tinkered with Val's answering machine and made it look like Ben had left her an urgent message. Val's friends doubted the message, but were reluctant to discourage a fragile Val's hopes. Pretending to be Val, Jill purchased a prescription of sleeping pills. While on a business conference in San Fransisco, Jill bought a gun. Making it look as if she was still in San Fransisco, Jill returned to Knots Landing, broke into Val's home, and forced her to swallow the sleeping pills. Before leaving, Jill penned a fake suicide note.

The ninth season opened with Val recovering from her force-fed pill overdose. Unfortunately, very few people believed her story that Jill tried to kill her. When evidence of Jill's guilt began to accumulate, a deranged Jill devised a scheme to destroy Gary by making it look like he killed her. Initially Gary was arrested for her murder, but was later cleared when police determined Jill had committed suicide.

Below: *Abby (Donna Mills) wreaked havoc in Knots Landing. Her schemes spread as far as Japan, where she eventually moved.*

Opposite page: *Greg Sumner (William Devane) looked like he was going to reform when he fell in love with Laura Avery (Constance McCashin). Sadly, she died of a brain tumor after giving birth to their daughter, Meg.*

KNOTS LANDING

DECEMBER 27, 1979–PRESENT CBS

Traveling to Mexico, Mack managed to rescue Paige, Johnny, and Michael. A gun battle left Manny dead. Abby's efforts to discourage Olivia's romantic interest in Harold backfired when Olivia married him. Abby cut Olivia off financially because of the marriage. Mack quit his government job to go into private practice. A case of middle-aged blues led him to fantasize about a sexual relationship with forest ranger Paula Vertosick. When a series of circumstances left them alone in a motel room one night, Mack and Paula agreed a fling between them would never work.

Johnny left town after stealing a valuable computer program Michael had intended to sell to Greg. Once it became clear that Michael had developed the program, Greg offered him a position at Sumner Group. Greg's affair with Paige was discouraged by public relations consultant Ted Melcher (played by Robert Desiderio). Greg hired Melcher because he was anxious to again enter the political arena. With Melcher's encouragement, Greg abruptly ended his relationship with Paige and married Abby. Discovering evidence of oil on the Lotus Point land, Abby enlisted the aid of adviser Rick Hawkins and quietly purchased the property under a fake name, Murakame. Later, Abby was forced to hire a Japanese actor to pose as Murakame. The actor surprised Abby by blackmailing her. In the interim, Abby had started sleeping with Ted Melcher. When the actor and Rick Hawkins threatened to expose the truth about Murakame, Melcher killed them. When Abby's permit to drill for oil was denied, she accepted a position as Trade Representative to Japan. It was the same position Greg hoped to snare. Discovering Abby's affair with Melcher, Greg ended their marriage and put aside his plans to run for political office. In the season cliff-hanger, Abby left for Japan with her son, Brian.

The Knots Landing *men: (left to right) Doug Sheehan, Kevin Dobson, Ted Schackelford, William Devane, and Hunt Block.*

The Knots Landing *women: (top, left to right) Lisa Hartman, Julie Harris, Constance McCashin, Teri Austin, (bottom) Michele Lee, Joan Van Ark, and Donna Mills.*

The tenth season opened with Melcher successfully managing to leave town, after blackmailing Greg with documents incriminating him in the Murakame scheme. Paige decided not to resume her affair with Greg, and instead had an affair with crooked police detective Tom Ryan (played by Joey Gian). Paige's mother, Anne, now broke, returned to Knots Landing and secretly began stealing money from Paige. Displeased by Paige's relationship with Tom, Greg initiated an investigation into Tom's background. On Paige's wedding day to Tom, Greg confronted Tom with evidence documenting his illegal past. Greg threatened to expose Tom if he didn't leave town. Paige was left at the altar.

Gary fell in love with Amanda (played by Penny Peyser), a woman he met when he accidentally dialed her phone number. By an odd coincidence, Val became involved with Amanda's estranged husband, Danny Waleska (played by Sam Behrens). Unknown to Val, Danny was still married to Amanda. Jealous of Gary's interest in

Amanda, Danny retaliated by raping Amanda. Unfortunately, Amanda showered, destroying all evidence of the rape, making it impossible for her to successfully press charges. To Gary's dismay, Amanda decided to leave Knots Landing.

After a whirlwind romance, Val accepted Danny's marriage proposal. Their honeymoon, however, was short-lived. Although Val originally didn't believe Amanda's rape accusation against Danny, evidence began mounting. When Val finally realized the truth, she took the twins and sought protective shelter at Gary's ranch. Angered by Val's desertion, Danny changed all the locks on her house. One evening while driving home drunk, Danny accidentally ran into Pat Williams. Pat died in the hospital, and Danny was charged with homicide.

As the season ended, Karen accepted a position as host of a popular TV-talk show. Soon after, she began receiving threats from an obsessed fan. The fan turned out to be her own associate producer, Jeff Cameron (played by Chris Lemmon).

LOVE IS A MANY SPLENDORED THING

SEPTEMBER 18, 1967–MARCH 23, 1973 CBS

rna Phillips developed this half-hour serial, loosely based on the feature film of the same name starring William Holden and Jennifer Jones. Like the movie, it was to explore the interracial romance between an American white male and an Eurasian female. A second story involved a novitiate nun falling in love with her sister's boyfriend. Shortly after the series premiered, letters from viewers trickled into CBS voicing dissatisfaction over the storylines. Getting cold feet, network executives ordered Phillips to write Mia, the Eurasian character, off the show and have Laura, the nun, abandon her habit. An angered Phillips quit.

Jane and Ira Avery, the show's new writers, decided to emphasize the love triangle between two sisters, Iris and Laura Donnelly, and Mark Elliott. Soon after, David Birney replaced Sam Wade as Mark and the ratings took off. The success the young characters had in drawing new viewers to the series inspired network executives to rethink their ideas about what the audience wanted to see in daytime soaps. Unfortunately, the show's success quickly dwindled when Leslie Charleson, Donna Mills, and David Birney left, reportedly because of contract disputes.

In an effort to strengthen the show's appeal, two new families were introduced to play off the Donnellys. Iris found herself attracted to Spence Garrison, a politician who was enmeshed in an unhappy marriage to an overly-possessive wife, Nancy. Spence's mother, Margaret, was reeling from the loss of her wealthy husband, Chandler Garrison. He had been stolen away by a manipulative, scheming, younger woman—Jean. By this time, Mark was married to Laura. Their marriage, however, nearly ended when Mark had an affair with Jean.

Iris and Laura's widowed father, Will Donnelly, a pathologist, married Lily Chernak, who had two adult children. Her son, Pete, was a brilliant neurosurgeon who restored Iris's sight after she was blinded in an accident. Paul Michael Glaser, best known for starring in *Starsky &*

Hutch, originated the role. Betsy, Pete's sister, was also a doctor. She considered pursuing a relationship with a married doctor, but was also attracted to a paraplegic patient. When activist Joe Taylor entered Betsy's life, it became clear he was the man she wanted to spend the rest of her life with. At first the couple lived together, but in the final episode they were married in a traditional ceremony.

Multiple cast changes, a refocusing on storylines involving political intrigue, and a switch to a less desirable time slot led to the serial's cancellation. Despite appeals from thousands of disappointed fans, CBS stood by its decision and replaced *Love Is a Many Splendored Thing* with a game show. Its final episode aired March 23, 1973.

Below: *Sisters Iris (Bibi Besch, left) and Laura Donnelly (Veleka Gray) fought over Mark Elliott. In fact, Laura left the convent to marry him.*

Opposite page, top: *Beverlee McKinsey played Martha Donnelly and Berkeley Harris played Jim Whitman.*

Opposite page, bottom: *Will Donnelly (Judson Laire) married Lily Chernak (Diana Douglas). A year later, the show went off the air.*

THE CAST

Cast

PETE CHERNAK	VINCE BAGGETTA
	MICHAEL ZASLOW
	(PAUL) MICHAEL GLASER
IRIS DONNELLY GARRISON	BIBI BESCH
	LESLIE CHARLESON
NANCY GARRISON	SUSAN BROWNING
MARGARET GARRISON	FLORA CAMPBELL
RICKY DONNELLY	SHAWN CAMPBELL
WALTER TRAVIS	JOHN CARPENTER
LILY CHERNAK DONNELLY	DIANA DOUGLAS
MARK ELLIOTT	TOM FUCCELLO
	VINCENT CANNON
	MICHAEL HAWKINS
	DAVID BIRNEY
	SAM WADE
ALFRED PRESTON	DON GANTRY
STEVE HURLEY	MARK GORDON
	PAUL STEVENS
SIMON VENTNOR	DAVID GROH
JIM ABBOTT	RON HALE
	ROBERT MILLI
SPENCE GARRISON	BRETT HALSEY
	ED POWER
	MICHAEL HANRAHAN
JIM WHITMAN	BERKELEY HARRIS
HELEN ELLIOTT DONNELLY	GLORIA HOYE
	GRACE ALBERTSON
MIA ELLIOTT	NANCY HUSEH
SANFORD HILLER	STEPHEN JOYCE
CELIA WINTERS	ABIGAIL KELLOGG
WILL DONNELLY	JUDSON LAIRE
NIKKI CABOT	JODY LOCKER
JEAN GARRISON	JANE MANNING
BETSY CHERNAK TAYLOR	ANDREA MARCOVICCI
MARTHA DONNELLY/JULIE RICHARDS	BEVERLEE McKINSEY
CHANDLER GARRISON	WILLIAM POST, JR.
	MARTIN WOLFSON
PAUL BRADLEY	NICHOLAS PRYOR
JOE TAYLOR	LEON RUSSOM
LAURA DONNELLY ELLIOTT	BARBARA STANGER
	VELEKA GRAY
	DONNA MILLS
ANGEL ALLISON CHERNAK	SUSAN KAYE STONE
TOM DONNELLY	ALBERT STRATTON
	ROBERT BURR
ANDY HURLEY	RUSS THACKER
	DON SCARDINO
MARIAN HILLER	CONSTANCE TOWERS
PHILLIP ELLIOTT	LEN WAYLAND

LOVE OF LIFE

SEPTEMBER 24, 1951–FEBRUARY 1, 1980 CBS

This serial has the distinction of being the second longest-running serial ever to be canceled. It's also the only serial to be presented for several years in a 25-minute format (the remaining five minutes went to a CBS newscast). Created by Roy Winsor (who also helped create *Search for Tomorrow* and *The Secret Storm*), *Love of Life* premiered on September 24, 1951, as a daily 15-minute serial. In 1958, it was the first 15-minute serial to expand to a half hour. Originally owned by American Home Products, the serial was sold to CBS in 1969. From the very first episode until its last one on February 1, 1980, Larry Auerbach served as principal director.

Roy Winsor's serial began with the story of two siblings, good-hearted Vanessa Dale and her selfish, neurotic sister, Meg. Winsor's characters were written in very broad strokes, inspiring critics to accuse them of being one dimensional and flat. Hildy Parks, who played Ellie, Vanessa's roommate, marveled at Peggy McCay's ability to pull the character off. "Peggy was a dedicated actress," she said. "I don't know how she put up with all that nobility, but she did. She made Van less obviously long-suffering than the way the story was written."

Love of Life's history can be divided into three specific periods. The first period carried the serial through the fifties. Immediately following graduation from high school in the small farm town of Barrowsville, New York, Van enrolled in art school. To parents Will and Sarah Dale's dismay, Meg announced she had no intention of continuing her education. Instead, she wanted to set her sights on finding a rich man to marry. In no time at all, wealthy businessman Charles Harper proposed marriage. It was his misfortune that Meg accepted.

Shortly after Meg married Charles, she gave birth to a baby boy, Ben (nicknamed "Beanie"). Bored with life in Barrowsville, Meg nagged Charles to find a home for them in New York. Van, now in her early twenties, was appalled by Meg's neglect of young Beanie. Feeling sympathy for Charles, Van lent an ear to his complaints about Meg's selfish behavior. Will and Sarah tried to impress upon Meg the negative effect she was having on those who loved her, but she wasn't interested.

Tragedy struck the Dale family when Will died unexpectedly. Complicating matters was Sarah's lingering illness. Van divided her time between visiting her mother in Barrowsville and attending to young Beanie in New York. Van even managed to find an apartment in New York, which she shared with Ellie Hughes. To support herself, Van found a job working as an artist for an advertising agency that produced television shows.

Meg got involved with an underworld figure, Miles Pardee (played by Joe Allen, Jr.). Unknown to Meg, Miles used his huge Long Island estate as a front for a smuggling operation. One night while Meg was visiting, a nervous Miles was waiting for the latest shipment of contraband. To pass the time, Meg drank too much alcohol. Before the evening ended, Miles was dead. A drunken Meg was arrested for his murder.

Van cleared her sister's name with the help of lawyer-turned-FBI-agent Paul Raven (played by Richard Coogan). Miles's real killer turned out to be a vengeful member of his illegal smuggling operation. Tired of Meg's shenanigans, Charles divorced her and moved to Europe. Meanwhile, Van discovered she was falling in love with Paul. Not long after, they married and moved back to Barrowsville.

Below: *Tess Prentiss's (Toni Bull Bua) husband was treated by Dr. Joe Corelli (Tony LoBianco) for a rare blood disease. Dr. Corelli fell in love with Tess, but she couldn't get over the death of her husband.*

Opposite page: *Marsha Mason played Judith Cole in 1972.*

To Van's sadness, she discovered she was unable to have children. Instead, the couple adopted Carol (played by Tirell Barbery), a six-year-old deaf mute. Soon after the adoption, a strange woman secretly began spying on Carol and her adoptive parents. To Paul's surprise, it was his ex-wife, Judith Lodge (played by Virginia Robinson). She wasn't pleased that Paul had married Van. In fact, Judith did everything in her power to break up the couple. Paul's untrustworthy brother, Ben (played by David Lewis), also worked overtime to undermine their relationship.

One evening, Sarah's house burned down. After the firemen extinguished the flames, they discovered Judith's body. Van's fingerprints were found on the murder weapon—a cane—and she was accused of murder. Before Van was sentenced, the real killer was uncovered. It was Paul's brother, Ben, who held a grudge against Judith.

Shortly after Van's release, little Carol regained her speech and hearing. Paul's mother, Althea (played by Joanna Roos, who rejoined the cast several years later as Van's mother, Sarah), took the young girl to live with her. Some time later, Van would suffer an even greater loss when she received word that Paul was killed in a plane crash. Meg's move to Europe with young Beanie marked the end of the serial's first decade.

Following Paul's death, Van (now played by Bonnie Bartlett) accepted a job as a TV-talk show host in New York. She replaced Tammy Forrest (played longest by Ann Loring), who was fired by executive producer Noel Penn (originally played by Gene Peterson) because of her drinking problem. At first, Tammy resented Van. But as Van helped Tammy face her alcoholism, the two became good friends.

Widower Bruce Sterling (played by Ron Tomme) would become a significant figure in Van's life. He was a teacher at Winfield Academy, a boy's prep school located in Rosehill, New York. Bruce had two teenage children—Barbara (played longest by Lee Lawson) and Alan (played longest by Dennis Cooney), who were being raised by their wealthy maternal grandparents, Henry (played longest by Jack Stamberger) and Vivian Carlson (originally played by Helene Dumas). Neither of Bruce's children approved of Van's growing friendship with their father. Bruce's late wife, Gaye, was reportedly killed in a car accident, but there was lingering suspicion that she had committed suicide. Before long, Bruce's friendship with Van turned to love. Van quit the TV-talk show and relocated to Rosehill. Audrey Peters took over the role at this point and played Van until the show's end.

THE CAST

Original Cast

WILL DALE	EDWIN JEROME
MRS. RIVERS	MARIE KENNEY
MEG DALE HARPER	JEAN McBRIDE
VANESSA DALE	PEGGY McCAY
ELLIE HUGHES	HILDY PARKS
BEN "BEANIE" HARPER	DENNIS PARNELL
CHARLES HARPER	PAUL POTTER
SARAH DALE	JANE ROSE

LOVE OF LIFE

SEPTEMBER 24, 1951–FEBRUARY 1, 1980 CBS

Bruce and Van announced their plan to marry. Vivian felt Bruce's remarrying would be an affront to her daughter's memory. Vivian was so upset that she initiated a custody hearing against Bruce. It turned out to be an uphill battle for Vivian because her husband discovered he liked Van. Vivian grudgingly accepted Bruce's remarriage and dropped her custody suit.

Barbara had her own ax to grind with Van. She blamed Van's interference for stopping her elopement to handsome Dr. Tony Vento (played by Ron Jackson). Barbara met Tony when a car she was in with her casual boyfriend, Ken Shea (played by Roger Stevens), struck him. Barbara began dating Tony and fell in love with him. One night, a giddy Barbara confided her plans to elope with Tony to her new stepmother. Quicker than Barbara could pack her overnight bag, Van told Bruce. He immediately prevented Barbara from carrying out her plans.

Eventually, Barbara's broken heart healed and she turned her attention to the dashing Rick Latimer (originally played by Paul Savior). Rick had been married to Julie Murano (originally played by Jessica Walter), an alcoholic. Van sensed that Rick was too rebellious and tried to persuade Barbara not to marry him. Her advice fell on deaf ears. The marriage proved disastrous. The battling couple had a son, Hank (played longest by Justin Carlton Stambaugh), before ending their marriage. Barbara suffered a nervous breakdown as a result of the divorce. After recovering, she left Rosehill with Hank.

Van's marriage to Bruce also had problems, thanks to the manipulations of scheming Dr. Jennifer Stark (played by Joan Bassie). A few years earlier, Van and Bruce's marriage had been threatened by Bruce's brief fling with Ginny Crandall (played by Barbara Barrie). This second indiscretion left a hurt Van with one option: divorce. In a sense, the fate of Van and Bruce's faltering marriage was already sealed when Van's first husband, Paul—who was believed dead— resurfaced in Rosehill. Having suffered amnesia, Paul now identified himself as Matt Corby (played by Robert Burr). Extensive plastic surgery prevented Van from first recognizing her former husband, but as they had more and more frequent conversations, Paul's memory returned.

Van came close to remarrying Paul, but just before the ceremony she discovered he had

What two things do Warren Beatty and Christopher Reeve have in common? Both were considered for the role of Superman in the hit feature film of the same name. (Beatty turned the part down after looking at himself in a full-length mirror wearing nothing but long underwear. Feeling less self-conscious about his appearance in long underwear, Reeve gladly accepted the role that transformed him into a major film star.)

Okay, that's half the answer. The second thing Beatty and Reeve share is that they were both former cast members of *Love of Life*. Beatty appeared briefly in the late fifties. Reeve joined the cast in 1974 and appeared for two years as Ben Harper.

Other famous alumni include Martin Balsam, Bonnie Bedelia, Bert Convy, Ja'net DuBois, Julia Duffy, Peter Falk, John Fink, Paul Michael Glaser, Anne Jackson, Tony LoBianco, Marsha Mason, and Roy Scheider.

Warren Beatty had a role that lasted a few weeks on Love of Life. *He played the disapproving son of one of Van's suitors.*

Two ill-fated couples were Cal Aleata and David Hart (Deborah Courtney and Brian Farrell, top) and Ben Harper (Christopher Reeve) and Betsy Crawford (Elizabeth Kemp).

already remarried. His wife, Evelyn (played by Lee Kurty), was a shrew. They had a daughter, Stacy (originally played by Cindy Grover). Evelyn turned up dead and Paul was fingered as the killer. He died a short while later when he led a prison riot.

Bruce gave up his teaching job and became the publisher of a Rosehill newspaper, the *Herald*. As time passed, Van's hurt over Bruce's affair with Jennifer dissolved. The two began seeing each other romantically and decided they were destined to spend the rest of their lives together. They remarried in the early seventies and, despite many difficulties, stayed married until the show's end.

Love of Life entered its third and final era owned by CBS. Recognizing that soap audiences had changed since the early fifties, the network transformed *Love of Life* into a sexier, faster-paced serial. Meg (now played by Canadian actress Tudi Wiggins) moved back to Rosehill with her adult children, Ben (now played by Christopher Reeve)

and Caroline "Cal" Aleata (played by Deborah Courtney). For a brief period, viewers responded favorably to the new-and-improved *Love of Life*. CBS was pleased to see an increase in the long-running serial's ratings.

Unfortunately, *Love of Life's* second wind of popularity turned out to be short-lived. Many cast changes and several different teams of headwriters caused the serial to lose its focus. In 1979, the network switched the show to a late afternoon time slot. This move lost even more viewers.

Sadly, longtime viewers of the show weren't even treated to a final episode tying up loose storylines. Realizing that *The Edge of Night* had made a successful move from CBS to ABC in 1976, the serial's producers held out for the slim possibility that *Love of Life* would also be resurrected. The final credits rolled accompanied by a record of Tony Bennett singing, "We'll Be Together Again." To date, no one has expressed interest in reviving *Love of Life*.

LOVING

*A*gnes Nixon developed this half-hour serial, along with headwriter Douglas Marland, with an eye toward the college audience. It was her third series for ABC (she had also created *One Life to Live* and *All My Children*). Douglas Marland's credentials were also impressive. He started as an actor and appeared on such soaps as *The Brighter Day* and *As the World Turns*. His break as a writer came in the midseventies when Harding Lemay appointed him assistant headwriter for *Another World*. Two years later, he was headwriting *The Doctors*. But his stint as *General Hospital's* headwriter in 1978 put him on the map. Marland turned the struggling serial around and made it the most popular daytime soap on television by creating the Laura storyline. Before *Loving*, he was *The Guiding Light's* headwriter.

The show is set in the eastern seaboard town of Corinth. It originally focused on three families: the wealthy Aldens, the middle-class Vocheks, and the blue-collar Donovans. Cabot and Isabelle Alden have two adult children: Clay and Ann. In the serial's early days, Ann was the only one of their children featured. She and her husband, Roger Forbes, the newly appointed president of Alden University, had two children: Jack, a college sophomore, and Lorna, soon to be enrolled as a freshman at Alden University. Living with the Aldens was Clay's spoiled, self-centered son, Curtis. Viewers would later discover that Clay and his ex-wife, Gwyneth, had two other children, Rick and Trisha.

To Ann's dismay, Roger was involved in an extramarital affair with news anchor Merrill Vochek. Merrill's brother, Jim, was a priest. Their sister, Noreen, was married to Vietnam vet Mike Donovan, a police officer.

Retired police officer Patrick Donovan and Rose, his wife, had three children. Besides Mike, they were Douglas, a drama professor at Alden University, and the youngest, Stacey.

Stacey's love story with Jack Forbes has been popular with viewers since *Loving's* early days. When the serial premiered, Jack was in love with Lily Slater. Unknown to Jack, Lily had been sexually abused by her father, Garth. Lily coped with the abuse by developing a spilt personality. Not surprisingly, Garth opposed Lily's relationship with Jack. When Garth turned up dead, Jack was accused of killing him. It was later revealed that Lily's mother, June, had killed her husband to prevent him from attacking Lily again. Although Jack was now free to marry Lily, she and her mother decided to leave town.

Stacey had always been attracted to Jack, but kept her feelings secret. When Tony Perelli (played longest by Richard McMurray) moved to Corinth, Stacey became involved with him. Stacey even agreed to marry Tony. But then she discovered that Jack's sister, Lorna, was pregnant with Tony's child.

Cabot (Wesley Addy) and Elizabeth Alden (Augusta Dabney) are the wealthy parents of Clay and Ann.

Noreen (Marilyn McIntyre) and Mike Donovan (James Kiberd) were childhood sweethearts whose marriage was threatened by Mike's flashbacks of Vietnam.

After breaking off with Tony, Stacey became romantically involved with Jack. Meanwhile, Lorna surprised Tony with news that she had an abortion. Stacey and Jack's relationship came to an abrupt end when Jack discovered that Dane Hammon (played by Anthony Herrera), his grandfather's vengeful rival, was his natural father.

Confused and hurt, Jack was vulnerable to the social-climbing Ava Rescott's (played longest by Roya Megnot) manipulations. Ava tricked Jack into marrying her with news that she was pregnant. Shortly after the marriage, Ava miscarried. In a desperate move to keep Jack tied to her, Ava convinced her sister, Sherri (originally played by Susan Wands), to let her raise Sherri's newborn baby, Johnny, as her own. Believing Ava was only interested in him for his money, Jack resumed his relationship with Stacey and headed for California with little Johnny. Hurt by Jack's rejection, Ava became involved with his cousin, Curtis.

Eventually, Jack and Stacey returned to Corinth with little Johnny. Jack and Stacey finally married. Jack learned the truth about Johnny and was heartbroken when he had to give him up.

THE CAST

Original Cast

CABOT ALDEN	WESLEY ADDY
LILY SLATER	JENNIFER ASHE
RITA MAE BRISTOW	PAMELA BLAIR
DOUGLAS DONOVAN	BRYAN CRANSTON
GARTH SLATER	JOHN CUNNINGHAM
ISABELLE ALDEN	MEG MUNDY
JIM VOCHEK	PETER DAVIES
ANN ALDEN FORBES	SHANNON EUBANKS
MERRILL VOCHEK	PATRICIA KALEMBER
ROSE DONOVAN	TERI KEANE
PATRICK DONOVAN	NOAH KEEN
MIKE DONOVAN	JAMES KIBERD
BILLY BRISTOW	TOM LIGON
CLAY ALDEN	RANDOLPH MANTOOTH
CURTIS ALDEN	CHRISTOPHER MARCANTEL
NOREEN VOCHEK DONOVAN	MARILYN McINTYRE
ROGER FORBES	JOHN SHEARIN
JACK FORBES	PERRY STEPHENS
STACEY DONOVAN	LAUREN-MARIE TAYLOR
LORNA FORBES	SUSAN WALTERS
JUNE SLATER	ANN WILLIAMS

LOVING

JUNE 26, 1983–PRESENT ABC

Fortunately, he and Stacey were expecting a child of their own. Soon after their baby boy, J. J., was born, Lily returned to Corinth. Against his better judgement, Jack began sleeping with Lily. When Jack learned Stacey and J. J. were almost killed in a bank hold-up, he broke off his affair with Lily. The damage, however, had already been done and his marriage was soon over.

Stacey discovered the truth about Jack's affair and threw him out. Even worse, she found comfort in the arms of Jack's spiteful cousin, Rick (played by Brian Fitzpatrick). Recognizing that Stacey had a natural talent for writing, Rick encouraged her to pen a novel. Stacey became even closer to Rick when he rescued her son from drowning.

Shortly after Stacey invited Rick to move in with her and J. J., Stacey's steamy sex novel, a thinly veiled story about her relationship with both Jack and Rick, was published. A morally outraged Jack decided to seek custody of J. J. In order to keep her son, Stacey ended her relationship with Rick. To Jack's surprise, Rick was scheming behind Stacey's back to have her lose the custody battle. In an unexpected move, Jack informed the judge that he and Stacey were reconciling. Privately, Jack informed Stacey that while they were living together they could maintain separate bedrooms. Not long after, Stacey discovered she was pregnant with Rick's child.

Stacey was horrified when J. J. disappeared one evening. Fortunately, Rick found the boy and returned him to Stacey. That same night, Rick bragged to friends that he and Stacey were making plans to marry. Later, Rick drugged an unknowing Stacey and persuaded her to go through with a marriage ceremony. Realizing that Rick had drugged her, Stacey quickly broke off their relationship. She was very angry that Rick may have endangered their unborn child's life. Soon after, Stacey gave birth to a healthy baby girl. Jack and Stacey were taking steps to resuming their relationship.

Below: *Shana (Susan Keith) is Cabot Alden's illegitimate daughter, so Dane Hammond (Anthony Herrera) brought her to Corinth hoping to wreak some havoc.*

Opposite page: *Ann Alden Forbes's (Shannon Eubanks) family founded Alden University, where her husband, Roger (John Shearin), is the president.*

183

MARY HARTMAN, MARY HARTMAN

1976–1978 SYNDICATED

Shortly after this satirical soap premiered in 1976, the general manager of a Boston television station phoned producer Norman Lear's office in Hollywood and announced, "I've got 75 people marching on my station this afternoon to protest *Mary Hartman...* I love it!" In Nashville, Tennessee, convicts in the state penitentiary banged cups on their prison cell bars every afternoon to warn guards they wanted the recreation hall television set tuned to *Mary Hartman* when their break came. *The Village Voice* enthusiastically called *Mary Hartman* "the most disconcertingly funny show ever on TV."

Overwhelmed by the response his new series generated, a delighted Norman Lear said, "In no way could I guess the kind of reception *Mary Hartman* would receive." Considering Norman Lear was forced to pitch his serial directly to local television stations after all three networks turned it down, it's easy to understand his surprise.

Aside from her Pollyanna housedress and braided pigtails, Mary Hartman was an ordinary housewife living in fictional Fernwood, Ohio. While she spent her days fretting over her kitchen floor's waxy yellow build-up, her husband, Tom, worked on the assembly line at the town factory. Their 12-year-old daughter, Heather, was constantly plotting to run away from home. Mary's parents, George and Martha Schumway, lived down the street. They shared their home with Mary's sex-crazed younger sister, Cathy, and Martha's father, Grandpa Larkin, also known as "The Fernwood Flasher." Living next door to Mary and Tom was middle-aged Charlie Haggers, who worked with Tom and George at the plant. Loretta, his wife, was a 22-year-old aspiring country singer.

The residents of Fernwood were inspired by an article Lear read in *Life* magazine about the hardships encountered by an assembly line worker who lived in Lordstown, Ohio. "We simply decided we'd put a tract of homes there," said Al Burton, the serial's creative supervisor, "and the father would work in the plant and the husband would work in the plant and the next door neighbor would work in the plant. If the plant went on strike, they'd all be out of work; if they're all laid off because of the economy, then we'd deal with the economy."

Gail Parent, a former writer for *The Carol Burnett Show*, assisted Norman Lear and Al Burton in creating the series. When Parent bowed out of the project, Ann Marcus, who'd written for daytime's *Love Is a Many Splendored Thing* and *Search for Tomorrow*, came on board as headwriter. Marcus stayed with the series through its first season.

The comic tone for the serial was set in the opening episode when an excited Loretta Haggers knocked on Mary's kitchen door and breathlessly announced, "You'll never believe what happened!"

"There was a mass murder on the next block," Cathy dryly responded.

"You mean somebody told you before me?" asked a wide-eyed Loretta, with more than just a touch of disappointment.

The murder of all five members of the Lombardi family, their two goats, and eight chickens was just the beginning. One crisis after another unfolded during the serial's two-year run.

Below: *Mary Hartman (Louise Lasser) is shocked by horrible news told to her by her neighbor, Loretta Haggers (Mary Kay Place).*

Opposite page, top: *Mary was often concerned with the waxy yellow build-up on her kitchen floor.*

Opposite page, bottom: *Mary and her husband, Tom (Greg Mullavey), discuss his impotency problem.*

THE CAST

Original Cast

GEORGE SCHUMWAY . . . . PHILIP BRUNS
MARTHA SCHUMWAY . . . . DODY GOODMAN
HAROLD CLEMENS . . . . ARCHIE HAHN
CHARLIE HAGGERS . . . . GRAHAM JARVIS
GRANDPA LARKIN . . . . VICTOR KILIAN
HEATHER HARTMAN . . . . CLAUDIA LAMB
MARY HARTMAN . . . . LOUISE LASSER
TOM HARTMAN . . . . GREG MULLAVEY
LORETTA HAGGERS . . . . MARY KAY PLACE
CATHY SCHUMWAY . . . . DEBRALEE SCOTT
DENNIS FOLEY . . . . BRUCE SOLOMON

Final Cast

MS. FINKEN . . . . LANE BINKLEY
GEORGE SCHUMWAY . . . . TAB HUNTER
DR. FERMIN . . . . OLIVER CLARK
MERLE JEETER . . . . DABNEY COLEMAN
BILLY PATTERSON . . . . MAURY COOPER
MAUREEN . . . . KATHLEEN DOYLE
MARTHA SCHUMWAY . . . . DODY GOODMAN
HAROLD CLEMENS . . . . ARCHIE HAHN
CHARLIE HAGGERS . . . . GRAHAM JARVIS
GRANDPA LARKIN . . . . VICTOR KILIAN
HEATHER HARTMAN . . . . CLAUDIA LAMB
MARY HARTMAN . . . . LOUISE LASSER
WANDA JEETER . . . . MARIAN MERCER
BARTH GIMBLE . . . . MARTIN MULL
TOM HARTMAN . . . . GREG MULLAVEY
MICKEY MOE . . . . TONY PALMER
LORETTA HAGGERS . . . . MARY KAY PLACE
DR. BARKIN . . . . LOGAN RAMSEY
MISS ADELINE . . . . FRAN RYAN
CATHY SCHUMWAY . . . . DEBRALEE SCOTT
BLUMBERG . . . . DONEGAN SMITH
DENNIS FOLEY . . . . BRUCE SOLOMON
BARTENDER . . . . ROBERT STONEMAN

MARY HARTMAN, MARY HARTMAN

1976–1978 SYNDICATED

Heather was held hostage by the mass murderer. Tom suffered from impotency, was laid off from work, and had an affair with Mae Olinsky, a lonely divorcee who also worked at the plant. Tom contracted venereal disease from Mae and passed it to Mary. Grandpa Larkin was arrested for exposing himself in public. Tom's former high school coach drowned in a bowl of Mary's chicken soup. Cathy fell in love with a priest, a deaf poet, and police Sergeant Dennis Foley. Sergeant Foley, who was secretly in love with Mary, proposed to Cathy. To protect her sister from marrying Sergeant Foley, Mary agreed to make love to him. That same night, Sergeant Foley suffered a mild heart attack.

An automobile crash with a station wagon full of nuns left Loretta Haggers temporarily paralyzed from the waist down. Eight-year-old evangelist Jimmy Joe Jeeter was electrocuted while watching television in his bathtub. While a guest on *The David Susskind Show*, Mary suffered a nervous breakdown and was committed to a mental institution. Mary's father, George Schumway, mysteriously vanished.

The phenomenal success of *Mary Hartman, Mary Hartman* prompted the networks to approach Norman Lear about carrying the show. Feeling a sense of loyalty toward the local stations that supported the serial from its first episode, Lear turned down the offers. He and his staff also enjoyed the freedom of creating a television program without network interference. "I don't have someone from the network calling me up eight, ten, twenty-two times a show," said Lear. "I don't enervate myself with telephone calls with somebody saying, 'Well, can't she say X... do they have to do Y?'"

In *Mary Hartman, Mary Hartman's* final episode, Mary ran off with Sergeant Dennis Foley. Despite their attempt to begin a new life, Mary still fretted over the waxy yellow build-up on her kitchen floor.

After two seasons, an exhausted Louise Lasser stepped down from her role as Mary Hartman. Philip Bruns, who played George Schumway, also quit. The serial continued with a new title, *Forever Fernwood*. Bruns was replaced by former film star Tab Hunter. It was explained that George Schumway had accidentally fallen in a chemical vat and had to have his face restored by plastic surgery. Tom Hartman inherited a new love interest, Eleanor Major, played by Shelley Fabares. *Forever Fernwood* wasn't able to match *Mary Hartman, Mary Hartman's* success and ceased production after six months. Reruns briefly resurfaced on CBS in 1980 and in syndication in 1983.

Louise Lasser became famous as a result of her starring role on the syndicated soap *Mary Hartman, Mary Hartman*. Lasser had no intentions of pursuing a career as an actress while she was growing up. In fact, she enrolled as a political science major in college.

In the early sixties, she decided to try performing and found she enjoyed it. Her early work included a role in Elaine May's New York-based improvisational revue, *The Third Ear*. More stage roles followed. In 1966, she married comedian Woody Allen. They divorced in 1970, but still maintain a close friendship. In fact, she appeared in the following Woody Allen directed feature films: *What's Up Tiger Lily?*, *Bananas*, and *Everything You Always Wanted to Know About Sex but Were Afraid to Ask*.

Her television credits include guest-appearances on *The Bob Newhart Show*, *The Mary Tyler Moore Show*, and the TV-movie *Coffee, Tea or Me?* In 1976, Norman Lear cast her as the lead in *Mary Hartman, Mary Hartman*. She stayed with the series for two seasons. In the early eighties, she appeared as a regular on the ABC situation-comedy *It's a Living*. She also appeared in a stage production of *A Coupla White Chicks Sitting Around Talking*.

The cast of Mary Hartman, Mary Hartman.

186

ONE LIFE TO LIVE

JULY 15, 1968–PRESENT ABC

Impressed by Agnes Nixon's success in transforming *Another World* into a top-rated soap, ABC executives approached the talented writer about creating a soap for their network. Nixon informed the executives she wanted to develop a serial that focused on the relationships between various classes, ethnic groups, and races. To her surprise, they were enthusiastic. "It certainly was a risk," said Nixon years later. "As far back as I can remember, the networks and producers have always had a parochial philosophy about daytime serials: 'Stay away from anything controversial.' As a writer I got tired of all the putdowns by the critics of the serials who said we never did anything relevant."

Ms. Nixon originally titled her new serial *Between Heaven and Hell*, but shortly before the premiere its title was changed to *One Life to Live*. The serial focused on three families in the fictional Pennsylvania city of Llanview: the wealthy Lords, the blue-collar Woleks, and the Irish Rileys. Widowed patriarch Victor Lord was publisher and founder of Llanview's leading newspaper, *The Banner*. He had two adult daughters, Victoria and Meredith. (Years later, viewers would learn Victor also fathered two illegitimate children—Tony Lord and Tina Clayton.)

Anna Wolek was a mother substitute to her two brothers, Vince, a truck driver, and Larry, an earnest medical student. The Woleks love for one another ran deep. To insure Larry's future as a doctor, Vince and Anna scraped together their hard-earned money to cover their baby brother's tuition. Anna's life became decidedly more upscale when she married Dr. Jim Craig. Jim had a teenage daughter from his first marriage named Cathy. Vince's best friend was Joe Riley. Joe's sister, Eileen, was married to successful Jewish lawyer Dave Siegel. They had two teenage children, Timmy and Julie.

One Life to Live immediately grabbed the audience's attention with its premiere storyline involving Jim's light-skinned secretary, Carla Gray. For the first four months, viewers thought Carla was white. It wasn't until Carla became romantically involved with Dr. Price Trainor that the audience realized she was black. To give her storyline authenticity, Nixon talked to Ellen Holly, who played Carla, about her experiences

growing up as a light-skinned black. In Nixon's sensitive and believable story, Price ultimately rejected Carla because of her skin color.

Although Carla's storyline was the serial's first socially relevant plot, it would not be the last. When Jim's teenage daughter, Cathy, developed a drug habit, viewers were taken inside New York's Odyssey House, a real-life rehabilitation center for teenage addicts. The serial taped Cathy in therapy sessions with actual adolescent clients seeking treatment at the center. A few years later, Cathy became a reporter and wrote a frank article for *The Banner* informing readers how venereal disease is contracted. The serial's audience was invited to write in for free copies of the article, which Nixon researched and wrote herself. Nixon's goal was to assist people in obtaining necessary information about a once-considered taboo subject.

Below: *Despite her father's objections, Viki (Erika Slezak) married Joe Riley (Lee Patterson).*

Opposite page: *The cast assembles for a twentieth anniversary party.*

Although *One Life to Live* worked diligently to present socially responsible stories, it also understood the importance of entertaining its audience. Victor's eldest daughter, Victoria ("Viki"), grew up being treated like the son Victor never had. He hoped that one day she would take over the family business.

Viki did her best to earn her father's approval, but there were times the pressure was overwhelming. Things finally came to a head when Viki fell in love with her father's top reporter, the affable, hard-drinking Joe Riley. She realized her father disapproved of Joe, but she wasn't willing to give him up.

Caving in to the stress she was facing, the staid, upstanding Viki developed a split personality and became Nikki Smith, a girl who cruised the riverfront bar scene. Unlike Viki, Nikki made no secret about her attraction to men. With the help of psychiatrist Dr. Marcus Polk (originally played by Norman Rose), Viki's split personality was eventually uncovered and treated. The emotional crisis brought Viki and Joe even closer and they soon married.

THE CAST

Original Cast

ANNA WOLEK	DORIS BELACK
KAREN MARTIN	NIKI FLACKS
TOM EDWARDS	JOSEPH GALLISON
VICTOR LORD	ERNEST GRAVES
CARLA GREY	ELLEN HOLLY
DAVE SIEGEL	ALLAN MILLER
JIM CRAIG	ROBERT MILLI
JOE RILEY	LEE PATTERSON
VINCE WOLEK	ANTONY PONZINI
EILEEN RILEY SIEGEL	PATRICIA ROE
PRICE TRAINOR	THURMAN SCOTT
VICTORIA LORD	GILLIAN SPENCER
LARRY WOLEK	PAUL TULLEY
MEREDITH LORD	TRISH VAN DEVERE

ONE LIFE TO LIVE

JULY 15, 1968–PRESENT ABC

Meanwhile, Victor's hands were filled trying to discourage Meredith's attraction to Larry Wolek. Victor didn't approve of Larry's working class background and felt Meredith could do better. He was particularly concerned about Meredith because she suffered from a rare blood ailment and was frequently bedridden. Larry's love for Meredith was intense and he persisted in seeing her. Realizing it was no longer in Meredith's best interest to prevent their relationship, a sensible Victor gave Larry his approval to marry Meredith.

Although *One Life to Live* was considered a moderate ratings success, it had the misfortune of being plagued by frequent casting changes. In its first three years, Viki, Larry, and Cathy were each played by three different performers. When James Storm, the second actor to play Larry Wolek, decided to give up the role in the late sixties, the producers offered it to his younger brother, Michael. To justify the change in Larry's physical appearance, the character became the victim of a flash fire. Larry's burns proved so extensive that doctors had to perform plastic surgery. When his bandages were removed, viewers saw Michael Storm for the first time as the new Larry.

When Lee Patterson informed the producers he wouldn't be renewing his contract, they decided against recasting the role. Instead, Viki learned Joe had been killed in a car accident. This opened the door for the writers to create a new love interest for Viki. Overwhelmed with grief over Joe's sudden death, Viki turned to Steven Burke (played by Bernard Grant) for solace. Eventually the two fell in love and planned to marry. Before the ceremony took place, Steve went on trial for killing his secretary, Marcy Wade (played by Francesca James). The deranged secretary was jealous of Steve's romantic interest in Viki. Marcy schemed to make it look like Viki had reverted to her alter ego, Nikki Smith. When Steve realized what Marcy was doing, he confronted her. She pulled a gun on Steve, they scuffled, and the gun went off. Marcy was killed. Unfortunately, the police weren't able to find any evidence of the gun, leading them to believe Steve had cold-heartedly killed Marcy.

While Steve was busy trying to clear himself, Joe Riley returned to Llanview. Shortly after his car accident, Joe developed amnesia and wandered aimlessly around the country. When he

resurfaced in Llanview, Wanda Webb (originally played by Marilyn Chris), a lovable waitress, took an interest in him. She did not realize who he was. While visiting Wanda at the diner where she worked, Joe collapsed from an aneurysm and was rushed to the hospital. While at the hospital, he was finally identified as Joe Riley. In the meantime, Steve was proven innocent of Marcy's death.

Viki now faced a dilemma: Whom would she choose to be married to? At first, Viki chose Steve. But then she realized she made a mistake and she remarried Joe. During their marriage, Viki and Joe were blessed with two sons, Kevin and Joey. Sadly, Joe didn't live long enough to see his second son. Months before Joey's birth, Joe died.

Pat Kendall (Jacqueline Courtney) married Paul (Tom Fuccello, left) but was in love with Tony Lord (Phillip MacHale, top).

190

Viki wasn't the only person in Llanview to lose her spouse. A few years earlier, Larry lost Meredith. One evening while Meredith was home alone with their baby, Danny, robbers broke in and held mother and son hostage. During the ordeal, Meredith was hit by a robber and she suffered a cerebral hemorrhage. She died soon after in the hospital.

Eileen lost her longtime husband, Dave, to a fatal heart attack. The pain of his death was so strong for Eileen that she became addicted to prescription pills. Eventually, Eileen was able to work through her grief and overcome her drug habit.

Even the crusty Victor Lord lost his life. This was shortly after he discovered the existence of his illegitimate son, Tony. Victor's second wife, Dorian Kramer Lord (originally played by Nancy Pinkerton) was not pleased by Tony's arrival in Llanview. She plotted with Matt McAllister

(originally played by Vance Jefferis), Victor's opportunistic protege, to keep father and son apart for as long as possible. Thanks to Dorian's manipulations, a misinformed Tony turned his back on Victor. Angered and hurt by his son's rejection, Victor cut him out of his will. By the time Victor learned the truth about Dorian's schemes, he died of a stroke, leaving the majority of his vast wealth to Dorian.

Whether people were ready to face it or not, changes were taking place in Llanview. In the midseventies, *One Life to Live* spearheaded a major casting coup when it signed George Reinholt and Jacqueline Courtney, two extremely popular performers from NBC's highly rated *Another World*, to appear as Tony Lord and his former girlfriend Pat Ashley. George Reinholt stayed with the serial for two years before leaving daytime television. Jacqueline Courtney was with the serial until 1983, when the show's headwriters had

ONE LIFE TO LIVE

JULY 15, 1968–PRESENT ABC

exhausted all possible stories for her character. Both actors later resurfaced on *Another World.*

One Life to Live was also undergoing changes in its format. In 1976, the show was expanded to 45 minutes. In 1978, it went to a full hour.

The introduction of Karen Wolek (originally played by Kathryn Breech) as Larry's new love interest sparked a dramatic increase in the serial's ratings. At first, the character was written as self-absorbed and manipulative. But when Breech was replaced by Judith Light, the writers saw an opportunity to add new dimensions to the character. Karen was blackmailed into prostitution by her ex-lover, pimp Marco Dane (played by Gerald Anthony). Karen's life careened out of control when she had an argument with Talbot Huddleston (originally played by Byron Sanders), a man she slept with for money, while in a speeding car. The car hit Tony and Pat's illegitimate son, Brian, resulting in his death.

Meanwhile, Viki also became the victim of blackmail at the hands of Marco Dane. When Marco was found murdered, Viki was accused of killing him. While on the witness stand, an emotional Karen was forced to admit she was a prostitute and revealed that Talbot Huddleston was not only responsible for Marco's death, but also young Brian's. It was later learned Talbot had killed Marco's identical brother, Mario, and that Marco had assumed his identity.

Upset by news of his wife's secret life as a prostitute, Larry divorced her. Years later, Larry realized he was still in love with Karen, but she left town with another boyfriend, counterfeiter Steve Piermont (originally played by Richard K. Weber, and later by Judith Light's real-life husband, Robert Desiderio).

In the late seventies, the Texas-bred, wealthy Buchanans joined the serial. Clint Buchanan (played by Clint Ritchie) arrived to take over *The Banner* from the ailing Joe Riley. He was followed by his impressionable young brother, Bo (played by Robert Woods). Finally, patriarch Asa (played by Philip Carey) surfaced, hoping to renew his strained relationship with his oldest son. Bo's first serious romance in Llanview was with Pat Ashley.

By the early eighties, the Buchanans had become the serial's leading family. Viki fell in love with Clint and later married him. Their marriage has survived many separations: Clint's infidelity; the discovery of a son Clint never knew he had—Cord Roberts (played by John Loprieno); Viki's discovery that she had an adult daughter—Megan Gordon (played by Jessica Tuck); Viki's nervous breakdown after learning Tina Clayton (played longest by Andrea Evans) was her illegitimate half-sister; the reemergence of Viki's split personality; and Viki's friendship with Roger Gordon (played by Larry Pine), Megan's natural father. Sometime during all their struggles, Viki and Clint took time out to have a child of their own, a baby girl named Jessica.

In the late eighties, *One Life to Live* developed a reputation for presenting storylines that broke the barriers of traditional soap opera plotting.

Below: *Tim Siegel (Tom Berenger) knows more than he's telling about the murder of Mark Toland. His mother, Eileen (Alice Hirson), pleads with him to tell the police all he knows.*

Opposite page: *Bo (Robert Woods) and Sarah Buchanan (Jenson Buchanan) have had a rough time trying to make their relationship work.*

ONE LIFE TO LIVE

JULY 15, 1968–PRESENT ABC

Although Erika Slezak is the third actress to play Victoria Lord Riley Buchanan, joining the series in 1971, she's the actress most identified with the role. The daughter of famous character actor Walter Slezak, she received her theatre training at the prestigious Royal Academy of Dramatic Arts in London. At age 19, she landed her first professional acting job with the Milwaukee Repertory Company. While living in Milwaukee, she married a local actor. Their marriage, however, was short-lived. After two years, Slezak filed for divorce. "We were very happy," she said, "but we simply had different goals in life. He was perfectly content in Milwaukee. My ambition was to get into theatre in New York." Following her divorce, Slezak landed acting jobs in Buffalo and Houston, before being cast as Victoria Lord Riley on March 17, 1971.

Referring to the character she's played for nearly 20 years, Slezak said, "We're not at all alike. I mean, we have the same color hair—but that's where the similarity begins and ends. There are some basic things in her character which I really hope aren't in mine.

"She's a pain in the neck. Everyone must do things right. She's so stubborn about certain things. She may be older and wiser now, but she still lives by that strict moral code she was raised with."

In the late seventies, Slezak married actor Brian Davies. They have two children, Michael, 10, and Amanda, 9.

The only downside Slezak sees to performing on *One Life to Live* is that it prevents her from spending more time with her family. "I hate to say it because it almost sounds ungrateful, but people who stay home don't know how lucky they are to have that time... and they're probably sitting at home saying, 'She doesn't know how lucky she is to get out.' It's true; the grass is always greener on the other side. We always want something we don't have."

While recovering from a brain operation in 1987, Viki had an out-of-body experience and visited heaven for two weeks. The storyline gave viewers an opportunity to catch up with beloved characters who had died. This included Viki's sister, Meredith; her late husband, Joe; and her half-brother, Tony Lord. It may have been disheartening for viewers to learn that a spirit's physical condition continues to age in heaven.

Tina Clayton Lord (Andrea Evans) has always had a way with men, including Cord Roberts (John Loprieno, right) and Max Holden (James DePaiva, left).

The exciting Buchanan men: (left to right) Clint (Clint Ritchie), Asa (Philip Carey), and Bo (Robert Woods).

In 1988, a conk on the head sent Clint back to the Old West, where he visited Buchanan City for several months. The same actors who played Viki, Cord, and Asa were seen as their ancestors. Clint even developed a romantic relationship with Viki's kind-hearted, gentle great-grandmother, Miss Ginny. Determined to locate her husband, Viki entered the time warp and convinced him to return to his own time.

In 1989, viewers discovered that a secret city called Eterna existed below Llanview. Eterna was built by Roger Gordon's father in the midsixties,

but an explosion buried the secret entrance. At one time, Viki knew the location, but had been brainwashed to forget. The villain Michael Grande, who survived the explosion, forced Viki to recall the location of the entrance. The following year, Michael was murdered. Several of Llanview's leading citizens became suspects in his death.

Famous alumni of the series include Judith Light, Tom Berenger, Tommy Lee Jones, Jameson Parker, Phylicia Rashad, Al Freeman, Jr., and Esther Rolle.

ONE MAN'S FAMILY

NOVEMBER 4, 1949–JUNE 21, 1952 NBC (PRIME TIME)
MARCH 1, 1954–APRIL 1, 1955 NBC (DAYTIME)

This serial, created by Carleton E. Morse, has the distinction of being the longest-running serial in radio history. It aired from 1932 until 1959, and totaled 3,256 episodes. Two different versions of the serial ran on television. It first premiered as a weekly, half-hour prime-time series on NBC in 1949 and enjoyed a two-year run. Later it surfaced as a daily, 15-minute serial in the daytime and ran for 13 months. While the radio serial continued its story, the television adaptions went back to the radio version's 1932 stories and set them in the present day. To accommodate this change, the television characters lost approximately 20 years from their ages. For instance, ten-year-old Jack in the television version was 32 years old in the radio serial and had six children. What made this even more interesting is that some actors from the radio series performed double-duty and also appeared in the television versions. Anne Whitfield, who played 19-year-old Claudia on television, played Claudia's adult daughter Penelope on the radio during the same period.

The television version boasted three names that would become familiar to the public: Eva Marie Saint, Tony Randall, and Mercedes McCambridge.

The serial was set in a Northern California suburb, Sea Cliff, which overlooked the Golden Gate Bridge. It focused on San Francisco banker Henry Barbour and his large family. While Henry was considered a firm disciplinarian, Fanny, his wife, lovingly struggled to respect their children's natural independence. Eldest son, Paul, was a

The radio version of the Barbour family in 1957: (left to right) Mother Barbour (Mary Adams), Jack (Page Gilman), Claudia (Barbra Fuller), Paul (Russell Thorson), Hazel (Bernice Berwin), and Father Barbour (J. Anthony Smythe). Some of the radio actors also were on the TV version.

quiet man, wise beyond his years. He was also the one other members of the family would turn to for guidance and support when they were in trouble. A World War II veteran, Paul earned his living as a pilot. He was single. Eldest daughter, Hazel, was 28 years old when the television serial premiered. Early scripts centered on her search to find a husband. At last, Hazel succeeded. She married Bill Herbert. Unfortunately, her marriage proved to be turbulent and came close to ending more than once. Next came the college-age twins, Claudia and Cliff, who attended Stanford University. The twins constantly rebelled against Henry's "old fashioned" values. Youngest son, Jack, kept the family amused with his good-natured antics. Paul added a new member to the family when he adopted orphan Teddy Lawton. To Henry's disappointment, Claudia married the adventure-seeking Johnny Roberts.

Five years after the daytime television version went off the air, the long-running radio serial was canceled. Disheartened by the show's demise, Carleton E. Morse wrote to fans in *The Los Angeles Times*. "My own sorrow," he wrote, "is not so much in the cessation of the show, as much as in the thought that one more happy, sober beacon to light the way has been put out. The signposts for sound family life are now few, and I feel the loss of *One Man's Family* is just another abandoned lighthouse."

Prime-time Cast

TEDDY LAWTON	MADELINE BELGARD
JOE YARBOROUGH	JIM BOLES
BILL HERBERT	WALTER BROOKE
	LES TREYMAINE
MRS. ROBERTS	MONA BRUNS
FANNY BARBOUR	MAJORIE GATESON
JOHNNY ROBERTS	MICHAEL HIGGINS
CLIFF BARBOUR	JAMES LEE
	BILL IDELSON
	FRANKIE THOMAS
MR. ROBERTS	RALPH LOCKE
HENRY BARBOUR	BERT LYTELL
SIR GUY VANCE	MAURICE MANSON
CLAUDIA BARBOUR	EVA MARIE SAINT
	NANCY FRANKLIN
HAZEL BARBOUR HERBERT	LILLIAN SCHAAF
BETH HOLLY	SUSAN SHAW
	MERCEDES McCAMBRIDGE
MAC	TONY RANDALL
GLENN HUNTER	CALVIN THOMAS
PAUL BARBOUR	RUSSELL THORSON
JACK BARBOUR	RICHARD WIGGINTON
	ARTHUR CASSELL

Daytime Cast

FANNY BARBOUR	MARY ADAMS
JACK BARBOUR	MARTIN DEAN
JOHNNY ROBERTS	JACK EDWARDS
HENRY BARBOUR	THEODORE von ELTZ
CLIFFORD BARBOUR	JAMES LEE
HAZEL BARBOUR	LINDA LEIGHTON
PAUL BARBOUR	RUSSELL THORSON
CLAUDIA BARBOUR	ANNE WHITFIELD

PEYTON PLACE

. . . .

SEPTEMBER 15, 1964–JUNE 2, 1969 ABC

"*Y*ou've never been in a small town before?" newspaper publisher Matt Swain asked newcomer Dr. Michael Rossi. "Well, someday you're going to wake up and realize you know every face in town and you're going to have a definite feeling about every one of them and they're going to have a definite feeling about you. They may love you or hate you, but they won't be indifferent."

And so began the first episode of *Peyton Place*, which succeeded in attracting an estimated 60 million viewers during its five-year run on prime-time television. "This show is like a narcotic," observed creator and producer Paul Monash. "If you tune in often enough, there is a very strong threat of addiction." Talk show host Jack Paar jokingly called it "television's first situation orgy."

Based on Grace Metalious's best-selling novel, the serial centered on the lives of people living in a small New England town. Like the daytime soaps, *Peyton Place* titillated viewers with plots involving adultery, illegitimacy, lurid secrets, and scorned romances. It aired up to three times per week, and often landed in the Nielsen's top 20 during its first two seasons.

Mia Farrow and Ryan O'Neal were the first young stars to emerge from the serial's cast. They played starcrossed lovers Allison Mackenzie and Rodney Harrington. After a highly publicized marriage to singer Frank Sinatra, Mia Farrow left the series in 1966. Ryan O'Neal stayed until the final episode and went on to star in *Love Story*, *Paper Moon*, and *What's up, Doc?*

Film star Dorothy Malone netted top billing for her role as Constance Mackenzie. When an illness forced her to leave the series in 1965, Lola Allbright was hired as a temporary replacement. Malone returned but permanently left the show in 1968. Ed Nelson, who played Michael Rossi, then received top billing. Other prominent actors included Gena Rowlands, Barbara Parkins, Ruth Warrick (best known today for her role as Phoebe Tyler Wallingford on *All My Children*), David Canary (also of *All My Children*, he plays the dual roles of brothers Adam and Stuart Chandler), Barbara Rush, Leslie Nielsen, Ruby Dee, Glynn Turman, Mariette Hartley, and Lee Grant. Grant won the show's only Emmy.

The behind-the-scenes struggle over creative control was as intriguing as anything viewers of *Peyton Place* were privy to on their TV screens. The two feuding were creator Paul Monash and story consultant Irna Phillips, who had created such popular daytime serials as *As the World Turns* and *The Guiding Light*.

Monash, who had written for *The Untouchables*, was approached by 20th Century Fox in 1962 to develop a television version of Metalious's best-selling racy novel. One of the book's most controversial storylines involved a rape scene between a drunken father and his

Allison Mackenzie (Mia Farrow) was in love with Rodney Harrington, but he was married.

Top: *Barbara Parkins played Betty Anderson, Rodney Harrington's wife.*

Bottom: *Constance Mackenzie (Dorothy Malone) married Elliott Carson (Tim O'Connor).*

THE CAST

Original Cast

MATTHEW SWAIN	WARNER ANDERSON
GEORGE ANDERSON	HENRY BECKMAN
NORMAN HARRINGTON	CHRISTOPHER CONNELLY
STEVEN CORD	JAMES DOUGLAS
ALLISON MACKENZIE	MIA FARROW
ELI CARSON	FRANK FERGUSON
LESLIE HARRINGTON	PAUL LANGTON
CONSTANCE MACKENZIE	DOROTHY MALONE
MICHAEL ROSSI	ED NELSON
RODNEY HARRINGTON	RYAN O'NEAL
BETTY ANDERSON	BARBARA PARKINS
JULIE ANDERSON	KASEY ROGERS
ROBERT MORTON	KENT SMITH

Final Cast

NORMAN HARRINGTON	CHRISTOPHER CONNELLY
ALMA MILES	RUBY DEE
STEVEN CORD	JAMES DOUGLAS
ELI CARSON	FRANK FERGUSON
TOM WINTER	ROBERT HOGAN
SUSAN WINTER	DIANA HYLAND
FRED RUSSELL	JOE MAROSS
RITA JACKS HARRINGTON	PATRICIA MORROW
RODNEY HARRINGTON	RYAN O'NEAL
BETTY ANDERSON	BARBARA PARKINS
HARRY MILES	PERCY RODRIGUEZ
JULIE ANDERSON	KASEY ROGERS
MARSHA RUSSELL	BARBARA RUSH
ADA JACKS	EVELYN SCOTT
LEW MILES	GLYNN TURMAN
CAROLYN RUSSELL	ELIZABETH "TIPPY" WALKER

PEYTON PLACE

teenage stepdaughter. "Everyone was frightened to death," Monash told *TV Guide* in 1965. "There was no precedent for this series. The network was concerned. The affiliated stations were leery. I was under a strict directive to make the show palatable. People were nervous and anxious about it." Instead of offering viewers stories packed with sex and violence, Monash's intention was to present "good family drama."

Late in 1963, an hour-long pilot was filmed, incorporating all the notable characters from the novel—including the drunken father, Lucas Cross, who worked as a janitor at the high school, and his teenage stepdaughter, Selena. After viewing the pilot, ABC enthusiastically gave Monash its seal of approval. A few months later, however, the network turned skittish and decided to protect its investment by hiring Irna Phillips as story consultant. Phillips had more than 30 years experience writing soap operas.

Phillips sat through the pilot and then recommended the network trash it and start over fresh. She told *TV Guide*, "I did not think this was the kind of thing to give an American public—a father seducing his stepdaughter." Instead, she suggested a storyline where Allison Mackenzie unknowingly falls in love with her half-brother, the son of the man who fathered her out of wedlock. The budding relationship would force Constance Mackenzie to finally reveal to her daughter she was illegitimate. Monash hated the idea. "I utterly reject this tasteless and profitless story area," said Monash. "It is meretricious, trite, and tawdry. Are we seriously expected to film a story in which Allison and this young man play out a full romance? Isn't this suggestion coming from the very writer who complained about a plethora of sex in the pilot?"

Monash and Phillips worked through their creative differences and a new pilot was filmed. Following Phillips's advice, Lucas Cross and his stepdaughter Selena were exorcised from the revised story. To Monash's relief, Phillips's proposed story was also vetoed.

The second major change Irna Phillips implemented was switching Michael Rossi's profession from high school principal to town doctor. "The reason for that," explained Ed Nelson, "was that after they showed the pilot to the public, they found that the audience

responded very favorably to Rossi and wanted to see more of him. They couldn't figure out how to keep a high school principal involved in the show once Ryan, Mia, and Chris graduated, so they decided to make him a doctor." To accommodate the switch, Matt Swain, the town doctor in the novel, became a newspaper publisher, still making it possible for him to have intimate knowledge of everyone living in Peyton Place.

Dorothy Malone on the set of Peyton Place.

Cast members of Peyton Place:
(left to right) James Douglas,
Barbara Parkins, Ryan O'Neal,
Tim O'Connor, Dorothy Malone,
and Ed Nelson.

Memorable stories included bookshop owner Constance Mackenzie's dark secret that her teenage daughter, Allison, was illegitimate. In May 1965, Constance finally married Allison's father, Elliot Carson, after he was released from prison. Allison's romance with wealthy playboy Rodney Harrington was also a viewer favorite. Complicating their relationship was Rodney's troubled marriage to Betty Anderson. Although Mia Farrow left the series in 1966, prompting the producers to have Allison mysteriously disappear, the character's presence was still prominent. An aggressive investigation into her whereabouts was launched by police authorities when a young

woman named Rachel Welles arrived in town wearing a bracelet that had belonged to Allison. In 1968, a second young woman, Jill Smith, turned up with a baby she claimed belonged to Allison.

By June 1969, *Peyton Place's* audience had dropped, and the series was canceled. Diehard viewers were disappointed that the final episode left a number of storylines unresolved. Would wheelchair-confined Rodney Harrington ever recover from his paralysis? Who finally inherited the late Martin Peyton's millions? Was Dr. Michael Rossi cleared of murder? Viewers' curiosity was satisfied three years later when NBC broadcast *Return to Peyton Place.*

RYAN'S HOPE

JULY 7, 1975–JANUARY 13, 1989 ABC

"*Ryan's Hope* used to be like a tiny restaurant that people used to like to come to all the time," explained Ron Hale, who played Roger Coleridge. "The quality of the food was great, the service was great, you could spend a lot of time there and no one rushed you.... Then, someone came along and bought that little restaurant and decided to 'improve' it. Make more money out of it, expand it, by buying up the building next door, getting new tables. Well, what happened was that the quality of the food went down, and it wasn't that quiet little restaurant anymore. It became a restaurant like any other restaurant. That's what happened to *Ryan's Hope*."

Set in New York City, this half-hour serial focused on a large, lower-class Irish Catholic family, the Ryans, who owned a bar. Immigrants Johnny and Maeve Ryan had five adult children: Frank, a politican; Cathleen, a homemaker and mother; Mary, a reporter; Patrick, a doctor; and Siobhan, a free spirit who later became a police officer.

The upscale Coleridges, headed by widowed patriarch Dr. Ed Coleridge, were also featured prominently. Frank, who was married to the clinging, neurotic Delia when the show premiered, loved Jillian Coleridge. His kid brother, Pat, was enamored with Jillian's younger sister, Faith. Meanwhile, the Coleridges' self-centered brother, Roger, was attracted to Delia.

When the series opened, Frank Ryan was seriously injured after being pushed down a flight of stairs by a self-absorbed Delia. Creators Claire Labine and Paul Avila Mayer intended to kill Frank, but ABC objected. The network persuaded Labine and Mayer to build a storyline around him.

Meanwhile, Mary Ryan's passionate romance with sexy, argumentative Jack Fenelli was an immediate hit with viewers. Complicating their relationship was Johnny Ryan's disapproval of Jack. After Kate Mulgrew, the first actress to play Mary, left, Michael Levin realized how special the chemistry between them was. "I remember when Katie left, I thought, 'Well, that was fun but now it'll be even more interesting,'" he said. "Sometimes it's hard to tell when you're doing the one that's most important. In fact, Katie was tough to work with. With really good actors, a lot of times you've gotta fight—you give it to them and they give it back. Oh, Katie was terrific."

Recasting key roles developed into a major headache for *Ryan's Hope* during its 14-year run. Frank and Siobhan Ryan were recast five times each. Mary Ryan Fenelli was played by four different actresses. Likewise for Pat Ryan, Faith Coleridge, and Delia.

Ryan's Hope was originally owned by Claire Labine and Paul Avila Mayer. Escalating production costs forced them to sell the series to ABC in 1979, a move that proved damaging for the earthy serial. Inspired by the success of its powerhouse line-up of one-hour serials, particularly *General Hospital,* the network wanted changes that would make *Ryan's Hope* more fast-paced and glamorous. "We had a very special flavor here," said Ron Hale. "All of a sudden, there were all these other characters. Once we did that—or the powers-that-be did that—it didn't work. They tried to make us more of a familiar show, but it didn't work for us."

The Ryans: (clockwise, from seated center) Johnny (Bernard Barrow), Siobahn (Sarah Felder), Pat (John Blazo), Frank (Daniel Hugh-Kelly), Mary (Kathleen Tolas), and Maeve (Helen Gallagher).

Maeve and Johnny had rough times, but they always had each other to keep them strong.

"There were choices and they were clear choices, business and creative choices, after we sold the show," explained creator Claire Labine. "Soap opera took a different direction after *General Hospital,* and then—and I underline *then*—management of daytime at ABC wanted *Ryan's Hope* to be different." To insure that changes would be made, ABC pink-slipped the serial's creators.

The first step the new writers took was to replace the Ryans with the super-wealthy Kirklands. Hollis Kirkland (played by Peter Haskell) was a former lover of television station owner Rae Woodard (played by Louise Shaffer). Hollis returned to New York City hoping to renew their relationship.

When Catsy (played by Christine Jones), Hollis's wife, learned her estranged husband intended to wed Rae, she refused to give him a divorce. Their fragile daughter, Amanda (originally played by Mary Page Keller), fell in love with Pat Ryan. Recalling that period, Ron Hale said, "We used to call it "Kirkland's Hope." Hollis Kirkland was the world's richest man. There's always one in every soap town. I used to get letters from fans who'd ask, 'Who is this person?'"

Original Cast

JILLIAN COLERIDGE	NANCY ADDISON-ALTMAN
JOHNNY RYAN	BERNARD BARROW
FAITH COLERIDGE	FAITH CATLIN
BUCKY CARTER	JUSTIN DEAS
NICK SZABO	MICHAEL FAIRMAN
SENECA BEAULAC	JOHN GABRIEL
MAEVE RYAN	HELEN GALLAGHER
PAT RYAN	MALCOLM GROOME
RAMONA GONZALEZ	ROSALINDA GUERRA
ROGER COLERIDGE	RON HALE
FRANK RYAN	MICHAEL HAWKINS
BOB REID	EARL HINDMAN
DELIA REID RYAN	ILENE KRISTEN
ED COLERIDGE	FRANK LATIMORE
JACK FENELLI	MICHAEL LEVIN
MARY RYAN	KATE MULGREW
CLEM MOULTRIE	HANNIBAL PENNY, JR.
NELL BEAULAC	DIANA VAN DER VLIS

RYAN'S HOPE

JULY 7, 1975–JANUARY 13, 1989 ABC

As the serial's ratings continued to slip, ABC persuaded Claire Labine and Paul Avila Mayer to return as headwriters. "We had that kind of wonderful George Steinbrenner-Billy Martin relationship—You're hired, you're fired, you're hired, we quit—between 1980 and 1983," joked Claire Labine. "But when Paul Mayer and I left in the fall of '83, we left at that time without rancor. It was really clear that they wanted to do something so profoundly different.... We had all the sturn und drang, we'd had all the fights, all the blood on the floor, and at that point they said they knew what they wanted it to be like, and they did what they needed to do, and the ratings went down and then they changed the timeslot and at that point it was irrevocable."

"That was the second killer," observed Ron Hale. "When ABC changed our time slot from 12:30 to 12:00, it was an economic decision. But we started seeing ratings we'd never seen in our lives! It was a shock to go from twenty points to a fifteen."

"We were affected very badly," executive producer Joseph Hardy concurred. "Noon was a bad time for any ABC station to take us because they usually have on their own local programming."

In 1987, ABC approached Claire Labine about returning. Against the advice of friends and family, Labine resumed her former duties and tried to put the struggling serial back on track. Despite her efforts, the serial continued to lose viewers. In October 1988, ABC announced it was canceling the series. Although the cast and crew had been expecting the news, they took it hard. "I'm angry at the politics of it all," said James Wlecek (who played Ben Shelly). "How can ABC let a good show like ours go off the air when it's better than one or two other shows that remain?"

"It was a wonderful thirteen-and-a-half years," said Claire Labine. "There's no way to regret it and there was no way to stop what happened, no way, given the confluence of events, given the people who were in charge, given everything."

Jack Fenelli (Michael Levin) was married to Siobahn's (Marg Helgenberger) sister Mary.

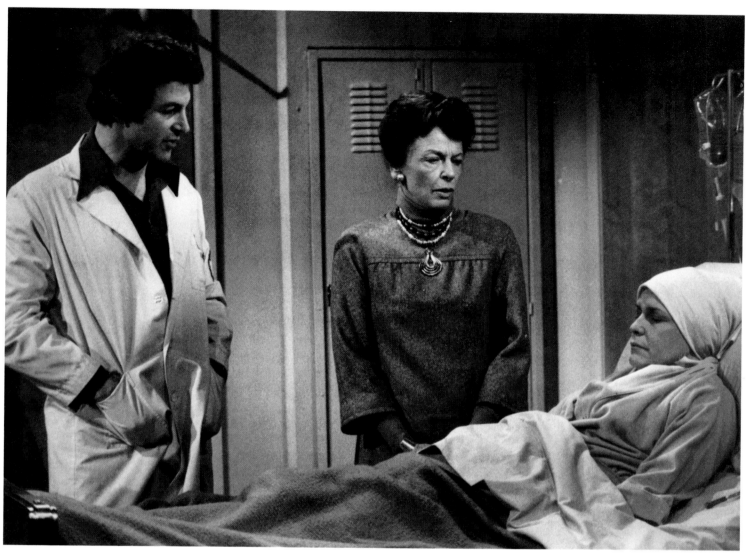

When Nell Beaulac (Diana Van Der Vlis) becomes ill, her mother-in-law, Marguerite (Gale Sondergaard), visits to be with her son, Seneca (John Gabriel).

Although it was a bittersweet opportunity, Labine looked forward to being the writer who would script the last episode. "I would hate like hell to have somebody else do it," she said, shortly after the serial's cancellation was made public. "And we will go off as we began. I want it to be Ryans. I want it to be Riverside. I want it to be the bar and I want it to be real, as real as it has been for all of us. I just want it to be what it is."

Taping the final episode proved to be an emotional experience for everyone involved. "Helen Gallagher said to me, 'Oh, God, just let me get through this,'" revealed Labine, "and I said, 'It doesn't matter if you don't. Nobody else is going to be dry-eyed...why should you?'"

In the final episode, Jack Fenelli, whose wife, Mary, was killed several years earlier in an explosion, finally put his first marriage behind him and wed Leigh Kirkland (played by Felicity LaFortune). Faith Coleridge returned for the wedding with her child, Grace, leading Pat to wonder if he was the father. The cliff-hanger was

deliberate. "I couldn't bear leaving the series in a static place," said Labine, "because you just don't go out on Friday in a serial in a static place. For me, I wanted to have a sense of life going on, yet I think there's a sense of fulfillment about the last show." The episode ended with Gallagher leading the cast in a wrenching rendition of "Danny Boy."

"I'm glad that if we had to go out, that we're leaving on a high note," said Ilene Kristen, who had returned two years earlier to reprise her role as Delia. "I think the stories have been among the best the soap has done, and I've enjoyed working with all the people on the show. As far as Delia is concerned, I've had a lot of wonderful experiences with her, and I'm glad that in the last couple of years Delia was allowed to become more her own person. She grew up and made important decisions about her own life. It's the end of a 14-year cycle, but also the start of another cycle and I feel very positive about my future."

"I wish we had six more months," concluded Labine. "I really do."

SANTA BARBARA

JULY 30, 1984–PRESENT NBC

*C*reators Jerome and Bridget Dobson had firsthand knowledge of their competitors, *The Guiding Light* and *General Hospital,* when *Santa Barbara* premiered on July 30, 1984. Besides serving as headwriters for both highly successful serials (and for *As the World Turns*), Bridget's parents, Frank and Doris Hursley, created *General Hospital. Santa Barbara* was the second soap to be launched in an hour-long format (the first was *Texas,* which was also scheduled opposite *General Hospital* and *The Guiding Light*).

Set in Santa Barbara, the serial focused on four families: the aristocratic Lockridges, the influential Capwells, the middle-class Perkinses, and a low-income Hispanic family, the Andrades. Two years later, only the Capwells and Lockridges would continue to be leading forces on the serial. Eighty-six-year-old stage actress Dame Judith Anderson appeared during the serial's early years as Minx, widow of T. MacDonald Lockridge. Marcy Walker, a popular performer from *All My Children* (she played self-centered Liza Colby), was cast in the pivotal role of Eden Capwell. Her father, millionaire C. C. Capwell, proved to be the most difficult role to cast. Three actors were hired and fired in rapid succession—Peter Mark Richman, Paul Burke, and Charles Bateman— before the producers finally selected a performer with the charisma needed to pull off the role. Jed Allan, who previously appeared as Don Craig on *Days of Our Lives,* was finally chosen.

The first episode opened with a lavish party set in 1979. Channing Capwell, Jr. (played by Robert Wilson) was discovered dead shortly after an argument with Kelly Capwell's fiance, Joe Perkins. The action moved forward to a present day party, where Kelly was celebrating yet another engagement, this time to Peter Flint, a social-climbing opportunist. Kelly's happiness was dampered by news that Joe Perkins, Channing's alleged killer, had been released from prison.

Finding the real killer of Channing Capwell, Jr. served as a leading storyline during *Santa Barbara's* early days. Anxious to find the killer, Detective Cruz Castillo (played by A Martinez) reopened the case. Meanwhile, an ostracized Joe Perkins was befriended by two off-beat characters. The eccentric, bored Augusta Lockridge, whose dogs wore diamond collars, hired Joe to work as her gardener, hoping to make him her new lover. Even odder was the mysterious beared-gentleman, Dominic, who slipped Joe valuable information regarding in-family fighting among the Capwells. Eventually, Dominic was revealed to be Sophia Capwell, a one-time Hollywood actress (formerly married to C. C.). Cruz finally managed to crack the case with a renactment of the crime. To everyone's surprise, Sophia (who was actually Channing's mother) had killed Channing. Her intention was to frighten ex-lover Lionel Lockridge with what she believed was an unloaded gun. Channing unexpectedly entered the library, startling Sophia and the gun went off. The incident was so traumatic that Sophia had erased it from her memory.

Minx Lockridge (Dame Judith Anderson, seated right) does not get along with her former daughter-in-law, Augusta (Louise Sorel, left), but Laken (Julie Ronnie, standing) mediates between her mother and grandmother.

The cast of Santa Barbara.

Concerned by the serial's low-ratings after four months on the air, the Dobsons decided to shake things up by staging an earthquake. (Ironically, the day the scenes were taped, the real Santa Barbara was hit with an earthquake registering 4.7 on the Richter scale.) The earthquake resulted in new faces being added to the cast. Dane Witherspoon was replaced by Mark Arnold (who played Gavin Wylie on *The Edge of Night*) as Joe Perkins, and Judith McConnell (she played Valerie Conway on *As the World Turns* and Nurse Augusta McLeod on *General Hospital*) took over for Rosemary Forsyth as Sophia. Discussing the serial's erratic beginning, A Martinez said, "The show had growing pains. I mean everything was subject to revamping.... It was really tough at the beginning because we came on with so much hype that I think everyone underestimated the task—to start an hour show from scratch, with every actor creating a character at once, and some of them didn't have a lot of experience. It was desperate around the set. The hours were staggering and the sense of pressure—it was too palpable—I mean you could cut it. You'd just get near the studio and you could feel your heart rate accelerating, literally. I'd never gone through anything like it in my life."

From the beginning, humor has been an important element of *Santa Barbara's* uniqueness. "We plan to have a lot of fun with this show," promised Bridget Dobson shortly before its debut.

Original Cast

MINX LOCKRIDGE	DAME JUDITH ANDERSON
MARISA PERKINS	VALORIE ARMSTRONG
JADE PERKINS	MELISSA BRENNAN
JOHN PERKINS	ROBERT ALLEN BROWNE
RUEBEN ANDRADE	ISMAEL CARLO
ROSA ANDRADE	MARGARITA CORDOVA
LIONEL LOCKRIDGE	NICOLAS COSTER
SOPHIA CAPWELL/DOMINIC	ROSEMARY FORSYTH
MASON CAPWELL	LANE DAVIES
SANTANA ANDRADE	AVA LAZAR
CRUZ CASTILLO	A MARTINEZ
PETER FLINT	STEPHEN MEADOWS
TED CAPWELL	TODD McKEE
WARREN LOCKRIDGE	JOHN ALLEN NELSON
DANNY ANDRADE	RUPERT RAVENS
C. C. CAPWELL	PETER MARK RICHMAN
LAKEN LOCKRIDGE	JULIE RONNIE
AUGUSTA LOCKRIDGE	LOUISE SOREL
EDEN CAPWELL	MARCY WALKER
JOE PERKINS	DANE WITHERSPOON
KELLY CAPWELL	ROBIN WRIGHT

SANTA BARBARA

JULY 30, 1984–PRESENT NBC

"Every character is going to have some humor. Soaps should be a pleasure to watch and not a pain. I hate to sit down in front of a TV and feel soggy." When Mason, the dastardly black sheep of the Capwell clan, was suspected by his own family of killing Channing, he responded, "All right, all of you are off my Christmas card list!" Explaining the initial in her husband's first name (T. MacDonald Lockridge), Minx answered, "T is for Tiger." Jealous of his girlfriend's (Jade Perkins) startstruck attraction to David Hasselhoff, who made a cameo appearance on the serial, Ted Capwell referred to the celebrity as "David Hasseldork." Mason's former fiance, Mary Duvall, was killed after the letter C from the Capwell Hotel sign struck her on the head. When Sasha Schmidt turned up dead, her body was temporarily hidden in Julia Capwell's freezer.

During *Santa Barbara's* early days, Kelly Capwell was featured as the serial's leading heroine. The creators soon discovered a special chemistry between Marcy Walker and A Martinez in the scenes they shared. Intrigued by what they saw, the Dobsons decided to regroup and explore the love relationship between Eden and Cruz. To date, it's been *Santa Barbara's* most enduring love story.

Eden and Cruz's relationship began five years before *Santa Barbara's* debut. They met in Europe, where Eden was pursuing her studies while giving herself distance from her overbearing family. Cruz was working undercover as a spy. They were immediately drawn to each other. Their brief affair, however, was interrupted when Eden's mother and stepbrother finally found her. They persuaded Eden to stand her lover up, leading Cruz to believe their affair had ended. When Eden returned to Santa Barbara several years later, Cruz was investigating her brother Channing's murder. Seeing one another again, they realized a spark of romance still existed between them, but were unwilling to admit it. Meanwhile, Cruz was heavily involved with Santana Andrade. To his dismay, Santana was busy pursuing C. C. Capwell, who she believed had information regarding her lost child. Recalling Cruz's turbulent relationship with Santana, A Martinez said, "It was real tough for me to play, that kind of yapping at her, begging for her charms, when she was off chasing this rich,

older man. I felt that was really stretching the believablity of the character. I thought he would just state his case once and then walk away. It was hard for me to play those things, but I was, of course, happy to have something to do."

Eden and Cruz's love kicked into high gear after C. C. suffered a stroke. While C. C. battled for his life, Eden stepped in as temporary head of Capwell Industries. Kirk Cranston (originally played by Joseph Bottoms), a coworker, became obsessed with Eden and wanted to marry her. By now, Eden knew she loved Cruz. C. C.'s young wife, Gina (originally played by Linda Gibboney, and later by Robin Mattson), viewed his stroke as an opportunity to inherit her ailing husband's fortune. Alone in his hospital room, a crafty Gina pulled the plug on C. C.'s respirator. Although C. C. didn't die, Kirk convinced an emotionally fragile Eden that she had pulled the plug.

Below: *The Capwells: (seated) Sophia (Judith McConnell), (left to right, middle) Eden (Marcy Walker), Kelly (Robin Wright), (rear) Mason (Lane Davies), Ted (Todd McKee), and C. C. (Jed Allan).*

Opposite page: *Eden (Marcy Walker) finally married Cruz in 1988.*

SANTA BARBARA

JULY 30, 1984–PRESENT NBC

Confused and frightened, Eden became more dependent on Kirk. Finally, she agreed to marry him. A short while later, Eden was pregnant with Kirk's baby. News of Eden's pregnancy prompted Cruz to marry Santana. A crazed Kirk intercepted love letters Eden wrote to Cruz and hatched a plot to kill her. Initially, Kirk enlisted Gina's help to carry out his devious plan. Gina and Eden got into a fight, but Gina realized she couldn't kill her. Unfortunately, the incident cost Eden her unborn baby. Determined to kill Eden, Kirk tossed her in a tank full of sharks. Thanks to Gina (who stepped forward with Kirk's plan), Cruz rescued Eden. The police arrived and arrested Kirk.

Tori Lane (played by Kristen Meadows), Cruz's ex-lover, came to town and created a new obstacle for Cruz and Eden. Jealous of Tori's hold on Cruz, Eden turned to sexy tennis pro Martin Ellia (played by John Wesley Shipp). She persuaded him to make a play for Tori. Shipwrecked alone with Tori, Cruz suffered a head injury and later made love to her. A short while later, both Tori and Eden were pregnant by Cruz! Eden didn't know she was pregnant until after she lost the baby in a car accident. Ironically, Tori was also involved in a car accident, but she survived—still pregnant. Concerned over his daughter's suffering, C. C. convinced his son, Mason, to marry Tori. Mason convinced everyone that he was the father of Tori's child (this turned out to be a noble step for Mason because his girlfriend, Julia Wainwright, was pregnant with his child).

Cruz and Eden came close to reuniting, but a psychotic woman, Elena Nikolas (played by Sherilyn Wolter), surfaced in Santa Barbara and kidnapped Eden. She hid Eden in a mountain cabin, guarded by Vietnam veteran Cain Garver (played by Scott Jacek). While a captive Eden watched Cain suffer from war flashbacks, Elena continued her vendetta against the Capwells. Meanwhile, the Capwells believed Eden was dead.

It was later discovered Elena was C. C.'s daughter by his first wife, Pamela. Thanks to the help of a reclusive mountain man, Eden managed to make it back to Santa Barbara. An accident, however, left Eden paralyzed and confined to a wheelchair. Cruz was anxious to reunite with Eden, but she discouraged him because of her paralysis. Later, Elena was killed and Cruz went on trial for her murder. While Cruz served time in prison, investigators discovered that Elena had

killed herself, influenced by Eden's psychotic ex-husband, Kirk. He was back in Santa Barbara creating trouble for Eden and the Capwells. Cruz was released from prison, Kirk was sent back to prison, and Eden regained the use of her legs. Eden and Cruz finally got married.

But the happy couple wasn't married long before their wedded bliss was shattered. Eden's doctor, Zack (played by Leigh McClosky), raped her. Not long after, Eden discovered she was pregnant. To Cruz's joy and relief, tests determined he was the father. A few months passed and Eden gave birth to a baby girl, Adriana. Before the baby took her first steps, she was kidnapped. Surprisingly, the kidnapper turned out to be Cruz's own sister-in-law, Hollis (Elizabeth Storm), who was desperately trying to

Below: *Despite once having been married to his father, Gina (Robin Mattson) had an affair with Mason (Lane Davies).*

Opposite page: *Kelly (Robin Wright) finally married Joe Perkins (Mark Arnold).*

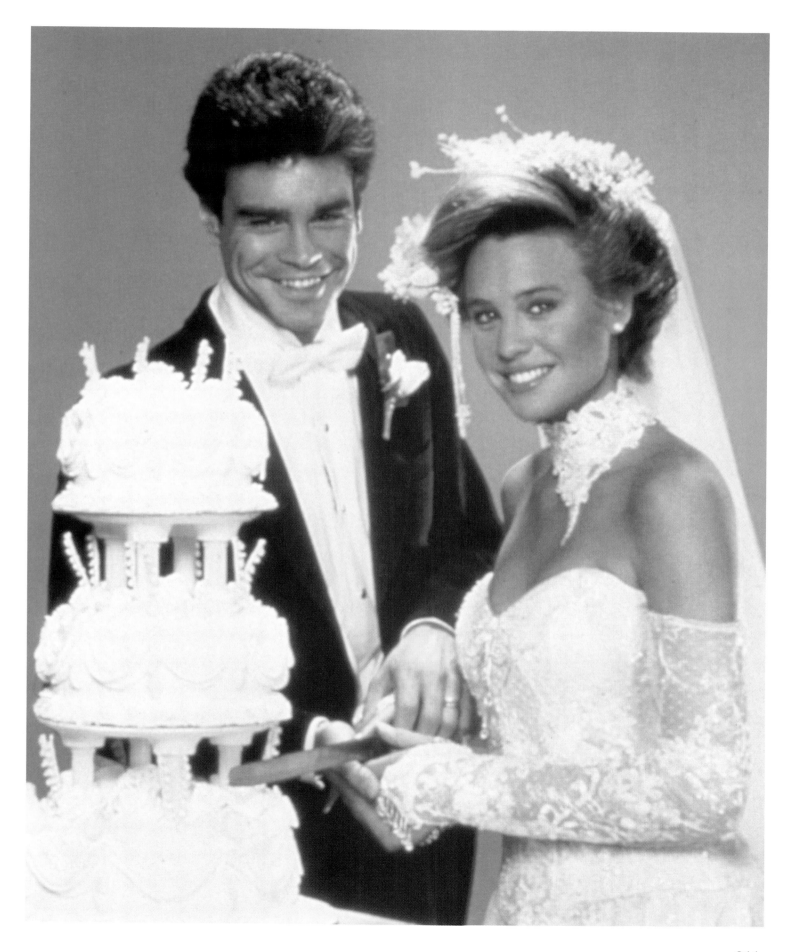

SANTA BARBARA

JULY 30, 1984–PRESENT NBC

replace her own dead child. Cruz and Eden managed to locate Adriana in Paris—following Zack's death from a rooftop. The baby was being raised by Hollis and Ric (played by Peter Love), Cruz's brother. Hollis returned Adriana to her natural parents, and then fell in a river and drowned.

It almost looked like Eden and Cruz would finally have a happy life together. Not long after their return to the States, however, Robert Barr (played by Roscoe Born), an old flame of Eden's, showed up in Santa Barbara. His presence forced Eden to confront her feelings. Did she love Cruz or Barr? Was it possible for her to love both of them? While Eden tried to sort out her feelings, Barr became romantically involved with Eden's sister, Kelly.

Describing Eden and Cruz's relationship, Martinez said, "[It] is really the old cliche of opposites attracting. They [the writers] did a good job of finding two people where one of them has a corner and the other one has a dent. But the bottom line that really makes it work is in the respect and the affection between Marcy and me." Martinez called his co-star "One of the bravest actors I've ever come across and it's inspiring. You know, all actors come from a different point of view, but there is a real clear view between us of what the other is doing and I respect her courage. We really care about each other and we know the difficulty that the other is addressing. Working with her is the most pleasant experience of my acting career—to mine the vein between those two

You can bet Laura Asher (Christopher Norris) and Mack Blake (Steve Bond) are up to no good.

Eden and Cruz (A Martinez) have been through many trials, but their love is always strong enough to bring them back together.

characters with her. If it was over tomorrow I would feel it was really worthwhile because I got to do that. It's just magic."

In 1990, John Conboy stepped in as executive producer. He had performed similar duties for *Capitol, The Young and the Restless,* and *Love Is a Many Splendored Thing.* Acknowledging Cruz and Eden's relationship as one of the serial's strengths, he said, "I think they are remarkable together, and that they are remarkable apart. I am going to introduce some major romantic stories that will involve Cruz and Eden, but they will involve a lot of other people on the show."

Evaluating the show, he said, "There needs to be more romance, with splashy, California coastline kinds of stories, with beautiful guys and beautiful girls. It has been down in the mines too much. It has been too dark. We are going to tell high adventure, and we are going to be on sailboats and beaches.... It hasn't been as romantic as it used to be, and I mean real, wild, escapism and romanticism, that guys as well as girls could say, 'I want to be there. I want to do that.' I want the feeling to be like a bumper sticker that says, 'I'd rather be watching *Santa Barbara.*'" Fans will be expecting the best from Conboy.

SEARCH FOR TOMORROW

SEPTEMBER 3, 1951–MARCH 26, 1982 (CBS)
MARCH 29, 1982–DECEMBER 26, 1986 (NBC)

*D*uring its 35-year history, this long-running serial followed the trials and tribulations of daytime television's most famous heroine, Joanne Gardner Barron Tate Vincente Tourneur (affecionately known as Jo). Creator Roy Winsor offered former MGM starlet Mary Stuart the role while lunching with her and her fiance, advertising executive Richard Krolik. "Mary Staurt had all the qualifications," explained Roy Winsor to writer Robert LaGuardia. "She was attractive, and I knew that she had the experience and was a hard worker. Obviously that first meeting brought us all tremendously good luck. I don't think we could have come up with a more perfect Joanne if we had searched the world."

Stuart accepted the role. Several weeks before the first live episode was broadcast, Roy Winsor and Procter & Gamble decided to change the name of their proposed serial from *Search for Happiness* to *Search for Tomorrow*. Agnes Eckhardt (later known as Agnes Nixon) was appointed headwriter for the first 13 weeks and then was replaced by Irving Vendig, who scripted the serial for the next seven years. (Ironically, Vendig, who lived in Sarasota, Florida, was never able to watch the series because the local television station in his town didn't carry it).

An early CBS press release described the serial as "the compelling story of the Barron family—father, mother, daughter-in-law, and grandchild. It is the story of an American family dominated by the 'old fashioned' elders, successful and secure. It is the story of a young widow and her child, and their pathetic struggle to voice the ideas of the young. It is the story of the folks next door, and the misunderstandings and heartbreaks that mar their lives."

The 15-minute serial was set in the small town of Henderson. It centered on a young married couple, Joanne and Keith Barron, and their little daughter, Patti. Creator Roy Winsor, who scripted several episodes of the radio soap *Ma Perkins*, saw Jo as "a kind of young Ma Perkins, the sort of woman who cared about her neighbors' problems, who could offer help to others, and who could face her own personal troubles with dignity." Keith's parents, Irene and Victor Barron,

figured heavily in the serial's early days, creating problems for Jo and Patti.

Shortly after the series' premiere, Jo acquired new next-door neighbors, the Bergmans. Stu (played by Larry Haines) and Marge (played by Melba Rae) also had a little girl, Janet (originally played by Ellen Spencer). The Bergmans, who had a keen sense of humor, were always quick with a joke or a smile. They provided a balance to the serial's melodramatic storylines. They were created for only a handful of episodes, but the audience responded so positively that they were made a part of the series. In 1971, Melba Rae died from a cerebral hemorrhage. *Search for Tomorrow* acknowledged the actress's death at the end of an episode, and a few months later her character quietly died off-camera.

Widow Jo Barron (Mary Stuart) had trouble raising her daughter, Patti (Lynn Loring), alone. Not the least of her worries was her meddlesome mother-in-law.

Mary Stuart was the only person to play Jo in all of the soap's 35 years.

Since these were the early days of television, production values, compared to the lavish serials seen today, were primitive. The budget for one week's worth of episodes in 1951 was $8,025.75 (it would cost more than $300,000 to produce a week's worth of episodes of a half-hour serial today). The sets were merely suggestions of living areas. Doors and window frames were hung on piano wire from a grid to show walls. Furniture was grouped together in an imaginary space. The home viewing audience saw black walls in every room because the walls of the studio were covered with black velour to absorb light and create the illusion of enclosed areas.

Live broadcasts also presented a series of unique problems. If an episode ended too early, Mary Stuart and Larry Haines were often asked by the show's director to fill the time by making up phone conversations. During an intimate scene played between two lovers in a park beneath a moonlight sky, a loud crash was suddenly heard. With an awareness of the show's audience, one of the actors justified the noise by muttering, "Those darn squirrels!"

Search for Tomorrow was the first soap to feature a pregnancy in its storyline. Following closely on the heels of Lucy Ricardo's famous pregnancy in the early fifties, Jo became pregnant and bore a son. The storyline was created to accomodate the real-life pregnancy of Mary Stuart. Like her television character, Stuart gave birth to a son. A few years later, much to the chagrin of Stuart, her television son was struck by a speeding automobile and later died from his

THE CAST

Original Cast

LOUISE BARRON	SARA ANDERSON
VICTOR BARRON	CLIFF HALL
IRENE BARRON	BESS JOHNSON
PATTI BARRON	LYNN LORING
NED HILTON	COE NORTON
JOANNE BARRON	MARY STUART
KEITH BARRON	JOHN SYLVESTER

Final Cast

CAGNEY McCLEARY	MATTHEW ASHFORD
DAVE GLENN	JACK BETTS
ESTELLE	DOMINI BLYTHE
HOGAN McCLEARY	DAVID FORSYTH
LIZA KENDALL	LOUAN GIDEON
WILMA	ANITA GILLETTE
BELLA	PAUL ESPEL
STU BERGMAN	LARRY HAINES
JERRY	TIM LOUGHLIN
SUNNY ADAMSON	MARCIA McCABE
KATE McCLEARY	MAEVE McGUIRE
QUINN McCLEARY	JEFF MEEK
PATTI McCLEARY	JACQUELINE SCHULTZ
JOANNE BARRON TOURNEUR	MARY STUART
MATT McCLEARY	PATRICK TOVATT

SEARCH FOR TOMORROW

SEPTEMBER 3, 1951–MARCH 26, 1982 (CBS)
MARCH 29, 1982–DECEMBER 26, 1986 (NBC)

injuries. "When that baby died, even if it happened only in the script, I was emotionally involved," said Stuart.

"You know, we couldn't show the baby on camera because of New York state laws. The writers gradually became bored trying to find ways to refer to him without showing him. That's when they decided to 'kill' him."

In 1968, *Search for Tomorrow* expanded to 30 minutes. Until then, the serial was followed by another 15-minute soap, *The Guiding Light*. Creator Irna Phillips felt confined by *The Guiding Light's* 15-minute format and once suggested to Mary Stuart they combine the two soaps, creating a new, single 30-minute serial. *Search for Tomorrow's* leading lady, understandably, was against the idea.

Weeks after *Search for Tomorrow's* debut, Keith was killed in a car accident. For the first time in her young life, a penniless Jo was forced to seek work. She finally found a job at Henderson Hospital. Keith's interfering mother, Irene, didn't approve of how Jo was raising Patti and tried to win custody of her granddaughter. When her legal maneuvers failed, a desperate Irene kidnapped Patti. Eventually, Patti was returned to Jo and Irene accepted her new role as a loving—though interfering—grandmother.

While working at Henderson Hospital, Jo fell in love with fellow employee Arthur Tate (originally played by Terry O'Sullivan). Soon after, Jo left her job at the hospital and began operating the Motor Haven (a roadside motel). She also accepted Arthur's marriage proposal. On the day

Jo and Patti hoped to be a happy family again when Jo married Arthur Tate (Terry O'Sullivan), but new troubles were brewing for Jo.

216

of their wedding, a woman arrived in town who claimed to be Arthur's believed-dead wife, Hazel (played by Mary Patton). Actually, she was the late Hazel's identical twin sister, Sue, who had been hired by the mob to prevent Jo and Arthur's wedding. The mob wanted to take over Jo's Motor Haven and use it as a front to traffic drugs.

Nathan Walsh (played by George Petrie), a close friend of Jo and Arthur's, discovered Sue was passing herself off as Hazel. Jo, Arthur, and Nathan staged a phony fire and hired an actress to impersonate Sue's late sister. Horrified by seeing her sister, Sue fled into the woods, where she was later found murdered. Jo was accused of the murder, but Nathan and Arthur were able to provide the police with the identity of the real killer (a mobster) and Jo was cleared of all charges. Unfortunately, Arthur was shot trying to clear Jo; the shot left Arthur paralyzed. Despondent over his condition, Arthur delayed their wedding plans.

After Arthur's death, Jo fell in love with Sam Reynolds, but his estranged wife, Andrea Whiting (Joan Copeland), refused to give him a divorce.

Meanwhile, the mob continued with their plans to take over the Motor Haven. Backed by the mob, Rose Peabody (originally played by Lee Grant, then Nita Talbot, and finally, Constance Ford) moved to Henderson and wormed her way into Jo and Arthur's lives. Accompanying Rose was her mute brother, Wilbur (played by Don Knotts). In an attempt to discredit Jo, Rose plotted to serve poisoned soup at the diner. At the last minute, Rose changed her mind and poured the soup down the drain.

Psychiatric treatment found that Wilbur was made mute by a traumatic experience. When he was a young boy, Wilbur witnessed Rose trying to kill their foster father after he tried to sexually assault her. Wilbur's revelation caused him to regain his voice. Soon after, he and his reformed sister left town.

Despite Arthur's paralysis, Jo convinced him to marry her. Jo became pregnant. The Motor Haven began having financial difficulties. To keep from going bankrupt, Arthur enlisted the financial help of his domineering rich aunt, Cornelia Simmons (played by Doris Dalton). Moving to Henderson, Cornelia took an instant dislike to Jo and tried to bust up her marriage. Jo was too busy caring for her new baby, Duncan, to notice Cornelia's intense animosity.

One day while Duncan was outside playing, a car struck and killed him. Compounding Jo's grief was news that her mother had also died. Jo's father, Frank Gardner (originally played by Eric Dressler), and her sister, Eunice (originally played by Marion Brash), soon moved to Henderson to join Jo.

Jo's marriage didn't have a happy ending. Arthur had a growing problem with alcoholism. And Eunice was immediately attracted to Arthur, whose paralysis was cured, and succeeded in seducing him. Even worse, a guilt-ridden Eunice later told Jo about the affair. Overcome with shame, Arthur accepted an offer from Cornelia that would mean moving to Puerto Rico. During Arthur's absence, Cornelia married an attractive younger man, Rex Twining (originally played by Larry Hugo). Before the ink dried on their wedding license, Eunice was sleeping with Rex.

Unhappy with his new job in Puerto Rico, Arthur returned to Henderson and was surprised to discover his aunt had been murdered. Eunice and Rex were tried for her murder and found guilty. The culprit turned out to be Cornelia's housekeeper, Harriet Baxter (originally played by Vicki Vola).

Arthur and Jo patched up their differences and resumed their lives as a married couple. But

SEARCH FOR TOMORROW

SEPTEMBER 3, 1951–MARCH 26, 1982 (CBS)
MARCH 29, 1982–DECEMBER 26, 1986 (NBC)

failed business ventures drove Arthur to develop a drinking problem. Not long after, he died from a heart attack.

After grieving Arthur's death, Jo fell in love with Sam Reynolds (originally played by Robert Mandan), a former business associate of Arthur's. Sam wasn't free to marry Jo because he was already married to Andrea Whiting (played longest by Joan Copeland). Despite being separated for several years, Andrea refused to give Sam a divorce. When Andrea learned Sam was in love with Jo, she tried to kill him by slipping a drug called Hemadol into Sam's drink. Confusing Sam's glass with her own, Andrea ended up taking the drink. While a poisoned Andrea was rushed to the hospital to have her stomach pumped, Sam was charged with attempted murder. Reluctant to see

Sam sentenced to prison, Andrea confessed. After seeing a psychiatrist for treatment, Andrea agreed to divorce Sam. Jo and Sam made wedding plans, but at the last minute, Sam was called to Africa on a business trip.

While Sam was out of the country, Jo was involved in a car accident and she lost her eyesight. While in the hospital recovering from the accident, friends gently informed her that Sam had been killed in Africa.

Tony Vincente (originally played by Anthony George), Jo's handsome doctor, was a great source of comfort as she worked through her latest crisis. Realizing Tony and Jo had fallen in love, Tony's wealthy, manipulative wife, Marcy (originally played by Jeanne Carson), pretended to be crippled so her husband wouldn't desert her.

Below: *The cast celebrates the 6,000th show of* Search for Tomorrow.

Opposite page: *NBC tried to revitalize the show in February 1986, by bringing Jo and her daughter Patti (Jacqueline Schultz) once again to the forefront. Unfortunately, the new structure was too late, the show was canceled in December of that year.*

218

SEARCH FOR TOMORROW

SEPTEMBER 3, 1951–MARCH 26, 1982 (CBS)
MARCH 29, 1982–DECEMBER 26, 1986 (NBC)

When Tony discovered she was faking her paralysis, he divorced her. In the meantime, Jo's eyesight returned. The happy couple immediately made plans to marry.

Before walking down the aisle with Tony, Jo received shocking news. Sam was alive and back in Henderson. He had spent the last few years as a political prisoner in a foreign country. Jo resumed her relationship with Sam and again agreed to marry him. But just before the ceremony, Jo suddenly lost her eyesight. A doctor determined that Jo's blindness was caused by emotional stress. Apparently, Jo was really in love with Tony and longed to be his wife. Unable to face up to her feelings, Jo went blind.

It was then apparent that Sam had developed mental problems as a prisoner. Afraid of losing Jo to Tony, a crazed Sam kidnapped Jo and hid her in a cabin deep in the woods. While Sam was holding Jo hostage, two dangerous hippies stumbled onto their hideaway in need of shelter and food. Armed with a gun, they shot and killed Sam. The shock of Sam's death caused Jo's eyesight to return. Back in Henderson, Jo proceeded with her plans to marry Tony.

Shortly after the ceremony, an attractive nurse named Stephanie Wilkins (played by Marie Cheatham) moved to Henderson. She accused Tony of fathering her young daughter, Wendy (originally played by Andrea McArdle). Stephanie's

Left: Ken Kercheval played Dr. Nick Hunter, but went on to bigger fame on the prime-time soap Dallas.

Right: Robert Mandan played Sam Reynolds, Jo's third husband. He become more well known when he appeared in Soap.

deception was exposed when Wendy's real father, Dave Wilkins (played by Dale Robinette), surfaced and claimed Wendy as his daughter. Soon after, Tony suffered a fatal heart attack when he was beaten up by drug mobsters in Henderson Hospital's stairwell.

Several years passed before Jo was able to fall in love again. In the meantime, she focused her attention on her business life and opened an inn with her best friend, Stu Bergman. One of their guests, Chris Delon (played by Paul Dumont), was hiding from gangsters. When the gangsters finally tracked him down, Jo was accidently shot. After being in a coma for a week, Jo's doctor, Bob Rogers (originally played by Carl Low), informed her she'd never walk again. Fortunately his prognosis turned out to be incorrect. A short while later, Jo was, indeed, on her feet again.

The wealthy Martin Tourneur (John Aniston) was the next lucky man to marry Jo. She was so in love with him she overlooked his compulsive drinking and gambling habits. Soon after they married, Jo discovered Martin in bed with her archrival, Stephanie. Betrayed by Martin's indiscretion, Jo filed for divorce.

Jo's last big storyline was in 1983, when she was kidnapped by a deranged man named Vargas (played by John Glover). He mistakenly believed Jo was his mother. Vargas was intent on killing Jo, but she persuaded him to contact her ex-husband Martin and demand a $250,000 ransom. When Vargas tried to collect the money, the police caught him and located Jo.

In 1982, CBS canceled *Search for Tomorrow* following a drop in the ratings (constant changes in the series' time slot were largely responsible for

SEARCH FOR TOMORROW

SEPTEMBER 3, 1951–MARCH 26, 1982 (CBS)
MARCH 29, 1982–DECEMBER 26, 1986 (NBC)

"To me, this woman I play, Joanne Tate, represents the mother of us," Mary Stuart told *TV Guide* in 1961. "As a result, I feel very strongly about what she says. I'd like the character to be an example not only to me but to every woman."

When Stuart shared her ideas about how she'd like to see women represented on television to creator Roy Winsor during a casual lunch, she didn't realize she was talking herself into a job that would last more than 35 years. "I really didn't know what to say to him," recalled Stuart, "so I just started making haphazard conversation. He was involved with television producing and I just happened to say that I felt that television wasn't satisfying the needs of women. Radio wasn't, either. 'Women are too perfect on radio and television shows,' I said. 'Women can't see themselves. Why can't television do something real for them?' I don't even think I was all that sure of what I was talking about, but I had to say something. Roy then said to me, 'You should play the lead in that kind of television program.'"

Stuart was raised in Tulsa, Oklahoma. At age 12, she was singing with local bands and performing for the USO. After graduating from high school, she landed a job as a photojournalist. Stuart saved the money she earned from her job to move to New York. She planned to pursue a career in theater.

Prior to beginning her role as Joanne Barron on *Search for Tomorrow* in 1951, Stuart was a contract player for MGM in Hollywood. "I had small parts in big pictures and big parts in small pictures," she explained. Her film credits include *The Girl from Jones Beach*, which also starred Ronald Reagan, *Colt 45* and *The Adventures of Don Juan* (both starring Errol Flynn), and *Thunderhoof.* By 1950, Stuart tired of Hollywood and had returned to New York. She intended to resume her stage career. Instead, she was cast on *Search for Tomorrow.*

When the show premiered, she was newly married to advertising executive Richard Krolik. They had two children, Cynthia and Jeffrey. Mary and Richard divorced in 1966. She later married Wolfgang Neumann.

A professional singer, Stuart has recorded two albums. She also published an autobiography, *Both of Me,* in 1980. Stuart was the first daytime performer to be nominated for an Emmy, competing against Shirley Booth and Mary Tyler Moore in 1962. In 1983, she was honored with a Lifetime Achievement Award.

Shortly after receiving the news about *Search for Tomorrow's* cancellation, Stuart told a reporter, "Let's be happy for the 35 years."

Mary Stuart relaxing after a hard day on the set.

its decline in popularity). Believing that the series had grown too old for the youthful audience the network desired, CBS replaced it with a sexier new soap, *Capitol.* NBC immediately picked up *Search for Tomorrow* and scheduled the serial in its original late morning time slot. Unfortunately, constant cast changes and various teams of producers and headwriters cost the show its focus. Despite many attempts to rescue the struggling series, Procter & Gamble finally decided to cancel it in December 1986, three months after the serial celebrated its thirty-fifth anniversary.

Story consultant Pam Long revealed that the writers had considered a wedding between Jo and Stu for the last episode, but nixed the idea. Explaining why the proposed wedding was scrapped, Long said, "I talked to Mary Stuart immediately after the show was canceled, and I think there was a feeling that there had been such a friendship for so many years that she for sure felt that was what it was. Certainly we played around with the idea that at least on his [Stu's] part it was probably unrequited love and had been for some time, that he could never find another woman who could quite compare to Jo. But, on the other hand, that doesn't mean she would return those feelings."

When asked how she'd like people to remember Jo, Mary Stuart told a reporter, "on her way to someplace—in motion."

In the final episode, Stu found himself alone with Jo following her daughter Patti's wedding. "What are you searching for," he quietly asked. "Tomorrow," replied Jo. "And I can't wait."

THE SECRET STORM

FEBRUARY 1, 1954–FEBRUARY 8, 1974 CBS

This long-running serial was originally titled *The Storm Within*. The title wasn't appealing to one of the show's sponsors, Bisodol (an antacid), who was worried it would inspire images of an upset stomach. To appease Bisodol, the serial was retitled *The Secret Storm*.

Set in the small town of Woodbridge, New York, the show centered on the newly rich, neurotic Ames family. In the first episode, patriarch Peter Ames was left to raise his three children alone after his wife, Ellen, was killed in an automobile accident. The audience would soon discover that sudden deaths, mental illnesses, exotic diseases, and extramarital affairs figured heavily in storylines.

Viewers became so involved with the serial that it wasn't uncommon for CBS to be flooded with thousands of angry letters following the death of a well-liked character. This was most evident when Jill and Hugh Clayborne, a popular couple on the series, were suddenly disposed of in a plane crash. Surprised by the overwhelmingly negative response they received, the producers regretted killing off the characters.

For a period during the fifties, the serial was produced in Liederkranz Hall, next door to the *Captain Kangaroo* set. Animals scheduled to appear on the children's series would often wander onto the soap set. One day, director Gloria Monty mistook a cow for a bull and barricaded herself in the control room until the studio manager was able to rescue her. Realizing Gloria's nervousness about the animals, one of the show's actors decided to play a trick on her. Before she arrived at the studio, he placed a chimpanzee in the control room. The late David O'Brien, who played Kip Rysdale, told a reporter, "Everybody had a lot of fun playing tricks on Gloria. She was always slightly on the ragged edge of hysteria. She was a terribly good director, but anything that had fur and crawled around made her hysterical."

The Secret Storm premiered as a 15-minute serial, then it expanded to 30 minutes in 1962. The Ames family figured prominetly during the serial's first 15 years. Peter was a widower with two teenage children, Susan and Jerry, and a nine-year-old daughter, Amy. Ellen's unexpected death had an especially painful effect on Peter and young Jerry. For awhile, the family feared

Peter was losing his mind. Later, he turned to alcohol for comfort.

Jerry tried to kill the man responsible for his mother's death, which led to his being sent to reform school. Susan attempted to deal with her mother's death by taking over her mother's responsibilities in the family. Unfortunately, the teenager was not equipped to handle such adult responsiblities and soon became bossy and domineering. Young Amy was lost in the shuffle.

Fate played with the lives of these residents of Woodbridge: (clockwise, starting at top) Nick Kane (Keith Charles), Paul Britton (Nicolas Coster), Valerie Hill Ames (Lori March), Amy Ames (Jada Rowland), Belle Clemens (Marla Adams), and Joan Borman Kane (Christina Crawford).

Top: *Ken Stevens (Joel Crothers) and Laurie Hollister Stevens (Stephanie Braxton) talk to Laurie's mother, Nola (Mary K. Wells).*

Bottom: *Susan Ames (Judy Lewis) took over the mothering role for her family after the death of her own mother. She later married Alan Dunbar, who had shady connections. He cleaned up his act after marrying Susan, and became an investment banker.*

THE CAST

Original Cast

GRACE TYRELL . . . . MARJORIE GATESON
J. T. TYRELL . . . . RUSSELL HICKS
PETER AMES . . . . PETER HOBBS
JERRY AMES . . . . ROBERT MORSE
SUSAN AMES . . . . JEAN MOWRY
AMY AMES . . . . JADA ROWLAND
PAULINE HARRIS . . . . HAILA STODDARD

Final Cast

KEVIN KINCAID . . . . DAVID ACKROYD
BELLE CLEMENS KINCAID . . . . MARLA ADAMS
JOANNA MORRISON . . . . ELLEN BARBER
DAN KINCAID . . . . BERNARD BARROW
LAURI HOLLISTER REDDIN . . . . STEPHANIE BRAXTON
BRIAN NEEVES . . . . KEITH CHARLES
NIELE NEEVES . . . . BETSY VON FURSTENBERG
MARK REDDIN . . . . DAVID GALE
ROBERT LANDERS . . . . DAN HAMILTON
VALERIE HILL AMES NORTHCOTE . . . . LORI MARCH
DOREEN POST . . . . LINDA PURL
AMY AMES . . . . JADA ROWLAND
LISA BRITTON . . . . JUDY SAFRAN
STACE REDDIN . . . . GARY SANDY
JESSIE REDDIN . . . . FRANCES STERNHAGEN

THE SECRET STORM

FEBRUARY 1, 1954–FEBRUARY 8, 1974 CBS

When Peter was finally ready to begin another relationship, he fell in love with the family's housekeeper Jane Edwards. But the relationship was threatened by his overly possessive daughter, Susan, and his meddling, disapproving sister-in-law, Pauline Harris. Before Peter had eloped with Ellen, he was romatically involved with Pauline. She always resented her sister's marriage to Peter and—although she was unwilling to admit it—still carried a torch for Peter. Digging into Jane's background, Pauline succeeded in locating her believed-dead husband, Bruce Edwards. Reunited with Bruce, Jane canceled her plans to marry Peter.

Peter eventually fell in love with attractive Myra Lake and married her. Once again, Susan and Pauline did their best to undermine the relationship. It didn't help that Myra's own family disapproved of Peter. Deciding their problems were too big, Peter and Myra quickly filed for divorce.

Amy blossomed into a beautiful young woman. Sadly, her chaotic childhood made it difficult for Amy to choose men wisely. When she was a high school student, she fell in love with the rebellious Kip Rysdale. His father, the wealthy Arthur Rysdale, had recently married Amy's aunt, Pauline. Both families hoped to see the young couple marry, but Kip got involved with Nina di Francisco, the daughter of his high school Spanish teacher. Kip accidentally killed the girl and was forced to serve a prison sentence. Amy forgave Kip for being unfaithful and promised to wait for him.

Life as a college student, however, made it difficult for Amy to keep her word. While attending Woodbridge University as a freshman, Amy fell in love with her history professor, Paul Britton. Paul returned Amy's affections, but explained he wouldn't divorce his wife, Terry, because of their young son. When Amy ended up pregnant, Paul finally offered to divorce Terry and marry her. Suspecting that Paul only wanted to marry her out of obligation, Amy refused. Instead, Amy vowed to raise her child alone.

Before the baby was born, Kip was released from prison. Although Kip knew Amy was pregnant with Paul's child, he was still in love with her and proposed marriage. Suddenly fearful about being a single mother, Amy accepted. A few months later, she gave birth to a baby girl, Lisa. To Kip's disappointment, Amy's lingering love for Paul made it impossible for her to engage in sexual relations with him. When a divorced Paul resurfaced in Woodbridge, he persuaded Amy to divorce Kip and marry him.

Peter finally found happiness with his third wife, Valerie. But their happiness proved to be short-lived. While away on a business trip, Peter suffered a fatal heart attack. Meanwhile, Jerry moved to Paris with his wife, Hope, a renowned painter.

Audrey Landers has played in many soaps, including The Secret Storm, *where she played Joanna Morrison. She is currently on* One Life to Live.

Cory Boucher (Terry Kiser) talks to Grace Tyrell (Eleanor Phelps) and Amy Ames (Jada Rowland).

Amy's marriage to Paul was threatened by her archrival, Belle Clemens. They became enemies after Belle's illegitimate daughter, Robin, died in a boating accident in which Amy was also involved. Although Robin's death was accidental, Belle blamed Amy and vowed to destroy her marriage to Paul. To Amy's anguish, Belle's efforts worked. A smitten Paul divorced Amy and soon married Belle.

Amy's sister, Susan, married a reformed criminal, Alan Dunbar. He was later listed as killed in action in Vietnam. After working through her grief, Susan fell in love with newspaper reporter Frank Craver. Soon after their marriage, Alan turned up alive in Woodbridge, psychotic from his war experiences. He got involved in an illegal drug operation headed by Dan Kincaid, who was running for governor.

Bored by her marriage to a college professor, Belle divorced Paul and set her sights on Dan, who she believed would be the state's next governor. Meanwhile, Amy had fallen in love with Dan's son, Kevin, a lawyer. In rapid succession, Belle married Dan, and Amy wed Kevin. Despite belonging to the same family, Belle and Amy continued to be enemies.

THE SECRET STORM

FEBRUARY 1, 1954–FEBRUARY 8, 1974 CBS

Belle's wish to become First Lady ended when Dan's criminal activities were exposed and he was sent to prison. In retaliation against Dan, Kevin was shot by one of Dan's mobster associates and paralyzed from the waist down. Susan went on trial for killing Alan, but it was soon discovered that Alan had died in a shootout with Dan's drug-dealing friends. Once Susan was cleared of murder, she married Frank and they quickly left town.

Shortly before Kevin was paralyzed, an excited Amy informed him she was pregnant. Her news was premature; she wasn't pregnant. Worried about depressing Kevin, who was also left impotent by the shooting, Amy secretly arranged to be artifically inseminated by her friend, Dr. Brian Neeves. Unknown to Amy, Brian was the donor. When Kevin inadvertently discovered the truth, he divorced Amy. She and her new daughter, Danielle, moved in with her stepmother, Valerie. Amy soon became romantically involved with Brian. Meanwhile, a wheelchair-confined Kevin made plans to move to London.

The Secret Storm remained one of daytime television's most popular serials until 1969, when it was purchased by CBS. The network executives were inexperienced at producing soap operas and began tinkering with the serial's format. Cast members were suddenly dropped without warning and new characters were constantly introduced, only to be written out a few months later. It was also switched to a less-desirable late-afternoon time slot. By 1974, the serial had gone through several writers and was daytime television's lowest-rated soap. CBS canceled the series in February 1974, and replaced it with a game show.

In the final episode, Amy realized why Kevin divorced her and ended her affair with Brian. She realized that Kevin was the only man she'd ever truly love. Amy returned home and found Kevin sitting in her living room. When she went to rush toward him, Kevin insisted she remain standing where she was. Kevin rose from his wheelchair and tried to walk to her. After a few steps, he fell to the floor. A happy, tearful Amy went to her ex-husband and lovingly hugged him. A few moments later, Valerie, Lisa, and baby Danielle joined the reunited couple on the floor, forming a circle of love.

In the late sixties, Joan Crawford's adopted daughter, Christina Crawford, was appearing on *The Secret Storm* as the self-centered Joan Kane. When an ailment forced Christina to be hospitalized, Joan volunteered to step in and perform her role on the popular daytime soap. Christina was surprised by her mother's offer and found it a little farfetched. After all, the character she played was 24 years old. At that time, Joan was 64.

But the serial's producers graciously accepted Joan's offer. CBS supported the move because they thought it would attract millions of new viewers to *The Secret Storm*. To accomodate Joan's schedule, the producers taped all her scenes in a single weekend and then aired them over a four-day period. Joan was paid $585, which she donated to her hairdresser.

Watching Joan's episodes from her hospital bed, Christina was disheartened to see her mother visibly drunk. The embarrassing, sad incident is described in detail in Christina's best-selling autobiography, *Mommie Dearest*.

Below: *Ken Kercheval played Archie Borman.*

Opposite page: *When Christina Crawford got sick, her mother, Joan Crawford, offered to play her part.*

SOAP

SEPTEMBER 13, 1977–APRIL 20, 1981 ABC

This weekly half-hour serial billed itself as a satire of soap operas. Storylines revolved around the wealthy Tates and the working-class Campbells. Chester Tate was a self-important, grandiose businessman who frequently engaged in extramarital affairs. His wife, Jessica, rarely had her head out of the clouds. Their oversexed eldest daughter, Corinne, changed boyfriends the way most people change their bedroom sheets. Their conservative middle daughter, Eunice, fell in love with a married politician and then a former convict. Billy, the adolescent son, was sexually pursued by his high school teacher. Also living with the Tates was Jessica's father, "The Major," who dressed in his old army uniform and still believed he was fighting World War II. Benson was their surly butler who couldn't keep his nose out of the family's personal affairs.

Living in the poorer section of town was Jessica's sister, Mary. Burt Campbell, Mary's second husband, was a construction worker. Mary's two sons from her first marriage lived with the Campbells: Danny, who was mixed up with the mob, and Jody, who was gay. Burt's ventriloquist son, Chuck, moved in with the Campbells midseason with his dummy, Bob.

The primary storyline during the serial's first season was the murder of Burt's other son, handsome tennis pro Peter Campbell (who spent more time in bed with his female students than on the courts). A jilted Corinne was first accused of killing Peter. Then the finger of blame pointed at Jessica, who was tried and convicted for the crime. In the serial's first season cliff-hanger, an off-screen narrator informed viewers of Jessica's innocence and challenged them to guess the identity of the real killer.

The cast of Soap.

Top: *By the time Danny Dallas (Ted Wass) realized he loved Elaine Lefkowitz (Dinah Manoff), she had already been killed by mobsters.*

Bottom: *Benson (Robert Guillaume) was the wise-cracking butler, who left the show to be on his own spin-off, titled* Benson.

THE CAST

Cast

MILLIE	CANDANCE AZZARA
BILLY TATE	JIMMY BAIO
CAROL DAVID	REBECCA BALDING
SAUNDERS	ROSCOE LEE BROWNE
DETECTIVE DONAHUE	JOHN BYNER
CORINNE TATE	DIANA CANOVA
JODIE DALLAS	BILLY CRYSTAL
MARY DALLAS CAMPBELL	CATHRYN DAMON
BENSON	ROBERT GUILLAUME
ALICE	RANDEE HELLER
JESSICA TATE	KATHERINE HELMOND
CHUCK/BOB CAMPBELL	JAY JOHNSON
THE GODFATHER	RICHARD LIBERTINI
CHESTER TATE	ROBERT MANDAN
ELAINE LEFKOWITZ	DINAH MANOFF
ALAN POSNER	ALLAN MILLER
SALLY	CAROLINE McWILLIAMS
POLLY DAWSON	LYNN MOODY
BURT CAMPBELL	RICHARD MULLIGAN
LESLIE WALKER	MARLA PENNINGTON
THE MAJOR	ARTHUR PETERSON
CLAIRE	KATHRYN REYNOLDS
MAGGIE CHANDLER	BARBARA RHOADES
DUTCH	DONNELLY RHODES
EUNICE TATE	JENNIFER SALT
EL PURECO VALDEZ	GREGORY SIERRA
PETER CAMPBELL	ROBERT URICH
FATHER TIM FLOTSKY	SAL VISCUSO
DANNY DALLAS	TED WASS
GWEN	JESSE WELLES

SOAP

SEPTEMBER 13, 1977–APRIL 20, 1981 ABC

When the serial's second season opened, Chester confessed to killing Peter. Chester was imprisoned for a short time before escaping with his cell mate, Dutch. Chester lost his memory and ended up on the West Coast, where he was employed as a fry cook at a greasy diner. Meanwhile, Dutch eloped with Eunice. Jessica hired Detective Donahue to find Chester, but then she fell in love with Donahue. When Chester resurfaced, she was forced to choose between them. Jessica picked Chester, but their reunion was short-lived. Her brief affair with South American revolutionary "El Puerco" led to their divorce.

Soon after saving Billy from a religious cult—the Sunnies—Benson quit his job and moved to supervise the kitchen staff for a governor's mansion (where he was featured in his own series). His position was filled by an equally snooty gentleman, Saunders. Corinne wed former priest Timothy Flotsky. Six weeks after the ceremony, she gave birth to a baby possessed by Satan. Her entire family rallied together to assist in the exorcism.

Burt was kidnapped by aliens and cloned. An unknowing Mary made love to the clone. She gave birth to a baby nine months later, but who was the father? Mary's gay son, Jodie, tried having a relationship with a woman, Carol David. Their brief union also produced a baby, followed later by a bitter custody battle.

Danny was forced to marry a mobster's daughter, Elaine Lefkowitz. By the time Danny realized he loved Elaine, she was kidnapped by thugs and murdered. He was also involved in an interracial romance with a woman named Polly Dawson. In the serial's final season, Danny questioned his feelings for a hooker, Gwen.

Faithful viewers of *Soap* were disappointed by its final episode, which ended as a cliff-hanger. No storylines were resolved. Just when Danny finally realized he loved Gwen, Jodie announced she was *his* new girlfriend. A shooting put Danny in the hospital, where doctors informed the family he'd need a compatible kidney donor to survive. Jodie volunteered, but an embarrassed Mary revealed that Danny and Jodie had different fathers. Meanwhile, Jessica was left facing a firing squad in a South American country.

Producers of the serial explained that ABC announced the cancellation of the series after the final episode was taped. There was talk of reuniting the cast and crew for one more episode to tie up loose ends, but it was decided against for financial reasons.

Below: *Despite being gay, Jodie Dallas (Billy Crystal) married and had a baby.*

Opposite page: *Corrine Tate (Diana Canova) married former priest Tim Flotsky (Sal Viscuso).*

SOMERSET

. . . .

MARCH 30, 1970–DECEMBER 31, 1976 NBC

*T*his half-hour serial began as a spin-off of *Another World* and was originally titled, *Another World—Somerset*. To lure viewers of the highly rated *Another World*, three popular characters from that soap moved to Somerset, located approximately 50 miles from Bay City, Michigan (the setting for *Another World*). They were Missy Palmer Matthews, lawyer Sam Lucas, and Lahoma, his southern wife. During the serial's first season, *Another World's* headwriter, Robert Cenedella, penned scripts for the new series.

The wealthy Delaneys served as the town's leading family (nearly half the town worked for the family-owned Delaney Brands). Widowed patriarch Jasper Delaney had three adult children: Robert, Peter, and Laura. When the serial began, Robert was trying to get out of his unhappy marriage to the self-centered India. Meanwhile, ditzy Laura was married to the noble Rex Cooper, who generously helped raise Laura's illegitimate son, Tony, as his own.

The middle-class Grants were in contrast to the powerful Delaneys. India's modest elder sister, Ellen, was married to Ben Grant, Sam Lucas's partner in a small law firm. Ben and Ellen, his wife, had two teenage children: Jill and David. Jill's tortured adolescent romance with Tony Cooper was a leading storyline in the serial's early days. Their relationship came to a screeching halt when Tony learned he was illegitimate. To Tony's horror, his real father turned out to be the shifty manager of the Riverboat Casino, Ike Harding.

Robert was romantically interested in singer Jessica Buchanan, who performed the lounge act for the Riverboat Casino. The only reason Robert didn't divorce India was his domineering father, who was cut from the same cloth as the manipulative India.

Jasper ended up being murdered, and Robert was first suspected of committing the crime. Actually, Ike Harding killed Jasper. News that Ike killed her father led a fragile Laura to believe she was partly responsible. She then suffered a nervous breakdown. With Jasper dead, Robert divorced India and married Jessica. Immediately following their wedding ceremony, Robert and Jessica left town. The following year, Robert surfaced in *Another World's* Bay City, devastated by the death of Jessica and their infant child in a plane crash. Settling down in Bay City, Robert found worked as an architect.

When Robert Cenedella stepped down as headwriter, Henry Slesar, *The Edge of Night's* longtime writer, took over. He was responsible for phasing out the Delaneys and moving *Somerset* toward a crime/mystery format similar to *The Edge of Night*. His most famous storyline involved the wealthy Moores. David Grant's new girlfriend,

Teenage siblings Jill (Susan McDonald) and David Grant (Ron Martin).

India Delaney's (Marie Wallace) and Ellen Grant's (Georgeann Johnson) husbands often were involved in business together.

the sickly but sweet Andrea Moore (played by Harriet Hall) was slowly being poisoned by a member of her own family. The suspects included her aristocratic mother, Emily (played by Lois Kibbee); her aspiring novelist brother, Dana (played by Christopher Pennock); her mother's money-grubbing husband, Philip Matson (played by Frank Schofield); his bizarre son, Carter (played by Jay Gregory); his neurotic daughter, Zoe (played by Lois Smith); or Zoe's former concert pianist husband, Julian Cannell (originally played by Joel Crothers). The culprit turned out to be Zoe, who suspected her husband was in love with Andrea.

In 1974, Henry Slesar resigned from *Somerset* to focus his full attention on *The Edge of Night.* Longtime soap veteran Roy Winsor (who helped create *Love of Life, The Secret Storm,* and *Search for Tomorrow*) stepped in and moved *Somerset* toward a more traditional format. The most obvious change was Julian's career switch. Realizing he had no interest in pursuing classical music again, Julian became the publisher of the local newspaper. Julian's various love interests would take up much of *Somerset's* final years. The widowed Ellen Grant's May/December romance with Dale Robinson (played by Jameson Parker), was also a viewer favorite.

NBC decided to cancel the low-rated serial in 1976. Its replacement, *Lovers and Friends,* was also a spin-off of *Another World.*

THE CAST

Original Cast

RICKY MATTHEWS	JASON BERNARD
TONY COOPER	DOUGLAS CHAPIN
SAM LUCAS	JORDAN CHARNEY
JASPER DELANEY	RALPH CLANTON
ROBERT DELANEY	NICOLAS COSTER
PETER DELANEY	LEN GOCHMAN
MARSHA DAVIS	ALICE HIRSON
ELLEN GRANT	GEORGANN JOHNSON
BEN GRANT	EDWARD KEMMER
DAVID GRANT	RON MARTIN
GERALD DAVIS	WALTER MATHEWS
JILL GRANT	SUSAN MacDONALD
MISSY PALMER MATTHEWS	CAROL ROUX
JESSICA BUCHANAN	WYNNE MILLER
RANDY BUCHANAN	GARY SANDY
REX COOPER	PAUL SPARER
RAFE CARTER	PHIL STERLING
LAURA DELANEY COOPER	DOROTHY STINNETTE
PAMMY DAVIS	PAMELA TOLL
INDIA DELANEY	MARIE WALLACE
LAHOMA LUCAS	ANNE WEDGEWORTH

TEXAS

AUGUST 4, 1980–DECEMBER 31, 1982 NBC

*T*his spin-off of NBC's *Another World* was the first serial to start with a 60-minute format. NBC executives were excited by the Houston, Texas, setting because prime time's *Dallas* was the most popular series on television. To insure that new viewers would flock to the series, a popular character from *Another World*, Iris Carrington Bancroft, relocated from Bay City to Houston. She was the central focus of *Texas*. Then, shortly after the premiere, Kin Shriner was pirated away from *General Hospital*, where he played Scotty Baldwin, with the hopes of attracting viewers from television's top-rated soap. He played Jeb Hampton on *Texas*.

Millionaire Iris Carrington Bancroft moved to Houston to join her grown son, Dennis Carrington, who owned an art gallery. Shortly after her arrival, Iris was reunited with an old flame, oil magnate Alex Wheeler. Their last encounter was 25 years ago, when they spent three passionate days making love on her father's yacht. Rather than tell Iris he was a poor seaman, Alex chose to exit her life. He vowed to reenter it again when he was rich and successful. Alex's abrupt abandonment had turned Iris into a self-centered, manipulative young woman. Now that Iris's first love was back in her life again, she softened and became a loving, generous person. To Alex's surprise, Iris revealed that Dennis was his son. It was a secret she had kept from everyone, including her first husband, Eliot Carrington.

Iris and Dennis believed Eliot, who was a war correspondent, had been killed in Vietnam. To their astonishment, he suddenly surfaced in Houston and explained he had been a P.O.W. Despite Eliot's presence in her life again, Iris decided to marry Alex. Meanwhile, Eliot was interested in renewing his relationship with Dennis. Shortly before Iris's wedding, Eliot learned Dennis wasn't his son, leaving him angry and bitter. While Iris and Alex exchanged wedding vows, a shot rang out, injuring Alex. By the time Alex recovered from his wound, investigators successfully apprehended his assailant. It was Eliot, who now carried a deep-rooted hatred for Alex. Iris finally married Alex, but their happiness was short-lived. The mob infiltrated Alex's oil business and then murdered him after he uncovered their illegal activities.

Another notable storyline included Dennis's romantic relationship with Dawn Marshall. Complications developed when Dawn learned Dennis was Alex Wheeler's son. Dawn's family blamed Alex for the suicide of her father, Mike Marshall, after Alex refused to loan him money to keep his fledgling oil business afloat. Dennis and Dawn's relationship came to a halt after Dawn was raped by former convict Billy Joe Wright.

Dennis next turned his sights on Dawn's social-climbing older sister, Paige. Their relationship, however, was doomed because Paige

Members of Iris Carrington's household: (left to right, bottom) Lacy Wheeler (Lily Barnstone), Iris (Beverlee McKinsey), Grant Wheeler (Donald May), (top) Vivien Gorrow (Gretchen Oehler), and Dennis Carrington (Jim Poyner).

Top: (left to right) Kate Marshall played Josephine Nichols, Philip Clark was Ryan Connor, Carla Borelli was Reena Cook, and Barbara Rucker played Ginny Marshall.

Bottom: Ruby Wright (Dianne Neil) had her eye—and a bit more—on self-made millionaire Mark Wheeler (Michael Woods).

was only interested in Dennis for his money. To make matters worse, soon after marrying Paige, Dennis discovered she was an ex-porn star. What put Dennis over the edge was the news that Paige was having an affair with Eliot Carrington. Shortly after Dennis's divorce from Paige, he left Houston with his widowed mother, Iris.

When *Texas* proved unsuccessful at making a dent in powerhouse *General Hospital's* ratings, NBC switched the serial to a late morning time slot. But even that did not save the show. News that NBC had decided to cancel *Texas* prompted thousands of viewers to write letters protesting the action. Nevertheless, its final episode aired on December 31, 1982.

THE CAST

Original Cast

VICTORIA BELLMAN . . . . ELIZABETH ALLEN
REENA COOK . . . . CARLA BORELLI
AHMED AL HASSIN . . . . MAHER BOUTROS
RYAN CONNOR . . . . PHILIP CLARK
BART WALKER . . . . JOEL COLODNER
JASMIN CEHDI . . . . DONNA CYRUS
STRIKER BELLMAN . . . . ROBERT GERRINGER
SHEIK CEHDI . . . . MITCH GRED
RIKKI DEKKER . . . . RANDY HAMILTON
MAX DEKKER . . . . CHANDLER HILL HARBEN
COURTNEY MARSHALL . . . . CATHERINE HICKLAND
JOEL WALKER . . . . CHARLES HILL
DAWN MARSHALL . . . . DANA KIMMELL
ALEX WHEELER . . . . BERT KRAMER
JUSTIN MARSHALL . . . . JERRY LANNING
PAIGE MARSHALL . . . . LISBY LARSON
NITA WRIGHT . . . . ELLEN MAXTED
BILLY JOE WRIGHT . . . . JOHN McCAFFERTY
SAMANTHA WALKER . . . . ANN McCARTHY
IRIS CARRINGTON . . . . BEVERLEE McKINSEY
MIKE MARSHALL . . . . STEPHEN D. NEWMAN
KATE MARSHALL . . . . JOSEPHINE NICHOLS
KEVIN COOK . . . . LEE PATTERSON
DENNIS CARRINGTON . . . . JIM POYNER
TERRY DEKKER . . . . SHANNA REED
ELENA DEKKER . . . . CARYN RICHMAN
GINNY MARSHALL . . . . BARBARA RUCKER
MAGGIE DEKKER . . . . SHIRLEY SLATER
CLIPPER CURTIS . . . . SCOTT STEVENSON

TRIBES

· ·

MARCH 5, 1990–JULY 13, 1990 FOX TELEVISION GROUP

This half-hour serial was created with the adolescent audience in mind. It focuses on issues facing today's teenagers. "It's about problems kids go through," explained Kim Valentine, who originated the role of Stacey Cox. "It's from our point of view, instead of an adult's."

Leah Laiman, the creator and executive story consultant of *Tribes*, stressed, "In order to appeal to the teenage audience, the show must impress young viewers with characters and situations that are real to them."

The serial looks at a group of students attending Westdale High, located in Southern California. They include Matt Kubiak, whose mother deserted him when he was a child; Anny Kubiak, Matt's cousin; Billy Pressfield, a star athlete; Chris Pressfield, Billy's easy-going, artistic kid brother; Melinda Cox, whose confidence attracts fellow students; Stacey Cox, Melinda's insecure younger sister; and Pete Sego, a charming con artist who passes himself off as wealthy when his family is poor.

In the opening episode, Anny Kubiak's friends became alarmed after she fainted during a dance party in the school gym. Anny blamed crash-dieting for her condition. Later she confided to Matt that she was pregnant. Anny confronted her boyfriend about her pregnancy, but he was unwilling to help her. She considered abortion, but was told she was too far along.

Pete Sego learned about Anny's pregnancy and decided it was the perfect opportunity to get rid of his heavy gambling debt. Pete persuaded her to give the baby up for adoption (he hoped to profit from the procedure by contacting an adoption lawyer). At the last minute, Anny changed her mind. When Anny's father discovered she was pregnant, he flew into a rage. Unable to deal with the tensions at home, Anny moved in with Lorraine, a dropout.

Despite his best efforts, Matt could no longer deny that he was attracted to his best buddy's girlfriend, Melinda Cox. The feeling was mutual and they started secretly seeing each other. After a brief period, the couple decided it would be best for everyone if they cooled their romance and remained friends. Matt even

offered to help Melinda smooth things over with Billy. Matt and Melinda soon discovered they were miserable apart.

Billy had difficulty accepting his father's new wife, Pamela. He believed his father, Big Bill, remarried too soon after his mother's death. Things came to a head when Billy refused to attend a family celebration honoring Big Bill's first wedding anniversary to Pamela. But finally Billy promised to try and accept Pamela. Pamela had a great relationship with Billy's younger brother, Chris.

Below: *Tribes was a soap specifically geared to high schoolers, and much of its action revolved around school.*

Opposite page: *The cast of* Tribes: *(left to right) Kim Valentine, Michael Aron, Ele Keats, Greg Watkins, Lisa Lawrence, Patrick Day, and Jill Witlow.*

Melinda and Stacey couldn't understand the sudden change in their parents' marriage. Visiting her father's office, Stacey discovered her father passionately kissing another woman. She realized he was having an affair. Distraught by the news, Stacey responded by undergoing a personality transformation. She dressed flashier and wore heavy make-up. When Mr. Stevens, the school science teacher, took a friendly interest in Stacey, she accused him of trying to rape her. Later, Stacey admitted she was looking for attention and Mr. Stevens was exonerated. Unable to deal with her emotions, Stacey briefly flirted with the idea of suicide.

Tribes ran on Fox television stations in six cities: New York, Los Angeles, Chicago, Washington, D.C., Dallas, Houston, and Boston. Ratings were rising in the cities it aired, but it never was syndicated nationwide and was not profitable enough to continue.

THE CAST

Cast

PETE SEGO	MICHAEL ARON
CHRIS PRESSFIELD	PATRICK DAY
MATT KUBIAK	SCOTT GARRISON
DARRYL JOHNSON	ZERO HUBBARD
ANNY KUBIAK	ELE KEATS
MELINDA COX	LISA LAWRENCE
SOPHIE KUBIAK	MICHELE MARSH
STACEY COX	KIM VALENTINE
BILLY PRESSFIELD, JR.	GREG WATKINS
LORRAINE DELANEY	JILL WITLOW

TWIN PEAKS

APRIL 7, 1990–PRESENT ABC

This prime-time serial was created by filmmaker David Lynch and Mark Frost. It was hailed by critics as the most unique series of the 1989-90 television season and received more Emmy nominations that season than any other show.

"We told [the network] we were going to give them a two-hour moody, dark soap opera murder mystery set in a fictional town in the Northwest, with an ensemble cast and an edge. And very early on, after we delivered the pilot, they said that we'd given them exactly what we said we were going to give them. And that what we'd done was so foreign to their experience that they couldn't presume to tell us how to do it any better or any different. Basically, they said, 'Guys, you go make the series, and we'll be real anxious to see what it looks like,'" explained Frost.

Twin Peaks follows the unraveling murder mystery in the small, sleepy town of Twin Peaks, in the Pacific Northwest, five miles south of the Canadian border and 12 miles from the state line. In the premiere episode, FBI agent Dale Cooper arrives to assist Sheriff Harry S. Truman in solving the mysterious murder of young Laura Palmer. Laura was homecoming queen, organizer of the Meals on Wheels program, and a tutor. But very soon, it becomes apparent that Laura also had a dark side.

Another high-school girl, Ronette Pulaski, is reported missing by her father the night Laura was killed. The next morning, Ronette walks into town, dazed and wounded, and still bound at the wrists. She ends up at the hospital in a coma.

This idyllic small town fascinates Agent Cooper, even down to the smallest details of plant and animal life. But soon, as the audience learns more and more about the town, it becames less and less idyllic. Suspects and clues begin to mount, all of which are recorded by Agent Cooper into his hand-held recorder for his secretary, Diane.

Cooper finds the first clue under Laura's nail—the letter R. In Laura's diary, he finds a key with some white powder on it, under the entry "Day One." Cooper believes the white powder is cocaine, but Truman is skeptical. There is also a videotape, found in Laura's room, which Cooper shows to Bobby (Laura's boyfriend) when he is questioned. Bobby knows nothing about the tape,

but Donna (Laura's best friend), who is also in the room being questioned, is also in the video. The last scene the audience sees is a close-up of Laura's face. Reflected in her eye is a motorcyle.

Cooper and Truman find an abandoned railway car that appears to be where Laura and Ronette were tortured. There is a mound of dirt, with half of a golden heart on a chain and a note nearby on which is written, in blood, "Fire walk with me." James Hurley, Laura's secret boyfriend and owner of the bike reflected in Laura's eye in the videotape, has the other half of the heart.

The key found in Laura's diary unlocks a safety deposit box that contains $10,000 in cash and a copy of *Flesh World* magazine. In the magazine are personal ads from Ronette Pulaski and Leo Johnson. Leo is a trucker married to Shelly, who is having a secret affair with Bobby.

Sheriff Harry S. Truman (Michael Ontkean) and Dr. William Hayward (Warren Frost) uncover a dead body wrapped in plastic.

Top: *James Hurley (James Marshall, right) is a suspect in Laura's murder. Laura's best friend, Donna Hayward (Lara Flynn Boyle), falls in love with James and tries to defend him to Sheriff Truman and her father, Dr. Hayward (left two characters).*

Bottom: *The dead beauty, Laura Palmer (Sheryl Lee).*

Donna tries to warn James that the police are looking for a biker and the owner of the other half of the heart necklace. Donna goes to the Road House, where she runs into Bobby and Mike, her jealous boyfriend. A fight breaks out and Big Ed (James's uncle) tries to protect Donna. She slips out and another biker takes her to James. James tells her that he was with Laura the night she died. He says, "Donna, she was a different person." Donna and Bobby bury the necklace, and then realize they are falling in love. James drives Donna home, but Truman and Cooper have been tailing them all night and they stop the pair on the motorbike. James is arrested and taken to jail, where Bobby and Mike are already locked up for fighting at the Road House.

THE CAST

Original Cast

SHELLY JOHNSON	MADCHEN AMICK
BOBBY BRIGGS	DANA ASHBROOK
BENJAMIN HORNE	RICHARD BEYMER
DONNA HAYWARD	LARA FLYNN BOYLE
JOSIE PACKARD	JOAN CHEN
LOG LADY	CATHERINE COULSON
LEO JOHNSON	ERIC De RE
AUDREY HORNE	SHERILYN FENN
WILLIAM HAYWARD	WARREN FROST
DEPUTY HAWK	MICHAEL HORSE
CATHERINE MARTELL	PIPER LAURIE
LAURA PALMER	SHERYL LEE
NORMA JENNINGS	PEGGY LIPTON
DALE COOPER	KYLE MacLACHLAN
JAMES HURLEY	JAMES MARSHALL
ED HURLEY	EVERETT McGILL
HARRY S. TRUMAN	MICHAEL ONTKEAN
PETE MARTELL	JACK NANCE
LUCY MORAN	KIMMY ROBERTSON
NADINE HURLEY	WENDY ROBIE
DR. JACOBY	RUSS TAMBLYN
LELAND PALMER	RAY WISE
SARAH PALMER	GRACE ZABRISKIE

TWIN PEAKS

APRIL 7, 1990–PRESENT ABC

Agent Cooper is an eccentric character. Besides his constant recording of the tiniest details for Diane, he is able, from body language he claims, to tell when two people are secretly seeing each other. Another quirk of Cooper's personality is his love of food, especially sweets, and "damn fine coffee." A good cherry pie or donuts and good coffee make Cooper extremely happy. As the series progresses, Cooper relies less and less on his hand-held recorder—is he losing his professional objectivity? Are his loyalties shifting toward the townspeople and away from the F.B.I.?

All this, and more, happen on just the first episode of *Twin Peaks*. We later find out that Laura had sex with three men the night she died, she had a cocaine habit, she liked brutal sex, and she had worked as a prostitute.

"Who killed Laura Palmer?" may be the most asked TV question of the 1989-90 season. Could it have been Leo, who brutalizes his wife and who came home with a blood-soaked shirt? Maybe it was Bobby, Laura's boyfriend who seems to be more in love with Shelley, Leo's wife. How about Laura's father, who may have been having an incestuous affair with his daughter? And Jacques Renault is not above suspicion.

And what about the strange clues? Agent Cooper dreamed of a one-armed man and a singing dwarf; what does this tell us about the murder? The Log Lady's log tells us about owls and the darkness pressing in on her—what does this mean? What do the Book House Boys have to do with the mystery? They fight the "evil in the woods," but does the evil have to do with Laura's murder? The strange Dr. Jacoby also seems to hold some clues to Laura's death, but what are they? And is Laura's cousin, Madeleine (exact look-alike except hair color), really her cousin? And what clues can we find in the series-within-a-series, *Invitation to Love?*

Lynch and Frost also provide some hidden clues to the viewers. In the movie *Laura*, Laura is stalked by Waldo Lydecker. In *Twin Peaks*, Laura is pecked by a bird and dies from blood loss. The bird's name is Waldo, who is a patient of the veterinarian Dr. Lydecker. And in the film *Vertigo*, Madeleine is thought to commit suicide but later appears disguised as another woman. Remember James's comment to Donna, "... she was a different person"?

By the end of the first season, viewers still didn't know who killed Laura Palmer. Thank goodness the show's ratings were healthy enough for ABC to renew it for a second season. The series has had a major cultlike following—many fans have parties on the night of *Twin Peaks*, complete with donuts, pies, and hot coffee.

When a reporter asked Mark Frost how he and David Lynch planned to continue the series once Laura's killer was revealed, he answered, "A hundred different stories are left. The murder of Laura has always been just the tip of the iceberg. It was never designed to carry the series. We'll come up with stories that are equally compelling. There will be more mysteries."

Below: *FBI Agent Dale Cooper (Kyle MacLachlan) and Sheriff Truman discuss the evidence.*

Opposite page, top: *Laura's distraught mother, Sarah (Grace Zabriskie), is medicated by Dr. Hayward while Sheriff Truman questions her.*

Opposite page, bottom: *What do Josie Packard (Joan Chen, front) and Catherine Martell (Piper Laurie, back) have to do with Laura's death?*

UPSTAIRS, DOWNSTAIRS

JANUARY 6, 1974–MAY 1, 1977 PBS

The audience for this unique British-produced serial was estimated to total more than one billion viewers in 40 different countries. The BBC produced *Upstairs, Downstairs* following the success of *The Forsyte Saga*.

Jean Marsh, who played Rose, came up with the idea for the series while vactioning with her friend, fellow actress Eileen Atkins. Their original intention was to create a comedy act that would serve as a showcase for their acting talent. While brainstorming, the two women discovered they both had parents who had been in domestic service. They realized an act based on domestic help could be funny. But why limit it to one routine? Why not a series for television? They pitched their idea to producer John Hawkesworth, who was enthusiastic. He didn't want to limit the series to just the domestic help. Instead, he suggested a balance between the downstairs domestic staff and the upstairs upper-class family. Building on Jean Marsh and Eileen Atkins's idea, Hawkesworth developed a series that chronicled the lives of the Bellamy family, who lived upstairs at 165 Eaton Place in London, and the tribulations of their domestic staff, who worked downstairs. The staff was spearheaded by the authoritarian butler, Angus Hudson, and the curmudgeonly cook, Kate Bridges.

In the premiere episode, Sarah, a new under-houseparlormaid, joined the downstairs staff. Annoyed by Sarah's pretensions and general laziness, the staff decided to teach Sarah a lesson by putting her in her place.

Later, Sarah found herself pregnant by young James Bellamy. Learning of her condition, James's parents made arrangements for Sarah to have the baby and then put it up for adoption. A short while passed and Sarah was pregnant again. This child was fathered by Thomas, the chauffeur. Before the baby's birth, Thomas proposed marriage and Sarah gracefully accepted.

Midway through the serial's run, Rachel Gurney, who played dignified matriarch Lady Marjorie Bellamy, challenged John Hawkesworth's creativity when she announced her plans to quit. Quickly meeting with story editor Alfred Shaughnessy, Hawkesworth began brainstorming about how to deal with Lady Marjorie's departure. They decided that she would be one of the passengers on the Titanic's fateful maiden voyage. News that his wife hadn't survived would devastate Richard Bellamy, forcing him to move on with his life in new, unanticipated directions.

"When Rachel said to John that she wasn't going on, and could not be talked out of it, I think he was in dispair," said the late Bill Bain (who directed many episodes of the series), "because Lady Marjorie was the backbone of that house, and John for awhile couldn't see his way around the fact. But when he did, when he and Freddie

The kitchen staff: (left to right) scullery maid Ruby (Jenny Tomasin), Hudson (Gordon Jackson), and Mrs. Bridges (Angela Baddeley).

Top: *The cast of* Upstairs, Downstairs.

Bottom: *Lesley-Anne Down played Lady Georgina.*

worked it out, I think it's what made the program take off. Because suddenly the series was plumbing more depths, getting into a different level of story. Into grief, real grief, not just showing off grief."

The aftermath of James's experiences in the war would also play a major role in later storylines. Despite marrying Lady Georgina, a despondent James committed suicide.

The success of *Upstairs, Downstairs* inspired a loosely based American version, *Beacon Hill,* on CBS. That series barely lasted three months and was not a smash with critics.

THE CAST

Cast

THE MARQUIS	ANTHONY ANDREWS
KATE BRIDGES	ANGELA BADDELEY
EDWARD	CHRISTOPHER BEENY
AUNT PRUE	JOAN BENHAM
SARAH	PAULINE COLLINS
EMILY	EVIN CROWLEY
LILY	KAREN DOTRICE
LADY GEORGINA	LESLEY-ANNE DOWN
VIRGINIA BELLAMY	HANNAH GORDON
LADY MARJORIE	RACHEL GURNEY
FREDERICK	GARETH HUNT
ALFRED	GEORGE INNES
ANGUS HUDSON	GORDON JACKSON
RICHARD BELLAMY	DAVID LANGTON
ROSE	JEAN MARSH
HAZEL BELLAMY	MEG WYNN OWEN
ELIZABETH BELLAMY	NICOLA PAGETT
RUBY	JENNY TOMASIN
DAISY	JACQUELINE TONG
KING EDWARD VII	LOCKWOOD WEST
JAMES BELLAMY	SIMON WILLIAMS

WHERE THE HEART IS

SEPTEMBER 8, 1969–MARCH 23, 1973 CBS

English professor Julian Hathaway didn't want to admit it, but his young second wife, Mary, was attracted to his college-age son, Michael. Even worse, the feeling was mutual. Michael harbored a long-standing grudge against his father. He blamed him for his mother's suicide years ago. Father and son would find themselves attracted to the same woman a second time when Julian tried to work through his middle-age crisis by impregnating Michael's live-in girlfriend, Elizabeth.

Both storylines prompted thousands of angry letters from offended viewers. Yet, they continued to watch. Nestled between two long-running conservative soaps, *Love of Life* and *Search for Tomorrow*, this innovative serial challenged its audience by taking it through unfamiliar territory. Women constantly found themselves pregnant by men they didn't love but were physically drawn to. One character killed her brother because he wouldn't reciprocate sexual feelings. Another character left his wife to live with his pregnant girlfriend, got bored with the relationship, and then cheated on his girlfriend by having sex with his estranged wife! Whether viewers approved or disapproved, this serial forced them to put the iron down, turn off the vacuum cleaner, and watch their television screens.

Set in the suburban town of Northcross, Connecticut, this half-hour drama focused on the wealthy Hathaway family and their friends. In the first episode, Kate Hathaway was adjusting to the death of her father, Judge Daniel Hathaway. Her brother, Julian, was too busy worrying about his wife's attraction to his son to spend time grieving over the loss of his father. News of Judge Hathaway's death brought Kate and Julian's shallow younger sister, Allison, back to town. To Kate's chagrin, her sister decided to stay after the funeral was over. Joining Allison was her weak-willed husband, Roy Archer, who had jilted Kate several years earlier.

Although *Where the Heart Is* netted a respectable-size audience, CBS decided to cancel the serial after three-and-a-half years because it wanted to attract younger viewers. News of the unexpected cancellation inspired 35,000 viewers to write passionate letters protesting CBS's action. Nevertheless, the network proceeded with its plans and on March 26, 1973, replaced *Where the Heart Is* with a fresher, more contemporary soap that boasted a cast of attractive, sexy, young performers, *The Young and the Restless*.

Two famous alumni of *Where the Heart Is* are Marsha Mason, who went on to do feature films, and Rue McClanahan, best known for her roll in TV's *Golden Girls*. Laurence Luckinbill, who played Steve Prescott, became a famous character actor and went on to win theater awards for his work. Another casting choice brought much attention to the show—Despo, the Andy Warhol star, had a two-week role as Athena Stefanopolis.

Below: *Joseph Mascolo was the last actor to play Ed Lucas.*

Opposite page, top: *Bernard Barrow played Earl Hana on* Where the Heart Is, *and later played Johnny Ryan on* Ryan's Hope, *then moved on to* Loving.

Opposite page, bottom: *Ron Harper played Steve Prescott.*

246

THE CAST

Cast

MICHAEL HATHAWAY	GREGORY ABELS
TONY MONROE	DAVID BAILEY
EARL DANA	BERNARD BARROW
PETER JARDIN	MICHAEL BERSELL
AMY SNOWDEN	CLARICE BLACKBURN
ROBERT JARDIN	KEITH CHARLES
HUGH JESSUP	DAVID CRYER
	REX ROBBINS
ATHENA STEFANOPOLIS	DESPO
DANIEL HATHAWAY	JOSEPH DOLEN
LORETTA JARDIN	ALICE DRUMMOND
RUTH MONROE	NANCY FRANKLIN
HOLLIS FORBES	JOSEPH GALLISON
STEVE PRESCOTT	RON HARPER
	LAURENCE LUCKINBILL
CHRISTINE CAMERON	DELPHI HARRINGTON
	TERRY O'CONNOR
ROY ARCHER	STEPHEN JOYCE
ARTHUR SAXTON	BERNARD KATES
BEN JESSUP	DANIEL KEYES
ELLIE JARDIN	ZOHRA LAMPERT
TERRY PRESCOTT	TED LePLAT
	DOUGLAS ROSS
ED LUCAS	JOSEPH MASCOLO
	CHARLES CIOFFI
	MARK GORDON
MARGARET JARDIN	RUE McCLANAHAN
	BARBARA BAXLEY
HOWARD SNOWDEN	THOMAS McDERMOTT
JOHN RAINEY	PETER MacLEAN
LAURA BLACKBURN	MARSHA MASON
NAN PRESCOTT	KATHERINE MESKILL
JULIAN HATHAWAY	JAMES MITCHELL
HELEN WYATT	MEG MYLES
STELLA O'BRIEN	BIBI OSTERWALD
ADRIENNE HARRIS	PRISCILLA POINTER
JOE PRESCOTT	WILLIAM POST, JR.
VICKY LUCAS HATHAWAY	LISA RICHARDS
	ROBYN MILLAN
LOIS SNOWDEN	JEANNE RUSKIN
JEFFREY JORDAN	GEOFFREY SCOTT
ALLISON JESSUP	LOUISE SHAFFER
LIZ RAINEY HATHAWAY	TRACY BROOKS SWOPE
KATE HATHAWAY PRESCOTT	DIANA VAN DER VLIS
MARY HATHAWAY	DIANA WALKER

THE YOUNG AND THE RESTLESS

MARCH 26, 1973–PRESENT CBS

Originally titled *The Innocent Years* in its planning stages, *The Young and the Restless* would rival the pioneering accomplishments of *General Hospital. Days of Our Lives* headwriter, William J. Bell, created *The Young and the Restless* in a three-week span when he decided to launch his own daytime drama. With the assistance of his wife, Lee Phillip Bell, he sought to create what he called a "broad base of wholesome, identifiable young people in situations that reflected a segment of contemporary life." In less than a year, critics were hailing it as the most sophisticated soap opera on the air. It rose zenithlike in the ratings where it has remained almost permanently for nearly two decades. Because of the triumphs of *The Young and the Restless*, William Bell's reputation surpassed even that of Gloria Monty.

The serial dealt with the stories of two families—one rich and one poor—in Genoa City, Wisconsin. The Brooks family was prominent as well as affluent. Stuart was the owner and operator of the city's newspaper, the *Genoa City Chronicle*. Jennifer was his socially admired wife. Their four daughters were Leslie, a budding classical pianist; Lauralee, an adventuress and author; Chris, a journalist; and Peggy, a college coed.

On the other side of the tracks was the Foster family. Liz worked at the local mill, Chancellor Industries. She struggled to support her three kids: William, Jr. ("Snapper"), a young doctor; Greg, a fledgling lawyer; and Jill, who worked in a beauty salon. Somewhere in the background lurked Bill Foster, who had abandoned his wife and children. His whereabouts were unknown.

One of the earliest and longest running storylines concerned the ill-fated love between sheltered Chris Brooks and charming Snapper Foster. There were the standard problems, seen in most soap operas, in the relationship: Stuart Brooks's fatherly disapproval and Greg Foster's attraction to Chris. What made this show unique was the freedom with which Chris and Snapper talked about the pressing matter of sex. Never before on a daytime serial had the issue been examined so openly, nor so realistically.

Another unprecedented device quickly followed when Chris was assaulted and raped by cavalier George Curtis. It was soon clear, as *The Young and the Restless* began to draw a huge following from younger urban viewers, that sexier and more taboo topics were producing excellent audience reactions. Other serials began jumping on the bandwagon by cooking up similar youth-oriented plots and characters who were coming into their own sexually.

Moreover, the production values of the serial, attributed to the mastery of producer John Conboy, were also setting the stylistic pace that other soaps tried to imitate. The show was noted for moody, low-lit, sensual scenes. Genoa City was mostly populated by citizens who, in addition to being young and restless, were also wonderfully attractive.

Stuart (Robert Colbert) and Jennifer Brooks (Dorothy Green) had four daughters.

Three actors from The Young and the Restless *off the set: (from left) Deidre Hall played Barbara Anderson, Tom Selleck played Jed Anthony, and Jamie Lyn Bauer played Lauralee Brooks.*

But these elements were not the only ones being emphasized. At the other end of the spectrum, Bell introduced storylines that centered on the hopes and desires of older characters. This included Kay Chancellor, a middle-aged socialite looking for love in all the wrong places. Universal personal problems, such as alcoholism and eating disorders, were highlighted with the same finesse that Bell brought to controversial topics, such as incest and homosexuality.

Over its first decade, *The Young and the Restless* maintained a powerful mix that combined traditional soap opera formulas and innovative, sometimes risky efforts. This fueled the serial's continuing success. Where other daytime dramas fell into a ratings rut by trying to break their own molds, the confines of Genoa City allowed characters the freedom to burst into song at any moment (a practice started early on). It was no wonder that, in 1976, the serial won an Emmy Award for Outstanding Series and then, in 1983,

THE CAST

Original Cast

PIERRE ROLLAND	ROBERT CLARY
STUART BROOKS	ROBERT COLBERT
SALLY McGUIRE	LEE CRAWFORD
SNAPPER FOSTER	WILLIAM GRAY ESPY
JENNIFER BROOKS	DOROTHY GREEN
LESLIE BROOKS	JANICE LYNDE
BRAD ELIOT	TOM HALLICK
GREG FOSTER	JAMES HOUGHTON
LIZ FOSTER	JULIANNA McCARTHY
PEGGY BROOKS	PAMELA PETERS
CHRIS BROOKS	TRISH STEWART

THE YOUNG AND THE RESTLESS

MARCH 26, 1973–PRESENT CBS

for Best Daytime Drama. It also received many other nominations and special recognitions.

The 1983 award came as a solid vote of confidence. *The Young and the Restless* had undergone major surgery during the previous year. The two founding families had been mostly disassembled, leaving only Jill Foster to carry on the legacy. This was done because prominent performers, including Jamie Lynn Bauer (Lauralee), left the series, and were not replaceable. So two new families were planted in Genoa City. The upscale Abbotts were represented by John Abbott, a sympathetic entrepreneur in the cosmetics business; his roguish son, Jack; gorgeous and business-minded daughter, Ashley; and youngest daughter, Traci, a university student fighting a weight problem. The middle class was represented by the Williams, with rebel son, Paul, captivating much interest.

Producer Conboy was replaced by H. Wesley Kenney, who had worked with Bell on *Days of Our Lives*. But the effect was simply an updated, tighter, and bolder look for the serial. One of its most popular characters was wild-spirited Nikki Reed—played by Melody Thomas—who caused an immense daytime splash. Soon, Nikki's romantic intrigues with unpredictable yet compelling Victor Newman (Eric Braeden) were a source of excitement.

The Young and the Restless embodied enough consistencies and surprising story turns that it never floundered in the ratings. Whatever special magic co-executive producers Bell and Kenney had up their sleeves, they weren't spilling the beans. But they remain loyal to their characters and give each strong storylines and they present them in believable shades of gray. They have also opted not to go in the science fiction or farfetched international escapade direction that has led many a solid serial down a blind alley. Furthermore, the drama has distinguished itself by carving a unique brand of interfamily love triangles, repeating them as variations on a theme.

The first complex triangle was between Leslie Brooks, Brad Eliot, and Laurie Brooks. Brad was a handsome newcomer to Genoa City and seemed to harbor secrets from his past. But he gained the admiration of Leslie's father, Stuart, who gave Brad a job at the paper. Stuart

encouraged the budding romance between Brad and his reserved musician daughter, Leslie. No sooner had Laurie returned from college to work at the paper then she found herself attracted to Brad. She began to plot the ruin of her sister's relationship with him. Portraying Brad as indifferent to Leslie's musical ambitions, Laurie managed to place doubt in Leslie's mind. At the same time, Laurie suggested to Brad that he was hurting Leslie's career as a pianist.

Below: *Kay Chancellor (Jeanne Cooper, right) couldn't keep her nose out of Jill Foster's (Brenda Dickson, left) and Derek Thurston's (Joe La Due) lives.*

Opposite page: *Despite her sister's manipulations, Leslie Brooks (Janice Lynde) and Brad Eliot (Tom Hallick) finally wed.*

THE YOUNG AND THE RESTLESS

MARCH 26, 1973–PRESENT CBS

Although Laurie's campaign took a good while to succeed, she finally broke up Brad and her sister. The final blow came when Leslie sent Brad a letter asking him to join her for an important recital. Laurie intercepted the letter and she led Brad to believe he had been jilted by Leslie. In a state of despair, Brad allowed Laurie to use her feminine wiles on him. Not only did they make love, but (upon Laurie's suggestion) they also planned to get married. Knowing nothing other than she had been betrayed, Leslie had a nervous breakdown. After Leslie was institutionalized, Brad discovered Laurie's falsehoods.

Taking control of the traumatic situation, Brad ended the romance with Laurie and went to Leslie's side. Her emotional and psychological health restored, Leslie agreed to marry Brad. He then told her the secrets he had told no one. As a surgeon in Chicago, he had fathered a son out of wedlock. Later, he was forced to operate on that same child.

When his son died during the difficult surgical procedure, Brad, in his grief and feeling inadequate, fled Chicago and his medical practice. Leslie and Brad were married at long last; they regretted that they'd ever listened to Laurie's malicious lies.

Cricket (Lauralee Bell) and Phillip Chancelor (Tom Bierdz) almost tied the knot, but Nina broke up their relationship.

Nikki Reed (Melody Thomas Scott, right) married womanizer Victor Newman (Eric Braeden, left), but their marriage ended rather quickly.

In time, however, Laurie would suffer her own heartbreak. After a handful of fun flings with an assortment of men, she fell deeply in love with Mark Henderson. When the two came forward with their wedding plans, Laurie's mother, Jennifer, almost collapsed in shock. Jennifer had just survived a mastectomy and had almost left Stuart for Mark's father—her ex-suitor Bruce Henderson. Jennifer was forced to reveal her age-old secret that she had conceived Laurie by Bruce, and that Laurie was Mark's half-sister! Mark's reaction at almost having married his half-sister was to flee Genoa City. Laurie reviled her mother for never having told the truth about her real parentage.

Tragedy fell upon Brad and Leslie when Brad began to go blind. Refusing to tell her about his degenerative disease, Brad made Leslie think he was no longer in love with her. Ironically, he sought refuge at Laurie's home where she attempted to make his plight more bearable by helping him to get around. Although specialists cured his loss of sight, Brad thought that he had alienated Leslie permanently, so he left town.

Another triangle was already in the works. Still in love with Brad, Leslie had a dalliance with Lance Prentiss, an ardent fan of her music. Realizing that loving anyone but Brad was in vain, Leslie politely dropped Lance. He then engaged Laurie's interests. What began as a mild flirtation heated up quickly. Things might have gone well for Laurie and Lance had not Lance's mother, Vanessa, come between them. At first, Lance tried to keep his strange, veiled mother a secret. She was fiercely competitive with any new woman in his life. Once Laurie learned of Vanessa's existence, she tried to befriend her by suggesting that Vanessa have plastic surgery to fix the disfigurement that

THE YOUNG AND THE RESTLESS

MARCH 26, 1973–PRESENT CBS

caused Vanessa to wear veils. Even though Laurie's advice was well taken, Vanessa still viewed her with venom.

Complicating Laurie's predicament was the fact that Leslie was not only falling in love with Lance, but had discovered she was pregnant by him. To protect Laurie, Leslie told her nothing. A good stroke of fortune happened when Lance's brother, sailor Lucas Prentiss, swept into town and became Leslie's suitor. Before long, Lucas proposed to Leslie, promising to help her rear her baby. Leslie found herself married but not in love with the kindly Lucas. Unfortunately, she still felt passion for Lance, but she couldn't tell him he was the father of her baby, Brooks.

In a nightmarish sequence of events, Leslie left Genoa City, trusting Brooks to the care of Laurie and Lance. Then she fought heatedly with Laurie and had another mental breakdown. This time she lost her memory. After a dismal period of aimless traveling, she returned to Genoa City. Although her sanity was restored, Leslie found herself being pressured by her husband, Lucas, and Jonas, a suitor she'd met along the way. At the end of her rope, Leslie chose to return to her career and left with her child for good, ending up in Europe on a long tour.

Another chronic participant in triangles was Jill Foster. After becoming a secretary to socialite Kay Chancellor, Jill got pregnant by Kay's husband, Phillip. In the meantime, Jill had been lured into living with Kay's son, Brock Reynolds. Kay, in fact, had engineered that arrangement. Phillip was outraged that Jill was living with Brock, but became further distraught when Jill informed him of the pregnancy. Dutifully, Phillip went out of the country to get a divorce from Kay. To retaliate when he returned, Kay drove her car (with Phillip as a passenger) over a cliff. Before he died in the hospital, Phillip was able to marry Jill in a hastily arranged ceremony. Since Kay hadn't been seriously maimed in the accident, Phillip wanted to go to his death knowing that Jill and his heir would be supported by Phillip's healthy estate.

Grief-ridden after Phillip died, Jill moved her working-class family into the Chancellor home. Kay, however, sued Jill on the grounds that the marriage wasn't legitimate. The court ruled in Kay's favor. Destitute again, Jill was left to her own devises. She went to work for an incredible-

looking hairdresser, Derek Thurston, who began to make life easier until Kay Chancellor laid eyes on him. Jill's worst fears materialized when Kay and Derek married. To spite everyone, Jill decided she was going to nab the heart of Stuart Brooks, by then a widower and also the new love of Jill's mother, Liz.

After wreaking her havoc, Jill found better prey in John Abbot, owner and an executive of Jabot Cosmetics. Despite the schemes of John's son, Jack, who'd made his own advances, Jill

Below: *Kate Linder plays Esther Valentine, Kay Chancellor's housekeeper.*

Opposite page: *Laurie (red dress) fought with her sister Leslie (Victoria Mallory, blue dress) over Lance Prentiss (Dennis Cole, left). Leslie eventually married Lance's brother, Lucas (Tom Ligon, right), though she was pregnant with Lance's child.*

THE YOUNG AND THE RESTLESS

MARCH 26, 1973–PRESENT CBS

married John. Once living at the Abbot mansion, Jill found another potential enemy in Ashley Abbot, John's daughter. A greater adversary would eventually haunt her doorstep when Dina Mergeron, the disappeared wife of John, came back to make Jill's life a living hell. But Jill's scheming finally broke apart their marriage.

The storylines of the late eighties and early nineties have been interwoven to a degree that all characters in Genoa City share equal importance. No major family takes center stage.

Heartthrob David Hasselhoff, whose role as Snapper led to the nighttime series *Knight Rider* and *Bay Watch,* was quoted while still working on *The Young and the Restless:* "Our series also gives strong storylines to characters who are young, a little older and those more mature.... The storylines never play down to any segment of the audience or play up any one segment in order to ignore the importance of any other group..."

Nighttime drama and feature film superstar Tom Selleck played Jed Andrews, a conquest of Laurie Brooks. Their sexy soap lathering scene in a shower was touted as the steamiest ever seen on

soap opera, not to mention the "soapiest." Unfortunately, he was a casualty of Laurie's fickle interest and he left town.

The runaway nonstop success of the serial shouldn't be surprising to insiders of the world of daytime drama, given William J. Bell's extraordinary previous feats. Bell, at age 29, got a job from Irna Phillips writing dialogue for *The Guiding Light.* Co-creating and headwriting credits, under Phillips's direction, followed for Bell with *Another World* and *As the World Turns.* From there, it was a hop and a skip to applause for his headwriting for *Days of Our Lives.* But *The Young and the Restless* has, beyond a shadow of a doubt, proven Bell's immeasurable contribution to daytime drama.

Responding with modesty and pride, Bell said of his work, "Characters dictate their own story to me, and all stories emerge from those characters. You can't just superimpose any story over any character.... The bottom line is that an audience is attracted to good characters and interesting story and I think that's what we're going to give them."

257

YOUNG DR. MALONE

DECEMBER 29, 1958–MARCH 29, 1963 NBC

This half-hour serial, which premiered on NBC after nearly 20 years on radio, had a unique debut. For starters, its characters were slowly introduced on *Today Is Ours*, the short-lived soap it replaced. Viewers who tuned in for the last episode of *Today Is Ours* on Friday, returned Monday to find the same characters on a new series called *Young Dr. Malone*. Also, although NBC was broadcasting the television version, the radio version continued on CBS for several months. Fans who followed both versions discovered that, while they shared the same title, they were different programs. The television version took place in a different setting and at a later time frame. (This was unusual. For example, in *The Guiding Light*, the television version would air and the same episode would be on radio later in the day.)

Radio's Dr. Jerry Malone continued to run his practice out of a modest clinic in the small town of Three Oaks, while television's Dr. Jerry Malone was promoted to Chief of Staff at Valley Hospital in urban Denison, Maryland. The TV serial focused on the professional and personal lives of Valley Hospital's staff.

Jerry had two adult children from his first marriage, David and Jill. David followed in his father's footsteps and became a dedicated doctor. For a brief period, he was engaged to Fran Merrill but later married the wealthy, volatile Gig Houseman. Her unexpected death had a major impact on David. To Jerry's dismay, Jill suffered through an unhappy marriage to a compulsive gambler, Larry Renfrew.

Jerry's second wife was Tracey. Their marriage was seriously challenged when Tracey became clinically depressed following the tragic death of one of her children. Tracey's younger sister, Faye, married Jerry's close friend, Dr. Stefan Koda. Tracey and Faye were the daughters of one of Denison's wealthiest men, Emory Bannister.

Emory's greedy, younger second wife, Clare, was one of the serial's most popular characters. After Emory died, Clare married Lionel Steele who was Larry Renfrew's uncle and a ruthless employee of Emory's. Lionel later reformed to become the first ambivalent villain, or anti-hero, on daytime television.

Reviewing *Young Dr. Malone*, *TV Guide* wrote, "It's only fair that [the series] has been put together by experts in the field, that the production values are good and that the acting is earnest and professional. We are surprised only that the form has undergone so few modernizations in the past twenty years." After nearly a five-year run, the serial was replaced by another hospital-based drama, *The Doctors*.

Mary Fickett (who played Miss Jones), Hugh Franklin (who played Fred McNeill), and Louis Edmonds (who played Rick Hampton) would go on to daytime stardom on *All My Children*. Fickett plays Ruth Brent Martin, Franklin played Dr. Charles Tyler, and Edmonds plays Langley Wallingford.

The Malone family: (front) Dr. Jerry (William Prince) and Tracey Malone (Augusta Dabney), and their children, (back) David (John Connell) and Jill (Freda Holloway).

Liz Gardner (Dorothy Ferris, top) was David Malone's (John Connell, bottom) new girlfriend.

THE CAST

Cast

LIONEL STEELE	MARTIN BLAINE
JODY BAKER	STEPHEN BOLSTER
FRAN MERRILL	PATRICIA BOSWORTH
TED POWELL	PETER BRANDON
DAVID MALONE	JOHN CONNELL
MATT STEELE	NICOLAS COSTER
	FRANKLYN SPODAK
	EDDIE JONES
FAYE BANNISTER	CHASE CROSLEY
	LENKA PETERSON
TRACEY MALONE	AUGUSTA DABNEY
	VIRGINIA DWYER
RICK HAMPTON	LOUIS EDMONDS
MISS JONES	MARY FICKETT
FRED McNEILL	HUGH FRANKLIN
GAIL PRENTISS	JOAN HACKETT
JILL MALONE	SARAH HARDY
	FREDA HOLLOWAY
	KATHLEEN WIDDOES
GIG HOUSEMAN MALONE	DIANA HYLAND
STEFAN KODA	MICHAEL INGRAM
MARGE WAGNER	TERI KEANE
EMORY BANNISTER	JUDSON LAIRE
PETER BROOKS	ROBERT LANSING
LISHA STEELE	PATTY McCORMACK
	SUSAN HALLARAN
	MICHELE TUTTLE
	ZINA BETHUNE
EILEEN SEATON	EMILY McLAUGHLIN
PHYLLIS BROOKS	BARBARA O'NEILL
JERRY MALONE	WILLIAM PRINCE
ERNEST COOPER	NICHOLAS PRYOR
	ROBERT DRIVAS
CLARA KERSHAW	JOYCE VAN PATTEN
LARRY RENFREW	DICK VAN PATTEN
ERIKA BRANDT	ANN WILLIAMS
CLARE BANNISTER STEELE	LESLEY WOODS

(Clockwise from left) Nicollette Sheridan, Terry Farrell, and Morgan Fairchild from the short-lived Paper Dolls.

Flashes in the Pan

Despite not having lasted many seasons, or not having been innovative or original, any soap has had some followers. Just as we begin to be interested in the lives of the characters in our soap, the network decides that ratings aren't good enough. While these may not be as important in the history of soaps, no history would be complete without mention of them. So, to complete the history, but more importantly, to remind viewers of their short-lived favorites, the flashes in the pan are profiled.

All that Glitters

ALL THAT GLITTERS
. . . .
APRIL 18, 1977–JULY 15, 1977 SYNDICATED

Producer Norman Lear used a reversal of the sexes to launch this offbeat series that was inspired by the phenomenal success of *Mary Hartman, Mary Hartman*. *All that Glitters* featured a society where women held positions of authority, both in the workforce and at home. Men were subservient. Although intended as satire, not enough viewers found the show funny or interesting. Thirteen weeks after its highly touted debut, *All that Glitters* was quietly canceled.

Cast members included future *Dallas* star Linda Gray, who played a transsexual; Gary Sandy, best known for his starring role on *WKRP in Cincinnati;* and Louise Shaffer, who would later win an Emmy for her performance as Rae Woodard on daytime's *Ryan's Hope*.

L.W. CARRUTHERS . . . . BARBARA BAXLEY
MA PACKER . . . . EILEEN BRENNAN
PEGGY HORNER . . . . . . VANESSA BROWN
NANCY BANKSTON . . . . ANITA GILLETTE
LINDA MURKLAND . . . . LINDA GRAY
MICHAEL McFARLAND . . DAVID HASKELL
BERT STOCKWOOD . . . . . CHUCK McCANN
CHRISTINA STOCKWOOD . . . .
. . . . LOIS NETTLETON
GLEN BANKSTON . . . . WES PARKER
DAN KINCAID . . . . GARY SANDY
ANDREA MARTIN . . . . . . LOUISE SHAFFER
GRACE SMITH . . . . MARTE BOYLE SLOUT
JOAN HAMLYN . . . . JESSICA WALTER

BEACON HILL
. . . .
AUGUST 25, 1975–NOVEMBER 4, 1975 CBS

It's easy to understand the thought process that preceded *Beacon Hill's* creation. At the time, *Upstairs, Downstairs,* which aired on PBS's *Masterpiece Theatre,* was a hit with critics as well as viewers. Inspired by that show's popularity, CBS executives thought, why not create a loosely based American version?

Instead of being about the disparity between an upper-class British family and the lower-class house servants, *Beacon Hill* was about the disparity between an upper-class American family and the lower-class house servants. Unfortunately, the result was like comparing *Gilligan's Island* to *Robinson Crusoe* because both were about shipwrecked survivors stranded on a desert island.

In his review of *Beacon Hill, Time* magazine's Richard Schickel wrote, "[*Upstairs, Downstairs's*] vulgar American cousin .... commercial television once again refusing to trust the intelligence of its audience..." Apparently, viewers agreed. Eleven weeks after it's debut, *Beacon Hill* was canceled.

The cast boasted such daytime soap alumni as *The Edge of Night's* Maeve McGuire, *Love of Life's* Nancy Marchand, *All My Children's* Susan Blanchard, and *Search For Tomorrow's* Kathryn Walker.

GRANT PIPER . . . . DON BLAKELY
MAUREEN MAHAFFEY . . . .
. . . . SUSAN BLANCHARD
TREVOR BULLOCK . . . . ROY COOPER
ROBERT LASSITER . . . . DAVID DUKES
BENJAMIN LASSITER . . STEPHEN ELLIOTT
RICHARD PALMER . EDWARD HERRMANN
MARY LASSITER . . . . . NANCY MARCHAND
MAUDE PALMER . . . . MAEVE McGUIRE
EMILY BULLOCK . . . . DeANN MEARS
GIORGIO BALANCI . . . . . MICHAEL NOURI
KATE MAHAFFEY . . . . LISA PELIKAN
BETSY BULLOCK . . . . LINDA PURL
MR. HACKER . . . . GEORGE ROSE
TERENCE O'HARA . . . . DAVID ROUNDS
BRIAN MALLORY . . . . PAUL RUDD
EMMALINE HACKER . . . .
. . . . BEATRICE STRAIGHT
MARILYN GARDINER . HOLLAND TAYLOR
FAWN LASSITER . . . . . . KATHRYN WALKER
WILLIAM PIPER . . . . RICHARD WARD
ROSAMUND LASSITER . . . . . . KITTY WINN

BEHIND THE SCREEN
. . . .
OCTOBER 9, 1981–JANUARY 8, 1982 CBS

Veteran film actor Mel Ferrer led the cast of this CBS 30-minute, weekly, late-night offering. The serial was created by David Jacobs. Two of Jacobs's earlier creations, *Dallas* and *Knots Landing*, were already firmly established hits on CBS's prime-time schedule when the network approached him about developing a third series. Drawing upon his background as creator of these two popular nighttime soaps, Jacobs's new series was a dramatized, behind-the-scenes look at a fictional TV soap opera, *Generations*.

Behind the Screen focused on the young star of *Generations*, Janie-Claire, who struggled to keep her life from being dominated by Zina, her mother who was confined to a wheelchair; her shark agent, Evan Hammer; and her co-star and romantic interest, Brian Holmby. Brian was given to abrupt mood swings.

After three months on the air, *Behind the Screen* ended its run with viewers still wondering who killed starlet Joyce Daniels. Making a cameo appearance in the show's final episode was *Knots Landing's* Michele Lee, who appeared as herself and was a guest at the party where Joyce Daniels was poisoned. When police questioned Michele, they mistakenly identified her as another famous celebrity — Mary Tyler Moore.

Not long after concluding her stint on *Behind the Screen*, Debbi Morgan, who appeared as Lynette Porter, was cast as Angie Baxter on daytime's *All My Children.*

Behind the Screen

Strangly enough, Debbi Morgan now stars on a current soap, titled *Generations* (she plays Chantal).

GERRY HOLMBY . . . . JOSHUA BRYANT
DORY HOLMBY . . . . LOYITA CHAPEL
BOBBY DANZIG . . . . . . BRUCE FAIRBAIRN
EVAN HAMMER. . . . . MEL FERRER
ZINA WILLOW . . . . JOANNE LINVILLE
LYNETTE PORTER . . . . . DEBBI MORGAN
JORDAN WILLOW . . . . SCOTT MULHERN
ANGELA ARIES . . . . . CLAUDETTE NEVINS
KARL MADISON . . . . MARK PINTER
BRIAN HOLMBY . . . . . . MICHAEL SABATINO
JANIE-CLAIRE WILLOW . . JANINE TURNER
JOYCE DANIELS . . . . ERICA YOHN

BEN JERROD, ATTORNEY AT LAW
APRIL 1, 1963–JUNE 28, 1963 NBC

This short-lived, Hollywood-based serial premiered on the same day as two other daytime soaps that would go on to enjoy long, successful runs—*General Hospital* and *The Doctors*. *General Hospital* and *The Doctors* were inspired by the success of nighttime's *Ben Casey* and *Dr. Kildare*, and used a hospital setting as the backdrop for their stories. But *Ben Jerrod* took its lead from two popular nighttime courtroom dramas, *Perry Mason* and *The Defenders*. Created by Roy Winsor, *Ben Jerrod* featured two lawyers and their practice in the small town of Indian Hill, Rhode Island. The first and only case *Ben Jerrod* handled was defending young socialite Janet Donelli, who was accused of murdering her husband.

Ben Jerrod had the distinction of being the first daytime soap to be broadcast in color. Three of the show's cast members, Denise Alexander, Peter Hansen, and Gerald Gordon, would become better known for the characters they later played on *General Hospital*. Michael Ryan later played John Randolph on *Another World*.

EMILY SANDERS . . . . DENISE ALEXANDER
LIL MORRISON . . . . . MARTINE BARTLETT
JANET DONELLI . . . . . . REGINA GLEASON
SAM RICHARDSON . . . . GERALD GORDON
PETER MORRISON. . . . . . . PETER HANSEN
JOHN ABBOTT . . . . . . ADDISON RICHARDS
BEN JERROD . . . . MICHAEL M. RYAN
JIM O'HARA . . . . KEN SCOTT
LT. CHOATES. . . . . LYLE TALBOT

The Bennetts

THE BENNETTS
JULY 6, 1953–JANUARY 8, 1954 NBC

The Bennetts was an early attempt by NBC to lure faithful viewers away from CBS's strong line-up of daytime soaps. On the surface, *The Bennetts* contained all the necessary soap elements. It concerned small town lawyer Wayne Bennett, his family, and their domestic problems. To add variety to the daily 15-minute serial, Bennett's law office was used for further plot complications. A prominent storyline featured the Bennetts' next door neighbors, Blaney and Meg Cobb. The couple could not have children so, because of their strong desire to have a baby, they got themselves entangled in an illegal adoption racket. Disappointed by *The Bennetts* very low ratings, NBC realized a new strategy was needed to take viewers away from CBS and quickly canceled the series.

SPEEDY WINTERS . . . . VI BERWICK
WAYNE BENNETT . . . . DON GIBSON
NANCY BENNETT . . . . . PAULA HOUSTON
BLANEY COBB . . . . JACK LESTER
GEORGE KONOSIS . . . . SAM SIEGEL
ALMA WELLS. . . . . KAY WESTFALL
MEG COBB . . . . BEVERLY YOUNGER

BERRENGER'S
JANUARY 5, 1985—MARCH 9, 1985 NBC

An upscale, New York department store was the backdrop for this short-lived, prime-time soap. The Berrenger clan was lead by patriarch Simon Berrenger, who was the ruthless head of the family business. His oldest son, Paul, was the sympathetic company president who disagreed with Simon's underhanded method of business. Daughter Babs was determined to make her mark in the family business. The youngest son, Billy, was an endearing but confused young man who tried to win his father's attention by getting himself into troublesome situations. Also on the scene was Paul's estranged, self-seeking wife, Gloria, played by Andrea Marcovicci.

A pivotal character was heroine Shane Bradley, the merchandising vice president. Her secret love affair with Paul could destroy her career. Former film starlet Yvette Mimieux returned to television to play Shane, after a 15-year absence. Unable to find a suitable time slot for *Berrenger's*, NBC canceled the series after 11 episodes.

STACEY RUSSELL. . . . . JONELLE ALLEN
LAUREL HAYES . . . . LAURA ASHTON
MELODY HUGHES . . CLAUDIA CHRISTIAN
JOHN HIGGINS . . . . JEFF CONAWAY
MAX KAUFMAN . . . . ALAN FEINSTEIN
TODD HUGHES. . . . . ART HINDLE
CAMMIE SPRINGER . . . . LESLIE HOPE
GLORIA BERRENGER . . . .
ANDREA MARCOVICCI
SHANE BRADLEY . . . . . YVETTE MIMIEUX
BABS BERRENGER . . . . ANITA MORRIS
PAUL BERRENGER . . . . BEN MURPHY
RINALDI . . . . CESAR ROMERO
DANNY KRUCEK . . . . JACK SCALIA
BILLY BERRENGER . . . . . . ROBIN STRAND
JULIO MORALES. . . . . EDDIE VELEZ
SIMON BERRENGER . . . SAM WANAMAKER

Berrenger's

The Best of Everything

BEST OF EVERYTHING
• •
MARCH 30, 1970–SEPTEMBER 25, 1970 ABC

*T*his series was loosely based on Rona Jaffe's best-selling novel about three young career women living in New York City. An earlier movie version starred Joan Crawford, Hope Lange, Suzy Parker, and Diane Baker. The inclusion of former child star Patty McCormack and Hollywood film veterans Gale Sondergaard and Geraldine Fitzgerald helped generate publicity for the daytime soap version, but it was not successful in attracting enough viewers.

EDDIE PERRONE . . . . VICTOR ARNOLD
JOANNA KEY . . . . . BONNIE BEE BUZZARD
GWEN MITCHELL . . . . GINNIE CURTIS
DEXTER KEY . . . . JAMES DAVIDSON
KATE FARROW . . . . M'EL DOWD
VIOLET JORDAN . . . .
                GERALDINE FITZGERALD
KEN LAMONT . . . . BARRY FORD
KIM JORDAN . . . . KATHERINE GLASS
JOHNNY LAMONT . . . . STEPHEN GROVER
ANNE CARTER . . . . DIANE KAGAN
RANDY WILSON . . . . TED LePLAT
LINDA WARREN . . . . . PATTY McCORMACK
BARBARA LAMONT . . . ROCHELLE OLIVER
JOSHUA JORDAN . . . . JOHN RUST
                PETER HARRIS
AMANDA KEY . . . . . GALE SONDERGAARD
MIKE CARTER . . . . JEAN-PIERRE STEWART
APRIL MORRISON . . . . . . SUSAN SULLIVAN
                JULIE MANNIX

THE CATLINS
• • • • • • • • • • • • • • • • • • •
APRIL 4, 1983–MAY 31, 1985 TBS

*T*ed Turner's Atlanta-based cable network launched its first daily, half-hour soap with this serial.

Taking its cue from the legendary Hatfield—McCoy feud, the soap focused on the rivalry between two successful Southern families, the Catlins and the Quinns.

Catherine Catlin's son, T.J., owned Catlin Enterprises. T.J. and Annabelle had five children: Jonathan, president of Catlin Enterprises; Matthew, a doctor; Maggie, a lawyer; Beau, a race-car driver; and Jennifer.

The devious, unscrupulous Medger Quinn had three children: Seth, a sniveling, sorry excuse for a man; Cullen, a convicted felon; and Eleanor, who was married to Jonathan Catlin.

During its two year run, *The Catlins* featured three storylines: Jennifer Catlin's trial for killing her unfaithful fiance, the war between Matt and Beau Catlin for Lauren Woodward, and the death of Eleanor Quinn Catlin.

MATT CATLIN . . . . DAN ALBRIGHT
BEAU CATLIN . . . . PETER BOYNTON
                LARRY JORDAN
ANNABELLE CATLIN . . PAMELA BURRELL
                MURIEL MOORE
CULLEN QUINN . . . . . . McLINN CROWELL
STUART BLAKE . . . . . STUART CULPEPPER
T. J. CATLIN . . . . MICHAEL FOREST
                J. DON FERGUSON
WOODY THORPE . . . . CHARLES HILL
JONATHAN CATLIN . . . . . . JERRY HOMAN
CRISSY CATLIN . . . . NANCY LEEP
                CANDY HOWARD
MEDGER QUINN . . . . DANNY NELSON
ROBERT GOODE . . . . DIRK RANDALL
DIRK STACK . . . . JOE RANIER
LAUREN WOODWARD . CHRISTINA REGULI
SETH QUINN . . . . BRETT RICE
MAGGIE CATLIN . . . . JULIE RIDLEY
                VICTORIA LOVING
ANDREA SMITH . . . . IRIS L. ROBERTS
CATHERINE CATLIN . . . .
                MARY NELL SANTACROCE
MEMPHIS MORGAN . . . .
                JUSTINE THIELEMAN
JENNIFER CATLIN . . . .
                TERRI VANDENBOSCH
                JENNIFER ANGLIN
                NANCY KENNEDY

THE CLEAR HORIZON
• •
JULY 11, 1960–MARCH 11, 1961 CBS
FEBRUARY 26, 1962–JUNE 11, 1962 CBS

*T*elevision's first space age soap opera was also one of the first daytime serials to be telecast from

Hollywood, California. Originally titled *Army Wife*, this serial focused on the lives of astronauts and their families stationed at Cape Canaveral, Florida.

In the debut episode, Roy Selby, an Air Force captain, was transferred from his former post in Alaska and reassigned to Cape Canaveral. *The Clear Horizon* failed to attract an audience and was placed on hiatus. A retooled version of the series returned to the airwaves a year later and was also unsuccessful in finding an audience. Notable cast members included Ted Knight, Lee Meriwether, and comedian George Gobel.

LOIS ADAMS . . . . DENISE ALEXANDER
ANN SELBY . . . . PHYLLIS AVERY
RICKY SELBY . . . . JIMMY CARTER
                CHARLES HERBERT
MITCHELL CORBIN . . RICHARD COOGAN
GREG SELBY . . . . CRAIG CURTIS
SIG LEVY . . . . MICHAEL FOX
ROY SELBY . . . . EDWARD KEMMER
COL. TATE . . . . TED KNIGHT
HARRY MOSEBY . . . . RUSTY LANE
ENID ROSS . . . . LEE MERIWETHER
FRANCES MOSEBY . . . . EVE McVEAGH
THEODORE ADAMS . . . WILLIAM ROERICK
BETTY HOWARD . . . . JAN SHEPARD

The Clear Horizon

CONCERNING MISS MARLOWE
• •
JULY 5, 1954–JULY 1, 1955 NBC

*F*ilm star Louise Allbritton, best known for her performance in *The Egg and I*, was enlisted by NBC to headline this short-lived, 15-minute daytime soap. Allbritton played Maggie Marlowe, an aging New York stage actress who decided to give up her career for marriage, but then her fiance was killed in a tragic accident.

Determined to overcome her loss, a grieving Maggie dedicated her energy to making a comeback in a new play. Along the way, she fell in a love with a married man. Unfortunately, Maggie's new play was a disaster. To further complicate matters, Maggie's performance was being sabotaged by a younger female member of the cast, Kit Christy. On another front, Maggie hired private detectives to locate her long-lost daughter. Maggie and her young daughter were separated 14 years earlier, thanks to a ditzy grandmother who lost the child in France. Before the series ended, Maggie discovered that Kit, her nemesis, was her daughter.

Concerning Miss Marlowe is best remembered because it was responsible for one of live television's funniest bloopers. During a scene between Miss Allbritton and an actress playing her French maid, a phone rang when it shouldn't have. Picking up the phone, a flustered Allbritton answered and then immediately handed the receiver to the maid, saying, "It's for you." While the panic-stricken actress struggled to ad-lib, Allbritton walked off the set. She left the frightened woman completely alone in front of the camera until a commercial break!

MARGARET MARLOWE . . . .
                   LOUISE ALLBRITTON
                   HELEN SHIELDS
CINDY CLAYTON . . PATRICIA BOSWORTH
TOMMY CLAYTON . . . . EDDIE BRIEN
HARRY CLAYTON . . . . JOHN GIBSON
HUGH FRASER . . . . . . LAUREN GILBERT
BILL COOKE . . . . JOHN RABY
DOT CLAYTON . . . . HELEN SHIELDS
HARRIET THE HAT . . . . . JANE SEYMOUR
RONALD BLAKE . . . . BERT THORN
KIT CHRISTY . . . . CHRIS WHITE
JIM GAVIN . . . . . . EFREM ZIMBALIST, JR.

Concerning Miss Marlowe

A DATE WITH LIFE
OCTOBER 10, 1955–JUNE 29, 1956 NBC

This 15-minute daytime serial was about life in a small town. The show was narrated by the editor of the fictional *The Bay City News*, Jim Bradley, and later by Jim's brother, Tom.

The soap experimented with the serial format by presenting its stories anthology-style. A storyline focusing on the lives of various community members in the small town of Bay City would last approximately five weeks and then be replaced by a new story with a different cast of characters. To give the series continuity, the Bradley brothers not only introduced the stories, but also provided editorial commentary.

Launching the series was a story featuring Barbara Britton as Laurie Dayton, a woman who received startling news the day before her wedding—she'd been adopted. Postponing her wedding, Laurie embarked on a journey to learn more about herself by finding her birth parents.

JIM BRADLEY . . . . LOGAN FIELD
TOM BRADLEY . . . . MARK ROBERTS

A Date with Life

THE EGG AND I
SEPTEMBER 3, 1951–AUGUST 1, 1952 CBS

Comic overtones set this daytime serial apart from the sudsy dramas viewers were used to watching. It was based on the best-selling book by Betty MacDonald. Before

reaching daytime, the book had been made into a popular feature film starring Claudette Colbert and Fred MacMurray. Following the lead set by the book and film, the daytime version focused on a sophisticated, urban couple who had relocated to northern Pennsylvania to oversee a chicken farm. Fourteen years later, *Green Acres* would have more success with a similar premise.

BOB MacDONALD . . . . JOHN CRAVEN
PAULA FRENCH . . . . KAREN HALE
BETTY MacDONALD . . . . . . PAT KIRKLAND
MA KETTLE . . . . DORIS RICH
JED SIMMONS . . . . GRADY SUTTON
LISA SCHUMACHER . . . INGEBORG THEEK
PA KETTLE . . . . FRANK TWEDELL

EMERALD POINT, N.A.S.
SEPTEMBER 26, 1983–MARCH 12, 1984 CBS

Hot on the heels of their success with *Dynasty*, creators Richard and Esther Shapiro developed this nighttime series for CBS. Against the unlikely backdrop of a combat-ready naval air station, *Emerald Point, N.A.S.* offered generous portions of romance and intrigue. The primary focus of the series was Rear Admiral Thomas Mallory and his family. Waging battle against Mallory was the unscrupulous Harlan Adams.

Like *Dallas* and *Dynasty*, *Emerald Point's* cast consisted of well known nighttime actors and veteran daytime soap performers. Disappointed by its low ratings, CBS did not renew the series.

MAGGIE FARRELL . . . . MAUD ADAMS
SIMON ADAMS . . . .
       RICHARD DEAN ANDERSON
DAVID MARQUETTE . . . .
         MICHAEL BRANDON
ALEXI GORICHENKNO . . . .
         MICHAEL CARVEN
LESLIE MALLORY . . . . DORAN CLARK
CELIA MALLORY WARREN . . . . SUSAN DEY
KAY MALLORY . . . . STEPHANIE DUNNAM
JACK WARREN . . . . CHARLES FRANK
YURI BUKHARIN . . . . ROBERT LOGGIA
GLENN MATTHEWS . . . ANDREW STEVENS
DEANNA KINCAID . . . . JILL ST. JOHN
HARLAN ADAMS . . . . . . ROBERT VAUGHN
         PATRICK O'NEAL
HILARY ADAMS . . . . SELA WARD
THOMAS MALLORY . . . . . DENNIS WEAVER

Executive Suite

EXECUTIVE SUITE
. . . .
SEPTEMBER 20, 1976–
FEBRUARY 11, 1977 CBS

*T*he Edge of Night's longtime headwriter Henry Slesar developed this series, based on on the novel by Cameron Hawley. *Executive Suite* attempted to take viewers inside the board room of corporate America, as well as highlight the after-hour lives of its successful business executives. A prominent plot line was the interracial romance between one of the executive's sons and his black girlfriend. Sharing co-writing chores with Henry Slesar were Barbara Avedon and Barbara Corday, who later achieved success for creating the popular police series *Cagney and Lacey*.

HELEN WALLING . . . . SHARON ACKER
MARK DESMOND. . . . . RICHARD COX
ASTRID RUTLEDGE . . GWYDA DONHOWE
HOWELL RUTLEDGE. . STEPHEN ELLIOTT
TOM DALESSIO. . . . . PAUL LAMBERT
BRIAN WALLING . . . . . LEIGH McCLOSKEY
PEARCE NEWBERRY . . . . BYRON MORROW
YVONNE HOLLAND . . . . . . TRISHA NOBLE
STACEY WALLING . . . . . . WENDY PHILLIPS
GLORY DALESSIO . . . . JOAN PRATHER
MALCOLM GIBSON . . . PERCY RODRIGUEZ
DAN WALLING . . . . MITCHELL RYAN
ANDERSON GAULT . . . WILLIAM SMITHERS
SUMMER JOHNSON . . . . . . BRENDA SYKES

FAIRMEADOWS, U.S.A.
. . . .
NOVEMBER 4, 1951–APRIL 27, 1952 NBC

*T*his series originally began as a Sunday afternoon serial, but temporarily left the airwaves in 1951. In 1952, it returned to television with a new title, *The House in the Garden*. The revised format was included in *The*

Kate Smith Hour as a continuing, daily, 15-minute serial. Character film actor Howard St. John starred as John Olcott, the owner of a general store in a small town. Besides Olcott, other members of his family and residents of the small town were featured.

JOHN OLCOTT . . . . LAUREN GILBERT
                          HOWARD ST. JOHN
ALICE OLCOTT . . . . . . RUTH MATTESON
EVVIE OLCOTT . . . . MIMI STRONGIN

FARAWAY HILL
. . . .
OCTOBER 2, 1946–
DECEMBER 18, 1946 DuMONT

*T*his early serial's premise was similar to *The Egg and I*. After losing her husband, widow Karen St. John left her life in New York City and began a new one in a small farm town. Considered network television's first dramatic serial, *Faraway Hill* had no choice but to experiment with the form. Each episode was allotted a $300 budget. In the premiere episode, writer/director David P. Lewis introduced viewers to his new characters by flashing their names and relationships on the screen. Borrowing from radio, the characters' thoughts were narrated by an off-camera voice. At each show's beginning, Karen reminded viewers what happened the week before.

Broadway actress Flora Campbell played Karen. Later, she would appear on *The Seeking Heart*, *Love of Life*, *The Edge of Night*, *The Secret Storm*, and *Valiant Lady*.

KAREN ST. JOHN . . . . . . FLORA CAMPBELL

THE FIRST HUNDRED YEARS
. . . .
DECEMBER 4, 1950–JUNE 27, 1952 CBS

*C*BS started its daytime soap schedule with this comic serial. Owned by Procter & Gamble, *The First Hundred Years* chronicled the problems a newlywed couple, Chris and Connie Thayer, encountered adjusting to married life. Meddlesome in-laws served as

the primary source of conflict for the young couple.

A crucial stumbling block to the show's success was casting former teen actor Jimmy Lydon as Chris Thayer. Lydon's claim to fame was playing the title role in the lucrative Henry Aldrich film series. His portrayal of the gawky, scatter-brained teenager left such a strong mark that viewers had difficulty accepting him in a romantic leading role. Critics accused the fledgling series of being a talky, televised radio program. Eighteen months into its run, CBS pulled the plug. *The First Hundred Years* was replaced by long-running *The Guiding Light*.

During the serial's brief run, character actor Larry Haines appeared in a featured role. His later role as Stu Bergman on *Search for Tomorrow* would earn him a permanent place in daytime's hall of fame.

MR. MARTIN . . . . . ROBERT ARMSTRONG
MRS. MARTIN . . . . NANA BRYANT
MRS. THAYER . . . . VALERIE COSSART
CHRIS THAYER . . . . JAMES LYDON
MARGY MARTIN . . . . NANCY MALONE
CONNIE THAYER . . . . . . ANNE SARGENT
                            OLIVE STACEY
MR. THAYER . . . . DON TOBIN

First Love

FIRST LOVE
. . . .
JULY, 1954–DECEMBER 30, 1955 NBC

*R*egarding this serial one thing was clear: Viewers who tuned in liked what they saw. The dilemma NBC faced was in persuading more people to watch. *First Love* centered on the troubled relationship between jet engineer Zach James and his new bride, Laurie Kennedy. An unhappy childhood made it difficult for Zach to truly accept Laurie's love. It also fueled Zach's obsession with achieving success in his professional life. The biggest test in Zach and Laurie's marriage came when Zach went on trial for murder. The police suspected that he had been having an affair with the dead woman.

Although considered a serious soap, a dramatic Friday cliff-hanger veered into unintentional comedy when Val Dufour, who played Zach, stumbled over a line—this show was filmed live. Moments earlier, Zach had watched his friend Chris perish in a tragic plane crash. When it came time to break the news to Chris's wife and Laurie, who were played by Rosemary Prinz and Patricia Barry, Dufour was supposed to say, "Chris cracked up the plane." Instead, he said, "Chris crapped—" Realizing his mistake, he paused and then added, "—on the plane." Unable to contain themselves, the three actors broke into laughter. Fortunately, viewer response to the players' spontaneous transgression was positive and they weren't reprimanded by the network.

Eighteen months into the serial's run, NBC lost confidence and abruptly canceled the show.

DORIS KENNEDY . . . . PEGGY ALLENBY
ZACH JAMES . . . . TOD ANDREWS
                              VAL DUFOUR
BRUCE McKEE . . . . JAY BARNEY
LAURIE JAMES . . . . PATRICIA BARRY
QUENTIN ANDREWS . . . FREDERIC DOWNS
MIKE KENNEDY . . . . JOHN DUTRA
MATTHEW JAMES . . . . PAUL McGRATH
PEGGY GORDON . . . HENRIETTA MOORE
AMY . . . . ROSEMARY PRINZ
JUDGE KENNEDY . . . . HOWARD SMITH
PAUL KENNEDY . . . . MELVILLE RUICK
CHRIS . . . . FRANKIE THOMAS
PHIL GORDON . . . . JOE WARREN

FOLLOW YOUR HEART
AUGUST 3, 1953–JANUARY 8, 1954 NBC

This serial was radio-soap creator Elaine Carrington's ill-fated attempt to make her mark in television. Lifting storylines from her long-running radio serial *When a Girl Marries*, Carrington created a television soap about a high-society heroine who stuns her upper-crust family by falling in love with a man beneath her social class. A few weeks into the fledgling serial's run, its romantic theme was abandoned in favor of an adventure storyline about spies. When the ratings didn't improve, NBC canceled it leaving every storyline unresolved. Carrington must have taken the criticism that she had written a radio serial with pictures literally. She sold the series to radio, where it enjoyed a six-year run.

JULIE FIELDING . . . . SALLIE BROPHY
MRS. MacDONALD . . . . . ANNE SEYMOUR
SAM FIELDING . . . . JOHN SEYMOUR
MRS. FIELDING . . . . . . NANCY SHERIDAN
SHARON RICHARD . . . . MAXINE STUART
JOCEYLYN FIELDING . . . . LAURA WEBER
PETER DAVIS . . . . GRANT WILLIAMS

FOR BETTER OR WORSE
JUNE 29, 1959–JUNE 24, 1960 CBS

This serial's odds for success were increased by its lead-in, *As the World Turns*. But it was another anthology-style serial, a format viewers rejected. Dr. James A. Peterson, a teacher and marriage counselor, was the host. He introduced stories about marriages in need of repair. Dyan Cannon made her daytime debut in "The Case of the Childish Bride." She played a self-centered, immature woman unable to handle the responsibilities of marriage.

For Better or Worse

For Richer, For Poorer

FOR RICHER, FOR POORER
DECEMBER 6, 1977–
SEPTEMBER 29, 1978 NBC

This show was a revamped version of the short-lived serial *Lovers and Friends*, which NBC had placed on temporary hiatus seven months earlier. Like its predecessor, *For Richer, For Poorer* centered on the class conflict between two families, the wealthy Cushings and the poorer Saxtons.

Taking over headwriting chores for creator Harding Lemay, Tom King introduced two new families, the upscale Brewsters and the downtrodden Fergusons. Besides quickening the show's pace, King also used elements that were considered staples to daytime television drama: adultery, amnesia, and the crime syndicate.

The serial's location stayed the same, the wealthy Chicago suburb of Point Clair. The young lovers, Megan Cushing and Rhett Saxton, were recast and Rhett's name was changed to Bill. To win new viewers for the series, NBC exploited the success of *Another World* by having two of its popular characters, Rachel and Mac Cory, played by Victoria Wyndham and Douglass Watson, make guest appearances. Despite everyone's best efforts, the series remained a ratings disappointment and was canceled ten months later, but much of the cast went on to other NBC soaps.

BENTLEY SAXTON	DAVID ABBOTT
AUSTIN CUSHING	ROD ARRANTS
JASON SAXTON	RICHARD BACKUS
EDITH CUSHING	LAURINDA BARRETT
VIOLA BREWSTER	PATRICIA BARRY
CONNIE FERGUSON	CYNTHIA BOSTICK
FRANK DAMICO	STEPHEN BURLEIGH
LEE FERGUSON	ROBERT BURTON
JOSIE SAXTON	PATRICIA ENGLUND
TESSA SAXTON	BREON GORMAN
BILL SAXTON	TOM HAPPER
AMY GIFFORD	CHRISTINE JONES
GEORGE KIMBALL	STEPHEN JOYCE
DESMOND HAMILTON	DAVID KNAPP
LAURIE BREWSTER	JULIA MacKENZIE
MEGAN CUSHING	DARLENE PARKS
ELEANOR KIMBALL	FLORA PLUMB
IRA FERGUSON	ROY POOLE
COLLEEN GRIFFIN	NANCY SNYDER
LESTER SAXTON	ALBERT STRATTON

FULL CIRCLE
JUNE 27, 1960–MARCH 10, 1961 CBS

A stranger, Gary Donovan drifted into the small town of Crowder, Virginia. He had a major impact on the lives of its residents, particularly the town's founding family. Dyan Cannon's brief stint on *For Better or Worse* led to a starring role on this CBS serial. She portrayed Lisa Linda Crowder, a young woman who married into the prominent Crowder family. Following the mysterious death of her husband, Loyal, Lisa inexplicably found herself drawn to Gary, who was a handsome drifter passing through town. This raised the town people's suspicions about her husband's untimely death. Gary stayed in Crowder and got tangled in the lives of its citizens.

Soon after the show's cancellation, Dyan Cannon retired temporarily from acting and she married movie-star Cary Grant. When their marriage ended in divorce, she resumed her career and received an Oscar nomination for her performance in *Bob & Carol & Ted & Alice*.

KIT ALDRICH	JEAN BYRON
LISA CROWDER	DYAN CANNON
DEPUTY	SAM EDWARDS
GARY DONOVAN	ROBERT FORTIER
CARTER TALTON	BYRON FOULGER
DAVID TALTON	BILL LUNDMARK
LOYAL CROWDER	JOHN McNAMARA
ELLEN DENKER	NANCY MILLARD
VIRGIL DENKER	MICHAEL ROSS
BETH PERCE	AMZIE STRICKLAND

Golden Windows

GOLDEN WINDOWS
JULY 5, 1954–APRIL 8, 1955 NBC

S how business served as the backdrop for this short-lived series. Against the wishes of her father and fiance, 22-year-old singer Juliet Goodwin left Maine to seek fame and fortune in New York City. Her new life in the Big Apple brought many changes to her life, especially in the area of romance. Although her fiance, John Brandon, was still interested in marrying her, a confused Juliet now found herself attracted to Tom Anderson, a man with an intriguing past. To further complicate matters, Juliet also wrestled with the notion that an elderly European man who visited her backstage after a performance might actually be her natural father.

HAZEL	BARBARA COOK
CHARLES GOODWIN	ERIC DRESSLER
JULIET GOODWIN	LELIA MARTIN
TOM ANDERSON	HERBERT PATTERSON
JOHN BRANDON	GRANT SULLIVAN

THE GREATEST GIFT
AUGUST 30, 1954–JULY 1, 1955 NBC

T his serial featured daytime television's first woman doctor. Medical school and a hitch in Korea, courtesy of the Army Medical Corps, barely prepared Dr. Eve Allen for the struggle she faced in taking over her uncle's medical practice. The understaffed clinic was financially-strapped and located on the wrong side of the tracks in a small town. Providing romance on the serial was Eve's entanglement with Dr. Phil Stone.

Broadway actress Anne Burr was cast to play Eve Allen. Jack Klugman, Anne Meara, and Martin Balsam also found work in featured roles on this short-lived series.

PETER BLAKE	HENRY BARNARD
EVE ALLEN	ANNE BURR
SAM BLAKE	JOSEF DRAKE
PHIL STONE	PHILIP FOSTER
HAROLD MATTHEWS	WILL HARE
	MARTIN BALSAM
PEG	MARGARET HENEGHAN
JIM HANSON	JACK KLUGMAN
BETTY MATTHEWS	ATHENA LORDE
HARRIET	ANNE MEARA
NED BLACKMAN	GENE PETERSON
	WARD COSTELLO
MRS. BLAKE	HELEN WARREN

The Greatest Gift

HAWKINS FALLS
JUNE 17, 1950–
AUGUST 19, 1950 (PRIME TIME)
APRIL 2, 1951–JULY 1, 1955 (DAYTIME) NBC

O ne of NBC's first successful serials, *Hawkins Falls* began as a prime-time series about the trials and tribulations of life in a small town. Its format combined drama and situation comedy, and was broadcast from Chicago. When the series returned to television as a daytime serial, most of the cast remained intact. What set *Hawkins Falls* apart from other daytime serials was its use of location scenery. It was shot in Woodstock, Illinois (the town the series was inspired by). Unfortunately, this made the series one of the most expensive to produce and led to its demise.

Hugh Downs, the current host of 20/20, served as the show's announcer. Character actor Tom Poston, famous for his long-running role on the prime-time series *Newhart*, appeared in a feature role.

FLOYD COREY . . . . . MAURICE COPELAND
MICHAEL GOLDA
ROY BETTERT . . . . BRUCE DANE
CLATE WEATHERS . . . . FRANK DANE
LONA DREWER COREY . . . .
BERNADINE FLYNN
TOBY WINFIELD . . . . TOM POSTON
SPEC BASSETT . . . . RUSS REED
ELMIRA CLEEBE . . . . . . ELMIRA ROESSLER
LAIF FLAIGLE . . . . WYN STRACKE
BELINDA CATHERWOOD . . HOPE SUMMERS
MILLIE FLAIGLE . . . . ROS TWOHEY

Hawkins Falls

HIDDEN FACES

DECEMBER 30, 1968–JUNE 27, 1969 NBC

Realizing that trying to compete with the homespun *As the World Turns* for ratings would be an uphill battle, NBC decided to counter-program with a serial more along the lines of *The Edge of Night*. In fact, this mystery-crime series was developed by *Edge's* creator, Irving Vendig. The show's leading character, lawyer Arthur Adams, was facing the toughest case of his legal career. He was defending Katherine Logan, a surgeon who'd been accused of causing a patient's death. During the course of the trial, Adams fell in love with his attractive client.

Although *Hidden Faces* was considered top-notch drama by its audience, initial low ratings caused NBC to lose confidence in the serial. Six months after its premiere, the series was canceled.

ALLYN JAFFE . . . . LINDA BLAIR
GRACE ENSLEY . . . . LUDI CLAIRE
ROBERT JAFFE . . . . JOSEPH DALY
ARTHUR ADAMS . . . . CONARD FOWKES
MIMI JAFFE . . . . RITA GAM
MARK UTLEY . . . . STEPHEN JOYCE
NICK CAPELLO TURNER . TONY LoBIANCO
EARL HARRIMAN . . . . NAT POLEN
MARTHA LOGAN . . . . . . LOUISE SHAFFER
WILBUR ENSLEY . . . . JOHN TOWLEY
KATHERINE LOGAN . . . .
GRETCHEN WALTHER

HIGH HOPES

1978 SYNDICATED

This show was the first daytime serial to be broadcast simultaneously in America and Canada. Taped in Toronto, *High Hopes* aired on the CBC network and was syndicated to local independent stations in America. The series centered on psychiatrist Neal Chapman's practice, which specialized in family counseling. Although Chapman was a whiz at guiding other families through a crisis, his own personal life was falling apart. Unfortunately, viewers were bored by the serial's languid pace. For the first few months, its front-burning storyline involved Chapman's daughter Jessie and her obsession with keeping a stray dog. In a last-ditch attempt to save the series, the producers added *Peyton Place* star Dorothy Malone to its cast.

AMY SPERRY . . . . GINA DICK
LOUISE BATES . . . . JAYNE EASTWOOD
WALTER TELFORD . . . . COLIN FOX
PAULA MYLES . . . . . . NUALA FITZGERALD
NEAL CHAPMAN . . . . BRUCE GRAY
TRUDY BOWEN . . . . BARBARA KYLE
JESSIE CHAPMAN . . . . MARIANNE McISSAC

CAROL TAUSS . . . . . . DOROTHY MALONE
DAN GERALD . . . . JAN MUSZINSKI
VICTOR TAUSS . . . . . NEHEMIAH PERSOFF
MEG CHAPMAN . . . . DORIS PETRIE

High Hopes

HOTEL COSMOPOLITAN

AUGUST 19, 1957–APRIL 11, 1958 CBS

CBS replaced the formerly successful *Valiant Lady* with this anthology-style serial. It was inspired by the film classic *Grand Hotel*. The series focused on the glamorous guests who stayed at the Cosmopolitan, a fictitious hotel in New York City. Perhaps if the producers had convinced the reclusive Greta Garbo to make a guest appearance, the series may have stood a chance at success. Unfortunately, the relatively unknown actors who did appear failed to ignite the audience's interest. Actor Donald Woods narrated the stories and Henderson Forsythe, who would later be successful as Dr. David Stewart on *As the World Turns*, played the Cosmopolitan's house detective.

HOUSE DETECTIVE . . . .
HENDERSON FORSYTHE
NARRATOR . . . . DONALD WOODS

The House on High Street

THE HOUSE ON HIGH STREET
. . . .
SEPTEMBER 28, 1959–
FEBRUARY 5, 1960 NBC

Juvenile delinquency and divorce were the basis of this dramatic anthology serial. Each story was based on an actual court case and was resolved in three to five episodes. Philip Abbott played probation officer John Collier, while real psychiatrists and judges appeared as themselves. The first story concerned a 16-year-old boy from a prominent family who was on trial for stealing a car.

The serial recruited talented stage actors for guest appearances, including Alan Alda, Sylvia Miles, Martin Balsam, Kay Medford, and Frances Sternhagen.

KING'S CROSSING
. . . .
JANUARY 16, 1982–
FEBRUARY 27, 1982 ABC

This prime-time serial had its roots in another nighttime sudser that had failed a year earlier, *Secrets of Midland Heights*. Producers Lee Rich and Michael Filerman hinted that *King's Crossing* would be a revised version of the earlier serial, but viewers found it completely different. Set in a small college town, *King's Crossing* centered around

English teacher Paul Hollister and his family. Paul's alcoholic drinking and abusive behavior were major sore points for the family.

Newharts' Mary Frann played Nan, Paul Hollister's wife, and *Beauty and the Beast's* Linda Hamilton had a co-starring role as Lauren Hollister. The cast featured other faces familiar to daytime audiences, including *The Guiding Light's* Michael Zaslow and *The Secret Storm's* Stephanie Braxton.

CAROL HADARY...STEPHANIE BRAXTON
JILLIAN BEAUCHAMP ....DORAN CLARK
PAUL HOLLISTER...BRADFORD DILLMAN
NAN HOLLISTER.........MARY FRANN
LAUREN HOLLISTER...LINDA HAMILTON
CAREY HOLLISTER.....MARILYN JONES
LOUISA BEAUCHAMP ....
.................BEATRICE STRAIGHT
JONATHON HADARY...MICHAEL ZASLOW
BILLY McCALL ....DANIEL ZIPPI

King's Crossing

KITTY FOYLE
. . . .
JANUARY 13, 1958–JUNE 27, 1958 NBC

It's understandable why NBC thought this serial would be a success. It had already been well received as a novel, radio serial, and feature film (Ginger Rogers won an Academy Award for her performance in the title role). Using Christopher Morley's novel as the springboard, the TV serial focused on a poor Irish girl who fell in love with a young man from a wealthy Philadelphia family. Producers of the serial

scoured the country, seeing two hundred actresses, in a well publicized talent search before selecting Kathleen Murray to play the title role. Critics quickly dismissed the series, citing weak writing.

OLIVIA STRAFFORD....VALERIE COSSART
ROSIE RITTENHOUSE ....LES DAMON
POP FOYLE.............RALPH DUNNE
ED FOYLE..............BOB HASTINGS
MOLLY SCHARF ....JUDY LEWIS
SOPHIE FOYLE.........KAY MEDFORD
KITTY FOYLE .....KATHLEEN MURRAY
WYN STRAFFORD....WILLIAM REDFIELD
MAC FOYLE...........LARRY ROBINSON
STACEY LEE BALLA....MARIE WORSHAM

Kitty Foyle

LOVERS AND FRIENDS
. . . .
JANUARY 3, 1977–MAY 6, 1977 NBC

Another World's headwriter Harding Lemay and producer Paul Rauch presented this serial. It was about the differences between two economically diverse families: the prosperous Cushings and the humble Saxtons. Set in Point Clair, a posh lakefront suburb of Chicago, *Lovers and Friends* emphasized character development over plot. The primary love story was the youthful romance between Rhett Saxton and Megan Cushing. Complicating matters was Rhett's brother Jason, who was also in love with Megan. Concerned by the show's low-ratings, NBC decided to put it on temporary hiatus. Six months later, NBC came out with a revamped version, retitled *For Richer, For Poorer*. It followed the more traditional soap format of the day (murder, mob action, etc.) and renamed

Rhett Saxton, its young male lead, a less pretentious "Bill."

BENTLEY SAXTON	DAVID ABBOTT
AUSTIN CUSHING	ROD ARRANTS
JASON SAXTON	RICHARD BACKUS
SOPHIA SLOCUM	MARGARET BARKER
TESSA SAXTON	VICKY DAWSON
JOSIE SAXTON	PATRICIA ENGLUND
MEGAN CUSHING	PATRICIA ESTRIN
CONNIE FERGUSON	SUSAN FOSTER
LESTER SAXTON	JOHN HEFFERNAN
AMY GIFFORD	CHRISTINE JONES
GEORGE KIMBALL	STEPHEN JOYCE
DESMOND HAMILTON	DAVID KNAPP
EDITH CUSHING	NANCY MARCHAND
ELEANOR KIMBALL	FLORA PLUMB
RHETT SAXTON	BOB PURVEY
RICHARD CUSHING	RON RANDELL

Lovers and Friends

MISS SUSAN
MARCH 12, 1951–DECEMBER 28, 1951 NBC

This serial's behind-the-scenes story was more compelling than what viewers saw on the screen. Former MGM starlet Susan Peters played the title role. While on a hunting trip in 1945, Peters was accidentally shot and was paralyzed from the waist down. She was confined to a wheelchair. She returned to work three years later with a starring role in the feature film, *The Sign of the Ram.* In 1951, she accepted NBC's offer to star in a serial developed especially for her. She played Susan Martin, an attorney that was wheelchair-bound, who had recently resumed her law practice in her hometown of Martinsville, Ohio.

An early storyline centered around Susan's engagement to a man who wanted to raise a large family. He didn't realize his intended bride couldn't bear children. Sensing the serial exploited Peters's misfortune, viewers stayed away in droves. Less than a year after the series went off the air, 30-year-old Susan Peters died.

MRS. PECK	KATHRYN GRILL
SUSAN MARTIN	SUSAN PETERS
BILL CARTER	MARK ROBERTS

MODERN ROMANCES
OCTOBER 4, 1954–SEPTEMBER 19, 1958 NBC

This anthology series enjoyed a successful four-year run. It dramatized stories from the popular magazine *Modern Romances.* Every Monday a new story would be introduced by the serial's host and narrator, Martha Scott. She was later replaced by Mel Brandt. When Brandt stepped down, guest hosts, including Jayne Meadows and Margaret Truman, were featured.

The premiere story revolved around a possessive husband who feared his wife was having an affair with their attorney. Ann Flood, who played Nancy Karr on *The Edge of Night,* and Georgann Johnson, who played Ellen Grant on *Somerset,* made frequent appearances. Mary K. Wells and Augusta Dabney, two other soap stars, also appeared.

Modern Romances

Moment of Truth

MOMENT OF TRUTH
JANUARY 4, 1965–NOVEMBER 5, 1965 NBC

The late Douglass Watson, who was most famous for his role as Mac Cory on *Another World,* starred in this Toronto-based serial. Watson played Dr. Robert Wallace, a professor and psychologist. The series focused on the lives of people living in a small Canadian community. Viewers responded more favorably to the low-rated serial's replacement, *Days of Our Lives.*

RUSSELL WINGATE	IVOR BARRY
GIL BENNETT	JOHN BETHUNE
JOHNNY WALLACE	MICHAEL DODDS
VINCE CONWAY	PETER DONAT
MONIQUE WINGATE	FERNANDE GIROUX
LINDA HARRIS	ANNA HAGAN
NANCY WALLACE	LOUISE KING
JACK WILLIAMS	STEPHEN LEVY
BARBARA HARRIS	MIRA PAWLUK
SHELIA WALLACE	BARBARA PIERCE
ROBERT WALLACE	DOUGLASS WATSON
DEXTER	CHRIS WIGGINS

MORNING STAR
SEPTEMBER 27, 1965–JULY 1, 1966 NBC

Anxious to give CBS a run for its money in daytime, an aggressive NBC premiered this serial and *Paradise Bay* on the same day. Both serials were based in Hollywood and presented in color. Ten months later, they disappeared from the airwaves on the same day. *Morning Star* was created by Ted Corday (who performed similar duties with Irna Phillips on *Days of Our Lives*). The serial revolved around Katy Elliott, who received devastating news the day before her wedding—her fiance had been killed in an automobile crash. Overcome with grief, Katy left her hometown and moved to New York City, where she pursued a career in fashion design. Soon, romance blossomed again in Katy's life and she became involved with Bill Riley. Despite her new happiness, Katy was plagued by memories of her former life in Springdale, Massachusetts. *Morning Star* was written by Carolyn Weston who flipped burgers at a Frosty-Freeze and penned romance stories in her free time.

The same week this serial was canceled, Edward Mallory, who played Bill Riley, was cast as Dr. Bill Horton on *Days of Our Lives*.

TIM BLAKE	WILLIAM ARVIN
MILLIE ELLIOTT	SHELIA BROMLEY
MIKE HALLORAN	TED deCORDA
EVE BLAKE	FLOY DEAN
ANN BURTON	OLIVE DUNBAR
GREGORY ROSS	BURT DOUGLAS
JAN ELLIOTT	ADRIENNE ELLIS
JOAN MITCHELL	BETTY LOU GERSON
GRACE ALLISON	PHYLLIS HILL
ERIC MANNING	RON JACKSON
BILL RILEY	EDWARD MALLORY
DANA MANNING	
	BETSY JONES MORELAND
KATY ELLIOTT	ELIZABETH PERRY
	SHARY MARSHALL
ED ELLIOTT	ED PRENTISS
STAN MANNING	JOHN STEPHANSON
	JOHN DEHNER

Morning Star

NEVER TOO YOUNG
SEPTEMBER 27, 1965–JUNE 24, 1966 ABC

Like Fox television's *Tribes*, this serial was told from a young adult's point of view. Rather than using a high school setting, however, *Never Too Young* chose Malibu Beach as its backdrop.

Leave It to Beaver's Tony Dow and *Lassie's* Tommy Rettig appeared in feature roles. Dack Rambo, who's known for his work on *All My Children, Dallas,* and *Another World,* was also a cast member. Ironically, ABC threw in the towel on this serial before giving young viewers an opportunity to sample it during summer vacation. It was probably just as well, considering the serial that replaced it—*Dark Shadows.*

TAD	MICHAEL BLODGETT
SUSAN	CINDY CAROL
BARBARA	PAT CONNOLLY
CHET	TONY DOW
JOY	ROBIN GRACE
FRANK	JOHN LUPTON
TIM	DACK RAMBO
JO-JO	TOMMY RETTIG
ALFIE	DAVID WATSON
RHODA	PATRICE WYMORE

A NEW DAY IN EDEN
1982–1983 SHOWTIME

This successful cable-TV serial was written by Douglas Marland, who has written for *General Hospital, As the World Turns, The Guiding Light, Loving,* and *The Doctors.* On the surface, *A New Day in Eden* functioned like most serials on network television. It explored the romantic lives of people living in a small midwestern town. Since this was cable television, however, the serial had the freedom to explore situations then unknown to soap audiences. This included an incestuous relationship between a father and his daughter, a love affair between two women, and an explicit romance between an older woman and a younger man.

Jack Wagner, who would later have major success in daytime television as Frisco Jones on *General Hospital,* was a featured performer. Jane Elliot, best known for her role as Tracy Quartermaine on *General Hospital,* co-starred. Lara Parker, who bedazzled viewers of *Dark Shadows* with her role as Angelique DuVall Collins, also starred on the serial.

JOHN COLLIER	STEVE CARLSON
MADGE SINCLAIR	JANE ELLIOT
BRYAN LEWIS	JIM McMULLAN
BETTY FRANKLIN	LARA PARKER
GREG LEWIS	LARRY POINDEXTER
MIRANDA STEVENS	MAGGIE SULLIVAN
CLINT MASTERSON	JACK P. WAGNER
LAUREL FRANKLIN	ANN WILKINSON
BIFF LEWIS	GRANT WILSON

The Nurses

THE NURSES
SEPTEMBER 27, 1965–MARCH 31, 1967 ABC

This serial began as a prime-time, one-hour weekly series starring Shirl Conway and Zina Bethune. It aired on CBS for three seasons (in its final season it was retitled *The Doctors and the Nurses*). Three weeks after it disappeared from CBS's prime-time schedule, *The Nurses* resurfaced as a daily daytime serial on ABC. Mary Fickett, who now plays Ruth Martin on *All My Children,* replaced Shirl Conway in the starring role as nurse Liz Thorpe. Melinda Plank took over for Zina Bethune as nurse Gail Lucas. The series was unable to duplicate its prime-time success in daytime. It was canceled 18 months after its premiere.

LIZ THORPE	MARY FICKETT
HUGH McLEOD	ARTHUR FRANZ
DONNA STEELE	CAROL GAINER
PAT STEELE	SALLY GRACIE
BRENDA McLEOD	PATRICIA HYLAND
CORA ALEXANDER	MURIEL KIRKLAND
JAMIE McLEOD	JUDSON LAIRE
JAKE STEELE	RICHARD McMURRAY
DOROTHY WARNER	LEONIE NORTON
BRAD KIERNAN	LEE PATTERSON
GAIL LUCAS	MELINDA PLANK
JOHN CRAGER	NAT POLEN
KEN ALEXANDER	NICHOLAS PRYOR
MRS. GROSSBERG	POLLY ROWLES
PAUL FULLER	PAUL STEVENS
MARTHA	JOAN WETMORE
VIVIAN GENTRY	LESLEY WOODS

THE O'NEILLS
SEPTEMBER 6, 1949–JANUARY 20, 1950
DuMONT

This prime-time, half-hour weekly series had enjoyed a nine-year run as a radio serial. Like the radio series, the TV version centered around widow Peggy O'Neill's struggle to raise her children. Jane West and Janice Gilbert returned to star as the same characters they played in the earlier radio version. Following her stint on *The O'Neills*, Vera Allen would find further work in daytime television. She played Kass, the Fraser family's maid on *From These Roots*, and Grandma Matthews on *Another World.*

PEGGY O'NEILL	VERA ALLEN
TRUDY LEVY	CELIA BUDKIN
MORRIS LEVY	BEN FISHBEIN
JANICE O'NEILL	JANICE GILBERT
DANNY O'NEIL	MICHAEL LAWSON
UNCLE BILL	IAN MARTIN
MRS. BAILEY	JANE WEST

OUR FIVE DAUGHTERS
JANUARY 2, 1962–SEPTEMBER 28, 1962 NBC

Silent film star Esther Ralston, nicknamed "The American Venus," came out of retirement to headline this serial. Shortly before joining the series, she had been working as a salesclerk at B. Altman & Company. She was forced to accept this position after losing her large fortune from her movie era days.

Ralston played Helen Lee, who was the mother of five unique daughters. Early on in the show, Helen's husband, Jim, was seriously hurt and lingered indefinitely as an invalid. Although the family tried valiantly to rebound, the tragedy left a permanent mark on their lives.

Jacqueline Courtney, who is best known to daytime audiences for her role as Alice Matthews on *Another World*, played her daughter Ann.

BARBARA LEE	PATRICIA ALLISON
ANN LEE	JACQUELINE COURTNEY
JANE LEE	NUELLA DIERKING
GEORGE BARR	RALPH ELLIS
PAT NICHOLS	EDWARD GRIFFITH
DON WELDON	BEN HAYES
MARJORIE LEE	IRIS JOYCE
JIM LEE	MICHAEL KEENE
MARY LEE WELDON	WYNNE MILLER
HELEN LEE	ESTHER RALSTON
UNCLE CHARLIE	ROBERT W. STEWART
GRETA HITCHCOCK	JANIS YOUNG

OUR PRIVATE WORLD
MAY 5, 1965–SEPTEMBER 10, 1965 CBS

This prime-time serial was a spin-off of *As the World Turns*. It starred Eileen Fulton as Lisa Hughes, the character she was famous for playing on the daytime soap. Inspired by the success of ABC's *Peyton Place*, CBS gave *Our Private World* a shot on its summer schedule. They aired the series at different times on Wednesday and Friday nights.

Fed up with her life in Oakdale, a divorced Lisa decided to forge ahead with a new life in Chicago. Renting a room from a middle-class family, she found a job at a hospital. Soon after, she fell in love with wealthy John Eldridge. Unfortunately, the series wasn't as fortunate as Lisa in building a new life. When its summer run was completed, CBS didn't renew the show.

ETHEL ROBERTSON	GRACE ALBERTSON
JOHN ELDRIDGE	NICOLAS COSTER
BRAD ROBERTSON	ROBERT DRIVAS
PAT	CATHERINE DUNN
HELEN ELDRIDGE	GERALDINE FITZGERALD
TOM ELDRIDGE	SAM GROOM
EVE ELDRIDGE	JULIENNE MARIE
FRANNY MARTIN	PAMELA MURPHY
TONY LARSON	DAVID O'BRIEN
SANDY LARSON	SANDRA SMITH
SERGEANT CLARK	MICHAEL STRONG
DICK ROBERTSON	KEN TOBEY

Paper Dolls

PAPER DOLLS
SEPTEMBER 23, 1984–
DECEMBER 25, 1984 ABC

A strong cast headed this prime-time serial set in Manhattan's glamorous fashion world. Morgan Fairchild played Racine (nicknamed "Racy"), the no-nonsense, cutthroat president of a high-powered modeling agency. Her primary career objective was building the careers of two teenage models, the eager-to-please Laurie Caswell and the less-than-enthusiastic Taryn Blake (played by *Knots Landing* star Nicollette Sheridan). Contrasting Racine's ruthless approach to business was the principled founder of Harper Cosmetics, Grant Harper. A major source of disappointment for Harper was Racine's romantic involvement with his son, Wesley. Despite glowing reviews, viewers were resistant to this serial. ABC canceled it midseason.

DAVID VENTON	RICHARD BEYMER
MARK BAILEY	ROSCOE BORN
CHRISTOPHER YORK	DON BOWREN
GRANT HARPER	LLOYD BRIDGES
RACINE	MORGAN FAIRCHILD
LAURIE CASWELL	TERRY FARRELL
SANDY PARIS	JONATHAN FRAKES
COLETTE FERRIER	LAUREN HUTTON
MARJORIE HARPER	NANCY OLSON
MICHAEL CASWELL	
	JOHN BENNETT PERRY
WESLEY HARPER	DACK RAMBO
JAKE LARNER	JOHN REILLY
BLAIR HARPER VENTON	MIMI RODGERS
SARA FRANK	ANNE SCHEDEEN
TARYN BLAKE	NICOLLETTE SHERIDAN
JULIA BLAKE	BRENDA VACCARO
JOHN WAITE	HIMSELF
DINAH CASWELL	JENNIFER WARREN

PARADISE BAY
. . . .
SEPTEMBER 27, 1965–JULY 1, 1966 NBC

This series began and ended the same days as *Morning Star* on NBC. The premiere episode of this short-lived daytime serial centered around the discovery of a young woman's dead body in a small Southern California beach community. Twenty-four years later, prime-time's *Twin Peaks* would use a similar approach to kick off its story. Film actor Keith Andes, best known for his performance in the film version of *The Farmer's Daughter*, starred as radio-station manager Jeff Morgan. An amusing storyline was Jeff and his wife Mary's bemusement at learning their teenage daughter Kitty had joined a rock band.

Marion Ross, best known for her role as mother Marion Cunningham on the popular situation-comedy *Happy Days*, played Mary.

JEFF MORGAN	KEITH ANDES
WALTER MONTGOMERY	
	WALTER BROOKE
JUDGE ELLIS	MONA BRUNS
CHARLOTTE BAXTER	PAULLE CLARKE
DUKE SPAULDING	DENNIS COLE
JUNE HUDSON	SUSAN CRANE
CHUCK LUCAS	CRAIG CURTIS
LUCY SPAULDING	JUNE DAYTON
FRED MORGAN	STEVE MINES
KITTY MORGAN	HEATHER NORTH
CARLOTTA CHAVEZ	ALICE REINHEART
MARY MORGAN	MARION ROSS
ESTELLE KIMBALL	K. T. STEVENS
JUDGE GRAYSON	FRANK M. THOMAS

Paul Bernard, Psychiatrist

PAUL BERNARD, PSYCHIATRIST
. . . .
1972 SYNDICATED

This anthology-style serial was produced in Canada. It centered around the psychiatric practice of Dr. Paul Bernard, who apparently specialized in treating women. The series dramatized therapy sessions between Dr. Bernard and his female clients, tackling such maladies as depression, loneliness, and parental intrusion. Following therapy, each client returned for a monthly visit to share her personal growth. The series was produced in cooperation with the Canadian Mental Health Association. Approximately 195 episodes were syndicated to American television markets.

PAUL BERNARD . . CHRISTOPHER WIGGINS

PORTIA FACES LIFE
. . . .
APRIL 5, 1954–JULY 1, 1955 CBS

This daytime TV serial was based on the popular radio version, which aired on the CBS-radio network from 1940 to 1951. The main character was a renowned woman lawyer, who was named after the Shakespearean heroine in *The Merchant of Venice*. Lucille

Wall, best known to television audiences for her 13-year hitch as head nurse Lucille March on *General Hospital*, played the title role on radio. Frances Reid, who plays Alice Horton on *Days of Our Lives*, originated the role on television. She was succeeded by Fran Carlon.

Like most radio serials, *Portia Faces Life* had a difficult time making the transition to television. It was retitled *The Inner Flame* (more typical of television's soap titles) and lasted only 14 months before getting the pink-slip.

PORTIA MANNING	FRAN CARLON
	FRANCES REID
DORIE BLAKE	JEAN GILLESPIE
BILL BAKER	RICHARD KENDRICK
SHIRLEY MANNING	GINGER McMANUS
	RENNE JARRETT
KARL MANNING	PATRICK O'NEAL
MORGAN ELLIOTT	BYRON SANDERS
WALTER MANNING	KARL SWENSON
	DONALD WOODS
DICKIE BLAKE	CHARLES TAYLOR
KATHY BAKER	ELIZABETH YORK

Portia Faces Life

RETURN TO PEYTON PLACE
. . . .
APRIL 3, 1972–JANUARY 4, 1974 NBC

This daytime serial was a continuation of the prime-time hit, *Peyton Place*, which completed its run on ABC in 1969. Since *Return to Peyton Place* was preceded by two best-selling books, two successful feature films, and the popular prime-time version, NBC believed it would be a hit. Unfortunately, only three cast members, Pat Morrow, Frank Ferguson, and Evelyn Scott, from the ABC series reprised their roles. Viewers had a difficult time adjusting to new faces playing familiar characters Allison and Constance Mackenzie, Rodney and Norman Harrington, and Michael Rossi. But the problem was made worse; almost all the major roles during the daytime version were recast in the first year. In 1974, the network replaced it with a new serial, *How to Survive a Marriage*.

Return to Peyton Place

BENNY TATE . . . . BEN ANDREWS
JASON TATE . . . . BEN ANDREWS
CONSTANCE MACKENZIE CARSON . . . .
                        SUSAN BROWN
                 BETTYE ACKERMAN
MONICA BELL . . . . BETTY ANN CARR
ED RIKER . . . . CHUCK DANIEL
ELI CARSON . . . . FRANK FERGUSON
D. B. BENTLEY . . . . MARY FRANN
STEVEN CORD . . . . JOSEPH GALLISON
LESLIE HARRINGTON . . . . . STACY HARRIS
                   FRANK MAXWELL
MARTIN PEYTON . . . . JOHN HOYT
BETTY ANDERSON HARRINGTON . . . .
                       LYNN LORING
                      JULIE PARRISH
SELENA CROSS ROSSI . . MARGARET MASON
RITA JACKS HARRINGTON . . . .
                  PATRICIA MORROW
NORMAN HARRINGTON . . . RON RUSSELL
ADA JACKS . . . . EVELYN SCOTT
ALLISON MACKENZIE. . . . PAMELA SHOOP
                   KATHERINE GLASS
ELLIOT CARSON . . . . . . WARREN STEVENS
MICHAEL ROSSI . . . . GUY STOCKWELL
RODNEY HARRINGTON. . . YALE SUMMERS
                   LAWRENCE CASEY
HANNAH CORD . . . . MARY K. WELLS

Rituals

RITUALS
· · · · · · · · · · · · · · · · · ·
SEPTEMBER 10, 1984–
SEPTEMBER 6, 1985 SYNDICATED

*R*ituals was the first evening half-hour dramatic serial to be syndicated to a large share of American TV stations. Taped in Hollywood, *Rituals* centered on the lives of families living in the small college town of Wingfield, Virginia. Typically scheduled in an early evening time slot, *Rituals* had a difficult time attracting viewers. Most were used to watching their soaps in the afternoon. The show ran for 52 weeks before being canceled.

Kin Shriner, who gained national attention when he played Scotty Baldwin on ABC's *General Hospital*, headlined the cast. Patti Davis, former-President Ronald Reagan's daughter, appeared briefly as the seductress Marissa Mallory. She was later replaced by Janice Heiden. Deciding the steamy love scenes she was required to play were against her born-again Christian values, actress JoAnn Pflug relinquished her role as Taylor Chapin. She was replaced by Tina Louise, who is best known for playing Ginger on *Gilligan's Island*. Before joining *Days of Our Lives* as Kayla Johnson, Mary Beth Evans appeared on *Rituals* as Dakota Lane.

TOM GALLAGHER . . . . KEVIN BLAIR
LUCKY WASHINGTON . . . RANDY BROOKS
SARA GALLAGHER . . . . . LAURIE BURTON

                 LORINNE VOZOFF
DAKOTA LANE . . . . MARY BETH EVANS
                 CLAIRE YARLETT
CHERRY LANE . . . . SHARON FARRELL
PATTY DUPONT . . . WINIFRED FREEDMAN
DIANDRA SANTIAGO . . . . GINA GALLEGO
MADDIE WASHINGTON . . . .
                 LYNN HAMILTON
C. J. FIELDS . . . . PETER HASKELL
MARISSA MALLORY . . . . . JANICE HEIDEN
                 PATTI DAVIS
CHRISTINA ROBERTSON . . . .
                 CHRISTINE JONES
NOEL GALLAGHER . . . . KAREN KELLY
LOGAN WILLIAMS . . . . GEORGE LAZENBY
BRADY CHAPIN . . . . JON LINDSTROM
                 MARC POPPEL
TAYLOR CHAPIN . . . . TINA LOUISE
                 JoANN PFLUG
CARTER ROBERTSON . . . .
                 MONTE MARKHAM
JULIA FIELDS. . . . . ANDREA MOAR
EDDIE GALLAGHER . . . . GREG MULLAVEY
PATRICK CHAPIN . . . . . . DENNIS PATRICK
LISA THOMPSON . . . .
            WESLEY ANN PFENNING
LUCAS GATES. . . . . ANTONY PONZINI
LACEY JARRETT. . . . . . PHILECE SAMPLER
MIKE GALLAGHER . . . . KIN SHRINER
BERNHARDT . . . . CAMERON SMITH
CLAY TRAVIS. . . . . MICHAEL WELDON

THE ROAD OF LIFE
· · · · · · · · · · · · · · · · · ·
DECEMBER 13, 1954–JULY 1, 1955 CBS

*L*ike the long-running radio version that preceded it, this television serial centered on wry-humored Dr. Jim Brent and his wealthy adversaries, the Overtons. The show's scripts were cleverly written by Charles Gussman, but the TV serial barely lasted six months. The radio version, however, which began in 1937, continued until 1959.

Don MacLaughlin, who is best known for his role as Chris Hughes on *As the World Turns*, played Dr. Jim Brent. Virginia Dwyer, who played Mary Matthews on *Another World* for 11 years, appeared as Jocelyn, his wife. John Larkin, who played Jim's newspaperman pal Frank Dana, went on to star on *The Edge of Night* as Mike Karr. Both played their roles on the radio version. Elizabeth Lawrence, best known for her role as Myra Murdoch on *All My Children*, played Francie Brent. Film actor Jack Lemmon appeared in a non-contract role.

SYBIL OVERTON FULLER	
	BARBARA BECKER
CONRAD OVERTON . . . . CHARLES DINGLE	
JOCELYN McLEOD BRENT	
	VIRGINIA DWYER
MALCOLM OVERTON	
	HARRY HOLCOMBE
FRANK DANA . . . . JOHN LARKIN	
	CHUCK WEBSTER
FRANCIE BRENT . . ELIZABETH LAWRENCE	
JOHN BRENT . . . . BILL LIPTON	
JIM BRENT . . . . DON MacLAUGHLIN	
REGGIE ELLIS . . . . DOROTHY SANDS	

ROAD TO REALITY
OCTOBER 17, 1960–MARCH 31, 1961 ABC

*R*oad to Reality was ABC's first daytime serial. It was an anthology-style soap and it used transcripts of actual group therapy sessions for its unusual format. Each episode featured five to ten actors who played participants in group therapy sessions.

John Beal headlined as Dr. Lewis, the show's fictional therapist. Scheduled against *Art Linkletter's House Party* and *The Loretta Young Theater*, this experimental drama got a stiff dose of reality when it discovered audiences avoided it. Six months after its premiere, ABC wisely decided to bring the sessions to a close and cancel the show. Beal would later play Jim Matthews on *Another World*.

DR. LEWIS . . . . JOHN BEAL

SCARLETT HILL
1965–1966 SYNDICATED

*T*his syndicated Canadian serial enjoyed a one-season run on a handful of local television stations. It concerned the lives of people living at a hotel in Scarlett Hill, New York. Landlady Kate Russell was a busybody who was up to date on everybody's business. She even knew about Dr. David Black's proposal to Janice Turner. Kate served as a constant source of amusement for viewers though her residents were not often amused.

WALTER PENDELTON . . . . . . IVOR BARRY	
JANICE TURNER . . . . . SUZANNE BRYANT	
KATE RUSSELL . . . . BETH LOCKERBIE	
HARRY . . . . ED McNAMARA	
SIDNEY . . . . ALAN PEARCE	
DAVID BLACK . . . . GORDON PINSENT	
GINNY . . . . LUCY WARNER	

Secrets of Midland Heights

SECRETS OF MIDLAND HEIGHTS
DECEMBER 6, 1980–JANUARY 24, 1981 CBS

*T*his was a prime-time serial designed for teenage viewers. Unfortunately, CBS placed the series in a Saturday evening slot where it was unlikely to reach its intended audience, who would not be home to watch. Rather than give the serial an opportunity to build an audience on a new night, CBS decided to cancel it after seven episodes. A revised version, retitled *King's Crossing*, resurfaced on ABC the next season.

Lorenzo Lamas appeared as frat-boy Burt Carroll. A year later he would become a familiar face to soap viewers for his role as Lance Cumson on the long-running *Falcon Crest*.

DOROTHY WHEELER . . . . BIBI BESCH	
GUY MILLINGTON	
	JORDAN CHRISTOPHER
ANN DULLES . . . . DORAN CLARK	
LISA ROGERS . . . . LINDA HAMILTON	
NATHAN WELSH . . . . . . ROBERT HOGAN	

HOLLY WHEELER . . . . . . MARILYN JONES	
	LINDA GROVERNOR
BURT CARROLL . . . . . . LORENZO LAMAS	
MARTIN WHEELER . . . . WILLIAM JORDAN	
CALVIN RICHARDSON . . . . . MARK PINTER	
MARGARET MILLINGTON	
	MARTHA SCOTT
TEDDY WELSH . . . . DANIEL ZIPPI	
JOHN GRAY . . . . JIM YOUNGS	

THE SEEKING HEART
JULY 5, 1954–DECEMBER 10, 1954 CBS

*P*roduced by Procter & Gamble, this short-lived serial used a hospital setting and focused primarily on Dr. John Adam. His marriage to his unfulfilled wife, Grace, was in jeopardy.

Complicating matters was Dr. Adam's growing attraction to his assistant, Dr. Robinson McKay. Realizing the feeling was mutual, John and Robinson struggled to keep their relationship strictly professional. A sympathetic CBS put them out of their misery by canceling the serial six months after its premiere.

ROBINSON McKAY . . . . FLORA CAMPBELL	
JOHN ADAM . . . . SCOTT FORBES	
GRACE ADAM . . . . DOROTHY LOVETT	

STRANGE PARADISE
1969 SYNDICATED

*T*his off-beat, supernatural serial was inspired by the success of *Dark Shadows*. Produced by an American production company, it was taped in Ottawa, Canada, and syndicated nationally in the United States. The story involved Jean Paul Desmond, whose efforts to bring his dead wife, Erica, back to life backfired. He inadvertently conjured up the spirit of his ancestor Jacques Eloi DeMonde. Eventually, Erica did return and created havoc for the inhabitants of the Carribbean Island of Maljardin, the serial's setting. Other interesting features included voodoo and ghosts. Harding Lemay would have better success as a writer on *Another World*.

HUACO . . . . PATRICIA COLLINS
HOLLY MARSHALL . . . . SYLVIA FEIGEL
JEAN PAUL DESMOND . . . . COLIN FOX
JACQUES ELOI DeMONDE . . . . . COLIN FOX
TIM STANTON . . . . BRUCE GRAY
DAN FOREST . . . . JON GRANIK
ALISON CARR . . . . . DAWN GREENHALGH
RAXIL . . . . COSETTE LEE
MATT DAWSON . . . . DAN MacDONALD
ELIZABETH MARSHALL . . . .
                              PAISLEY MAXWELL
VANGIE . . . . ANGELA ROLAND
QUITO . . . . KURT SCHIEGL
ERICA DESMOND . . . . TUDI WIGGINS
HELENA . . . . TUDI WIGGINS
DINAH . . . . TRUDY YOUNG

The Survivors

THE SURVIVORS
. . . .
**SEPTEMBER 9, 1969–
SEPTEMBER 17, 1970 ABC**

This highly promoted prime-time serial served as a comeback vehicle for film star Lana Turner. Unfortunately, it was short-lived. Created by best-selling novelist Harold Robbins, it co-starred George Hamilton, Kevin McCarthy, and Jan-Michael Vincent.

Actually, the behind-the-scenes goings-on were more interesting than the show itself. Not only had Robbins departed, but also three producers and a number of other workers. Lana Turner slapped one producer, who slapped her back. He very quickly lost his job.

The serial dealt with the lives of two rival banking families. Originally plotted by Robbins to run for two seasons, ABC, disappointed by its dismal ratings, pulled the plug on the expensive, high-budgeted series after 15 episodes. A few weeks later, a new series titled *Paris 700* materialized and starred George Hamilton. He was the lone surviving cast member from the failed show, but it ran for only ten episodes then it was also canceled.

MARGUERITA . . . . DONNA BACCALLA
CORBETT . . . . MICHAEL BELL
BAYLOR CARLYLE . . . . . RALPH BELLAMY
RIAKOS . . . . ROSSANO BRAZZI
SHEILA . . . . KATHY CANNON
MARK JENNINGS . . . . CLU GULAGER
DUNCAN CARLYLE . . GEORGE HAMILTON
JONATHAN . . . . LOUIS HAYWARD
TOM STEINBERG . . . . ROBERT LIPTON
PHILIP HASTINGS . . . . KEVIN McCARTHY
BELLE . . . . DIANA MULDAUR
JEAN VALE . . . . LOUISE SOREL
ROSEMARY PRICE . . . . PAMELA TIFFIN
TRACY CARLYLE HASTINGS . . . .
                                  LANA TURNER
MIGUEL SANTERRA . . . . ROBERT VIHARO
JEFFREY HASTINGS . . . .
                        JAN-MICHAEL VINCENT

THESE ARE MY CHILDREN
. . . .
JANUARY 31, 1949–FEBRUARY 25, 1949 NBC

The first daytime soap to premiere on a major television network also had one of the shortest runs—barely a month. Created by Irna Phillips, and broadcast from Chicago, the experimental serial centered around a self-sacrificing widow who operated a boarding house. She fought valiantly to support her three children and recently acquired daughter-in-law, Jean. Reviews of Phillips's efforts were less than glowing, especially one appearing in *Television World*, which wrote: "There is no place on television for this type of program, a blank screen is preferable." Phillip had better success with *The Guiding Light*, *Another World*, *Days of Our Lives*, *Peyton Place*, and *Love Is a Many Splendored Thing*.

JEAN HENEHAN . . . . JOAN ARLT
PATRICIA HENEHAN . . JANE BROOKSMITH
AUNT KITTY HENEHAN . . . .
                        MARGARET HENEGHAN
JOHN HENEHAN . . . . GEORGE KLUGE
KAY CARTER . . . . ELOISE KUMMER
PENNY HENEHAN . . . . MARTHA McCLAIN
MRS. HENEHAN . . . . ALMA PLATTS
MRS. BERKOVITCH . . MIGNON SCHREIBER

Three Steps to Heaven

THREE STEPS TO HEAVEN
. . . .
AUGUST 3, 1953–DECEMBER 31, 1954 NBC

This early NBC serial concerned the trials and tribulations of Mary Jane "Poco" Thurmond, a small town girl. She moved to New York City hoping to become a successful model. While trying to get her career off the ground, Poco met and fell in love with writer Bill Morgan. He lived at the same boarding house as Poco. A major stumbling block in their romance was Bill's difficulty overcoming painful memories of his experiences as a soldier in World War II. Mobster Vince Bannister also presented trouble for Poco by involving her brother Barry in his criminal activities. Before the series drew to an end, Poco finally married Bill.

During the serial's 16-month run, the pivotal roles of Poco Thurmond and Bill Morgan were recast three times. The show was created and written by Irving Vendig, who went on to create *The Edge of Night*.

BETH WARING . . . . . MADELINE BELGARD
MIKE . . . . JOE BROWN, JR.
CHARLOTTE DOANE . . . . . . MONA BRUNS
ALAN ANDERSON . . . . DORT CLARK
NAN WARING . . . . BETH DOUGLAS
WALTER JONES . . . . EARL GEORGE
JASON CLEVE . . . . LAUREN GILBERT
PIGEON MALLOY . . . . EATA LINDEN
POCO THURMOND . . . .
                          KATHLEEN MAGUIRE
                          DIANA DOUGLAS
                          PHYLLIS HILL

JENNIFER ALDEN	LORI MARCH
VINCE BANNISTER	JOHN MARLEY
ANGELA	GINGER McMANUS
MRS. DOANE	DORIS RICH
BILL MORGAN	MARK ROBERTS
	GENE BLAKELY
	WALTER BROOKE
BARRY THURMOND	ROGER SULLIVAN
UNCLE FRANK	FRANK TWEDWELL
ALICE TRENT	LAURIE VENDIG
CHIP MORRISON	ROBERT WEBBER

A Time for Us

A TIME FOR US
DECEMBER 28, 1964–
DECEMBER 16, 1966 ABC

This 30-minute serial premiered as a drama about class conflict in a small town. It was originally titled *Flame in the Wind*. Six months after its debut, Irna Phillips was appointed story editor and she made significant changes. Besides gaining a new title, romantic stories were featured using youthful characters. The leading family, the ethnic Skerbas, lost their name and became the Driscolls.

During its two-year run, three actresses who played Linda Driscoll would become familiar faces to daytime audiences. Joanna Miles played Anne Tyler on *All My Children*. Barbara Rodell played Leslie Jackson during the early seventies on *All My Children*. Jane Elliot appeared on several daytime soaps, but is most closely

associated with her role as Tracy Quartermaine on *General Hospital*.

JASON FARRELL	WALTER COY
STEVE REYNOLDS	TOM FIELDING
	GORDON GRAY
PAUL DAVIS	CONRAD FOWKES
JANE DRISCOLL	BEVERLY HAYES
	MARGARET LADD
ROXANNE REYNOLDS	MAGGIE HAYES
LESLIE FARRELL	RITA LLOYD
DAVE SIMON	TERRY LOGAN
KATE AUSTEN	KATHLEEN MAGUIRE
LINDA DRISCOLL	JOANNA MILES
	JANE ELLIOT
	BARBARA RODELL
LOUISE AUSTEN	JOSEPHINE NICHOLS
SUE MICHAELS	JILL O'HARA
MARTHA DRISCOLL	LENKA PETERSON
AL DRISCOLL	ROY POOLE
CRAIG REYNOLDS	FRANK SCHOFIELD
TONY GREY	MORGAN STERNE
CHRIS AUSTEN	RICHARD THOMAS
MIRIAM BENTLEY	LESLEY WOODS

A Time to Live

A TIME TO LIVE
JULY 5, 1954–DECEMBER 31, 1954 NBC

An aspiring newspaper reporter was the focal point for this 15-minute serial based in Chicago. Shortly after realizing her goal of becoming a reporter, former proofreader Julie Byron became romantically involved with reporter Don Riker. One of the first newspaper stories Julie tackled was trying

to prove Greta Powers's innocence after she'd been accused of committing a heinous crime. Greta's defeatist attitude made Julie's job difficult.

GRETA POWERS	ZOHRA ALTON
MADGE BYRON	VIOLA BERWICK
RUDY	ZACHARY CHARLES
MILES DOW	DORT CLARK
LUCY	NELL CLARK
JUSTINE POWERS	JOHN DEVOE
DR. CLAY	DANA ELCAR
LENORE	BARBARA FOLEY
DAPHNE	TONI GILMAN
DON RIKER	JOHN HIMES
ANN	LARRY KERR
	ROSEMARY KELLY
CARL SHERMAN	JACK LESTER
JULIE BYRON	PAT SCULLY
CHICK BUCHANAN	LEN WAYLAND
PATRICIA	BEVERLY YOUNGER

Today Is Ours

TODAY IS OURS
JUNE 30, 1958–DECEMBER 26, 1958 NBC

Patricia Benoit was Wally Cox's love interest, nurse Nancy Remington, on prime-time's *Mr. Peepers*. She then moved to daytime to star in this 30-minute serial. Benoit played Laura Manning, the divorced assistant principal of Bolton Central High School. A relationship with architect Glenn Turner blossomed into love for Laura. Disappointed by the serial's poor showing, NBC canceled it after six months. A few of its characters resurfaced on the serial's replacement, *Young Dr. Malone.*

LAURA MANNING . . . . . PATRICIA BENOIT
RHODA SPENCER . . . . . AUDREY CHRISTIE
GLENN TURNER . . . . ERNEST GRAVES
NICKY MANNING . . . . PETER LAZAR
LESLIE MANNING . . . . JOYCE LEAR
MAXINE WELLS . . . . . . BARBARA LODEN
ADAM HOLT . . . . JOHN McGOVERN
KARL MANNING . . . . . . PATRICK O'NEAL
BETTY WINTERS . . . . . NANCY SHERIDAN

Valiant Lady

VALIANT LADY
. . . .
OCTOBER 12, 1953–AUGUST 16, 1957 CBS

Fans of the long-running radio serial were in for a surprise when they turned into this TV version. The only thing that remained the same was the title. Instead of being about Joan Barrett's fight to keep her husband on the straight and narrow, the serial centered around Helen Emerson, a recent widow and mother of three children.

Film actress Nancy Coleman, who appeared in *King's Row* and *Mourning Becomes Electra,* starred as Helen Emerson. Overwhelmed by having to memorize a new script every day, she stepped down after one year. She was replaced by Flora Campbell, who was best known for her work on television's first network soap, *Faraway Hill.* James Kirkwood, who

wrote several best-selling novels and won a Pulitzer Prize for *A Chorus Line,* played Helen's son, Mickey. Margaret Hamilton, famous for her role as the wicked witch in *The Wizard of Oz,* appeared briefly in a featured role. During the serial's four-year run, the role of Helen's teenage daughter, Diane, was recast four times.

JOEY GORDON . . . . MARTIN BALSAM
HELEN EMERSON . . . . . FLORA CAMPBELL
 NANCY COLEMAN
FRANK EMERSON . . . . . . JEROME COWAN
BONNIE WITHERS . . . SHIRLEY EGLESTON
 JOAN LORING
LAWRENCE WALKER . . . . . JOHN GRAHAM
HAL SOAMES . . . . EARL HAMMOND
LINDA KENDALL . . . . FRANCES HELM
MICKEY EMERSON . . . .
 JAMES KIRKWOOD, JR.
DIANE EMERSON SOAMES . . . .
 LELIA MARTIN
 SUE RANDALL
 DOLORES SUTTON
 ANNE PEARSON
ELLIOTT NORRIS . . . . . TERRY O'SULLIVAN
ROBERTA WILCOX . . . . BETTY CAKES
KIM EMERSON . . . . BONNIE SAWYER
 LYDIA REED
CHRIS KENDALL . . . . . LAWRENCE WEBER

The Verdict Is Yours

THE VERDICT IS YOURS
. . . .
**SEPTEMBER 2, 1957–
SEPTEMBER 28, 1962 CBS**

This unscripted, anthology-style courtroom drama aired for five successful seasons on CBS. Each case was featured for nine episodes before

reaching a conclusion. Actors were presented a brief outline stating the situation and then they improvised when cross-examined by real lawyers. Members of the studio audience were chosen to play the jurors, who ruled on the case's outcome, giving new meaning to the phrase, "audience participation." Actresses were encouraged to go full blast with their emotions and occasionally the real lawyers became dupes of their own histrionics. In one memorable episode, a lawyer became so frustrated with how his case was evolving he stormed off the set. He left the stunned courtroom reporter, played by Jim McKay, with the thankless task of ad-libbing until the show's conclusion.

Forrest Compton, best known for playing Mike Karr on *The Edge of Night,* Audrey Peters, who played Vanessa Sterling for 21 years on *Love of Life,* and film star Ellen Burstyn (then known as Ellen McRae) were frequent guest stars.

COURT REPORTERS . . . . JIM McKAY
 BILL STOUT
 JAKE WHITTAKER
COURT BALIFF . . . . MANDEL KRAMER

Way of the World

WAY OF THE WORLD
. . . .
JANUARY 3, 1955–OCTOBER 7, 1955 NBC

This anthology-style serial dramatized stories adapted from women's magazines. The stories generally lasted a week and were introduced by hostess Linda Porter, played by actress Gloria Louis. One story, heavily influenced by the feature film *Lifeboat*, centered around the survivors of a plane crash who were stranded in the wilds of Newfoundland during a freezing cold spell.

Gena Rowlands, Constance Ford (best known for her role as Ada Davis on *Another World*), Thomas Tryon (who later became a best-selling novelist), Louise Allbritton, and William Prince appeared as guest stars during the serial's ten-month run.

LINDA PORTER . . . . GLORIA LOUIS

A WOMAN TO REMEMBER
· ·
FEBRUARY 21, 1949–JULY 15, 1949 DuMONT

This soap entry aired on the old DuMont network. It took its audience behind the scenes of an imaginary radio soap opera. Actress Christine Baker was the main character. Plots revolved around Christine's romance with co-star Steve Hammond, and the competitive Carol Winstead's dastardly efforts to undermine Christine's career. Filling out the cast were Christine's actress friend Bessie Thatcher, and Charley Anderson, a sound man.

This show was a very early pioneer of the soap opera. It operated on a budget of $1,750 per week, and only had one camera, but it formed the roots of the modern-day soap.

A Woman To Remember originally premiered as a daytime serial but was later moved to an early evening slot, where it languished for two more months before finally being canceled.

CAROL WINSTEAD . . . . JOAN CATLIN
BESSIE THATCHER . . . . . RUTH McDEVITT
STEVE HAMMOND . . . . JOHN RABY
CHARLEY ANDERSON . . . .
. . . . FRANKIE THOMAS
CHRISTINE BAKER . . . . . PATRICIA WHEEL

WOMAN WITH A PAST
· ·
FEBRUARY 1, 1954–JULY 2, 1954 CBS

Constance Ford, who is best known as Ada Davis on *Another World*, starred in this early CBS serial. She played Lynn Sherwood, a New York dress designer who constantly found herself caught in an assortment of romantic entanglements. On the scene to make Lynn's life even more difficult was her chief foe, Sylvia Rockwell.

Constance Ford's career has spanned stage, television, and film. Her critically acclaimed film appearances include *A Summer Place*, *All Fall Down*, and *The Caretakers*. On nighttime television, she has guest-starred in such memorable shows as *East Side, West Side*, *Perry Mason*, *Alfred Hitchcock Presents*, *Twilight Zone*, *Naked City*, *Dr. Kildare*, and *The Untouchables*. Following her daytime stint on *Woman with a Past*, she played regular roles on *Search for Tomorrow* and *The Edge of Night* before settling on *Another World* as Ada.

Jean Stapleton, best known for her role as Edith Bunker on *All in the Family*, appeared in a featured role as Gwen.

SYLVIA ROCKWELL . . . .
. . . . GERALDINE BROOKS
. . . . MARY SINCLAIR
LYNN SHERWOOD . . . . CONSTANCE FORD
PEGS . . . . ANN HEGIRA
TIFFANY BUCHANAN . . . LINDA LAUBACH
STEVE ROCKWELL . . . . GENE LYONS
DIANE SHERWOOD . . . . . BARBARA MYERS
. . . . FELICE CAMARGO

A WORLD APART
· ·
MARCH 30, 1970–JUNE 25, 1971 ABC

Scheduled against the long-running and popular *Search for Tomorrow*, this half-hour drama had its work cut out for it. Irna Phillips served as story editor for her adopted daughter Katherine's creation, which was partly autobiographical. The serial centered on a woman very similar to Irna Phillips. Betty Kahlman was an unmarried soap opera writer who lived in Chicago and had single-handedly raised two adopted children. The serial attempted to examine the differences between generations and the steps they took toward understanding and accepting one another. Contrasting the turbulent Kahlman family was the stable Sims family. Since these were changing times, however, Dr. Ed Sims and his conservative wife, Adrian, had their hands full coping with their free-spirited daughter, Becky.

Susan Sarandon played Betty's adopted daughter, Patrice. Recalling her early soap role, Susan says, "I was the girl everything happened to, so I learned a lot [about acting]. My character took off with a Weatherman type, and he got thrown in jail, and then he volunteered for medical experiments. By this time I had aged a few years. I had seduced him and became pregnant as he was dying of mercury poisoning. God knows what our child was going to look like."

A World Apart

OLIVER HARRELL	DAVID BIRNEY
BECKY SIMS	ERIN CONNOR
BUD WHITMAN	KEVIN CONWAY
CHRIS KAHLMAN	MATTHEW COWLES
BETTY KAHLMAN BARRY	
	AUGUSTA DABNEY
	ELIZABETH LAWRENCE
MATT HAMPTON	CLIFTON DAVIS
NATHANIEL FULLER	JOHN DEVLIN
JACK CONDON	STEPHEN ELLIOTT
JOHN CARR	ROBERT GENTRY
T. D. DRINKARD	TOM LIGON
JULIE STARK	DOROTHY LYMAN
LINDA PETERS	HEATHER MacRAE
ADRIAN SIMS	KATHLEEN MAGUIRE
MEG JOHNS	ANNA MINOT
ED SIMS	JAMES NOBLE
NEIL STEVENS	ALBERT PAULSEN
RUSSELL BARRY	WILLIAM PRINCE
PATRICE KAHLMAN	SUSAN SARANDON
NANCY CONDON	SUSAN SULLIVAN
FRED TURNER	NICOLAS SUROVY
OLIVIA HAMPTON	JANE WHITE
LOUISE TURNER	CAROL WILLIARD

THE WORLD OF MR. SWEENEY
. . . .
JUNE 30, 1954–DECEMBER 31, 1955 NBC

This comic serial was based in New York, and was first introduced as a continuing segment on *The Kate Smith Hour.* NBC scheduled it as a prime-time serial in the summer of 1954, airing it on Tuesdays, Wednesdays, and Fridays. The following fall, it moved to daytime as a daily comic serial. Character actor Charles Ruggles, who had appeared in such popular feature films as *Charley's Aunt* and *Bringing up Baby,* headlined as general store owner Cicero P. Sweeney, who was the town's leading "wise, old man." His shop was the primary meeting place for the good-natured, small-town residents of Mapleton. Critics regarded the serial as a welcome departure from the usual melodramatic fare dished up on network daytime television. Low ratings, however, caused NBC to cancel the series after an 18-month run.

Helen Wagner, best known for playing Nancy Hughes on *As the World Turns,* made her television debut appearing as Sweeney's daughter, Marge. Film actor Christopher Walken played Marge's son, Kippie.

TIMMY THOMPSON	JIMMY BAIRD
HENRIETTA	JANET FOX

ABIGAIL MILLIKAN	BETTY GARDE
ED	BOB HASTINGS
SUE THOMPSON	SUSAN ODIN
EVA	LYDIA REED
CICERO P. SWEENEY	CHARLIE RUGGLES
ALICE FRANKLIN	MIMI STRONGIN
MARGE FRANKLIN	HELEN WAGNER
KIPPIE FRANKLIN	
	GLENN (CHRISTOPHER) WALKEN
LIZ THOMPSON	HELEN WARNOW

The World of Mr. Sweeney

THE YOUNG MARRIEDS
. . . .
OCTOBER 5, 1964–MARCH 25, 1966 ABC

ABC scheduled this half-hour, Hollywood-based serial after its only successful soap, *General Hospital.* It focused on the problems faced by four newlywed couples adjusting to marriage.

After the serial's cancellation in 1966, a number of its cast members would become popular to daytime viewers on other soaps. They included three future *Days of Our Lives* cast members: Susan Seaforth, who played Julie Williams; Peggy McCay, who plays Caroline Brady (and was the original Vanessa Dale on *Love of Life*); and Brenda Benet, who played Lee Dumonde before committing suicide in 1982.

Before achieving success in films, Charles Grodin appeared on *The Young Marrieds.*

JILL McCOMB	BRENDA BENET
	BETTY CONNOR
BUZZ KORMAN	LES BROWN, JR.
ANN REYNOLDS	SUSAN BROWN
LENA KARR GILROY	NORMA CONNOLLY
LIZ FORSYTHE STEVENS	FLOY DEAN
MATT STEVENS	SCOTT GRAHAM
	CHARLES GRODIN
SUSAN GARRETT	PEGGY McCAY
WALTER REYNOLDS	MICHAEL MIKLER
IRENE FORSYTHE	CONSTANCE MOORE
DAN GARRETT	PAUL PICERNI
ROY GILROY	BARRY RUSSO
CAROL WEST	SUSAN SEAFORTH
AUNT ALEX	IRENE TEDROW

Gregg Marx with the Emmy he won for playing
Tom Hughes on As the World Turns.

Additional Information

Soap Operas are not just daytime TV. They are an important part of TV history. Daytime programming achievements were recognized in 1966. Then, in 1971, daytime serials received separate Emmy categories. By 1976, they had their own branch of the Emmys. Fans of soap operas are interested in the background of their favorite shows, and in graduates of these shows. For additional information, we have provided a chronology of soap operas, Emmy awards for daytime performers and shows, addresses of fan clubs and studios, and graduates of daytime serials.

CHRONOLOGY OF AMERICAN
TV NETWORK SERIALS

Faraway Hill	Dumont	1946
These Are My Children	NBC	1949
A Woman to Remember	Dumont	1949
The O'Neills	Dumont	1949-50
One Man's Family	NBC	1949-55
Hawkins Falls	NBC	1950-55
The First Hundred Years	CBS	1950-52
Miss Susan	NBC	1951
Search for Tomorrow	CBS, NBC	1951-86
Love of Life	CBS	1951-80
The Egg and I	CBS	1951-52
Fairmeadows, U.S.A.	NBC	1951-52
The Guiding Light	CBS	1952-
One Man's (Woman's) Experience	Dumont	1952-53
The Bennetts	NBC	1953-54
Three Steps to Heaven	NBC	1953-54
Follow Your Heart	NBC	1953-54
Valiant Lady	CBS	1953-57
The Brighter Day	CBS	1954-62
Woman with a Past	CBS	1954
The Secret Storm	CBS	1954-74
The World of Mr. Sweeney	NBC	1954-55
Portia Faces Life	CBS	1954-55
The Seeking Heart	CBS	1954-55
First Love	NBC	1954-55
A Time to Live	NBC	1954
Concerning Miss Marlowe	NBC	1954-55
Golden Windows	NBC	1954-55
The Greatest Gift	NBC	1954-55
Modern Romances	NBC	1954-58
Road of Life	CBS	1954-55
Way of the World	NBC	1955
A Date with Life	NBC	1955-56
As the World Turns	CBS	1956-
The Edge of Night	CBS, ABC	1956-84
Hotel Cosmopolitan	CBS	1957-58
The Verdict Is Yours	CBS	1957-62
Kitty Foyle	NBC	1958
Today Is Ours	NBC	1958
From These Roots	NBC	1958-61
Young Dr. Malone	NBC	1958-63
For Better or Worse	CBS	1959-60
The House on High Street	NBC	1959-60
Full Circle	CBS	1960-61
The Clear Horizon	CBS	1960-62
Road to Reality	ABC	1960-61
Our Five Daughters	NBC	1962
Ben Jerrod, Attorney at Law	NBC	1963
The Doctors	NBC	1963-82
General Hospital	ABC	1963-
Another World	NBC	1964-
Peyton Place	ABC	1964-69
The Young Marrieds	ABC	1964-66
A Time for Us	ABC	1964-66
Our Private World	CBS	1965
Morning Star	NBC	1965-66
Paradise Bay	NBC	1965-66
Never Too Young	ABC	1965-66
The Nurses	ABC	1965-67
Days of Our Lives	NBC	1965-
Confidential for Women	ABC	1966
Dark Shadows	ABC	1966-71
Love Is a Many Splendored Thing	CBS	1967-73
One Life to Live	ABC	1968-
Hidden Faces	NBC	1968-69
Where the Heart Is	CBS	1969-73
The Survivors	ABC	1969-70
Bright Promise	NBC	1969-72
All My Children	ABC	1970-
The Best of Everything	ABC	1970
A World Apart	ABC	1970-71
Somerset	NBC	1970-76
Return to Peyton Place	NBC	1972-74
The Young and the Restless	CBS	1973-
How to Survive a Marriage	NBC	1974-75

Ryan's Hope	ABC	1975-89	*Dynasty*	ABC	1981-89
Beacon Hill	CBS	1975	*Behind the Screen*	CBS	1981-82
Executive Suite	CBS	1976-77	*Falcon Crest*	CBS	1981-90
Lovers and Friends	NBC	1977	*Capitol*	CBS	1982-87
Soap	ABC	1977-81	*Loving*	ABC	1983-
For Richer, For Poorer	NBC	1977-78	*Emerald Point, N.A.S.*	CBS	1983-84
Dallas	CBS	1978-	*Santa Barbara*	NBC	1984-
Knots Landing	CBS	1979-	*Paper Dolls*	ABC	1984
Texas	NBC	1980-82	*Berrenger's*	NBC	1985
Number 96	NBC	1980-81	*The Bold and the Beautiful*	CBS	1987-
Secrets of Midland Heights	CBS	1980-81	*Generations*	NBC	1989-
Flamingo Road	NBC	1981-82	*Twin Peaks*	ABC	1990-

SYNDICATED (AMERICAN PRODUCED)

Doctor Hudson's Secret Journal	1955	*Young Lives*	1981
Scarlett Hill	1965-66	*Romance Theater*	1982-83
Mary Hartman, Mary Hartman	1976-78	*Rituals*	1984-85
All That Glitters	1977	*Tribes*	1990
Life and Times of Eddie Roberts	1980		

CABLE (AMERICAN PRODUCED)

Another Life	CBN	1981-84	*The Catlins*	TBS	1983-85
A New Day in Eden	SHOWTIME	1982-83			

AUSTRALIAN

Prisoner: Cell Block H	SYNDICATED	1980

BRITISH

The Forsyte Saga	NET	1969-70	*Upstairs, Downstairs*	PBS	1974-77
Coronation Street	SYNDICATED 1972; 1982-83		*Eastenders*	PBS	1987-

CANADIAN

Strange Paradise	SYNDICATED	1969	*High Hopes*	SYNDICATED	1978

EMMY WINNERS

(winner in bold)

1971-72
OUTSTANDING ACHIEVEMENT IN DAYTIME DRAMA—PROGRAMS

The Doctors—NBC
General Hospital—ABC

1972-73
OUTSTANDING ACHIEVEMENT IN DAYTIME DRAMA

Days of Our Lives—NBC
The Doctors—NBC
The Edge of Night—CBS
One Life to Live—ABC

OUTSTANDING ACHIEVEMENT BY AN INDIVIDUAL IN DAYTIME DRAMA

Macdonald Carey (Tom Horton, *Days of Our Lives*)
Mary Fickett (Ruth Brent, *All My Children*)
Norman Hall (director, *The Doctors*)
H. Wesley Kenney (director, *Days of Our Lives*)
Peter Levin (director, *Love Is a Many Splendored Thing*)
David Pressman (director, *One Life to Live*)
Victor Pagnuzzi (scenic designer, *Love Is a Many Splendored Thing*)
John A. Wendell (set director, *Love Is a Many Splendored Thing*)

1973-74
OUTSTANDING DAYTIME DRAMA SERIES

Days of Our Lives—NBC
The Doctors—NBC
General Hospital—ABC

OUTSTANDING ACTOR IN A DAYTIME DRAMA SERIES

John Beradino (Steve Hardy, *General Hospital*)
Macdonald Carey (Tom Horton, *Days of Our Lives*)
Peter Hansen (Lee Baldwin, *General Hospital*)

OUTSTANDING ACTRESS IN A DAYTIME DRAMA SERIES

Rachel Ames (Audrey Baldwin, *General Hospital*)
Mary Fickett (Ruth Martin, *All My Children*)
Elizabeth Hubbard (Althea Davis, *The Doctors*)
Mary Stuart (Joanne Vincente, *Search for Tomorrow*)

1974-75
OUTSTANDING DRAMA SERIES

Another World—NBC
Days of Our Lives—NBC
The Young and the Restless—CBS

OUTSTANDING ACTOR IN A DAYTIME DRAMA SERIES

John Beradino (Steve Hardy, *General Hospital*)
Macdonald Carey (Tom Horton, *Days of Our Lives*)
Bill Hayes (Doug Williams, *Days of Our Lives*)

OUTSTANDING ACTRESS IN A DAYTIME DRAMA SERIES

Rachel Ames (Audrey Baldwin, *General Hospital*)
Susan Flannery (Laura Horton, *Days of Our Lives*)
Susan Seaforth (Julie Banning, *Days of Our Lives*)
Ruth Warrick (Phoebe Tyler, *All My Children*)

1975-76
OUTSTANDING DAYTIME DRAMA SERIES

All My Children—ABC
Another World—NBC
Days of Our Lives—NBC
The Young and the Restless—CBS

OUTSTANDING ACTOR IN A DAYTIME DRAMA SERIES

John Beradino (Steve Hardy, *General Hospital*)

Macdonald Carey (Tom Horton, *Days of Our Lives*)
Larry Haines (Stu Bergman, *Search for Tomorrow*)
Bill Hayes (Doug Williams, *Days of Our Lives*)
Michael Nouri (Steve Kaslow, *Search for Tomorrow*)
Shepperd Strudwick (Victor Lord, *One Life to Live*)

OUTSTANDING ACTRESS IN A DAYTIME DRAMA SERIES

Denise Alexander (Lesley Williams, *General Hospital*)
Helen Gallagher (Maeve Ryan, *Ryan's Hope*)
Frances Heflin (Mona Kane, *All My Children*)
Susan Seaforth Hayes (Julie Anderson, *Days of Our Lives*)
Mary Stuart (Joanne Vincente, *Search for Tomorrow*)

1976-77

OUTSTANDING DAYTIME DRAMA SERIES

All My Children—ABC
Another World—NBC
Days of Our Lives—NBC
The Edge of Night—ABC
Ryan's Hope—ABC

OUTSTANDING ACTOR IN A DAYTIME DRAMA SERIES

Val Dufour (John Wyatt, *Search for Tomorrow*)
Farley Granger (Will Vernon, *One Life to Live*)
Larry Haines (Stu Bergman, *Search for Tomorrow*)
Lawrence Keith (Nick Davis, *All My Children*)
James Pritchett (Matt Powers, *The Doctors*)

OUTSTANDING ACTRESS IN A DAYTIME DRAMA SERIES

Nancy Addison (Jillian Coleridge, *Ryan's Hope*)
Helen Gallagher (Maeve Ryan, *Ryan's Hope*)
Beverlee McKinsey (Iris Carrington, *Another World*)
Mary Stuart (Joanne Vincente, *Search for Tomorrow*)
Ruth Warrick (Phoebe Tyler, *All My Children*)

1977-78

OUTSTANDING DAYTIME DRAMA SERIES

All My Children—ABC
Days of Our Lives—NBC
Ryan's Hope—ABC
The Young and the Restless—CBS

OUTSTANDING ACTOR IN A DAYTIME DRAMA SERIES

Matthew Cowles (Billy Clyde Tuggle, *All My Children*)
Lawrence Keith (Nick Davis, *All My Children*)
Michael Levin (Jack Fenelli, *Ryan's Hope*)
James Pritchett (Matt Powers, *The Doctors*)
Andrew Robinson (Frank Ryan, *Ryan's Hope*)
Michael Storm (Larry Wolek, *One Life to Live*)

OUTSTANDING ACTRESS IN A DAYTIME DRAMA SERIES

Mary Fickett (Ruth Martin, *All My Children*)
Jennifer Harmon (Cathy Craig, *One Life to Live*)
Laurie Heineman (Sharlene Frame, *Another World*)
Susan Lucci (Erica Kane, *All My Children*)
Beverlee McKinsey (Iris Bancroft, *Another World*)
Susan Seaforth Hayes (Julie Williams, *Days of Our Lives*)
Victoria Wyndham (Rachel Cory, *Another World*)

1978-79

OUTSTANDING DAYTIME DRAMA SERIES

All My Children—ABC
Days of Our Lives—NBC
Ryan's Hope—ABC
The Young and the Restless—CBS

OUTSTANDING ACTOR IN A DAYTIME DRAMA SERIES

Jed Allan (Don Craig, *Days of Our Lives*)
Nicholas Benedict (Phillip Brent, *All My Children*)
John Clarke (Mickey Horton, *Days of Our Lives*)
Joel Crothers (Miles Cavanaugh, *The Edge of Night*)
Al Freeman, Jr. (Ed Hall, *One Life to Live*)
Michael Levin (Jack Fenelli, *Ryan's Hope*)

OUTSTANDING ACTRESS IN A DAYTIME DRAMA SERIES

Nancy Addison (Jillian Coleridge, *Ryan's Hope*)
Irene Dailey (Liz Matthews, *Another World*)
Helen Gallagher (Maeve Ryan, *Ryan's Hope*)
Beverlee McKinsey (Iris Bancroft, *Another World*)
Susan Seaforth Hayes (Julie Williams, *Days of Our Lives*)
Victoria Wyndham (Rachel Cory, *Another World*)

OUTSTANDING SUPPORTING ACTRESS IN A DAYTIME DRAMA SERIES

Rachel Ames (Audrey Hardy, *General Hospital*)
Susan Brown (Gail Adamson, *General Hospital*)
Lois Kibbee (Geraldine Whitney Saxon,
  The Edge of Night)
Frances Reid (Alice Horton, *Days of Our Lives*)
Suzanne Rogers (Maggie Horton, *Days of Our Lives*)

OUTSTANDING SUPPORTING ACTOR IN A DAYTIME DRAMA SERIES

Lewis Arlt (David Sutton, *Search for Tomorrow*)
Bernard Barrow (Johnny Ryan, *Ryan's Hope*)
Joseph Gallison (Neil Curtis, *Days of Our Lives*)
Ron Hale (Roger Coleridge, *Ryan's Hope*)
Peter Hansen (Lee Baldwin, *General Hospital*)
Mandel Kramer (Bill Marceau, *The Edge of Night*)

1979-80

OUTSTANDING DAYTIME DRAMA SERIES

All My Children—ABC
Another World—NBC
The Guiding Light—CBS

OUTSTANDING ACTOR IN A DAYTIME DRAMA SERIES

John Gabriel (Seneca Beaulac, *Ryan's Hope*)
Michael Levin (Jack Fenelli, *Ryan's Hope*)
Franc Luz (John Bennett, *The Doctors*)
James Mitchell (Palmer Cortlandt, *All My Children*)
William Mooney (Paul Martin, *All My Children*)
Douglass Watson (Mac Cory, *Another World*)

OUTSTANDING ACTRESS IN A DAYTIME DRAMA SERIES

Julia Barr (Brooke English, *All My Children*)
Leslie Charleson (Monica Quatermaine, *General Hospital*)
Kim Hunter (Nola Madison, *The Edge of Night*)
Judith Light (Karen Wolek, *One Life to Live*)
Beverlee McKinsey (Iris Bancroft, *Another World*)
Kathleen Noone (Ellen Shepard, *All My Children*)

OUTSTANDING SUPPORTING ACTRESS IN A DAYTIME DRAMA SERIES

Deidre Hall (Marlena Craig, *Days of Our Lives*)
Francesca James (Kelly Cole, *All My Children*)
Lois Kibbee (Geraldine Whitney Saxon,
  The Edge of Night)
Elaine Lee (Mildred Trumble, *The Doctors*)
Valerie Mahaffey (Ashley Bennett, *The Doctors*)

OUTSTANDING SUPPORTING ACTOR IN A DAYTIME DRAMA SERIES

Warren Burton (Eddie Dorrance, *All My Children*)
Vasili Bogazianos (Mickey Dials, *The Edge of Night*)
Ron Hale (Roger Coleridge, *Ryan's Hope*)
Julius LaRosa (Renaldo, *Another World*)
Shepperd Strudwick (Timothy McCauley, *Love of Life*)

OUTSTANDING CAMEO APPEARANCE IN A DAYTIME DRAMA SERIES

Sammy Davis, Jr. (Chip Warren, *One Life to Live*)
Joan Fontaine (Page Williams, *Ryan's Hope*)
Kathryn Harrow (Pat Reyerson, *The Doctors*)
Hugh McPhillips (Hugh Pearson, *Days of Our Lives*)
Eli Mintz (locksmith, *All My Children*)

1980-81

OUTSTANDING DAYTIME DRAMA SERIES

All My Children—ABC
General Hospital—ABC
Ryan's Hope—ABC

OUTSTANDING ACTOR IN A DAYTIME DRAMA SERIES

Larry Bryggman (John Dixon, *As the World Turns*)
Henderson Forsythe (David Stewart, *As the World Turns*)
Anthony Geary (Luke Spencer, *General Hospital*)
James Mitchell (Palmer Cortlandt, *All My Children*)
Douglass Watson (Mac Cory, *Another World*)

OUTSTANDING ACTRESS IN A DAYTIME DRAMA SERIES

Julia Barr (Brooke Cudahy, *All My Children*)
Helen Gallagher (Maeve Ryan, *Ryan's Hope*)

Judith Light (Karen Wolek, *One Life to Live*)
Susan Lucci (Erica Kane, *All My Children*)
Robin Strasser (Dorian Lord Callison, *One Life to Live*)

OUTSTANDING SUPPORTING ACTRESS IN A DAYTIME DRAMA SERIES

Randall Edwards (Delia Coleridge, *Ryan's Hope*)
Jane Elliot (Tracy Quartermaine Williams,
General Hospital)
Lois Kibbee (Geraldine Whitney Saxon,
The Edge of Night)
Elizabeth Lawrence (Myra Murdoch, *All My Children*)
Jacklyn Zeman (Bobby Spencer, *General Hospital*)

OUTSTANDING SUPPORTING ACTOR IN A DAYTIME DRAMA SERIES

Richard Backus (Barry Ryan, *Ryan's Hope*)
Matthew Cowles (Billy Clyde Tuggle, *All My Children*)
Justin Deas (Tom Hughes, *As the World Turns*)
Larry Haines (Stu Bergman, *Search for Tomorrow*)
William Mooney (Paul Martin, *All My Children*)

1981-82
OUTSTANDING DAYTIME DRAMA SERIES

All My Children—ABC
General Hospital—ABC
The Guiding Light—CBS
Ryan's Hope—ABC

OUTSTANDING ACTOR IN A DAYTIME DRAMA SERIES

Larry Bryggman (John Dixon, *As the World Turns*)
Stuart Damon (Alan Quartermaine, *General Hospital*)
Anthony Geary (Luke Spencer, *General Hospital*)
James Mitchell (Palmer Cortlandt, *All My Children*)
Richard Shoberg (Tom Cudahy, *All My Children*)

OUTSTANDING ACTRESS IN A DAYTIME DRAMA SERIES

Leslie Charleson (Monica Quartermaine, *General Hospital*)
Ann Flood (Nancy Karr, *The Edge of Night*)
Sharon Gabet (Raven Whitney, *The Edge of Night*)
Susan Lucci (Erica Kane, *All My Children*)
Robin Strasser (Dorian Lord Callison, *One Life to Live*)

OUTSTANDING SUPPORTING ACTRESS IN A DAYTIME DRAMA SERIES

Elizabeth Lawrence (Myra Murdoch, *All My Children*)
Dorothy Lyman (Opal Gardner, *All My Children*)
Meg Mundy (Mona Aldrich Croft, *The Doctors*)
Louise Shafer (Rae Woodard, *Ryan's Hope*)

OUTSTANDING SUPPORTING ACTOR IN A DAYTIME DRAMA SERIES

Gerald Anthony (Marco Dane, *One Life to Live*)
David Lewis (Edward Quartermaine, *General Hospital*)
Douglas Sheehan (Joe Kelly, *General Hospital*)
Darnell Williams (Jesse Hubbard, *All My Children*)

1982-83
OUTSTANDING DAYTIME DRAMA SERIES

All My Children—ABC
Days of Our Lives—NBC
General Hospital—ABC
One Life to Live—ABC
The Young and the Restless—CBS

OUTSTANDING ACTOR IN A DAYTIME DRAMA SERIES

Peter Bergman (Cliff Warner, *All My Children*)
Stuart Damon (Alan Quartermaine, *General Hospital*)
Anthony Geary (Luke Spencer, *General Hospital*)
James Mitchell (Palmer Cortlandt, *All My Children*)
Robert S. Woods (Bo Buchanan, *One Life to Live*)

OUTSTANDING ACTRESS IN A DAYTIME DRAMA SERIES

Leslie Charleson (Monica Quartermaine, *General Hospital*)
Susan Lucci (Erica Kane, *All My Children*)
Dorothy Lyman (Opal Gardner, *All My Children*)
Erika Slezak (Victoria Lord Buchanan, *One Life to Live*)
Robin Strasser (Dorian Lord Callison, *One Life to Live*)

OUTSTANDING SUPPORTING ACTRESS IN A DAYTIME DRAMA SERIES

Kim Delaney (Jenny Gardner, *All My Children*)

Eileen Herlie (Myrtle Fargate, *All My Children*)
Robin Mattson (Heather Webber, *General Hospital*)
Louise Shaffer (Rae Woodard, *Ryan's Hope*)
Brynn Thayer (Jenny Janssen, *One Life to Live*)
Marcy Walker (Liza Colby, *All My Children*)

OUTSTANDING SUPPORTING ACTOR IN A DAYTIME DRAMA SERIES

Anthony Call (Herb Callison, *One Life to Live*)
Al Freeman, Jr. (Ed Hall, *One Life to Live*)
David Lewis (Edward Quartermaine, *General Hospital*)
Howard E. Rollins, Jr. (Ed Harding, *Another World*)
John Stamos (Blackie Parrish, *General Hospital*)
Darnell Williams (Jesse Hubbard, *All My Children*)

1983-84

OUTSTANDING DAYTIME DRAMA SERIES

All My Children—ABC
Days of Our Lives—NBC
General Hospital—ABC

OUTSTANDING ACTOR IN A DAYTIME DRAMA SERIES

Larry Bryggman (John Dixon, *As the World Turns*)
Joel Crothers (Miles Cavanaugh, *The Edge of Night*)
Stuart Damon (Alan Quartermaine, *General Hospital*)
Terry Lester (Jack Abbott, *The Young and the Restless*)
Larkin Malloy (Sky Whitney, *The Edge of Night*)
James Mitchell (Palmer Courtlandt, *All My Children*)

OUTSTANDING ACTRESS IN A DAYTIME DRAMA SERIES

Ann Flood (Nancy Karr, *The Edge of Night*)
Sharon Gabet (Raven Alexander Whitney, *The Edge of Night*)
Deidre Hall (Marlena Evans Brady, *Days of Our Lives*)
Susan Lucci (Erica Kane Chandler, *All My Children*)
Erika Slezak (Victoria Lord Buchanan, *One Life to Live*)

OUTSTANDING SUPPORTING ACTRESS IN A DAYTIME DRAMA SERIES

Loanne Bishop (Rose Kelly, *General Hospital*)
Christine Ebersole (Maxie McDermont, *One Life to Live*)
Judi Evans (Beth Raines, *The Guiding Light*)

Eileen Herlie (Myrtle Fargate, *All My Children*)
Lois Kibbee (Geraldine Whitney Saxon, *The Edge of Night*)
Marcy Walker (Liza Colby, *All My Children*)

OUTSTANDING SUPPORTING ACTOR IN A DAYTIME DRAMA SERIES

Anthony Call (Herb Callison, *One Life to Live*)
Justin Deas (Tom Hughes, *As the World Turns*)
Louis Edmonds (Langley Wallingford, *All My Children*)
David Lewis (Edward Quartermaine, *General Hospital*)
Paul Stevens (Brian Bancroft, *Another World*)

1984-85

OUTSTANDING DAYTIME DRAMA SERIES

All My Children—ABC
Days of Our Lives—NBC
General Hospital—ABC
The Guiding Light—CBS
The Young and the Restless—CBS

OUTSTANDING ACTOR IN A DAYTIME DRAMA SERIES

Larry Bryggman (John Dixon, *As the World Turns*)
David Canary (Adam/Stuart Chandler, *All My Children*)
Terry Lester (Jack Abbott, *The Young and the Restless*)
James Mitchell (Palmer Cortlandt, *All My Children*)
Darnell Williams (Jesse Hubbard, *All My Children*)

OUTSTANDING ACTRESS IN A DAYTIME DRAMA SERIES

Deidre Hall (Marlena Evans Brady, *Days of Our Lives*)
Susan Lucci (Erica Kane, *All My Children*)
Gillian Spencer (Daisy Cortlandt, *All My Children*)
Robin Strasser (Dorian Lord, *One Life to Live*)
Kim Zimmer (Reva Shayne Lewis, *The Guiding Light*)

OUTSTANDING SUPPORTING ACTRESS IN A DAYTIME DRAMA SERIES

Norma Connolly (Ruby Anderson, *General Hospital*)
Eileen Herlie (Myrtle Fargate, *All My Children*)
Maeve Kinkead (Vanessa Chamberlain Lewis, *The Guiding Light*)

Elizabeth Lawrence (Myra Murdoch Sloane,
All My Children)
Beth Maitland (Traci Abbott Romalotti,
The Young and the Restless)

OUTSTANDING SUPPORTING ACTOR IN A DAYTIME DRAMA SERIES

Anthony Call (Herb Callison, *One Life to Live*)
Louis Edmonds (Langley Wallingford, *All My Children*)
Larry Gates (H. B. Lewis, *The Guiding Light*)
David Lewis (Edward Quartermaine, *General Hospital*)
Robert LuPone (Zach Grayson, *All My Children*)

OUTSTANDING INGENUE IN A DAYTIME DRAMA SERIES

Kristian Alfonso (Hope Williams Brady,
Days of Our Lives)
Tracey E. Bregman (Lauren Fenmore Williams,
The Young and the Restless)
Melissa Leo (Linda Warner, *All My Children*)
Lisa Trusel (Melissa Anderson, *Days of Our Lives*)
Tasia Valenza (Dottie Thornton Martin, *All My Children*)

OUTSTANDING JUVENILE/YOUNG MAN IN A DAYTIME DRAMA SERIES

Brian Bloom (Dustin Donovan, *As the World Turns*)
Steve Caffrey (Andrew Preston Cortlandt,
All My Children)
Michael Knight (Tad Gardner Martin, *All My Children*)
Michael O'Leary (Rick Bauer, *The Guiding Light*)
Jack P. Wagner (Frisco Jones, *General Hospital*)

1985-86

OUTSTANDING DAYTIME DRAMA SERIES

All My Children—ABC
As the World Turns—CBS
General Hospital—ABC
The Young and the Restless—CBS

OUTSTANDING SUPPORTING ACTOR IN A DAYTIME DRAMA SERIES

Scott Bryce (Craig Montgomery, *As the World Turns*)
Larry Bryggman (John Dixon, *As the World Turns*)
David Canary (Adam/Stuart Chandler, *All My Children*)

Nicolas Coster (Lionel Lockridge, *Santa Barbara*)
Terry Lester (Jack Abbott, *The Young and the Restless*)
Robert S. Woods (Bo Buchanan, *One Life to Live*)

OUTSTANDING ACTRESS IN A DAYTIME DRAMA SERIES

Elizabeth Hubbard (Lucinda Walsh, *As the World Turns*)
Susan Lucci (Erica Kane, *All My Children*)
Peggy McKay (Caroline Brady, *Days of Our Lives*)
Erika Slezak (Victoria Lord Buchanan, *One Life to Live*)
Kim Zimmer (Reva Shayne, *The Guiding Light*)

OUTSTANDING SUPPORTING ACTRESS IN A DAYTIME DRAMA SERIES

Dame Judith Anderson (Minx Lockridge, *Santa Barbara*)
Uta Heagen (Hortense, *One Life to Live*)
Eileen Herlie (Myrtle Fargate, *All My Children*)
Leann Hunley (Ana DiMera, *Days of Our Lives*)
Kathleen Widdoes (Emma Snyder, *As the World Turns*)

OUTSTANDING SUPPORTING ACTOR IN A DAYTIME DRAMA SERIES

Louis Edmonds (Langley Wallingford, *All My Children*)
Al Freeman, Jr. (Ed Hall, *One Life to Live*)
Larry Gates (H. B. Lewis, *The Guiding Light*)
Gregg Marx (Tom Hughes, *As the World Turns*)
John Wesley Shipp (Doug Cummings,
As the World Turns)

OUTSTANDING INGENUE IN A DAYTIME DRAMA SERIES

Martha Byrne (Lily Walsh, *As the World Turns*)
Debbi Morgan (Angie Hubbard, *All My Children*)
Ellen Wheeler (Marley/Victoria Love, *Another World*)
Robin Wright (Kelly Capwell, *Santa Barbara*)

OUTSTANDING YOUNG MAN IN A DAYTIME DRAMA SERIES

Brian Bloom (Dustin Donovan, *As the World Turns*)
Jon Hensley (Holden Snyder, *As the World Turns*)
Vincent Irizarry (Lujack, *The Guiding Light*)
Michael Knight (Tad Martin, *All My Children*)
Don Scardino (Chris Chapin, *Another World*)

1986-87

OUTSTANDING DAYTIME DRAMA SERIES

All My Children—ABC
As the World Turns—CBS
Santa Barbara—NBC
The Young and the Restless—CBS

OUTSTANDING ACTOR IN A DAYTIME DRAMA SERIES

Eric Braeden (Victor Newman, *The Young and the Restless*)
Scott Bryce (Craig Montgomery, *As the World Turns*)
Larry Bryggman (John Dixon, *As the World Turns*)
Terry Lester (Jack Abbott, *The Young and the Restless*)
A Martinez (Cruz Costillo, *Santa Barbara*)

OUTSTANDING ACTRESS IN A DAYTIME DRAMA SERIES

Elizabeth Hubbard (Lucinda Walsh Dixon,
 As the World Turns)
Susan Lucci (Erica Kane, *All My Children*)
Frances Reid (Alice Horton, *Days of Our Lives*)
Marcy Walker (Eden Capwell, *Santa Barbara*)
Kim Zimmer (Reva Shayne, *The Guiding Light*)

OUTSTANDING SUPPORTING ACTRESS IN A DAYTIME DRAMA SERIES

Lisa Brown (Iva Snyder, *As the World Turns*)
Robin Mattson (Gina Capwell, *Santa Barbara*)
Peggy McKay (Caroline Brady, *Days of Our Lives*)
Kathleen Noone (Ellen Chandler, *All My Children*)
Kathleen Widdoes (Emma Snyder, *As the World Turns*)

OUTSTANDING SUPPORTING ACTOR IN A DAYTIME DRAMA SERIES

Anthony Call (Herb Callison, *One Life to Live*)
Justin Deas (Keith Timmons, *Santa Barbara*)
Richard Eden (Brick Wallace, *Santa Barbara*)
Al Freeman, Jr. (Ed Hall, *One Life to Live*)
Gregg Marx (Tom Hughes, *As the World Turns*)

OUTSTANDING INGENUE IN A DAYTIME DRAMA SERIES

Tracey E. Bregman (Lauren Fenmore,
 The Young and the Restless)

Martha Byrne (Lily Walsh, *As the World Turns*)
Jane Krakowski (T. R. Kendall, *Search for Tomorrow*)
Krista Tesreau (Mindy Lewis, *The Guiding Light*)
Robin Wright (Kelly Capwell, *Santa Barbara*)

OUTSTANDING YOUNG ACTOR IN A DAYTIME DRAMA SERIES

Brian Bloom (Dustin Dononvan, *As the World Turns*)
Jon Hensley (Holden Snyder, *As the World Turns*)
Michael Knight (Tad Martin, *All My Children*)
Grant Show (Rick Hyde, *Ryan's Hope*)
Billy Warlock (Frankie, *Days of Our Lives*)

1987-88

OUTSTANDING DAYTIME DRAMA SERIES

All My Children—ABC
As the World Turns—CBS
General Hospital—ABC
Santa Barbara—NBC
The Young and the Restless—CBS

OUTSTANDING ACTOR IN A DAYTIME DRAMA SERIES

Larry Bryggman (John Dixon, *As the World Turns*)
David Canary (Adam/Stuart Chandler, *All My Children*)
Robert Gentry (Ross Chandler, *All My Children*)
A Martinez (Cruz Castillo, *Santa Barbara*)
Stephen Nichols (Steve "Patch" Johnson,
 Days of Our Lives)

OUTSTANDING ACTRESS IN A DAYTIME DRAMA SERIES

Helen Gallagher (Maeve Ryan, *Ryan's Hope*)
Elizabeth Hubbard (Lucinda Walsh Dixon,
 As the World Turns)
Susan Lucci (Erica Kane Montgomery, *All My Children*)
Erika Slezak (Victoria Lord Buchanan, *One Life to Live*)
Marcy Walker (Eden Capwell, *Santa Barbara*)/

OUTSTANDING SUPPORTING ACTRESS IN A DAYTIME DRAMA SERIES

Lisa Brown (Iva Snyder, *As the World Turns*)
Eileen Fulton (Lisa Mitchell, *As the World Turns*)
Maeve Kinkead (Vanessa Chamberlain, *The Guiding Light*)

Robin Mattson (Gina Capwell, *Santa Barbara*)
Arleen Sorkin (Calliope Jones Bradford,
   Days of Our Lives)
Ellen Wheeler (Cindy Parker, *All My Children*)

OUTSTANDING SUPPORTING ACTOR IN A DAYTIME DRAMA SERIES

Bernie Barrow (Johnny Ryan, *Ryan's Hope*)
Nicolas Coster (Lionel Lockridge, *Santa Barbara*)
Justin Deas (Keith Timmons, *Santa Barbara*)
Mark La Mura (Mark Dalton, *All My Children*)
David Lewis (Edward Quartermaine, *General Hospital*)

OUTSTANDING INGENUE IN A DAYTIME DRAMA SERIES

Tichina Arnold (Zena Brown, *Ryan's Hope*)
Andrea Evans (Tina Lord Roberts, *One Live to Live*)
Lauren Holly (Julie Chander, *All My Children*)
Julianne Moore (Sabrina/Frannie Hughes,
   As the World Turns)
Robin Wright (Kelly Capwell, *Santa Barbara*)

OUTSTANDING YOUNGER ACTOR IN A DAYTIME DRAMA SERIES

Scott DeFreitas (Andy Dixon, *As the World Turns*)
Robert Duncan McNeill (Charlie Brent,
   All My Children)
Andy Kavovit (Paul Stenbeck, *As the World Turns*)
Ross Kettle (Jeffrey Conrad, *Santa Barbara*)
Billy Warlock (Frankie, *Days of Our Lives*)

1988-89

OUTSTANDING DAYTIME DRAMA SERIES

All My Children—ABC
As the World Turns—CBS
General Hospital—ABC
The Guiding Light—CBS
Santa Barbara—NBC
The Young and the Restless—CBS

OUTSTANDING ACTOR IN A DAYTIME DRAMA SERIES

Larry Bryggman (John Dixon, *As the World Turns*)
David Canary (Adam/Stuart Chandler,
   All My Children)

A Martinez (Cruz Castillo, *Santa Barbara*)
James Mitchell (Palmer Cortlandt, *All My Children*)
Douglass Watson (Mac Cory, *Another World*)

OUTSTANDING ACTRESS IN A DAYTIME DRAMA SERIES

Jeanne Cooper (Katherine Chancellor Sterling,
   The Young and the Restless)
Elizabeth Hubbard (Lucinda Walsh Dixon,
   As the World Turns)
Susan Lucci (Erica Kane, *All My Children*)
Marcy Walker (Eden Capwell Castillo, *Santa Barbara*)

OUTSTANDING SUPPORTING ACTRESS IN A DAYTIME DRAMA SERIES

Jane Elliot (Angelica Curtin, *Days of Our Lives*)
Nancy Lee Grahn (Julie Wainwright, *Santa Barbara*)
Robin Mattson (Gina Capwell Timmons, *Santa Barbara*)
Debbi Morgan (Angie Hubbard, *All My Children*)
Arleen Sorkin (Calliope Bradford, *Days of Our Lives*)

OUTSTANDING SUPPORTING ACTOR IN A DAYTIME DRAMA SERIES

Joseph Campanella (Harper Deveraux,
   Days of Our Lives)
Justin Deas (Keith Timmons, *Santa Barbara*)
David Forsyth (John Hudson, *Another World*)
Quinn Redeker (Rex Sterling, *The Young and the Restless*)

OUTSTANDING INGENUE IN A DAYTIME DRAMA SERIES

Noelle Beck (Trisha Alden Sowolsky, *Loving*)
Martha Byrne (Lily Walsh, *As the World Turns*)
Anne Heche (Victoria Frame/Marley McKinnon,
   Another World)
Kimberly McCullough (Robin Scorpio,
   General Hospital)

OUTSTANDING YOUNG ACTOR IN A DAYTIME DRAMA SERIES

Justin Gocke (Brandon Capwell, *Santa Barbara*)
Andrew Kavovit (Paul Stenbeck, *As the World Turns*)
Darell Utley (Benjy, *Days of Our Lives*)

FAN CLUB ADDRESSES

AS THE WORLD TURNS
As the World Turns Fan Club
c/o Deanne Turco
212 Oriole Drive
Montgomery, NY 12549

THE BOLD AND THE BEAUTIFUL
The Bold and the Beautiful Fan Club
Suite 3371
7800 Beverly Blvd.
Los Angeles, CA 90036

DAYS OF OUR LIVES
National "Days" Fan Club
424 A Johnson Street
Sausalito, CA 94965

A Touch of Days
116 Boston Avenue
North Arlington, NJ 07032

GENERAL HOSPITAL
Fans of General Hospital
Sue Corbett
P.O. Box 8023
Westchester, OH 45069

THE GUIDING LIGHT
Guiding Light Fan Club
c/o Sharon Kearns
104 St. George Drive
Camillus, NY 13031

ONE LIFE TO LIVE
One Life to Live Fan Club
Carol Dickson, President
1218 North Main Street
Glassboro, NJ 08028

SANTA BARBARA
Santa Barbara Fan Club
c/o Kim Jalet
P.O. Box 9080
Albany, NY 12209

THE YOUNG AND THE RESTLESS
The Young and the Restless Fan Club
8033 Sunset Blvd.
Los Angeles, CA 90046

For more information about fan clubs, contact:

National Association of Fan Clubs
2730 Baltimore Avenue
Pueblo, CO 81003

STUDIO ADDRESSES

ALL MY CHILDREN
c/o ABC-TV
77 West 66th Street
New York, NY 10023

ANOTHER WORLD
c/o NBC-TV
30 Rockefeller Plaza
New York, NY 10112

AS THE WORLD TURNS
c/o CBS-TV
51 West 52nd Street
New York, NY 10019

THE BOLD AND THE BEAUTIFUL
c/o CBS-TV
7800 Beverly Blvd.
Los Angeles, CA 90036

DALLAS
c/o CBS-TV
7800 Beverly Blvd.
Los Angeles, CA 90036

DAYS OF OUR LIVES
c/o NBC-TV
3000 West Alameda Avenue
Burbank, CA 91523

GENERAL HOSPITAL
c/o ABC-TV
4151 Prospect Avenue
Hollywood, CA 90067

GENERATIONS
c/o NBC-TV
3000 West Alameda Avenue
Burbank, CA 91523

THE GUIDING LIGHT
c/o CBS-TV
51 West 52nd Street
New York, NY 10019

KNOTS LANDING
c/o CBS-TV
7800 Beverly Blvd.
Los Angeles, CA 90036

LOVING
c/o ABC-TV
77 West 66th Street
New York, NY 10023

ONE LIFE TO LIVE
c/o ABC-TV
77 West 66th Street
New York, NY 10023

SANTA BARBARA
c/o NBC-TV
3000 West Alameda Avenue
Burbank, CA 91523

TWIN PEAKS
c/o CBS-TV
77 West 66th Street
New York, NY 10023

THE YOUNG AND THE RESTLESS
c/o CBS-TV
7800 Beverly Blvd.
Los Angeles, CA 90036

Kevin Bacon

GRADUATES OF DAYTIME SOAPS

Alan Alda

Warren Beatty *Love of Life*

Bonnie Bedelia Sandy Porter, *Love of Life*

Robby Benson
Bruce Carson, *Search for Tomorrow*

Tom Berenger Tim Siegel, *One Life to Live*

Corbin Bernsen Ken Graham, *Ryan's Hope*

Ellen (McRae) Burstyn
Dr. Kate Bartok, *The Doctors*
The Verdict Is Yours

Dyan Cannon
For Better or Worse
The Doctors
Lisa Crowder, *Full Circle*

Alan Alda
Gilbert Parker, *The House on High Street*

Ana Alicia Alicia Nieves, *Ryan's Hope*

Susan Anspach Angela Carter, *The Doctors*

Armand Assante
Johnny McGhee, *How to Survive a Marriage*
Mike Powers, *The Doctors*

Kevin Bacon Tod Adamson, *Search for Tomorrow*
Tim Werner, *The Guiding Light*

Martin Balsam
Harold Mathews, *The Greatest Gift*
The House on High Street
Joey Gordon, *Valiant Lady*
Love of Life

Warren Beatty

Kate Capshaw	Jinx Avery, *The Edge of Night*
Nell Carter	Ethel Green, *Ryan's Hope*
Jill Clayburgh	
	Grace Bolton, *Search for Tomorrow*
James Coco	*Search for Tomorrow*
Gary Coleman	*The Edge of Night*
Margaret Colin	
	Margo Montgomery, *As the World Turns*
	Paige Madison, *The Edge of Night*

Dana Delany

Ted Danson

Ted Danson	Tom Conway, *Somerset*
Brad Davis	
	Alexander Kronos, *How to Survive a Marriage*
Ruby Dee	Martha Frazier, *The Guiding Light*

Dana Delany	Amy Russell, *Love of Life*
	Hayley Wilson, *As the World Turns*
Sandy Dennis	Alice Holden, *The Guiding Light*
Robert DeNiro	*Search for Tomorrow*
Olympia Dukakis	
	Dr. Barbara Moreno, *Search for Tomorrow*
Patty Duke	Ellen Dennis, *The Brighter Day*
Sandy Duncan	Helen, *Search for Tomorrow*
Charles Durning	Gil McGowan, *Another World*
Dana Elcar	Clinton Wheeler, *The Edge of Night*
	George Paterson, *Dark Shadows*
	Dr. Clay, *A Time to Live*
Peter Falk	*Love of Life*

Jill Clayburgh

Morgan Fairchild
Jennifer Pace, *Search for Tomorrow*

Mike Farrell   Scott Banning, *Days of Our Lives*

Mike Farrell

Mary Frann
D. B. Bentley, *Return to Peyton Place*
Amanda Howard, *Days of Our Lives*
Nan Hollister, *King's Crossing*

Anthony Geary   Luke Spencer, *General Hospital*
Rapist, *The Young and the Restless*
David Lockhart, *Bright Promise*

(Paul) Michael Glaser   Peter Chernak,
Love Is a Many Splendored Thing
Dr. Joe Corelli, *Love of Life*

Scott Glenn   Calvin Brenner, *The Edge of Night*

Lee Grant   Rose Peabody, *Search for Tomorrow*

300

Charles Grodin
Matt Stevens, *The Young Marrieds*

Joan Hackett   Gail Prentiss, *Young Doctor Malone*

Larry Hagman   Ed Gibson, *The Edge of Night*

Mark Hamill   Kent Murray, *General Hospital*

Kathryn Harrold   Nola Dancy, *The Doctors*

David Hasselhoff
Snapper Foster, *The Young and the Restless*

Joel Higgins   Bruce Carson, *Search for Tomorrow*

Hal Holbrook
Grayling Dennis, *The Brighter Day*

Jackée (Harry)   Lily Mason, *Another World*

Anne Jackson   *Love of Life*

Hal Holbrook

Mark Hamill

Tommy Lee Jones (right, with Bubba Smith)

Kate Jackson   Daphne Harridge, *Dark Shadows*

James Earl Jones
Dr. Jerry Turner, *As the World Turns*
Dr. Jim Frazier, *The Guiding Light*

Tommy Lee Jones
Mark Toland, *One Life to Live*

Raul Julia   Miguel Garcia, *Love of Life*

Ken Kercheval
Larry Kirby, *How to Survive a Marriage*
Archie Borman, *The Secret Storm*
Dr. Nick Hunter, *Search for Tomorrow*

Richard Kiley
R. Moseley Bradshaw, *The Edge of Night*

Kevin Kline   Woody Reed, *Search for Tomorrow*

Don Knotts
Wilbur Peabody, *Search for Tomorrow*

Diane Ladd   Kitty Styles, *The Secret Storm*

Audrey Landers   Heather Kane, *Somerset*
Joanna Morrison, *The Secret Storm*
One Life to Live

Judith Light   Karen Wolek, *One Life to Live*

Hal Linden   Larry Carter, *Search for Tomorrow*

Audra Lindley   Liz Matthews, *Another World*
Laura Tomkins, *From These Roots*
Sue Knowles, *Search for Tomorrow*

Tony LoBianco   Joe Corelli, *Love of Life*
Nick Capello Turner, *Hidden Faces*

Robert Loggia
Anthony Vincente, *Search for Tomorrow*

Raul Julia (with Sonia Bragga)

Andrea McArdle
Wendy Wilkins, *Search for Tomorrow*

Rue McClanahan
Caroline Johnson, *Another World*
Margaret Jardin, *Where the Heart Is*

Judith Light

Marsha Mason

Nancy Marchand
    Therese Lamonte, *Another World*
    Vinnie Phillips, *Love of Life*

Marsha Mason   Judith Cole, *Love of Life*
    Laura Blackburn, *Where the Heart Is*
    Vampire Girl Lily, *Dark Shadows*

George Maharis
    Bud Gardner, *Search for Tomorrow*

Bette Midler   *The Edge of Night*

Donna Mills   Rocket, *The Secret Storm*
    Laura Donnelly,
    Love Is a Many Splendored Thing

Bette Midler

Demi Moore
    Jackie Templeton, *General Hospital*

Kate Mulgrew   Mary Ryan, *Ryan's Hope*

Michael Nader
    Kevin Thompson, *As the World Turns*

Patricia Neal   *The Secret Storm*

Christopher Reeve

Barry Newman   John Barnes, *The Edge of Night*

Lois Nettleton
    Patsy Hamilton, *The Brighter Day*

Michael Nouri   Steve Kaslo, *Search for Tomorrow*
    Tom Conway, *Somerset*

Jameson Parker   Brad Vernon, *One Life to Live*
    Dale Robinson, *Somerset*

Phylicia (Ayers-Allen) Rashad
    Courtney Wright, *One Life to Live*

Christopher Reeve   Ben Harper, *Love of Life*

Eric Roberts   Ted Bancroft, *Another World*

Tom Selleck

Wayne Rogers   Slim Davis, *Search for Tomorrow*

Gena Rowlands
        Paula Graves, *The Way of the World*

Susan Sarandon

Gena Rowlands

Meg Ryan   Betsy Stewart, *As the World Turns*

Eva Marie Saint   *The Edge of Night*

Gary Sandy   Hank Barton, *As the World Turns*
            Randy Buchanan, *Somerset*
        Stacey Reddin, *The Secret Storm*

Susan Sarandon
        Patrice Kahlman, *A World Apart*
    Sarah Fairbanks, *Search for Tomorrow*

Roy Scheider   Bob Hill, *The Secret Storm*
            Jonas Falk, *Love of Life*
        Dr. Wheeler, *Search for Tomorrow*

David Selby   Quentin Collins, *Dark Shadows*

Tom Selleck
        Jed Andrews, *The Young and the Restless*

Roy Scheider

Ted Schackelford   Ray Gordon, *Another World*

Martin Sheen   Roy Sanders, *The Edge of Night*

Rick Springfield
Dr. Noah Drake, *General Hospital*

Beatrice Straight   Vinnie Phillips, *Love of Life*

Dolph Sweet   Gil McGowan, *Another World*

Susan Sullivan   Lenore Curtin, *Another World*
April Morrison, *Best of Everything*
Nancy Condon, *A World Apart*

Richard Thomas
Tom Hughes, *As the World Turns*
Chris Austen, *A Time for Us*

Blair Underwood

Roy Thinnes
Alex Crown (Coronal), *One Life to Live*
Phil Brewer, *General Hospital*

Daniel J. Travanti
Spence Andrews, *General Hospital*

John Travolta   *The Edge of Night*

Kathleen Turner   Nola Dancy, *The Doctors*

Cicely Tyson   Martha Frazier, *The Guiding Light*

Blair Underwood   *One Life to Live*

Joan Van Ark
Janene Whitney, *Days of Our Lives*

Abe Vigoda   Ezra Braithwaite, *Dark Shadows*
Leo Coronal, *One Life to Live*

Kathleen Turner

Rick Springfield

JoBeth Williams

Billy Dee Williams

(Glenn) Christopher Walken
Mike Bauer, *The Guiding Light*
Kippie Franklin, *The World of Mr. Sweeney*

Jessica Walter   Julie Murano, *Love of Life*

Sigourney Weaver   Avis Ryan, *Somerset*

Billy Dee Williams
Dr. Jim Frazier, *The Guiding Light*

JoBeth Williams   Carrie Wheeler, *Somerset*
Brandy Shelooe, *The Guiding Light*

Efrem Zimbalist, Jr.
Jim Gavin, *Concerning Miss Marlowe*

Sigourney Weaver (with Harrison Ford)

Christopher Walken

311

Index

Peterson, Arthur, 231
Peterson, Gene, 177, 268
Peterson, Lenka, 259, 278
Peterson, Pat, 165
Petrie, Doris, 269
Petrie, George, 217
Pettet, Joanna, 93
Peyser, Penny, 173
Peyton Place, 13, 64, 165, 198-201, 269, 273, 274, 277, 284
Pfenning, Wesley Ann, 275
Pflug, JoAnn, 275
Phelps, Eleanor, *227*
Phillips, Irna, 9, 28, 34, 35, 36, 37, 40, 48, 84, 154, 156, 174, 198, 200, 216, 257, 272, 277, 278, 280
Phillips, John, 135
Phillips, Katherine, 36, 280
Phillips, Michelle, 169
Phillips, Wendy, 123, 266
Picerni, Paul, 281
Pickett, Cindy, 158
Pierce, Barbara, 271
Pillar (Carpenter), Gary, 51
Pine, Larry, 192
Pinkerton, Nancy, 191, *191*
Pinsent, Gordon, 276
Pinter, Mark, 263, 276
Place, Mary Kay, *184*, 185
Plank, Melinda, 272, 273
Platts, Alma, 277
Pleshette, John, 165, *165*
Plumb, Flora, 268, 271
Poindexter, Larry, 272
Pointer, Priscilla, 247
Polen, Nat, 37, 191, 269, 273
Pollock, Eileen, 140
Pollock, Robert Mason, 140
Ponzini, Antony, 189, 275
Poole, Roy, 268, 278
Poppel, Marc, 275
Porter, Eric, 135, *135*
Porter, Nyree Dawn, 135
Portia Faces Life, 8, 9, 274, *274*, 284
Post, William (Jr.), 175, 247
Poston, Tom, 269
Potter, Allen, 159
Potter, Paul, 177
Power, Ed, 175
Powers, Hunt, 139
Powers, Leona, 35
Poyner, Jim, *236*, 237
Prather, Joan, 266
Prentiss, Ed, 272
Presley, Priscilla Beaulieu, *65*, 70
Pressman, David, 286
Prince, William, 29, *258*, 259, 280, 281
Principal, Victoria, 65, *67*, 70, *72*
Pringle, Joan, 151
Prinz, Rosemary, 17, 37, *37*, 162, 163, *163*, 266
Prisoner: Cell Block H, 285
Pritchett, James, 92, *92*, 93, 287
Pryor, Nicholas, 29, 175, 259, 273
Purl, Linda, 225, 262
Purvey, Bob, 271

R
Rabin, Al, 86, 90
Raby, John, *265*, 280
Rae, Charlotte, 136, 137
Rae, Melba, 214

Rahn, Patsy, 140
Raines, Cristina, 133, *133*
Ralston, Esther, 273
Rambo, Dack, 272, 274
Ramsey, Gail, 151
Ramsey, Logan, 185
Randall, Dirk, 264
Randall, Sue, 279
Randall, Tony, 196, 197
Randell, Ron, 271
Ranier, Joe, 264
Rapelye, Mary Linda, *14*
Rashad, Phylicia (Ayers-Allen), 195, 305
Ratcliff, Sandy, 115
Reed, Donna, 66, 70
Reed, Lydia, 279, 281
Reed, Russ, 269
Reed, Shanna, 59, 237
Reeve, Christopher, 178, 179, *179*, 305, *305*
Reguli, Christina, 264
Reid, Frances, 84, *84*, 85, 86, *87*, 91, 274, 288, 292
Reilly, John, 274
Reinheart, Alice, 274
Reinholt, George, 29, 30, 191
Rennick, Nancy, 49
Rettig, Tommy, 272
Return to Peyton Place, 201, 274-275, *275*, 284
Reynolds, Kathryn, 231
Rhoades, Barbara, 151, 231
Rhodes, Donnelly, 231
Rice, Brett, 264
Rich, Chris, *28*
Rich, Doris, 265, 278
Rich, Lee, 270
Richard, Wendy, 114, 115
Richards, Addison, 263
Richards, Lisa, 75, 247
Richman, Caryn, 237
Richman, Peter Mark, 206, 207
Ridley, Julie, 264
Right to Happiness, The, 9, 11
Riseman, Naomi, 27
Ritchie, Clint, 192, *195*
Rituals, 275, *275*, 285
Road of Life, The, 9, 275-276, 284
Road to Reality, 276, 284
Roat, Richard, 92, 151
Robards, Glenn, 133
Robbins, Harold, 277
Robbins, Rex, 247
Roberts, Eric, 305
Roberts, Iris L., 264
Roberts, Mark, 265, 271, 278
Robertson, Dale, 101
Robertson, Kimmy, 241
Robie, Wendy, 241
Robinette, Dale, 221
Robinson, Andrew, 287
Robinson, Chris, 140
Robinson, Larry, 270
Robinson, Virginia, 177
Rodan, Robert, 75
Rodd, Marcia, 133
Rodell, Barbara, *157*, 278
Rodgers, Mimi, 274
Rodriguez, Percy, 199, 266
Roe, Patricia, 189
Roerick, William, 264

Roessler, Elmira, 269
Rogers, Kasey, 199
Rogers, Suzanne, 288
Rogers, Tristan, *146*
Rogers, Wayne, 307
Roland, Angela, 277
Roland, Christopher, 27
Rolle, Esther, 195
Rollins, Howard E. (Jr.), 290
Romance of Helen Trent, The, 9
Romance Theater, 285
Romero, Cesar, 124, *124*, 263
Ronnie, Julie, *206*, 207
Roos, Joanna, 177
Rose, George, 262
Rose, Jane, 123, 177
Rose, Norman, 189
Ross, Douglas, 247
Ross, Jarrod, 158
Ross, Katherine, 58, 59
Ross, Marion, 274
Ross, Michael, 268
Rounds, David, 262
Roundtree, Richard, 150, 151, *151*
Roux, Carol, 29, 235
Rowland, Jada, 93, *224*, 225, *227*
Rowlands, Gena, 198, 280, 307, *307*
Rowles, Polly, 273
Rubin, Benny, 49
Rucker, Barbara, 237, *237*
Rudd, Paul, 167, 262
Ruggles, Charles, 281
Ruick, Melville, 267
Runyeon, Frank, *14*, *39*
Rush, Barbara, 132, *132*, 133, 198, 199
Ruskin, Jeanne, 247
Russell, Ron, 275
Russo, Barry, 281
Russom, Leon, 175
Rust, John, 264
Rutherford, Kelly, 151, *151*
Ryan, Fran, 185
Ryan, Meg, *39*, 307
Ryan, Michael, 26, 27, 263
Ryan, Mitchell, 75, 266
Ryan's Hope, 202-205, *247*, 262, 285, 287, 288, 289
Rydell, Mark, 37

S
Sabatino, Michael, 168, 263
Sader, Alan, 27
Safran, Judy, 225
Saint, Eva Marie, 196, 197, 307
St. Clement, Pat, 115
St. John, Howard, 266
St. John, Jill, 265
St. John, Kristoff, *150*, 151
Salih, Nejdet, 115
Salt, Jennifer, 231
Samms, Emma, 59, *59*, 62, *110*, *112*, 148
Sampler, Philece, 275
Sampson, Robert, *53*
Sanders, Byron, 137, 192, 274
Sanders, David, *137*
Sandor, Alfred, 75
Sands, Dorothy, 276
Sandy, Gary, 225, 235, 262, 307
Santa Barbara, 13, *95*, 140, 206-213, 285, 292, 293
Santacroce, Mary Nell, 264

Sarandon, Susan, 280, 281, 307, *307*
Sargent, Anne, 266
Saulsberry, Rodney, 53
Savior, Paul, 139, 178
Sawyer, Bonnie, 279
Scalia, Jack, 263
Scannell, Susan, 27
Scarboro, David, 115
Scardino, Don, 175, 291
Scarlett Hill, 276, 285
Schaaf, Lillian, 197
Schackelford, Ted, *164*, 165, *165*, *168*, 308
Schedeen, Anne, 274
Scheider, Roy, 178, 307, *307*
Schiegl, Kurt, 277
Schnetzer, Stephen, *32*
Schofield, Frank, 235, 278
Schreiber, Mignon, 277
Schultz, Jacqueline, 215, 219
Scoggins, Tracy, 59, *61*
Scollay, Fred J., 92, 93
Scott, Debralee, 185
Scott, Evelyn, 199, 275
Scott, Geoffrey, 247
Scott, Judson, 59
Scott, Kathryn Leigh, 77, 79, 80
Scott, Ken, 263
Scott, Martha, 271, 276
Scott, Synda, 51
Scott, Thurman, 189
Scully, Pat, 278
Scully, Terry, 135
Seaforth, Susan. *See* Hayes, Susan Seaforth
Search for Tomorrow, 9, 11, 13, 26, 133, 138, 176, 184, 214-223, 235, 246, 262, 266, 280, 284
Second Mrs. Burton, The, 11
Secrets of Midland Heights, 270, 276, *276*, 284
Secret Storm, The, 11, 13, 170, 176, 224-229, 235, 266, 270, 284
Seeking Heart, The, 266, 276, 284
Seely, Diane, 27
Selby, David, 77, 78, 79, 80, 123, *129*, *130*, 132, 133, 307
Selleck, Tom, 148, *249*, 257, *306*, 307
Seymour, Anne, 267
Seymour, Jane, 265
Seymour, John, 267
Shaffer, Louise, 203, 247, 262, 269, 289, 290
Shannon, James, 163
Shapiro, Esther, 100, 265
Shapiro, Richard, 100, 265
Sharon, Fran, 29
Shaughnessy, Alfred, 244
Shaw, Lana, 79
Shaw, Steve, 165
Shaw, Susan, 197
Shearin, John, 99, 133, 181, *183*
Sheehan, Douglas, 168, *172*, 289
Sheen, Martin, 308
Sheinkopf, David, 123
Shepard, Jan, 264
Sheridan, Nancy, 267, 279
Sheridan, Nicollette, 169, *260*, 273, 274
Shields, Helen, 137, 265
Shipp, John Wesley, 159, 210, 291
Shirley, Tom, 137

318